The Pottery from Arroyo Hondo Pueblo
and
The Stone Artifacts from Arroyo Hondo Pueblo

ARROYO HONDO ARCHAEOLOGICAL SERIES

DOUGLAS W. SCHWARTZ
GENERAL EDITOR AND PROJECT DIRECTOR

ARROYO HONDO ARCHAEOLOGICAL SERIES

*Publication of this book was made possible
by a grant from the National Science Foundation
and by generous support from
Marianne and J. Michael O'Shaughnessy.*

Part I

The Pottery from Arroyo Hondo Pueblo, New Mexico

Tribalization and Trade in the Northern Rio Grande

Judith A. Habicht-Mauche

with contributions by
Richard W. Lang and Anthony Thibodeau

Part II

The Stone Artifacts from Arroyo Hondo Pueblo

Carl J. Phagan

SCHOOL OF AMERICAN RESEARCH PRESS

ARROYO HONDO ARCHAEOLOGICAL SERIES, VOLUME 8

School of American Research Press
Post Office Box 2188
Santa Fe, New Mexico 87504-2188

Library of Congress Cataloging-in-Publication Data

Habicht-Mauche, Judith A., 1959–
    The pottery from Arroyo Hondo Pueblo, New Mexico :
tribalization and trade in the northern Rio Grande / Judith A.
Habicht-Mauche with contributions by Richard W. Lang and
Anthony Thibodeau. The stone artifacts from Arroyo Hondo
Pueblo / Carl J. Phagan. — 1st ed.
        p.   cm. — (Arroyo Hondo archaeological series ; v. 8)
    Includes bibliographical references (p.   ) and index.
    ISBN 0-933452-34-9 (paperback only) : $30.00
    1. Arroyo Hondo Site (N.M.)   2. Pueblo Indians—Pottery.
3. Pueblo Indians—Implements.   4. Pueblo Indians—
Commerce.   5. Pottery—New Mexico—Arroyo Hondo Site—
Analysis.   6. Pottery—New Mexico—Arroyo Hondo Site—
Classification.   7. Stone implements—New Mexico—Arroyo
Hondo Site.   I. Lang, Richard W.   II. Thibodeau, Anthony,
1965–   .III. Phagan, Carl James.   Stone artifacts from Arroyo
Hondo Pueblo.   1993.   IV. Title.   V. Title: Stone artifacts
from Arroyo Hondo Pueblo. VI. Series.
E99.P9A784   1993
978.9'53—dc20   93-20322
                                                            CIP

Cover: Detail from painting of the Arroyo Hondo area,
Susan Cooper, 1975.

Contents

Illustrations and Tables

TABLES

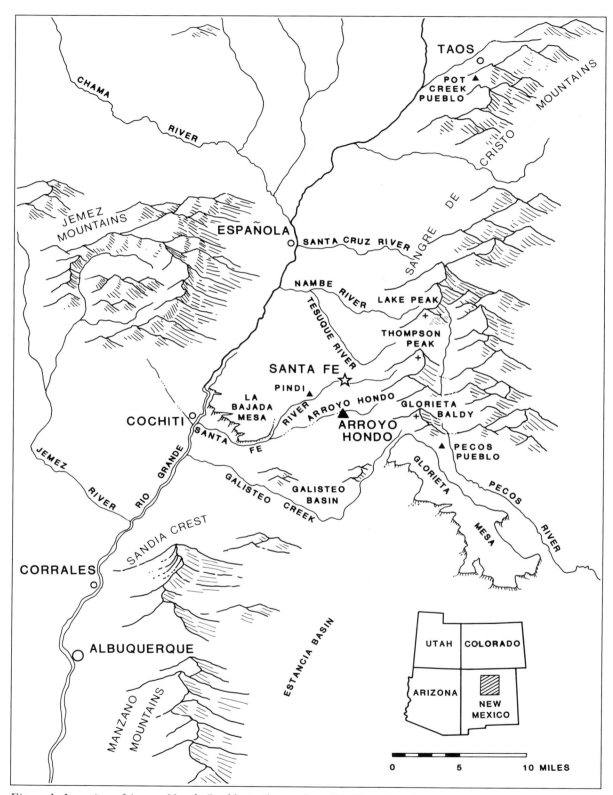

Figure 1. Location of Arroyo Hondo Pueblo in the northern Rio Grande region.

Foreword

At the base of the Sangre de Cristo Mountains five miles southeast of what is now Santa Fe, New Mexico, a major new settlement arose during the early years of the fourteenth century A.D. (fig. 1). Named Arroyo Hondo Pueblo by archaeologists, this community grew rapidly from a few residences to nearly a thousand rooms and perhaps as many occupants by the year 1330. For the northern Rio Grande valley at this time, it was a massive settlement. Although abandoned by 1425, Arroyo Hondo was both forerunner and prototype for other Puebloan settlements that arose in the century prior to the arrival of the Spaniards.

Arroyo Hondo Pueblo has provided fundamental information about fourteenth-century life in the northern Rio Grande valley, in part because of the site's relatively short period of occupation, in part because no large prehistoric or historic pueblo was later constructed on top of it. The sequence of its settlement and construction, and of its many changes over time, are therefore clearly visible in the archaeological record.

Five excavation seasons at Arroyo Hondo and almost two decades of analysis and writing have provided an extraordinary opportunity to examine the life of this community and its region. The present volume, the eighth in the Arroyo Hondo series, is a detailed analysis of the site's pottery and of the changes in style, production, and distribution that occurred during the life of the settlement. The study opens a window onto the complex interactions that linked the different ethnic groups of the northern Rio Grande region into a single, integrated "tribal" network by the end of the fourteenth century. In so doing, it makes an important contribution to our understanding of Rio Grande and Southwestern prehistory.

Archaeological Background

The northern Rio Grande valley lagged significantly behind the rest of the Anasazi world in population size and cultural complexity. Although the region had been occupied for thousands of years, its first farming villages did not appear until about A.D. 700. For the next three centuries, Rio Grande settlers lived in small, scattered farmsteads, existed on a mix of foraging and horticulture, resided in circular pithouses or aboveground adobe rooms, and moved seasonally to take advantage of the widest variety of resources. Throughout this period, the region was marginal to the more highly developed Four Corners Anasazi.

In the middle of the 1200s, population in the northern Rio Grande valley began to increase, and the first medium-sized villages appeared—settlements with a dozen to 150 rooms, some containing two or more sets of roomblocks facing a plaza with a kiva. Though larger, these villages were constructed in a manner similar to earlier sites in the region, and their inhabitants used locally made pottery.

The late thirteenth century saw a transition in settlement pattern throughout the Southwest, as towns far larger than most earlier communities—with the exception of Snaketown and some Chaco Canyon sites—began appearing in widely scattered locations. Sites such as Point of Pines and Grasshopper in central Arizona, Awotovi in the Hopi country of northern Arizona, Casas Grandes in northern Mexico, and others in the Zuni country south of Gallup, New Mexico, and in the Montezuma Valley near Mesa Verde had from five hundred to two thousand rooms. Arroyo Hondo was one of the first of these larger communities to be built in the northern Rio Grande valley. The reasons behind this transition from small villages to major towns were among the central questions addressed by the Arroyo Hondo project.

Arroyo Hondo Pueblo

During a time of increased precipitation early in the fourteenth century, a few families found and settled a special location: a good building site with a nearby free-flowing spring, well-watered soil in an adjacent canyon, and easy access to a number of richly diverse ecological zones. Taking advantage of these qualities, the founders of the pueblo built an alignment of masonry rooms along the edge of the 125-foot-deep Arroyo Hondo gorge.

From the start, agriculture was important to the pueblo's economy. Arroyo Hondo's bottomlands could support irrigation or floodwater farming, while the surrounding higher areas could be dry-farmed during years of high precipitation. The settlers probably planted the first fields of corn, beans, and squash in the arroyo and supplemented their harvests by gathering seasonally available wild greens, seeds, and nuts throughout what came to be the pueblo's eighty-square-mile territory. Among the more than ninety species of animals available, deer provided the major source of protein, and rabbits, antelope, bison, and domesticated turkeys were significant additions to the diet.

Residents of Arroyo Hondo traded actively with other communities in the region, probably exchanging food as well as locally made ceramics. They also obtained resources from more distant areas: painted turtles from villages just to the south, shells from the Pacific coast, and—probably indirectly—live macaws from what is now northern Mexico.

Arroyo Hondo experienced rapid growth during its first decades and ultimately expanded to twenty-four roomblocks of one- and two-story apartments clustered around ten plazas (fig. 2). But soon after 1335 the population shrank dramatically: rooms were abandoned, and some were filled with trash or windblown dirt after their roofs and walls collapsed. By 1345 Arroyo Hondo was virtually abandoned. For the next thirty years, the derelict pueblo was inhabited at most by a small remnant population, or perhaps only seasonally by small groups. This abandonment marks the end of the Component I occupation.

Why the pueblo was abandoned is not entirely clear, but environmental change was certainly part of the problem. Annual precipitation began to decrease significantly during the late 1330s and may have resulted in food shortages. But even without drought, the very presence of so many people in one place must have depleted the environment. Over the years, firewood must have been increasingly difficult to obtain and deer and other animals in the local area may have been hunted almost to extinction. Such factors may have exacerbated existing weaknesses within the cultural system itself.

Skeletal remains suggest that the residents of Arroyo Hondo did suffer from food shortages. Malnutrition and iron deficiency, complicated by disease, resulted in the death of over half of all children under the age of five (Palkovich 1980).

Consistent food shortages and declining firewood supplies could have sparked other social complications as well. The founders of Arroyo Hondo had all come from much smaller communities, where methods of conflict resolution between families and individuals may have been well established. But at Arroyo Hondo, population increase may have come so rapidly that the necessary social mechanisms to allocate land and settle disputes may have proved inadequate. Social tensions could have hastened the abandonment of the pueblo.

Arroyo Hondo's second phase of settlement, designated Component II, began sometime during the 1370s and corresponded with a new period of increased moisture. This pueblo was built over the ruins of the earlier town but at its peak was much smaller, comprising only two hundred rooms organized in nine roomblocks around three plazas (fig. 3). Within forty years, however, the region was again impacted by drought. As before, rooms were abandoned and demolished as the population declined, and sometime after 1410 a catastrophic fire destroyed much of the settlement. A few years later, the drought reached a severity unprecedented in the history of the pueblo—the lowest annual precipitation in the thousand years represented in the dendroclimatological record. With this last adversity, the second and final occupation of Arroyo Hondo Pueblo came to an end.

Before the Spaniards arrived and settled much of the unoccupied land, Pueblo people moved their villages frequently. Whether the reasons were environmental, social, or a combination of the two, moving and rebuilding villages—even very large settlements—was apparently a common practice (Lekson 1990). Arroyo Hondo is an excellent example of just how rapidly these large villages were constructed and how rapidly they could be abandoned.

History of the Arroyo Hondo Project

The Arroyo Hondo project was begun in 1970 with three central objectives: (1) to use the most modern and comprehensive techniques to expand our understanding of northern Rio Grande Pueblo culture; (2) to explore the growth and dynamics of a large Pueblo IV settlement as exemplified at Arroyo Hondo; and (3) to use Arroyo Hondo Pueblo along with comparative ethnographic analysis to examine the cross-cultural implications of rapid population growth and of cultural and environmental change (Schwartz 1971).

Field research to determine the nature of the site began in the summer of 1970 with a survey and test excavations. Based on this and later work, funds to support

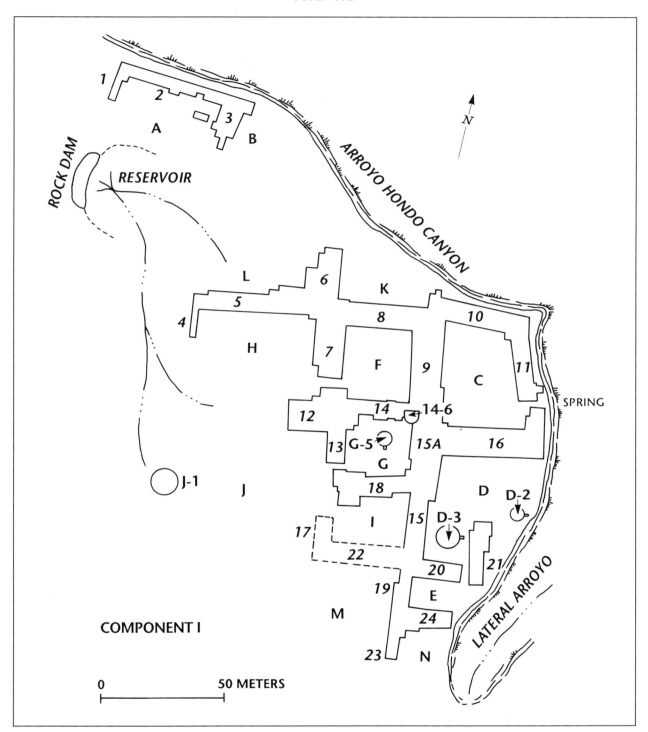

Figure 2. Schematic plan of Arroyo Hondo Pueblo, Component I.

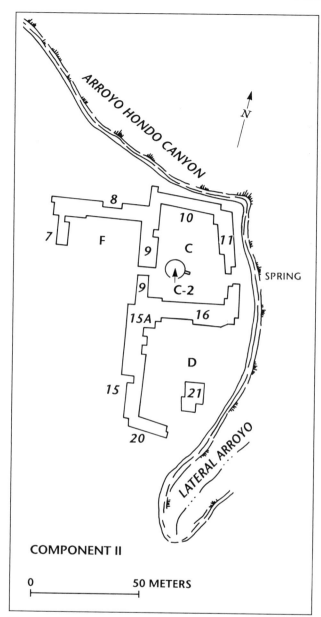

Figure 3. Schematic plan of Arroyo Hondo Pueblo, Component II.

the field phase of the project (1971–74) were received from the National Science Foundation (grants GS-28001 and GS-42181). A systematic program of excavation during these years covered room and roomblock architecture, site organization and growth, residential configuration, and the character of plazas and kivas. In addition, a regional archaeological survey was conducted, along with an extensive ecological analysis.

During the course of the excavations, interim results were published in three reports (Schwartz 1971, 1972; Schwartz and Lang 1973). Upon completion of the fieldwork, in 1974, a film—*The Rio Grande's Pueblo Past*—illustrating the history of the project and presenting some initial conclusions was made with support from the National Geographic Society. A preliminary synthesis of the project was published after several years of analysis had been completed (Schwartz 1981).

The Arroyo Hondo project was first conceived and the excavation and related projects were initiated over twenty years ago. Since then a great deal has been learned about the pueblo and its region. The project itself led me to think seriously about the pursuit of major, long-term archaeological projects. Undertakings the size of the Arroyo Hondo project have problems of continuity in personnel; they require the progressive, interrelated analysis of vast amounts of varied data; and they demand great perseverance to follow the steps necessary to reach final publication. In the course of this process, the original questions that stimulated research will be greatly refined and elaborated as the results of the analyses and ongoing developments in archaeological thinking are incorporated.

The Arroyo Hondo Publication Series

Arroyo Hondo was clearly a large and complex site to tackle. From the beginning of the project, I felt that the best results would be obtained by involving a number of scholars with specialized backgrounds and knowledge in each phase of the project. The main research questions to be addressed with the Hondo data were identified during the first year of fieldwork. During the first and second field seasons, I recruited individuals with unique expertise to work on specific aspects of the research. My intention was that each of these researchers would follow the project from fieldwork to analysis to writing and final publication. The objective was to produce a series of volumes in which individual authors would contribute to the project through presentation of their own research and, it was hoped, would add important new ideas to the development of Southwestern archaeology.

This plan succeeded admirably for the first six volumes in the series, all written by scholars who had joined the project during the fieldwork stage. Some of these authors were advanced graduate students who were invited to use the Arroyo Hondo material for theses (Kelley 1980) or dissertations (Dixon 1979; Palkovich 1980; Wetterstrom 1986); others were members of the School of American Research archaeological staff working with outside experts (Lang and Harris 1984), or were consultants analyzing some phase of the project (Rose, Dean, and Robinson 1981).

Another National Science Foundation grant (BNS 76–83501) provided partial support for the publication of the data volumes. The composition of the series changed as the potential contribution of the various topics emerged from the research and could be better assessed. Some studies originally planned as full volumes, such as the analyses of pollen and lithics, developed into shorter reports or appendixes. Other work originally intended as shorter reports resulted in major monographs, as was the case with dendroclimatology.

The latest two volumes of the series, on architecture and ceramics, were initiated by members of the SAR staff soon after the excavations at Arroyo Hondo were completed. Richard W. Lang undertook a comprehensive analysis of the ceramics, and John D. Beal compiled a preliminary manuscript on architecture. But Lang and Beal left the School before their final manuscripts could be completed. Judith Habicht-Mauche was asked to rework and complete this volume on the pottery from Arroyo Hondo Pueblo. She has taken a broad look at the site's ceramics in their regional context and has been able to draw important conclusions about the development and organization of prehistoric northern Rio Grande society. Winifred Creamer was asked to further develop Beal's architecture manuscript, using the data to examine the construction details, growth, organization, and decline of the Arroyo Hondo community. Both Habicht-Mauche and Creamer were assisted by Tony Thibodeau, the School's archaeological laboratory coordinator.

To date, published volumes in the Arroyo Hondo series have covered contemporary ecology (Kelley 1980); regional site survey (Dickson 1979); skeletal and mortuary remains (Palkovich 1980); dendroclimatology (Rose, Dean, and Robinson 1981); faunal analysis (Lang and Harris 1984); archaeobotany (Wetterstrom 1986); architecture (Creamer 1993); and ceramics (this volume). Shorter reports have been published on regional metric comparisons of skeletal collections (Mackey 1980); pollen studies (Bohrer 1986); artifacts of wood (Lang 1986); bone artifacts (Beach and Causey 1984); shell artifacts (Venn 1984); and hide, fur, and feathers (Lang 1984). The present volume on ceramics also includes shorter reports on lithics, stratigraphic ceramic samples, and miscellaneous ceramic artifacts. The volume on architecture contains an appendix on the site's dendrochronology by Lang and Thibodeau.

A final volume in the series is also planned, in which I will synthesize the results of the total project, returning to the original questions and examining new issues that emerged during the course of the project—some of which relate to problems that reach far beyond Arroyo Hondo and its culture history. This concluding synthesis is currently in preparation.

In spite of delays, changes in authors, and the additional expense of restarting unsuccessful or incomplete writing projects, I believe the use of numerous skilled individuals as analysts and authors has been highly advantageous. The Arroyo Hondo project was an immense undertaking. Research efforts focusing on small sites may yield faster results, but the amount of data and the depth of the interpretation that can emerge from work at larger sites justifies the extended effort. As I look back over each of the volumes that have now been published, I feel they have accomplished our original objectives and added significantly to our understanding of both Arroyo Hondo and Southwestern prehistory.

Completing a series of this sort is challenging and requires a solid core of continuity: a guiding force who will keep all aspects of the work moving forward and who will find ways around inherent and unanticipated difficulties. Each year, time must be dedicated to coordinating analyses, raising necessary funds, motivating authors, exercising quality control over the publication process, and assessing the progress of the total project in order to provide feedback to its constituent parts. The high quality of the volumes produced by the many scholars who devoted themselves to the interpretation of Arroyo Hondo Pueblo has made this effort extremely worthwhile.

The Ceramics of Arroyo Hondo

Judith Habicht-Mauche performs in this volume a tour-de-force of archaeological analysis and interpretation. Building on an exhaustive study of the mineralogical and chemical analyses of the pottery from Arroyo Hondo Pueblo, she has produced an extremely impressive consideration of the range of stylistic diversity in the ceramic collection, an account of the origins of pottery manufacture, and a report on changes in the relative frequency of ceramic types through time. Instead of analyzing the distribution of ceramic types within the pueblo itself, Habicht-Mauche focuses on Arroyo Hondo's position within and relationship to the larger region. The analysis provides the foundation for her conclusions on changes in the structure of social and economic alliances and their significance for an understanding of population expansion, resource competition, regional trade, craft specialization, ethnic diversity, and the rise of tribal networks in the northern Rio Grande area during the fourteenth and early fifteenth centuries.

The contribution of this monograph is enhanced by three separately authored reports. Carl J. Phagan presents here for the first time a valuable reconstruction and interpretation of the stone artifact assemblage from Arroyo Hondo—materials originally analyzed some two decades ago. Richard W. Lang presents an analysis and seriation of stratigraphic ceramic samples from the site, and Tony Thibodeau describes the pueblo's miscellaneous ceramic artifacts, including pipes and effigy figures.

Judith Habicht-Mauche's objective in writing this monograph was to demonstrate how archaeological ceramic analysis can move beyond reconstructions of chronology and site history to provide a clearer understanding of the structure and organization of prehistoric societies. Her success in this effort comes through in a clearly written and well-organized work. I am proud to present this monograph as part of the Arroyo Hondo series.

Douglas W. Schwartz

The Pottery from Arroyo Hondo Pueblo

Part I

The Pottery from Arroyo Hondo Pueblo, New Mexico

Tribalization and Trade in the Northern Rio Grande

Judith A. Habicht-Mauche

with additional reports by
Richard W. Lang and Anthony Thibodeau

Acknowledgments

The study and analysis of ceramic materials from the excavation of Arroyo Hondo Pueblo have been conducted, on and off, over the course of the last twenty years. My own involvement with the project began in the spring of 1988, when I was asked by Douglas Schwartz of the School of American Research to undertake an analysis of the materials and produce a monograph for publication in the present series. I am extremely grateful to Dr. Schwartz for his unwavering confidence and support throughout this project.

Although it is always difficult to take over a project in mid-course, I am deeply indebted to all those researchers and laboratory assistants who preceded me for the quality and thoroughness of their work. Special thanks must go to Richard Lang, who more than any other person laid the foundation for my analysis and interpretation of the pottery from Arroyo Hondo Pueblo. He was responsible for coordinating the processing, sorting, and typing of all the ceramics from the 1971 through 1974 field seasons and for recording type frequencies for most of the excavated proveniences. His work established the basic standards of type identification and description at the site, especially in regard to the white wares. Although we sometimes differ on certain nuances of typology and its cultural-historical significance, I would not have been able to reach the conclusions I did without the basic framework he provided. Dick is also responsible for working out the details of the very complex seriational sequence at the site. Unlike other large sites in the northern Rio Grande (e.g., Pecos), Arroyo Hondo had no deep stratified midden deposits from which to reconstruct the ceramic sequence. Instead, the sequence had to be reconstructed from isolated well-dated proveniences located throughout the site. I doubt that this task could have been duplicated by anyone who did not have Dick's extensive first-hand knowledge of the site and its stratigraphy or his careful attention to detail. The results of his seriational analysis appear as a separate report in this volume. It represents an important and lasting contribution to our understanding of the history of Arroyo Hondo Pueblo.

My own research has focused on evaluating the relationship between stylistic diversity, as it was reflected in the ceramic record from Arroyo Hondo, and changes in the structure of social and economic alliances in the northern Rio Grande during the fourteenth and early fifteenth centuries. This study consisted of two distinct phases of data collection and analysis. In the first phase, a series of standard physical attributes was recorded for a sample of previously typed pottery fragments from the site. The degree of attribute variability within and between types was evaluated in order to determine the source and standardization of stylistic diversity associated with each and to record changes in stylistic diversity through time. Invaluable help with this phase of the project was provided by my lab assistants, Cary Virtue and Anthony Thibodeau. Cary was responsible for sorting and recording attributes for much of the culinary ceramics analyzed for this project—a task that required a great deal of patience and dedication. Tony combed through voluminous stacks of site records to consolidate the type frequency by provenience data presented in appendix A—another tedious but extremely important task. Tony also took charge of the analysis of the miscellaneous ceramic objects from the site, including pipes and figurines. The results of his analysis appear in this volume as a separate report.

In the second phase of the study, a sample of each ceramic type from each component was subjected to mineralogical and chemical analyses. The petrographic thin sections were expertly prepared by Dave Mann of Mann Petrographic in Los Alamos, New Mexico. A true craftsman, Dave treated my broken potsherds with the same care and attention he usually devotes to moon rocks and meteorites. I conducted the petrographic analysis while a guest scientist with the Geology/Geochemistry group at Los Alamos National Laboratory. This arrangement was facilitated by Dr. W. Scott Baldridge, who also provided important help in collecting geological field specimens and interpreting the petrographic and chemical data. Chemical analyses of ceramic samples, using x-ray fluorescence, were run by Bart Olinger, also of

Los Alamos National Lab. Both Scott and Bart provided very thorough and helpful comments on early drafts of chapter 3.

I am also extremely grateful for the comments made by John Speth, Gary Feinman, and other members of the 1989–90 class of resident scholars at the School of American Research, on material presented in chapters 1 and 4. Their challenging insights and thought-provoking discussion pushed me to critically evaluate and greatly focus the theoretical framework of this research.

A special note of appreciation must go to Patricia Crown for her very thorough critical review of the manuscript. Her thoughtful comments and suggestions especially helped me clarify the technical discussion of the compositional analyses and their interpretation.

The present study was also greatly enriched by numerous discussions of Rio Grande archaeology, in general, and Arroyo Hondo, in particular, with Jonathan Haas and Winifred Creamer. Their tenure at SAR made for a lively and enriching community of scholars.

Finally, I would like to thank Jane Kepp (director of publications), Joan O'Donnell (editor), Beverly Oneglia (copy editor), and Deborah Flynn Post (art director) for taking my manuscript and turning it into a beautiful book. Katrina Lasko executed the maps and line drawings in the book, and Herbert Lotz took the artifact photographs. The professionalism, high standards, and careful attention to detail of these talented individuals instilled great confidence in a young author just a little afraid to relinquish her hard-wrought research to the dark, unknown mysteries of "publication."

The ceramic collections from Arroyo Hondo Pueblo are large and complex and beyond the scope of any single study. They should continue to be an important resource for archaeological research well into the future. My hope is that the present study will shed some light on ways in which ceramic analysis in archaeology can help us move beyond reconstructions of chronology and site history to a clearer understanding of the structure and meaning of prehistoric societies.

Judith A. Habicht-Mauche

Chapter 1

Introduction

Pottery studies are a time-honored tradition in northern Rio Grande archaeology. In the early decades of this century, ceramic analysis focused largely on the development of relative chronologies based on changes in the design of ceramic vessels recovered from stratigraphic contexts (e.g., Nelson 1914, 1916; Kidder 1915; Kidder and Amsden 1931; Kidder and Shepard 1936; Mera 1933, 1935). When the "types" defined by these seriational studies were linked to the rapidly expanding tree-ring sequence of the Southwest (Smiley et al. 1953; Breternitz 1966), pottery became a powerful tool for dating archaeological sites in the region. Site chronology remains the central focus of most archaeological studies of Rio Grande pottery up to the present day.

Along with changes through time, spatial differences in local pottery styles were noted. This ceramic variation appeared to correspond to local distinctions in other aspects of material culture, architecture, settlement pattern, and culture history, and it resulted in the recognition of various archaeological "districts" within the Rio Grande area (e.g., Mera 1940; Shepard 1942; Wetherington 1968; Cordell 1979a) (fig. 4). Although not always explicitly stated, this spatial variation in material remains was assumed to correlate with the presence of distinct sociolinguistic groups in the area. In particular, differences in ceramic styles were viewed as the result of the migration of various ethnic groups into the northern Rio Grande, each of them bearing a distinct and recognizable set of cultural traits (e.g., Reed 1949; Wendorf 1954; Wendorf and Reed 1955; Ford et al. 1972; and Lang 1982). Every ceramic development, through time or across space, was seen as reflecting either the diffusion of ideas or the actual migration of people from the more culturally "advanced" regions of the Southwest, such as the Colorado Plateau, into the culturally "backward" and "underdeveloped" areas of the northern Rio Grande.

Over the last thirty years, these largely historical schemes have gradually been replaced by studies that seek to explain culture change in the northern Rio Grande in terms of the internal ecological dynamics of the area rather than as a response to external influences (Cordell and Plog 1979; Cordell 1979a, 1979b, 1984,

1989; Snow 1981; Stuart and Gauthier 1981; Wilcox 1981). Technological, economic, and sociopolitical innovations, recorded in the archaeological record of the northern Rio Grande, were viewed as components of a systemic "adaptive strategy" that developed in response to demographic and environmental stresses.

Recent critiques of cultural ecological models (e.g., Leonard 1989; Hodder 1986) point out that by acting on the level of "cultures" and "systems," these explanations fail to take into account the importance of the actions of individuals as reflected in material culture. In particular, such models do not address how people use material objects to create meaning in social contexts. The standard ecological models of northern Rio Grande prehistory, for example, fail to explain why locally distinct black-on-white ceramic styles developed after ca. A.D. 1250, or why these styles were largely replaced by the homogeneous spread of glaze-painted pottery throughout much of the same region a century later.

In the following study, I will present an alternative model of culture change for the period between A.D. 1250 and 1400 in the northern Rio Grande, based on an analysis of changes in pottery style, production, and distribution at Arroyo Hondo Pueblo (LA 12). According to this model, northern Rio Grande inhabitants used stylistic diversity, as manifested in the proliferation of local white ware styles after about 1250, to structure social relations and promote the stability and predictability of interactions between competing ethnic groups in an increasingly complex social landscape. Subsequently, the centralized production and widespread trade of glaze-painted pottery acted to sustain a system of complementary and reciprocal interactions that linked these various ethnic groups into a single, integrated "tribal" network by the end of the fourteenth century.

Style, Ethnicity, and Social Boundaries

Central to the following discussion is the concept of "style" in material culture. I accept a fairly broad definition of style as any combination of physical attributes that are diagnostic of a specific time and place (Sackett

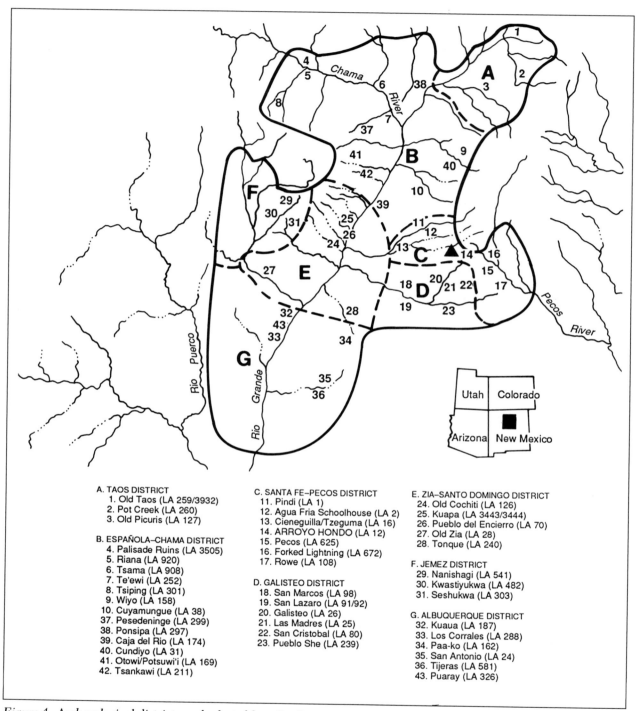

Figure 4. Archaeological districts and selected late Coalition–early Classic sites in the northern Rio Grande region of New Mexico.

A. TAOS DISTRICT
1. Old Taos (LA 259/3932)
2. Pot Creek (LA 260)
3. Old Picuris (LA 127)

B. ESPAÑOLA–CHAMA DISTRICT
4. Palisade Ruins (LA 3505)
5. Riana (LA 920)
6. Tsama (LA 908)
7. Te'ewi (LA 252)
8. Tsiping (LA 301)
9. Wiyo (LA 158)
10. Cuyamungue (LA 38)
37. Pesedeninge (LA 299)
38. Ponsipa (LA 297)
39. Caja del Rio (LA 174)
40. Cundiyo (LA 31)
41. Otowi/Potsuwi'i (LA 169)
42. Tsankawi (LA 211)

C. SANTA FE–PECOS DISTRICT
11. Pindi (LA 1)
12. Agua Fria Schoolhouse (LA 2)
13. Cieneguilla/Tzeguma (LA 16)
14. ARROYO HONDO (LA 12)
15. Pecos (LA 625)
16. Forked Lightning (LA 672)
17. Rowe (LA 108)

D. GALISTEO DISTRICT
18. San Marcos (LA 98)
19. San Lazaro (LA 91/92)
20. Galisteo (LA 26)
21. Las Madres (LA 25)
22. San Cristobal (LA 80)
23. Pueblo She (LA 239)

E. ZIA–SANTO DOMINGO DISTRICT
24. Old Cochiti (LA 126)
25. Kuapa (LA 3443/3444)
26. Pueblo del Encierro (LA 70)
27. Old Zia (LA 28)
28. Tonque (LA 240)

F. JEMEZ DISTRICT
29. Nanishagi (LA 541)
30. Kwastiyukwa (LA 482)
31. Seshukwa (LA 303)

G. ALBUQUERQUE DISTRICT
32. Kuaua (LA 187)
33. Los Corrales (LA 288)
34. Paa-ko (LA 162)
35. San Antonio (LA 24)
36. Tijeras (LA 581)
43. Puaray (LA 326)

1977, 1982; Lechtman and Steinberg 1979). Although rarely explicitly defined, this general notion of style has been used intuitively by archaeologists as the basis for most typological classifications of material culture. Like Sackett (1977, 1982), I find fault not with the way in which style in material culture has been identified by archaeologists but rather with the interpretation of its meaning and significance within traditional cultural-historical frameworks.

Attribute variability in material culture is the result of cognitive and behavioral choices made by the artisan during the process of manufacture. To a large extent these choices are determined by the intended function of an object—that is, the use to which it is put or the role it plays in society. Within the confines of these utilitarian constraints, however, all material culture is the product of technologies (i.e., behaviors) that are inextricably linked to the specific cultures in which they operate. Aspects of culture, such as systems of learning, the management of resources and labor, concepts about the natural and social environment, and the class and gender of the artisan, are all determinative in shaping the structure or style of technological systems and their material by-products.

As Lechtman and Steinberg (1979:139) point out, "In asking what the cultural component of technology is, we are also asking what technology can tell us about culture. We must be concerned . . . not only with the materials, processes and products of technology, but also with what technologies express." From this perspective, style in technology and material culture can be viewed as one of several fundamental modes of cultural expression and communication—similar to language, art, music, dance, costume, or gesture—all of which are based on fundamental, culturally determined patterns of cognition, learning, and performance (see Conkey 1978; Hodder 1979; and Kintigh 1985 for similar perspectives). Thus, if we claim that technology manifests cultural choices and values, it is our task to explain the nature of that manifestation (i.e., its style) and to determine how it can be read in the material record.

According to Wobst (1977), style can be defined as that part of variability in material culture related specifically to information exchange. This more restricted view of style differs from the one presented here, which defines style as any aspect of variability in material culture associated with a specific temporal or spatial context. Stylistic variability does provide an excellent medium for the self-conscious exchange of information, but the symbolic significance and social meaning of that information is not necessarily structurally inherent in the variability itself. Rather, it is determined by the way in which stylistic behavior is manipulated by individuals and groups within specific social contexts. The question then becomes, What conditions select for an emphasis on stylistic variability as a means of conveying social information, and what are the types of messages most often expressed through stylistic behavior?

Recent studies of style and information exchange, especially those related to pottery (e.g., Graves 1985; Kintigh 1985; Hegmon 1990), seem to imply that stylistic messages are limited to certain nonfunctional or nonutilitarian attributes—in particular, decoration. It is my contention, however, that any attribute or suite of attributes that results in visually recognizable distinctions in functionally equivalent forms of material culture can be manipulated symbolically to convey social information. Sackett (1982) referred to these functionally equivalent but stylistically distinct variants as "isochrestic forms." There is probably no better example of the concept of isochrestic form than the black-on-white painted bowls that dominated the decorated ceramic assemblages of the northern Rio Grande during the late thirteenth and early fourteenth centuries. Vessels from throughout the region are remarkably similar in form, size, and even decorative layout, yet variations in paste composition, slipping, and finishing techniques allow us consistently to identify local styles or types of the basic white ware bowl.

Since stylistic variability is by definition diagnostic of a particular cultural context, such variation is most useful as a means of exchanging symbolic information about individual social identity and participation in certain social and economic networks (Braun and Plog 1982). Wobst (1977) and Hodder (1979) have both documented the use of stylistic behavior as a means of expressing ethnic identity and establishing ethnic boundaries. I follow Barth's (1969) definition of ethnic groups as categories of ascription and self-identification that have the characteristic of organizing interactions between individuals. From this viewpoint, the sharing of a common culture and value system is seen as the result of the formation of ethnic identity rather than as a primary and defining characteristic of ethnic groups. Thus, "culture" does not equal "ethnicity," but cultural diversity can be an effective means of marking and reinforcing ethnic identity.

There persists in anthropology in general, and archaeology specifically, a view that geographical and social isolation have been critical factors in generating and sustaining ethnic and cultural diversity (see Plog 1980, 1983 for an extensive critique of this and other underlying principles of what he refers to as "social interaction theory"). Other empirical investigations (Barth 1969; Hodder 1979), however, have shown that ethnic diversification does not depend on an absence of mobility, contact, and information exchange but rather on conscious, social processes of exclusion and incorporation. Stable, persistent, and critically important social and economic relations are maintained across ethnic boundaries and are often based precisely on the dichotomy and complementarity of the participating ethnic groups. Under conditions of intense interethnic contact and interaction, material culture can be an important mechanism for maintaining ethnic boundaries by providing objective criteria for signaling membership and exclusion. Boundary maintenance is critical to the existence of stable interethnic relations because it provides a structure and context for social and economic transactions.

When two or more ethnic groups are in contact, the nature of their relationships and interdependence will take on different forms, depending on their differential access to resources, labor, and power in specific social and environmental settings (Hodder 1979). These conditions will directly affect the ways in which ethnic dichotomies are expressed, both culturally and materially. Thus, changes in style through time, and in the distribution of styles across the cultural landscape, can be interpreted as reflecting changes in the structure of social and economic relationships between ethnic groups. At the same time, stylistic change may result from changes in the role that cultural diversity plays in mediating these transactions.

Tribalization and Trade

According to Barth (1969), when two or more ethnic groups come into contact, their relationship may take on one of the following forms:

1. They may exploit clearly distinct niches in the natural environment and thus be in minimal competition for resources. Under these circumstances, interaction will be limited despite coresidence in the same area.
2. They may control separate, adjoining territories, in which case they will be in competition for resources at their borders, and their articulation will involve conflict and negotiation along those borders and, possibly, in other sectors of society.
3. They may occupy reciprocal and interdependent niches, in which case they may provide important goods and services for each other. Where these groups occupy relatively equivalent statuses within a social or economic network, this situation approaches a "mutualistic" relationship (e.g., Spielmann 1982). If statuses are unequal, as is the case in most states, empires, and colonial situations,

the relationship may entail a more complex system of economic and political interdependence involving issues of dominance and exploitation.
4. Finally, they may be interspersed within the same niche and may be in at least partial competition for the same resources. Such a situation is inherently unstable, and with time one would expect one group to displace the others or an accommodation involving increasing complementarity and interdependence to develop. Again, the form that accommodation and interdependence will take will depend on the relative statuses and differential access to resources that exist among the participating ethnic groups.

When access to critical resources and power is roughly equal and social structures are largely unstratified, that accommodation is most likely to result in the formation of social networks of the type known as "tribes." I see tribalization, the process by which tribal networks evolve, as primarily a mechanism for structuring and stabilizing social and economic relations between individuals and ethnic groups in an otherwise highly competitive environment.

The concepts of "tribe" and "ethnic group" should not be confused. Whereas ethnicity represents a system of self-identity that arises within the context of social interaction, tribes are characterized as networks of social and economic integration that function both within and across ethnic boundaries. Tribes or tribal networks can be defined as social networks integrated by cross-cutting pan-residential institutions (e.g., sodalities) but lacking class structure or a prescribed system of hierarchy (Sahlins 1968; Service 1971; Braun and Plog 1982). These networks range in complexity and scale from short-lived, personally negotiated alliances between individuals to formally negotiated and symbolically maintained regional alliances between ethnic groups. Previously, I have referred to the latter regional and interethnic alliances as "complex tribes" (Habicht-Mauche, Hoopes, and Geselowitz 1987; Habicht-Mauche 1988b).

Tribal alliances can be viewed as lines of communication and cooperation that facilitate the transmission of materials and information (Braun and Plog 1982) between individuals and groups. The stability and interdependence of these cooperative alliances are sustained through a process of complementarity and reciprocity. For example, the exchange of localized resources is often a central feature of tribal interactions. If resources are fairly homogeneous throughout a given region, complementarity may be established through role differentiation and the subsequent exchange of specialized goods or services. In the context of forming and sustaining tribal networks, then, trade is more than a simple economic transaction; it is also a social act of negotiation that symbolically and materially links groups in a web of interdependency based on reciprocity and mutual obligation (Mauss 1967).

Stable interethnic relations presuppose the existence of a mutually intelligible set of prescriptions governing situations of contact and interaction. As a result, one would expect the process of tribalization to reduce ethnic and cultural diversity in a region because shared behaviors, values, and symbols are both required and generated by the level of cooperation and communication needed to sustain these networks. The widespread exchange of certain resources and specialized crafts would also serve to reduce local stylistic diversity within the region of tribal integration.

Arroyo Hondo Pueblo and the Rio Grande Classic Transition

The northern Rio Grande culture area has been defined as stretching from Isleta Pueblo on the south to Taos Pueblo on the north, and west to east from the Jemez Mountains to the upper drainage of the Pecos River (Wendorf and Reed 1955) (see fig. 4). The site of Arroyo Hondo Pueblo (LA 12) is located near the eastern periphery of this region at the base of the western foothills of the Sangre de Cristo Mountains, about five miles southeast of Santa Fe, New Mexico (fig. 5).

The pottery collections from Arroyo Hondo provide a rare opportunity to address the issue of the structural relationship between changes in stylistic diversity in material culture and changes in the nature and organization of social and economic interaction in the northern Rio Grande area. Inhabited, off and on, between ca. A.D. 1300 and 1425, the occupation at Arroyo Hondo spanned a period of major restructuring in northern Rio Grande society. In archaeological terms, these years mark the transition between the so-called late Coalition and early Classic periods (Wendorf and Reed 1955; Cordell 1989) (table 1). This transition was marked by dramatic changes in population size, settlement structure, local and regional social organization, ceremonialism, craft specialization, and economic integration. The following study will focus on documenting patterned changes in ceramic styles at Arroyo Hondo and integrating these patterns into a new model of ethnic diversity, social organizational change, and economic integration in the northern Rio Grande during this transitional period.

In the early 1970s, Arroyo Hondo Pueblo became the focus of an extensive archaeological research project directed by Douglas W. Schwartz of the School of American Research in Santa Fe. As a result of five summers of excavation, nearly 20,000 fragments of decorated pottery and almost seven times that number of corrugated culinary ware fragments were recovered from excavated roomfill and plaza tests across the entire site. This collection represents one of the largest and best-documented archaeological samples of fourteenth- and early fifteenth-century Rio Grande pottery ever assembled from a single site. As such, it is a vital record of changes in regional ceramic production and trade in the northern Rio Grande during the late Coalition and early Classic periods.

Arroyo Hondo Pueblo was among the largest communities in the northern Rio Grande during this critical transitional period. The earliest tree-ring dates indicate that the town was first settled around A.D. 1300, during an episode of increased precipitation that allowed Pueblo farmers to take full advantage of the agricultural potential of this otherwise marginal upland location (Rose, Dean, and Robinson 1981; Wetterstrom 1986). During the first three decades of the fourteenth century, the pueblo prospered and grew rapidly. At its height in the 1330s, the town consisted of over 1,000 rooms in 24 multistoried roomblocks arranged around 10 plazas, and it supported a population of between 500 and 1,000 individuals (Wetterstrom 1986).

Shortly after A.D. 1335, however, seasonal precipitation became highly variable and unpredictable (Rose, Dean, and Robinson 1981). These climatic fluctuations may have had a negative impact on Arroyo Hondo's subsistence base. Both plant and faunal remains from the site indicate increasing food shortages after the 1330s (Wetterstrom 1986). Skeletal remains also reveal evidence of dietary stress and high infant mortality (Palkovich 1980; Wetterstrom 1986). Suffering from malnutrition and disease, the town's population declined dramatically. Tree-ring dates show a slump in building activities between A.D. 1335 and 1355 and again between 1360 and 1370 (Lang and Harris 1984). Trash deposits from the site indicate that by 1345 much of the pueblo may have been abandoned (Schwartz 1986). For the next thirty years the pueblo was inhabited, at most, by a small, remnant population, perhaps seasonally, and at times it may have been totally vacant. This period of abandonment marks the end of what has been designated the Component I occupation at Arroyo Hondo (see fig. 2).

The Component I occupation at Arroyo Hondo corresponds to a time of dramatic population growth and settlement expansion in the northern Rio Grande area. The rapidity and scale of this expansion suggest that the population increase may have been due, in part, to either a direct migration from the northern San Juan (Cordell 1989) or the retreat southward of groups from

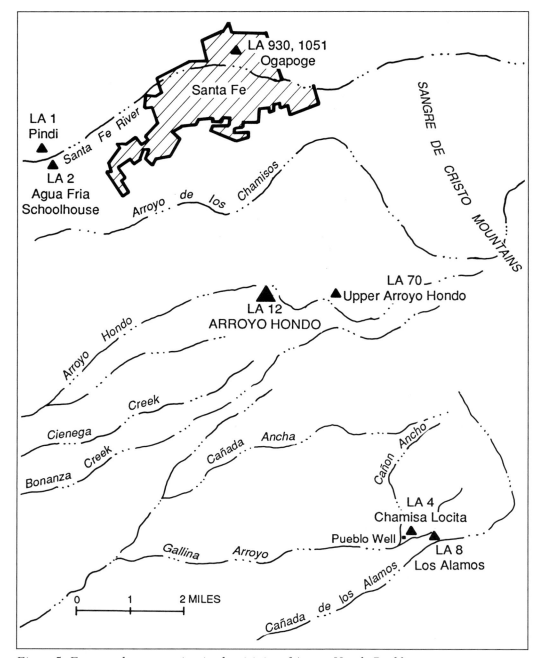

Figure 5. Fourteenth-century sites in the vicinity of Arroyo Hondo Pueblo.

the northwest periphery of the northern Rio Grande in the face of this movement of people out of the San Juan. In either case, as a result of this external demographic pressure, new social and ethnic alliances would have been forged as these immigrants merged with the indigenous inhabitants of the northern Rio Grande to form large, aggregated settlements. Competition and conflict over access to limited resources, such as agricultural land, may have intensified between these emerging ethnic groups as a result of the increasing density and decreasing mobility of population in the area.

The period was also marked by increased local patterning in material remains. This patterning is most clearly reflected in the diversity of local black-on-white ceramic styles recognizable in the archaeological record of the turn of the fourteenth century. This emphasis on

TABLE 1
Temporal framework for Arroyo Hondo Pueblo.

Dates A.D.	Periods	Arroyo Hondo Sequence	Pottery Sequence
1600	Late Classic		
1500	Early Classic	Component II	Glaze B
1400	Classic Transition	Component I	Glaze A
1300	Coalition		Galisteo B/W Wiyo B/W
1200			Santa Fe B/W
1100			

cultural diversity may represent a mechanism for validating cultural identity and ethnic boundaries in an increasingly complex and competitive social landscape.

Correlating with another episode of increased moisture, a second phase of settlement began at Arroyo Hondo in the 1370s. The second component village was built atop the ruins of the first, but it never achieved the areal extent or scale of its predecessor. At its peak around A.D. 1400, the Component II village consisted of only 200 single-story rooms organized in 9 roomblocks around 3 plazas (see fig. 3). Population probably never exceeded 200 to 300 inhabitants (Wetterstrom 1986). Recurrent drought returned to the area sometime after 1415, and the second occupation of the site was terminated rather abruptly after a fire destroyed a large part of the village during the 1420s (Schwartz 1986).

The Component II occupation at Arroyo Hondo represented a relatively small village by early Classic period standards, when large, aggregated towns were increasingly becoming the norm. Structural changes in the nature of craft production and trade, initiated during this period, served to link dispersed aggregated settlements and settlement clusters in the northern Rio Grande into a single, integrated social and economic network. The nature and extent of this new network is most clearly reflected in the manufacture and distribution of the early glaze-painted ceramics. Local centers of glaze-ware production emerged in the Zia–Santo Domingo, Albuquerque, and Galisteo districts that appear to have controlled the manufacture and trade of glaze-painted pottery to large areas of the northern Rio Grande and beyond (Shepard 1942; Warren 1970). Although the ceramic remains from Arroyo Hondo are dominated by black-on-white ceramics throughout, there is a dramatic increase in the frequency of glaze-on-red (G/R) ceramics, especially from the Galisteo district, in the second component assemblage.

The emergence of local craft specialization and long-distance regional trade, such as that exemplified by the distribution of the glaze wares, is indicative of the diversification and complementarity characteristic of stable tribal networks. Along with revealing something about the basic nature of culture change in the Rio Grande area during the Rio Grande Classic transition, the analysis of ceramic collections from Arroyo Hondo should increase our understanding of the changing structural role of ceramic stylistic diversity in the emergence of these new social and economic networks.

Chapter 2

The Pottery from Arroyo Hondo Pueblo

The pottery used and discarded by the residents of Arroyo Hondo Pueblo belonged to a long-standing ceramic tradition that has been a characteristic feature of northern Rio Grande culture for over a thousand years. Archaeologists have divided this pottery into a series of named types in an attempt to systematize analysis and description and in order to gain a clearer understanding of the spatial, temporal, and cultural relationships that existed among the various manifestations of this ceramic tradition. By studying the pottery from Arroyo Hondo within the context of these standardized types, one can begin to analyze the processes of site growth, use, decline, and abandonment in both historical and regional perspective. Furthermore, comparisons of ceramic assemblages can reveal something of the level of social, economic, and technological interaction that existed between the people of Arroyo Hondo and their neighbors.

This chapter presents a brief history and critique of the existing northern Rio Grande ceramic typologies. Adaptations and revisions of these schemes are proposed based on information gained from the study of the Arroyo Hondo pottery collections and on the need to simplify and clarify the existing systems. Brief descriptions of each of the major types recovered from Arroyo Hondo are presented, and their frequency and distribution across the site are recorded.

In addition to the classical taxonomic schemes, attribute analysis is used to identify and quantify variability both within and between types and to escape the traditional limitations of strictly normative modes of analysis. For example, attribute analysis allows for the identification of new analytical categories that can be used to address issues of form, function, technology, and style that crosscut the simple time-space framework of the traditional typologies.

Northern Rio Grande Ceramic Typologies

Adolph Bandelier, beginning in the 1880s, was probably the first anthropologist to use formal pottery types as a tool for studying the prehistoric ruins of the Southwest (Bandelier 1881, 1890, 1892). Kidder (1915) expanded on Bandelier's techniques in his doctoral dissertation on the pottery from the Pajarito Plateau, but it was not until Nelson's (1913, 1914, 1916, 1917) stratigraphic excavations in the Galisteo Basin that the validity and analytical usefulness of such a strategy were proven.

In the decades that followed, the focus of ceramic studies in the northern Rio Grande was on the identification, description, and formalization of distinct pottery types from throughout the region. These types acted primarily as cultural-historical markers, allowing researchers to order sites sequentially through time and to organize them into cultural units based on the distribution of certain stylistic attributes across space.

Two early contributions to this work were seminal to the formation of the general system of ceramic classification still in use by most Rio Grande archaeologists. The work of Kidder and his colleagues at Pecos Pueblo (Kidder and Kidder 1917; Kidder 1927; Kidder and Amsden 1931; Kidder and Shepard 1936) provided detailed descriptions of most of the major ceramic types found in the northern Rio Grande valley and established the stylistic criteria on which the discrimination between types in the area would be based. Mera's (1933, 1934, 1935) studies of surface collections at the Laboratory of Anthropology in Santa Fe provided a basic outline of the spatial and temporal distribution of specific pottery types throughout the northern Rio Grande region. Mera also introduced the binomial system of classification to Rio Grande ceramic studies.

Kidder once defined a pottery type as "the totality of characteristics which make a given ceramic group different from all others" (Kidder and Amsden 1931:221–22). This concept of type corresponds more or less with Spaulding's (1953) definition of artifact types as "non-random clusters of attributes." All attributes and forms of variability, however, are not weighted equally in the identification of Rio Grande ceramic types. Traditionally, emphasis has been placed on identifying suites of characteristics that covaried through time and space, with little attention paid to the analysis of formal or decorative variability within temporal-spatial contexts. Also, unlike Spaulding and his colleagues, researchers in the northern Rio Grande created types based largely on intuitively derived sorting categories rather than on statistically derived attribute clusters. As a result, there has been little or no standardization of the criteria on which divisions between groupings are based. This method has led to the definition of pottery types of varying specificity and differing temporal and spatial relevance. For example, both Santa Fe Black-on-white pottery, which was produced throughout much of the northern Rio Grande for over two hundred years, and Pindi Black-on-white, whose production was limited to a single river drainage and possibly a single site, for only a few decades, have both been considered types despite the fact that they clearly represent hierarchically different units of analysis.

In an attempt to address just such problems of comparability, integration, and interpretation, the type-variety system of classification was developed in the late 1950s (Wheat et al. 1958; Phillips 1958; Smith et al. 1960; Willey, Culbert, and Adams 1967). The type-variety system is a hierarchical taxonomy in which pottery is incorporated into increasingly inclusive groups based on similarities in certain well-defined attributes. Such a system helps clarify the technological and stylistic connections between groups, as well as their temporal, spatial, and cultural relationships. Furthermore, it allows for the identification of analytical units of varying size and complexity.

Despite these advantages, the type-variety system of ceramic classification has never penetrated the older, more established Rio Grande typology. There are several reasons why ceramicists have been reluctant to adopt the type-variety system in this area. First, the Kidder-Mera classification has long-standing precedence, and any attempt to modify the existing system substantially would drastically affect the comparability and usefulness of the older site reports from the region. Second, the criteria on which type distinctions are based in the northern Rio Grande focus primarily on paste characteristics and surface treatment. The hierarchical arrangement of such technologically oriented attributes is somewhat less straightforward than is the more common use of other attributes, such as form and decoration.

In the following summary, I have attempted to bring the Rio Grande classification into compliance with the basic structure of the type-variety system. I have tried, as far as possible, to retain existing sorting categories, while at the same time explicitly systematizing and standardizing the criteria on which they are based. These categories have been arranged in a hierarchical framework which will help clarify technological, cultural, and temporal relationships among groups of ceramics.

An outline of the classificatory system used in this study is summarized in table 2. Four levels of categories were used: ware, series, type, and variety. Wheat, Gifford, and Wasley (1958:34–35) defined a ware as "a large grouping of pottery types which has little temporal or spatial implication but consists of stylistically varied types that are similar technologically and in method of manufacture." Based on these criteria, the Rio Grande ceramics from the Arroyo Hondo pottery collections can be divided into three basic ware categories: Rio Grande Gray Ware (Colton 1953:26), Pajarito White Ware (basically equivalent to Colton's [1953] Pajarito Gray Ware), and Rio Grande Glaze Ware (Mera 1933). Along with representing major technological categories, these three wares probably represent distinct functional classes of ceramics, as well. Most of the rare, exotic trade ceramics from the site can be classified into one of two ware categories: Cibola White Ware (Colton 1953) or White Mountain Red Ware (Colton 1953; Carlson 1970).

As used by Colton (1953:52), a series is a sequence of types that has a more restricted geographical distribution than the ware of which it is a part and is composed of types that generally succeed one another through time. The series concept was extremely useful for organizing and analyzing the carbon-painted white wares from the northern Rio Grande, which, after A.D. 1300, clearly break down into a number of distinct local styles. It was far less useful, however, in dealing with the glaze ware ceramics, whose developmental sequence is fairly uniform throughout their distribution. As a result, the glaze wares have not been subdivided into geographical series but rather into temporal groupings that follow the traditional Glaze A(I), Glaze B(II), and so forth, sequence devised by Kidder (Kidder and Shepard 1936) and Mera (1933).

As noted above, types, within the Rio Grande classification system, have been viewed implicitly as unique clusters of attributes characteristic of a particular time and place. Thus defined, this concept of artifact type is more or less equivalent to the general definition of artifact style presented in chapter 1. Within the context of the present study, then, the two terms can be used interchangeably. Unlike other areas of the northern Southwest, in the northern Rio Grande distinctions between ceramic styles or types have been based primarily on physical or technological attributes rather than decorative or formal attributes. Those attributes that are most often recognized as having stylistic or typological significance include (1) paint type; (2) paste composition, texture, and color; and (3) surface treatment and finish.

While aligning themselves with the basic concept of a ceramic type as a "cluster of attributes," Wheat, Gifford,

TABLE 2
The classification of pottery from Arroyo Hondo Pueblo.

Classification	Estimated Dates
I. Rio Grande Gray Ware	
Santa Fe Series	
Rio Grande Corrugated	1025–1300
Tesuque Gray	1250–1500
II. Cibola White Ware	
Puerco-Chaco Series	
Red Mesa Black-on-white	900–1050
Rio Grande Series	
Kwahe'e Black-on-white	1025–1175
Socorro Series	
Socorro Black-on-white	1050–1300
Chupadero Black-on-white	1175–1545
III. Pajarito White Ware	
Jemez Series	
Vallecitos Black-on-white	1230–1400
Jemez Black-on-white	1360–1660
Pajarito Series	
Santa Fe Black-on-white, *var. Santa Fe*	1175–1425
var. Pindi	1300–1400
Wiyo Black-on-white	1250–1425
Abiquiú Black-on-white	1340–1450
Galisteo Series	
Galisteo Black-on-white, *var. Galisteo*	1270?–1425
var. Kendi	1350–1400
Pecos Series	
Rowe Black-on-white, *var. Poge*	1300–1425
var. Arroyo Hondo	1380–1425
IV. Jeddito Yellow Ware	
Jeddito Series	
Jeddito Black-on-yellow	1300–1450
V. White Mountain Red Ware	
Zuni Series	
St. Johns Polychrome	1175–1300 +
Heshotauthla Polychrome	1275–1400
VI. Rio Grande Glaze Ware	
Glaze A Red	
Los Padillas Polychrome	1300–1350
Agua Fria Glaze-on-red	1315–1425
San Clemente Glaze Polychrome	1340–1425
Sanchez Glaze-on-red	1400–1425
Glaze A Yellow	
Cieneguilla Glaze-on-yellow	1370–1425
Glaze B	
Largo Glaze-on-red/Glaze-on-yellow	1400–1450

and Wasley (1958:34–35) recognized that "some method is needed to designate entities which do not differ markedly from a described type and yet are useful if given separate recognition." To meet this requirement they suggested the use of a classificatory unit known as a "variety." "A variety differs from the type to which it is related only in one or more minor particulars [attributes]. In terms of geographical distribution and time span it may be equal to that of the type, although generally it is more restricted in one or both of these elements" (Wheat, Gifford, and Wasley 1958:34–35).

Attribute Analysis

Several valid theoretical and methodological criticisms can be leveled against the standard normative classification system presented above. One of the most important of these criticisms is that by pigeonholing sherds and vessels into these idealized "types," one tends to obscure a great deal of variability that may have important temporal, behavioral, or cultural significance. A second problem is that the questions that researchers can ask of the ceramic data are to some extent limited by the structure of the classification system used. For example, the Rio Grande ceramic typologies were originally set up to act as cultural-historical markers, and as such they have functioned reasonably well over the last fifty or so years. This system, however, is not well suited to studies of pottery function that are dependent on the analysis of vessel size and shape—attributes that are rarely of classificatory significance in Rio Grande ceramic typologies.

In order to overcome some of these limitations, a modified form of attribute analysis was used in the study of the pottery from Arroyo Hondo Pueblo. In this case, attribute analysis was not used to create a new statistically derived typology. Rather, by working within the existing structure of defined types, the statistical analysis of attribute variability was used to clarify type descriptions and to validate the stylistic significance of pottery groupings. This method was also used to monitor changes in individual attributes through time. Finally, analyses of vessel shape, size, and decoration facilitated the study of pottery function and design.

Methods of Analysis

The remains of approximately 17,700 painted vessels were recovered from room and kiva excavations at Arroyo Hondo. This estimate was achieved by recording all mendable or matching sherds from the collection as single vessels, while counting each isolated sherd as an individual vessel. Virtually all of the sherds had been sorted and typed by Richard Lang and his assistants during the early 1970s. Spot-checking of pottery lots from a variety of proveniences revealed that Lang's sorting criteria corresponded more or less with my own. As a result, Lang's original pottery classifications were used as the basis for the analysis of the temporal and spatial distribution of ceramic types at the site. An inventory of all the analyzed pottery by type and provenience appears in appendix A.

About 1,700 decorated sherds from selected test units within plazas at the site were also inventoried and appear in appendix A. Unfortunately, plaza trash deposits tended to be shallow and unstratified. Much of the ceramic material from plaza tests has never been inventoried or typed and, as a result, was largely excluded from the following study.

The painted pottery from 17 of the 64 excavated rooms from Component I, and 12 of the 52 excavated rooms from Component II, was examined personally by the author as part of the attribute analysis. The ceramic material from one kiva from each component was also analyzed. These proveniences are listed in table 3. This nonrandom sample was selected to insure representation of pottery from areas widely scattered across both the early and the late villages. Totals of 2,543 Component I decorated sherds and 4,163 Component II decorated sherds were analyzed. These sherds represent approximately 40 percent of the inventoried decorated ceramics from excavated room proveniences and plaza tests at Arroyo Hondo.

Virtually all the pottery in this sample is from roomfill trash. Isolated abandoned rooms appear to have functioned as trash dumps for the inhabitants of adjacent occupied rooms and roomblocks. Thin layers of windblown trash deposits are also present in most roomfill. Finally, some portion of the trash fill from rooms may have melted out of collapsed adobe walls after abandonment. Unlike other large adobe sites in the northern Rio Grande (Patricia L. Crown, personal communication, 1991), however, excavation records indicate that melted adobe was probably not a significant factor in the composition of roomfill at Arroyo Hondo.

Because of the nature of these site formation processes, it is clear that this sample of roomfill is virtually useless for synchronic functional studies of room use or site activity areas. Fine-scale diachronic analyses are also difficult because most roomfill trash could only be dated within very general parameters. For example, trash from certain Component I rooms must date from after the latest structural tree-ring date for the room but before the

TABLE 3
Proveniences sampled for attribute analysis.

Component I	Component II
Trash-filled rooms	Trash-filled rooms
12-4-2	12-7-6
12-5-4	12-9-6
12-5-6	12-9-8*
12-5-11	12-9-10
12-9-7	12-10-3
12-11-4	12-11-7
12-11-6	12-15A-7
12-11-8	12-15-6
12-11-9	12-16-1
12-12-4*	12-16-13
12-14-5	12-16-18
12-15-7	12-16-20
12-15A-9*	12-16-25
12-16-30	12-20-4*
12-16-35	Kivas
12-18-7	12-C-2
12-18-14	
12-18-15	
12-20-6*	
12-24-3	
Kivas	
12-D-2	
Plaza middens	
12-C-3 (lower levels)	

*Culinary ware only.

construction date of the overlying Component II room. As a result of these limitations, all the roomfill trash analyzed from each component was combined into a single analytical sample. The two resulting samples could then be used to make very general "early versus late" diachronic comparisons of attribute and type frequencies.

A combination of qualitative and quantitative data on 36 different attributes—relating to vessel shape, vessel size, paste characteristics, surface characteristics, and decoration—were recorded for each sherd, using a standard database program (Excel®) on a Macintosh® personal computer. The attribute data were then summarized and analyzed using a statistics package (Data Desk®) on the Mac. The most diagnostic attributes for each of the major types are outlined below along with a discussion of temporal trends and other comparative patterns in the data.

Analysis of design was limited to either whole or partially reconstructed vessels. Despite the extensive nature of excavations at the site, the sample of whole or partially

reconstructed decorated vessels from Arroyo Hondo is surprisingly small (only around 45 vessels). For each vessel, information was recorded in a database on paint type, overall design layout, and individual decorative elements. These data are summarized in the discussion of decoration that follows the overall type descriptions.

The analysis of gray ware from Arroyo Hondo posed a number of methodological problems. Many of these are representative of problems that plague the study of Southwestern utility wares in general. For one thing, the sheer volume of the excavated assemblage is somewhat daunting. It has been estimated that corrugated sherds outnumber painted sherds in the assemblage on the order of roughly 10 to 1 (Schwartz and Lang 1973). The author's own estimate suggests that the ratio may be closer to 6.5 to 1. These estimates would indicate that the total number of corrugated sherds from excavated room proveniences from Arroyo Hondo is somewhere between 100,000 and 150,000+.

Gray ware ceramics analyzed in the 1970s were typed using at least three different, noncomparable classificatory systems. The most detailed information on the largest volume of corrugated sherds exists for the material collected in 1973. To increase this sample size, comparable data were recorded for all of the corrugated ceramics from the proveniences used in the attribute analysis of the decorated ceramics (see table 3). Data on each of the whole or partially reconstructed culinary vessels were also recorded. This resulted in a total sample of corrugated pottery of 43,402 sherds and 28 whole or partial vessels. This figure has been estimated to reflect approximately 30 to 40 percent of the total assemblage of Rio Grande Gray Ware recovered from room excavations and plaza tests at the site. Data recorded for each sherd or vessel included information on surface treatment and paste characteristics. Additional information on vessel shape and size was recorded for whole and partial vessels. The results of this analysis are summarized in the discussion of Rio Grande Gray Ware.

The Pottery from Arroyo Hondo Pueblo
Rio Grande Gray Ware

The so-called utility or culinary wares have long been the poor stepchild of Southwestern ceramic studies. Unfortunately, the degree of confusion that exists in the literature related to these ceramics is inversely proportional to the amount of attention they have received from researchers. Even in detailed site reports, the description and analysis of utility wares is often limited to a brief and very generalized discussion. In fact, most of the utility pottery from prehistoric ruins in the northern Rio Grande has yet to be divided into standardized, named types. These ceramics are so often neglected because they generally reflect much slower rates of stylistic change and have fewer easily observable and measurable attributes. These characteristics have made it extremely difficult to segregate utility pottery into neat taxonomic units and have limited the ware's usefulness for establishing relative chronologies and studying diachronic cultural change (Ford, Schroeder, and Peckham 1972:37; Lang 1975a:90d). This utility pottery, however, does reflect a long-standing and more or less stable technological tradition that functioned as an integral part of the domestic lifeways of the Eastern Pueblos for hundreds of years.

Probably the most comprehensive analysis of Rio Grande utility ceramics was presented by Kidder in his report on the pottery from Pecos (Kidder and Shepard 1936). Kidder used strictly descriptive terminology to segregate utility pottery on the basis of differences in surface treatment (i.e., Indented Corrugated, Indented Blind Corrugated, etc.). In his more cursory treatment of the subject, Mera (1935) attempted to bring the utility ware classification into compliance with his standard binomial system. He identified three types that are of significance to the present study: Tesuque Smeared Indented, Cundiyo Micaceous Smeared Indented, and Cordova Micaceous Ribbed. The identity of these types was based on a supposed combination of paste characteristics and surface treatment. In reality, however, the surface treatments used to distinguish Mera's types grade into one another, and hybrid vessels are common. For example, smeared indented corrugation and ribbed coiling often occur on the same vessel (fig. 6). Paste distinctions are also not as clear-cut as Mera suggested. Sherds assignable to Tesuque Smeared Indented on the basis of surface treatment run the range from pastes tempered with sand or crushed rock containing no mica to pastes containing highly micaceous, decomposed, metamorphic rocks (i.e., gneiss or schist). Not all "ribbed" vessels, however, are made from the friable, residual clays that are generally associated with so-called micaceous pottery of the Rio Grande area.

The fact that Mera's types are virtually impossible to find in any given culinary sherd collection is probably responsible for the fact that descriptive terminology akin to that of Kidder continues to be used by most researchers. These descriptive units (Indented Corrugated, Smeared Indented Corrugated, Ribbed, etc.) are not equivalent, however, to ceramic "types," per se, but

rather represent useful and convenient descriptive sorting categories.

Continued research of this problem may reveal a greater degree of seriational and spatial patterning in the variability that characterizes utility pottery from the northern Rio Grande than is readily apparent in the material from the Arroyo Hondo collection. Identification of such patterning would justify the division of this ware into a number of named types and varieties. At present, however, the author agrees with Lang (1975a) that most of the utility pottery from Arroyo Hondo can be divided into two broadly defined types, which he has designated Rio Grande Corrugated and Tesuque Gray. Both types incorporate a large range of variability in surface treatment and paste composition that will be discussed in greater detail in the sections that follow. Both types belong to a single developmental sequence that Lang (1975a) named the Santa Fe Series. Colton (1953:26) offered the name Rio Grande Gray Ware to cover all of the utility ware pottery from the northern Rio Grande, and that name is retained here out of convenience and precedence.

SANTA FE SERIES

RIO GRANDE CORRUGATED. This type is more or less synonymous with Kidder and Shepard's (1936:304) Indented Corrugated. Pots of this type are characterized by being fully indented over their entire conspicuously corrugated exteriors, with little or no evidence of subsequent smearing. This surface treatment is extremely rare at Arroyo Hondo, accounting for only 0.4 percent (154 sherds) of the analyzed sample. Occasionally, the basal region of the pot was scraped over to leave a plain, smooth surface. This variant surface treatment probably accounts for many of the 342 "plain" gray-ware sherds analyzed.

Paste textures are coarse to very coarse. Composition is variable and does not appear to be correlated with variation in surface treatment. Color is usually masked by carbon but tends to range from gray to very dark gray.

Culinary pottery with all-over indented corrugations is most commonly found in association with Kwahe'e B/W and early Santa Fe B/W decorated ceramics (ca. 1025–1250). Toward the end of the thirteenth century, however, quality of workmanship began to decline perceptibly, and overall smearing of corrugations became more and more common (Mera 1935:14). The relative paucity of sherds exhibiting conspicuously indented corrugations at Arroyo Hondo suggests an upper limit of production for Rio Grande Corrugated of around A.D. 1300.

Figure 6. Tesuque Gray Ware sherds, showing a combination of surface treatments.

TESUQUE GRAY. The type name Tesuque Gray has been adopted to cover a wide range of variation in paste composition and surface treatments that proliferated throughout the northern Rio Grande valley during the late Coalition and early Classic periods (ca. A.D. 1250–1500). The geographic designation has been retained after the first of Mera's (1935) named types, Tesuque Smeared Indented. Due to the variability in surface texturing found in this type, the color-descriptive "gray" has replaced "smeared indented" in the binomial designation. Although gray hues are typical, colors in fact range from

black to reddish yellow. The type, as defined here, subsumes (1) Mera's (1935) Tesuque Smeared Indented, Cundiyo Micaceous Smeared Indented, and Cordova Smeared Ribbed, as well as his unnamed smeared indented pottery of the Jemez and Galisteo drainages; (2) Indented Blind Corrugated, Clapboard Corrugated, Unindented Corrugated, and Unindented Blind Corrugated pottery of the upper Pecos and adjacent areas (Kidder and Shepard 1936); (3) smooth diagonal indented corrugated and ribbed indented corrugated ceramics of the Cochiti area (Honea 1968); and (4) Pajarito Smeared

14

Indented (Sundt 1972), as well as most other "smeared," "blind," or "obliterated" corrugated ceramics described from the northern Rio Grande.

Nearly 99 percent of the culinary pottery analyzed from Arroyo Hondo falls within the Tesuque Gray category. The range of surface treatments represented in the collection and their frequencies are listed in table 4. As the table indicates, smeared indented corrugations and smeared corrugations dominate the assemblage; however, smeared ribbed, ribbed, and smeared banded treatments are also common. In addition, as can be seen from the table, combinations of two or more surface treatments often occur on the same pot. One of the most common combinations consists of a banded or ribbed treatment on the rim, neck, or upper body and smeared or smeared indented corrugations over the lower body and base.

Two paste types dominate the culinary ware assemblage from Arroyo Hondo. These paste types crosscut all recorded surface treatments. The first and more common paste is composed of a coarse- to very coarse-textured residual clay containing large fragments of pink to pinkish orange granite, gneiss, and platy gold mica. This paste type characterizes up to 89 percent of the Component I assemblage and 86 percent of the Component II assemblage. The second paste type is distinguished by the use of highly micaceous residual clays containing abundant medium to coarse fragments of platy mica and angular fragments of white quartz-mica schist. These micaceous clays were used in about 11 percent of the culinary ware from Component I and increased slightly to 14 percent of Component II. The sources of the raw materials used in the production of this culinary pottery were probably the various metamorphic clay and rock outcroppings of the Sangre de Cristo Mountains east and northeast of Arroyo Hondo Pueblo (see chap. 3).

Cibola White Ware

This ware category incorporates all of the mineral-painted pottery recovered from Arroyo Hondo. Mineral-painted pottery is extremely scarce at the site, making up about 0.1 percent of the inventoried collection of decorated ceramics. These ceramics fall into two distinct categories. The first category consists of sherds from vessels whose production substantially predates the major occupations at Arroyo Hondo and which have, by one mechanism or another, found their way into the later deposits at the site. The Kwahe'e and Red Mesa sherds fall into this category. The second category consists of sherds from contemporaneous exotic vessels from the Rio Abajo area of New Mexico that probably reached Arroyo Hondo through trade with the pueblos of either the Socorro or Salinas districts. This category includes the Socorro Black-on-white and Chupadero Black-on-white material.

PUERCO-CHACO SERIES

RED MESA BLACK-ON-WHITE. One sherd of Red Mesa B/W was recovered from Component II trash deposits dating prior to 1381, but it is obviously a piece of much earlier date. During the tenth century the occurrence of Red Mesa B/W spread eastward from its Cibola heartland to cover essentially all of the Rio Grande area. By the middle of the eleventh century, however, it was largely being replaced in the northern Rio Grande by the indigenous Kwahe'e B/W (Sundt 1987:127).

The isolated specimen from Arroyo Hondo is from a bowl, thickly slipped on both surfaces, although the slip failed to obscure paste color completely. Slip color is a brilliant white. Both surfaces have been polished. The mineral paint is very dark gray (10yr3/1) with a slight brownish cast (all color designations follow Munsell Soil Color Charts, 1975 ed.). The lip is decorated with a painted line. A thin upper framing line is present on the interior well below the lip, and the single element of design remaining of the primary composition is a solid right triangle, pendent from the upper band line and embellished with dots. The rim is direct and contracting with a rounded lip. Paste color is a uniform gray (7.5yr6/0), and temper consists of crushed light gray to black sherd (Lang 1975a).

RIO GRANDE SERIES

KWAHE'E BLACK-ON-WHITE. One sherd of Kwahe'e B/W came from the pit room below room 12-11-6. Kwahe'e was the dominant painted pottery type in most of the northern Rio Grande, with the possible exception of the Taos district, during much of the eleventh and twelfth centuries. Clearly an indigenous product, it marks the beginning of a succession of black-on-white types unique to the northern Rio Grande area. Stylistic influences from the west and northwest, however, remained strong (Sundt 1987:127–28).

The most distinguishing characteristic of the Kwahe'e sherd from Arroyo Hondo is its paint, which is composed of iron with a carbon binder. Paint color is dark gray to very dark gray (7.5yr4/0, 7.5yr3/0). The specimen represents a bowl with a contracting, direct rim and a flattened lip. Both surfaces are smooth but unslipped. The interior is lightly polished over the paint. Both surfaces

TABLE 4
Frequency of Rio Grande Gray Ware surface treatments at Arroyo Hondo Pueblo.

Surface Treatment	Types	Component I		Component II	
		No.	%	No.	%
Plain	Tesuque Gray/Rio Grande Corrugated	163	0.6	179	1.0
Indented corrugated	Rio Grande Corrugated	104	0.4	49	0.3
Indented corrugated/banded	Rio Grande Corrugated	–	–	1	–
Banded	Tesuque Gray	188	0.7	206	1.1
Banded/ribbed	Tesuque Gray	2	–	2	–
Smeared banded	Tesuque Gray	344	1.4	164	0.9
Smeared banded/banded	Tesuque Gray	1	–	–	–
Smeared banded/banded/ smeared ribbed/smeared indented corrugated	Tesuque Gray	1	–	–	–
Ribbed	Tesuque Gray	319	1.3	215	1.2
Ribbed/smeared banded	Tesuque Gray	–	–	3	–
Smeared ribbed	Tesuque Gray	561	2.2	33	0.2
Smeared corrugated	Tesuque Gray	4,309	17.1	3,201	17.5
Smeared corrugated/smeared indented corrugated	Tesuque Gray	19	0.1	2	–
Smeared corrugated/banded	Tesuque Gray	–	–	6	–
Smeared corrugated/smeared banded	Tesuque Gray	1	–	13	0.1
Smeared corrugated/ribbed	Tesuque Gray	38	0.2	3	–
Smeared indented corrugated	Tesuque Gray	18,524	73.6	13,675	74.8
Smeared indented corrugated/ indented corrugated	Tesuque Gray	1	–	–	–
Smeared indented corrugated/ ribbed	Tesuque Gray	66	0.3	47	0.3
Smeared indented corrugated/ smeared ribbed	Tesuque Gray	99	0.4	18	0.1
Smeared indented corrugated/ banded	Tesuque Gray	29	0.1	88	0.5
Smeared indented corrugated/ smeared banded	Tesuque Gray	63	0.3	34	0.2
Unknown	Tesuque Gray/Rio Grande Corrugated	325	1.3	334	1.8
TOTAL		25,157	100.0	18,273	100.0

are gray (10yr6/1). Paste color is homogeneous and similar in color to the surfaces. The paste consists of an untempered, silty clay containing abundant grains of frosted quartz and soft, yellow-white calcium carbonate. This paste is similar to that which characterizes some of the later Santa Fe B/W ceramics at the site.

SOCORRO SERIES

SOCORRO BLACK-ON-WHITE. Two specimens of Socorro B/W were recovered from late Component I deposits in rooms 12-11-8 and 12-18-7. Socorro B/W is a poorly dated, mineral-painted, black-on-white ceramic type from the lower Rio Grande area, most at home on the west bank of the river. It appears to have been produced from the middle of the eleventh century to around A.D. 1300 (Mera 1935; Sundt 1987). Its presence at Arroyo Hondo may reflect early, low-level trade connections with people of the Rio Abajo area.

The sherd from room 12-11-8 represents a small jar. The interior is smooth but shows faint wiping or scraping striations. The exterior is covered by a thick, even (if somewhat pocked), light gray slip (10yr7/1). The exterior appears to have been polished prior to painting. The pigment is iron, and paint color ranges from a dark reddish brown (5yr3/2) to very dark gray (10yr3/1). The design is composed of opposed hatched elements. The paste is a uniform dark gray (7.5yr4/0), edged with white (10yr8/1) on the exterior margin. The temper is black sherd mixed with quartz sand (Lang 1975a).

The second sherd is from a bowl. The interior surface is white (10yr8/1), well smoothed but unpolished, and is pocked. The exterior surface is light gray (10yr7/2) and pitted. The mineral paint is an even, very dark gray (2.5y3/0). The paste color is white (10yr8/1) with a gray (7.5yr6/0) core. Temper is similar to the previous specimen.

CHUPADERO BLACK-ON-WHITE. A total of 14 Chupadero B/W vessels are represented in the inventoried collections from Arroyo Hondo. Ten vessel fragments came from Component I contexts, mostly from proveniences associated with the period between 1330 and 1350; however, the type has been found in proveniences dating from as late as the first quarter of the fifteenth century (Lang, this volume).

Chupadero B/W was the dominant decorated white ware pottery along the southeastern fringes of Pueblo country for over three hundred years. The earliest dates for the occurrence of the type cluster around 1175, but it continued to be produced well into the 1540s. The core area of its production and distribution was in the vicinity of Chupadera Mesa, adjacent portions of the Tularosa Basin, the upper Jornada del Muerto, and the Rio Grande valley between Belen and Socorro (Hayes 1981). The type was widely traded, however, particularly to the south and east. It is common on sites in northern Chihuahua and is a ubiquitous component of sites as far east as the south Texas Plains (Hayes 1981). It is found in low frequency as a trade ware on most northern Rio Grande sites as well.

I analyzed 8 of the 14 Chupadero specimens from Arroyo Hondo. All had dense, well-fired pastes that ranged in color from gray (2.5yr6/0, 10yr6/1) to white (10yr8/1), with most being a uniform light gray (10yr7/1, 7.5yr7/0). The specimens were tempered with moderate to abundant, fine to medium fragments of dark gray to black crushed sherd. Petrographic analysis (see chap. 3) revealed that schist-tempered culinary sherds were favored for temper.

Seven of the eight vessel fragments were from jars. Chupadero jars from various sites have been shown to conform to amazingly uniform standards of both shape and size (Hayes 1981; Beckett 1985), and the vessels from Arroyo Hondo do not appear to be an exception. The one measurable base fragment was from a large globular jar with a flattened base, approximately 30 cm in height and nearly 37 cm wide at the shoulder (fig. 7b). It has been estimated that vessels of this size could hold nearly 15 quarts (Hayes 1981:70). The rim fragments are also suggestive of the standard globular jar with a short narrow neck (11.5 cm in diameter) and slightly flaring rim (fig. 7a). The two handles present in the collection are of the vertical double loop type, formed of two rolls of clay placed parallel to each other and compressed together slightly. One of the handles is attached at the base of the neck, and the other example is attached just below the lip. Both examples terminate at the upper body of the jar, above the point of greatest diameter.

One rim fragment is from a hemispherical bowl with a direct rim and rounded lip. The thinness of the sherd (3.75 mm) indicates that it is from a relatively small vessel.

The interior surface of all of the jars and the exterior surface of the bowl all exhibit the rough, deep, horizontal striations so diagnostic of Chupadero B/W (Mera 1931). Jar exteriors are covered with a thick, but irregularly applied, off-white (5yr8/1, 10yr8/1) to light gray (10yr7/1–2) slip. Fire clouding is common. The light gray slip on the interior of the bowl is thin and streaky. Slipped surfaces are generally well polished.

The iron paint ranges in color from a good dense black (7.5yr2/0) to very dark gray (10yr3/1) to dark grayish brown (10yr4/2). The paint is often quite faint and subject to abrasion.

Design layouts consist of continuous or paneled bands filled with opposed hatched and solid elements like those described by Mera (1931:1), Kidder (Kidder and Shepard 1936:348), and Hayes (1981:70–71). These broad bands cover much of the body surface above and below the point of maximum diameter. In one case, a similar but narrow band of design is present on the jar neck. Another rim sherd has short, broad lines pendent from the lip. One handle fragment has been decorated with a series of four horizontal lines (Lang 1975a).

Pajarito White Ware

JEMEZ SERIES

VALLECITOS BLACK-ON-WHITE. Five fragments of Vallecitos B/W were found at Arroyo Hondo. One specimen was found in the fill of room 12-5-9 in a horizon believed to have been associated with the abandonment of

Figure 7. Chupadero Black-on-white jar sherds: a, *rim (left); neck and handle;* b, *base.*

the first village (Lang 1975a). Vallecitos B/W is essentially a regional variant of Santa Fe B/W, whose development and distribution were largely limited to the upper drainage of the Jemez River and its higher tributaries (Mera 1935). This type was the predominant decorated white ware pottery in that area from the mid-thirteenth to the mid-fourteenth century, when it began to be replaced by Jemez Black-on-white (Sundt 1987). Production, however, may have continued as late as A.D. 1400 (Mackey 1982).

The pastes of the Arroyo Hondo specimens range in color from very light gray (2.5y8/0) to light reddish brown (5yr6/4). Temper consists of fine quartz sand and volcanic ash, with dark particles of pyroxene and muscovite and coarser fragments of glassy pumice. One fragment also contained fine, angular, crushed sherd.

All five sherds are from medium-sized unrestricted hemispherical bowls. One rim is direct with a flattened lip and has an estimated maximum diameter of about 22 cm. Vessel interiors are covered with a distinctive thick, even, cream-colored (10yr8/2) slip that has been polished to a high gloss. The exterior surfaces of two of the specimens are unslipped; the third is slipped but unpolished. The carbon paint ranges from a dark gray (2.5y4/0) to a dense black (2.5y2/0).

JEMEZ BLACK-ON-WHITE. A total of five Jemez B/W bowl fragments were recovered from room and kiva excavations at Arroyo Hondo. Three are from Component I contexts, and two are from proveniences assigned to Component II. The scarcity of Jemez B/W at Arroyo Hondo conforms to the commonly held notion that the type was not widely traded. The core range of Jemez B/W is essentially the same as that of Vallecitos B/W (Mera 1935). The type was exceptionally long-lived, being produced in the Jemez district for nearly three hundred years, from the mid-fourteenth through the mid-seventeenth century (Sundt 1987).

The Arroyo Hondo specimens are typical in having pastes that range in color from grayish brown (10yr5/2) to brown (7.5yr5/4) and are tempered with coarse vesicular pumice and volcanic ash. Petrographic analysis (see chap. 3) showed that this pumice-ash is of a more dacitic composition than that which characterizes Pindi B/W, having a higher percentage of plagioclase feldspars and dark accessory minerals.

One rim sherd is from a restricted spheroidal bowl with an inverted rim and rounded lip. Average wall thickness is 4.9 mm. All but one specimen have a thick, crackled, creamy white (10yr8/1–2) slip on both surfaces; the exception is slipped only on the interior. Interiors are well polished. Polishing on exteriors is more

irregular, and flaking and fire clouding are both common. The carbon paint has the typical range of gray to brownish gray hues.

PAJARITO SERIES

SANTA FE BLACK-ON-WHITE, VAR. SANTA FE. This indigenous carbon-painted pottery spread rapidly throughout the northern Rio Grande during the thirteenth century. It is commonly found on sites from the eastern foothills of the Sangre de Cristo Mountains between Springer and the Pecos River to the lower drainages of the Puerco west of San Ysidro, and from Tijeras Canyon north to the Chama River (fig. 8) (Mera 1935; Stubbs and Stallings 1953). Associated dendrochronological dates indicate that the type first developed sometime between 1175 and 1200 and was common throughout the area as late as 1350 (Smiley, Stubbs, and Bannister 1953:25–26, 58; Stubbs and Stallings 1953:16–17, 48, 156–62; Breternitz 1966:95; Honea 1968:161, 163; Sundt 1987).

Tree-ring dates from Arroyo Hondo, however, suggest that Santa Fe B/W vessels continued to be produced in substantial quantities in the northern Rio Grande until sometime after 1410. Archaeomagnetic dates from the site also confirm the presence of the type through the end of the first quarter of the fifteenth century (Lang 1975a). These data indicate that large quantities of Santa Fe B/W pottery continued to be made and used far longer than has been previously accepted. Its production spans almost 250 years, from the late Developmental period through the beginning years of the middle Classic, making Santa Fe B/W one of the longest-lived carbon-painted white ware types in the northern Rio Grande and probably the most widely distributed as well.

Santa Fe B/W pottery accounted for 17.5 percent and 18 percent, respectively, of the Component I and Component II ceramic assemblages from Arroyo Hondo (table 5). More detailed seriational studies (see Lang, this volume), however, show that the frequency of Santa Fe pottery at the site was not as stable through time as these combined data would indicate. The type is seen to drop from an average frequency of over 70 percent in the earliest dated components of the site to a low of about 6 percent during the middle of the first component (ca. 1330). Its popularity appears to rebound, until by the beginning of Component II it again represents nearly 30 percent of the decorated ceramics from the site.

Because other black-on-white ceramic types, such as Rowe, *var. Poge,* and Santa Fe, *var. Pindi,* whose popularity peaked during the first component, do not show a similar resurgence in frequency during the second component, it seems unlikely that the high percentages of Santa Fe B/W sherds recovered from Component II

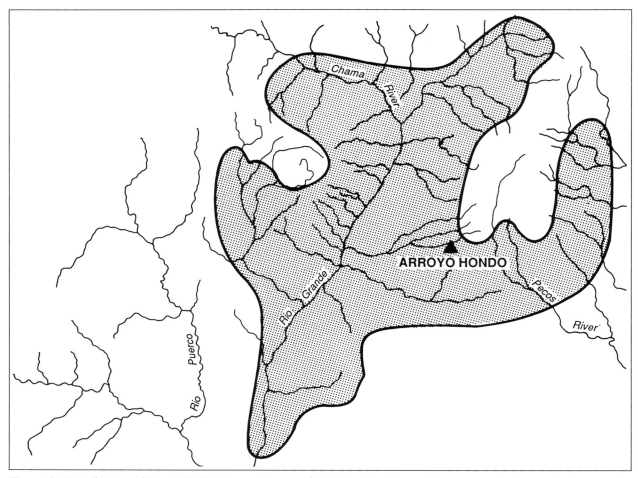

Figure 8. Distribution of Santa Fe Black-on-white pottery during the thirteenth century.

roomfill are simply the result of contamination from earlier trash fill or dissolved adobe walls. Rather, these radical shifts in the popularity of Santa Fe B/W probably reflect periodic changes in the nature of social and economic relations between Arroyo Hondo and its northern neighbors in the Tesuque and Pojoaque valleys. They may also reflect the periodicity and instability of occupation in that area of the Española-Chama district throughout the fourteenth century. Attribute values were recorded for 1,669 fragments of Santa Fe B/W vessels from the site (783 from Component I and 886 from Component II). The most diagnostic characteristics of this type are related to paste composition and color, sherd thickness, and surface treatment.

Amsden (Kidder and Amsden 1931:23) referred to Santa Fe B/W as Blue-Gray Type, emphasizing the distinctiveness of its paste color. Santa Fe B/W pastes are remarkably uniform in both color and texture. Core color is generally gray (10yr5/1, 10yr6/1) to light gray (10yr7/1). Carbon streaks are rare. Nonplastic inclusions are numerous but are of a fine to very fine texture, often invisible without the aid of a microscope or hand lens. Microscopic examination revealed two major types of inclusions: fine to very fine subrounded quartz silt/sand and very fine angular volcanic ash. There appears to be an almost continuous range of pastes, from those that contain quartz silt/sand exclusively, through those with a relatively even mixture of silt and ash, to those that have ash temper with few, if any, silty/sandy inclusions. Lang (this volume) noted that whereas silty/sandy pastes characterize the early end of the seriational sequence, the addition of ash temper appears to increase through time, with the very fine-textured, ash-tempered pastes dominating the Santa Fe B/W sherds from the second component.

Sherd thickness ranges from 2.5 mm to 9.2 mm, with

TABLE 5
Frequency of decorated ceramic types from Arroyo Hondo Pueblo.

Type	Component I		Component II	
	No.	%	No.	%
Indeterminate white ware	702	8.6	962	10.0
Santa Fe B/W, *var. Santa Fe*	1,429	17.5	1,723	18.0
Santa Fe B/W, *var. Pindi*	1,033	12.7	415	4.3
Wiyo B/W	1,475	18.1	1,925	20.1
Abiquiú B/W	12	0.1	151	1.6
Galisteo B/W (includes *vars.* *Galisteo* and *Kendi*)	1,169	14.3	1,288	13.5
Rowe B/W (includes *vars.* *Poge* and *Arroyo Hondo*)	1,973	24.2	1,519	15.9
Vallecitos/Jemez B/W	4 (1/3)	–	6 (4/2)	0.1
Red Mesa B/W	0	–	1	–
Kwahe'e B/W	1	–	0	–
Chupadero B/W	10	0.1	4	–
Socorro B/W	2	–	0	–
White Mountain Red Ware	0	–	5	0.1
St. Johns Polychrome	10	0.1	5	0.1
Heshotauthla Polychrome	8	0.1	8	0.1
Indeterminate Early G/R	225	2.8	1,139	11.9
Los Padillas Polychrome	19	0.2	10	0.1
Agua Fria G/R	38	0.5	219	2.2
San Clemente G/P	6	0.1	62	0.6
Sanchez G/R	1	–	2	–
Largo G/R	4	–	45	0.5
Cieneguilla G/Y	32	0.4	95	1.0
Largo G/Y	2	–	0	–
Jeddito B/Y	0	–	1	–
TOTAL	8,155	100.0	9,585	100.0

a mean of 4.9 mm and a standard deviation of ± 0.8 mm. The relative thinness of Santa Fe B/W vessels contrasts with the increasing thickness of succeeding types in the series. The overwhelming majority of the Santa Fe B/W sherds from Arroyo Hondo represent the remains of bowls. In contrast, jar fragments are extremely rare.

A great deal of variability exists in the treatment of decorated surfaces (i.e., bowl interiors and jar exteriors). Both slipped and unslipped (or self-slipped) examples occur. The distribution of slipped versus unslipped variants of Santa Fe B/W does not seem to pattern either temporally or spatially at the site. Also, both surface treatments crosscut paste categories. As a result, the data from Arroyo Hondo do not support the division of Santa Fe B/W into named varieties on the basis of surface treatment, as has been proposed by Honea (1968).

Unslipped or self-slipped surfaces are very close or identical in color to the vessel paste, with gray (10yr5/1, 10yr6/1, 10yr6/2) and light gray (10yr7/1, 10yr7/2) predominating. When special slip clays are applied, a dirty white (10yr8/1, 10yr8/2, 5yr8/1) surface is achieved. The majority (70%) of these surfaces are polished over both slip and paint, although the quality may vary from extremely uniform to streaked to very cursory. Poorly polished slips tend to slough off and wear easily.

Bowl exteriors are generally unslipped and rarely polished. Unslipped exterior surfaces exhibit the same range of light gray to dark gray colors that characterize pastes. Slips, when present, are usually thin and sloppily applied. In rare instances, the slip has been used as a paint to draw a broad, sloppy zigzag or loop design on the exterior. The surface is generally well smoothed; however, horizontal wiping and scraping striations are sometimes visible (7–9% of examples). Smeared indented or ribbed corrugations occur on the exteriors of less than 1 percent of the sample analyzed. Faint fingernail punctations were noted on four specimens.

The exteriors of another four specimens were covered by deep impressions, indicating that they had been molded inside baskets. These basket-impressed vessels appear to represent an early variant of Santa Fe B/W. Examples were relatively common in the deposits at the Forked Lightning site (LA 672) but rare in the later black-on-white assemblage from Pecos Pueblo (Kidder and Shepard 1936:383–85). The bowls were produced by pressing successive coils of clay into a small basket. When the edge of the basket was reached, a broad, free-standing rim was usually added, giving the vessel a distinctly "collared" appearance (fig. 9). The interiors were then usually smoothed, slipped, and painted.

The paint on Santa Fe B/W vessels is always carbon. The color on Arroyo Hondo samples is most often very dark gray (2.5y3/0), dark gray (2.5y4/0), or gray (2.5y5/0), although specimens with a slightly brownish tinge are common (10yr3/1, 10yr4/1, 10yr5/1). Although Santa Fe paints generally may be said to penetrate and adhere well, a watery consistency is suggested by their relative translucence and the smudging of larger, solid elements in the designs. In many cases, especially those with unslipped or self-slipped surfaces, the contrast between background and design is subtle at best (fig. 9).

Decoration is generally limited to a band of geometric designs on the interior of bowls and exterior of jars. Solid and hatched elements predominate. Framing lines and panel divisions are common. A more detailed and comparative discussion of design is presented below.

Santa Fe Black-on-white, var. Pindi. Shepard was the first to identify a coarse, pumice-tempered variety of Santa Fe B/W (Blue-Gray Type) (Kidder and Shepard 1936:463). Stratigraphic tests indicated that the variety underwent a short but dramatic spurt of popularity during the latter part of the black-on-white period at Pecos (ca. 1300–50). In their analysis of pottery from Pindi Pueblo, Stubbs and Stallings (1953:50) elevated this pottery group to a type, naming it Pindi B/W. They noted that the distribution of this pottery was rather restricted, being limited to a crescent area following the southern and western flanks of the Sangre de Cristo Mountains from Pecos Pueblo to Pindi Pueblo, in the vicinity of Santa Fe.

Associated tree-ring dates from Pindi (LA 1) suggest that this pottery was produced between 1300 and 1350, with the greatest popularity at ca. 1325. Dates from Arroyo Hondo indicate the appearance of Pindi B/W at

the site by around 1300, with continued occurrence in deposits dated as late as ca. 1425. There are no strong indications, however, that the type was actually being produced after about 1370. Pindi B/W ceramics reached their greatest popularity at Arroyo Hondo around the middle of the first component (ca. 1330–50), with frequencies dropping off sharply after ca. 1370 (Lang, this volume, and 1989).

Given its relatively restricted temporal and spatial distribution, I follow Shepard in viewing this pottery as a late, localized variety of Santa Fe B/W. The designation "Pindi," however, has been retained as the name of the variety.

The single most distinctive attribute of the *Pindi* variety of Santa Fe B/W is its temper. In place of the fine volcanic ash characteristic of both classic Santa Fe and Wiyo pastes, *Pindi* potters used a coarse, pumiceous ash temper, which shows up as large, brittle, white inclusions in a soft gray (10yr5/1, 10yr6/1) to light brownish gray (10yr6/2) paste.

About half of all *Pindi* bowl interiors are covered with a thin, streaky to moderately even slip, although sloughing and flaking of slips are common. White, light gray, and light brownish gray slips predominate. Interior surfaces are usually well polished over the paint. Exterior surface treatment is more variable. Slips occurred on only about 10 percent of the sample. Exterior surfaces are generally well scraped but grainy, with coarse fragments of pumice temper protruding, giving the surface a somewhat pitted appearance.

As in the *Santa Fe* variety, geometric paneled band designs predominate. The greater emphasis on solid versus hatched elements, however, is diagnostic of all white wares from the northern Rio Grande dating to the fourteenth century. The quality of the carbon paint sometimes achieves the density and deep black color characteristic of the best Wiyo specimens, but watery, more translucent examples are also known (fig. 10).

Wiyo Black-on-white. This type was originally called Biscuitoid by Amsden (Kidder and Amsden 1931)—a name that clearly reflects the close technological relationship of the type to the succeeding "biscuit wares" of the area. The distribution of Wiyo B/W is substantially restricted when compared to that of the classic variety of Santa Fe B/W, being limited largely to the traditional Tewa regions of the lower Chama, northern Pajarito Plateau, and Española Valley. The Santa Fe River and its tributaries mark the southern boundary of its major distribution (fig. 11).

Associated tree-ring dates suggest the appearance of

Figure 9. Santa Fe Black-on-white sherds.

Wiyo B/W in this core area by ca. 1250–75 and continuing through ca. 1400–25 (Stubbs and Stallings 1953: 16–17, 23; Smiley, Stubbs, and Bannister 1953:58; Breternitz 1966:104; Wendorf 1953:54; Traylor and Scaife 1982; Sundt 1987). The data from Arroyo Hondo do not substantially alter these associations, although they support the temporal data from Pindi in suggesting that the type did not become locally common in the Santa Fe area until after 1300. The seriational data indicate that Wiyo B/W was present in low to moderate frequencies (ca. 3–14%) throughout much of the first component of Arroyo Hondo, achieving its maximum

23

Figure 10. Santa Fe Black-on-white, var. Pindi, *sherds.*

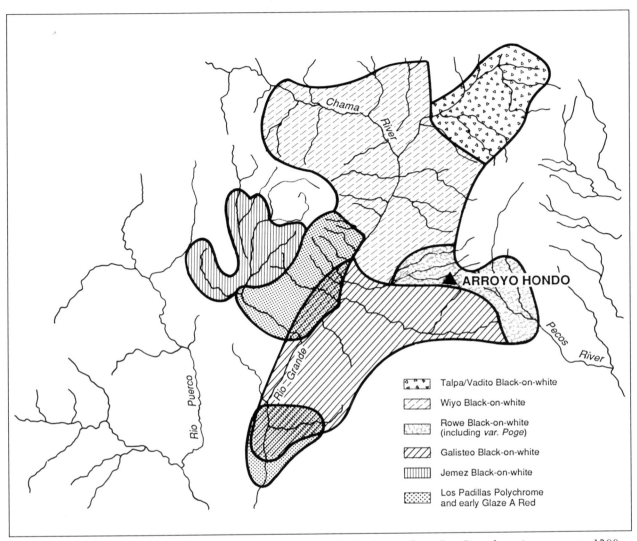

Figure 11. Primary distribution of local decorated ceramic styles in the northern Rio Grande region, ca. A.D. *1300.*

popularity (ca. 25%) at the site during the 1350s. The frequency of Wiyo B/W remains fairly stable throughout the second component, generally ranging between around 15 and 20 percent (Lang, this volume).

Wiyo B/W is distinguished from its predecessor, Santa Fe B/W, by its softer pastes and more oxidized colors. Wiyo pastes from Arroyo Hondo, although predominantly gray (10yr6/1) to light gray (10yr7/1), tend more toward light brownish gray (10yr6/2), pale brown (10yr6/3), very pale brown (tan) (10yr7/3), and light pinkish gray-brown (7.5yr6/3). A definable firing core is rare, but in a majority of specimens there is a distinct gradation in paste color from interior to exterior. In general, exteriors tend to be darker (lower value) and grayer (lower chroma),

whereas interiors tend to be lighter and browner. This gradation is indicative of a differential exposure of the two surfaces of the vessel to heat and air during the firing process.

Very fine, angular, volcanic ash is clearly the predominant tempering material. Although silty/sandy inclusions and coarse pumice fragments are common, the trend appears to be toward increasingly finer-textured pastes. At the same time, vessel walls increase in thickness, probably in response to the decreased plasticity and workability of the new finer-textured clays. Wiyo B/W sherds in the Arroyo Hondo sample range in thickness from 2.8 to 9.2 mm, with a mean of 5.3 mm and a standard deviation of ±0.9 mm.

One of the outstanding characteristics of Wiyo B/W vessels is the smoothness and evenness of their decorated surfaces. Bowl interiors and jar exteriors are either slipped or floated. In over three-quarters of the specimens examined, the surface has been rubbed with a hard object (i.e., polishing stone) while wet, causing a migration of clay particles to the surface. Two modes of slipping dominate the sample, the more common being a self-slip, in which the same clay that is used to produce the vessel body is applied to its surface. Less often, a distinct, lighter-firing slip clay is used. Both types of slips are thin but evenly applied and adhere well to the body. Surfaces are soft, however, and tend to abrade easily. Both slipped and floated surfaces are generally well polished to a satiny luster.

Jar interiors are unslipped and exhibit shallow to deep scraping marks. Over 95 percent of bowl exteriors are unslipped but usually well smoothed, exhibiting fine, horizontal striations. Fire clouding is common, being recorded for over 20 percent of the analyzed sample.

The denseness, blackness, and overall good quality of Wiyo B/W paint is one of the defining hallmarks of the type. The predominant paint colors range from gray (2.5y5/0) to black (2.5y2/0), with dark gray (2.5y4/0) to very dark gray (2.5y3/0) most common.

In the vast majority of bowls, paint is confined to the interior surface; on jars, to the exterior surface above the base. Lip embellishments (dots, dashes, etc.) are common. Wiyo designs are heavier than in Santa Fe B/W, with thicker brush lines and a greater use of solid elements (fig. 12). Paneled bands predominate. Many of the Wiyo vessels from Arroyo Hondo, however, have a distinctly "late" feel to them. Designs exhibiting bilateral and quadrilateral symmetry, reminiscent of early biscuit ware and glaze ware designs, are common.

ABIQUIÚ BLACK-ON-WHITE. This type, also referred to as Biscuit A (Kidder and Amsden 1931), is the first in the series of so-called biscuit wares whose distribution centers on the Chama Valley and Española Basin north of Santa Fe. Biscuit wares are characterized by their thick walls and fine-textured light gray to white pastes, which were thought to resemble unfired porcelain, or "bisque." This light paste forms an attractive contrasting background for the vessels' characteristically heavy, black designs. Biscuit wares were produced by Northern Tewa potters well into the seventeenth century.

Abiquiú B/W first appeared in the northern Rio Grande around the middle of the fourteenth century and continued in use for about a century (Breternitz 1966:70; Smiley, Stubbs, and Bannister 1953; Honea 1968:138;

Sundt 1987). These early biscuits are only a very minor component of ceramic collections from Arroyo Hondo, representing less than one percent of the entire decorated assemblage. Most of this material comes from Component II contexts, indicating that Abiquiú B/W vessels were rarely traded outside the Española-Chama district prior to ca. 1370. Similar chronometric data are available from the site of Las Madres (LA 25) in the Galisteo Basin, where Biscuit A does not appear until Period III, which has been dated to ca. 1360–70 (Schaafsma 1969).

There are many strong resemblances in terms of design and temper between the earliest biscuit wares and Wiyo B/W. In fact, the major difference between the two types appears to be in the kind of clay used. The small sample of Abiquiú B/W sherds from Arroyo Hondo is characterized by light gray (10yr7/1–2), very pale brown (10yr7/3), and white (10yr8/1) pastes. Shepard (Kidder and Shepard 1936:492–93) suggested that bentonite clays from the north side of the Jemez caldera were used to produce biscuit wares. These light-firing clays are characterized by high shrinkage and poor cohesiveness and workability. Such properties may explain the excessive thickness of biscuit ware vessels. The average thickness of Abiquiú B/W sherds from Arroyo Hondo is between 6.0 mm and 6.7 mm for both components, with vessel walls becoming thicker, on the average, through time.

Over 80 percent of the Abiquiú B/W sherds analyzed are tempered with fine-textured volcanic ash. In about 20 percent of the examples, coarser fragments of pumice and clear, angular quartz and feldspar fragments are visible.

Interior bowl surfaces are generally well finished, being either floated (83%) or slipped (17%). Slips are thin, even, and dense, but have a tendency to flake and wear off. Slip color is usually slightly lighter than that of the paste body. Decorated surfaces are well smoothed and polished but attain only a rather dull luster. Exterior surfaces are universally unslipped and unpolished. Fine to coarse scraping and wiping striations are often visible. Dark fire clouding of vessel exteriors is also common.

Abiquiú paints adhere well and have a deep, rich, very dark gray (2.5y3/0) to black (2.5y2/0) color. Decoration is confined to the interiors and lips of bowls and is similar to that described for Wiyo B/W (fig. 13).

GALISTEO SERIES

GALISTEO BLACK-ON-WHITE, VAR. GALISTEO. First described by Amsden (Kidder and Amsden 1931) as Crackle Type, Galisteo B/W exhibits a strong technological and stylistic relationship to the black-on-white ceramics from

Figure 12. Wiyo Black-on-white sherds.

the Mesa Verde region. In fact, early examples of the type are not easily distinguishable from Mesa Verde B/W. Shared attributes include sherd and volcanic rock temper; thick, white, well-polished slips that have a tendency to craze or crackle; carbon paint; square rims; and similar designs (Stubbs and Stallings 1953:50).

Galisteo B/W suddenly becomes the dominant decorated ceramic type on northern Rio Grande sites south of the Santa Fe drainage after ca. A.D. 1300 (see fig. 11), but there is evidence to suggest that it may have been produced in smaller quantities as early as ca. 1270 (Stubbs and Stallings 1953:16, 23; Honea 1968; Schaafsma 1967). Galisteo reached its peak of popularity and widest distribution during the mid- to late fourteenth century. Associated tree-ring dates from several sites including Arroyo Hondo, however, indicate that Galisteo continued to be produced and traded throughout the fifteenth century, well after glaze wares came to dominate the southern half of the northern Rio Grande region (Honea 1968; Lang, this volume, and 1989).

The classic variety of Galisteo B/W, as it is represented in the Arroyo Hondo collections, is characterized by light-firing, gray to white pastes (10yr5–8/1–2, 7.5yr5/0 to 8/0) that contrast markedly with the generally darker and browner pastes of the Pajarito Series. Dark-firing cores are present in about 30 percent of the specimens sampled. Temper is, universally, crushed sherd that appears as conspicuous medium to coarse, gray to black angular fragments in the light paste. A wide variety of accessory lithic and mineral inclusions are also visible.

Thick, hard slips that have a tendency to crackle or craze are a diagnostic feature of Galisteo B/W. Decorated surfaces (bowl interiors and jar exteriors) are consistently slipped. Bowl exteriors also were slipped in over 80 percent of the sample examined. Slip colors are predominantly white (10yr8/1,2) to light gray (10yr7/1,2 to 6/1).

The organic paints used to decorate Galisteo B/W vessels normally penetrate well. Paint color is generally a rich gray to very dark gray (2.5y3/0 to 5/0), with dark gray predominating (2.5y4/0). Decoration is generally limited to geometric paneled bands on bowl interiors and jar exteriors, although some bowls with overall quadrilateral symmetry were noted. Opposed hatched and solid elements are common. Secondary elements, such as pendent dots and rim ticking, are also common. Designs tend to be more complex and better executed on Galisteo vessels than on contemporaneous Pajarito Series vessels (fig. 14).

GALISTEO BLACK-ON-WHITE, VAR. KENDI. Approximately 6 percent of the Galisteo B/W sherds examined from Arroyo Hondo were tempered with intermediate volcanic rock fragments in place of the more common sherd temper. Stubbs and Stallings (1953:50) also identified Galisteo B/W pottery from Pindi Pueblo that was tempered with crushed volcanic rock (andesite). Similar ceramics were recovered from excavations at Las Madres, where they were given the type name Kendi Black-on-white. Stratigraphic data from Las Madres indicate that this variety of Galisteo B/W was most common between ca. A.D. 1360 and 1390 (Schaafsma 1969:21–23).

Honea (1968:137) also described a "Kendi variety of Galisteo Black-on-White" in the ceramic assemblage from the Alfred Herrera site (LA 6455) in the Cochiti Reservoir area. He noted that Kendi differed from the classic variety of Galisteo in having "a coarser tannish brown paste," as well as volcanic rock temper (Honea 1968:137). The distinction in paste texture and color noted by Honea, however, was not evident in the Arroyo Hondo sample.

PECOS SERIES

ROWE BLACK-ON-WHITE, VAR. POGE. Local, poor-quality variants of the Galisteo style appeared along the northern and eastern periphery of the type's distribution in the northern Rio Grande. This heterogeneous group of ceramics has been described variously under the designations Late Crackle Type (Kidder and Amsden 1931:26), Rowe Black-on-white (Kidder and Shepard 1936:474–75), and Poge Black-on-white (Stubbs and Stallings 1953:55–56). Rowe B/W is retained here as the type name for this group of ceramics because it is the binomial designation with precedence in the published literature.

The variety names *Rowe* and *Poge* are suggested to distinguish between related ceramic material from the upper Pecos and Santa Fe drainages, respectively. A third and newly defined variety of the type, *Arroyo Hondo*, also was identified. Ceramic material previously described in the literature as Rowe B/W, Poge B/W, or Late Crackle probably represents a mixture of all three varieties, and possibly other undifferentiated material.

The distribution of Rowe B/W parallels that of the *Pindi* variety of Santa Fe, ranging from Rowe Pueblo on the east, up the Pecos River, around the southern and western flanks of the Sangre de Cristo Mountains, and up the Santa Fe drainage as far west as Pindi (LA 1) and Agua Fria (LA 2) (see fig. 11).

At Pecos, Rowe B/W reached its peak of popularity toward the end of the "Black-on-White" period (around

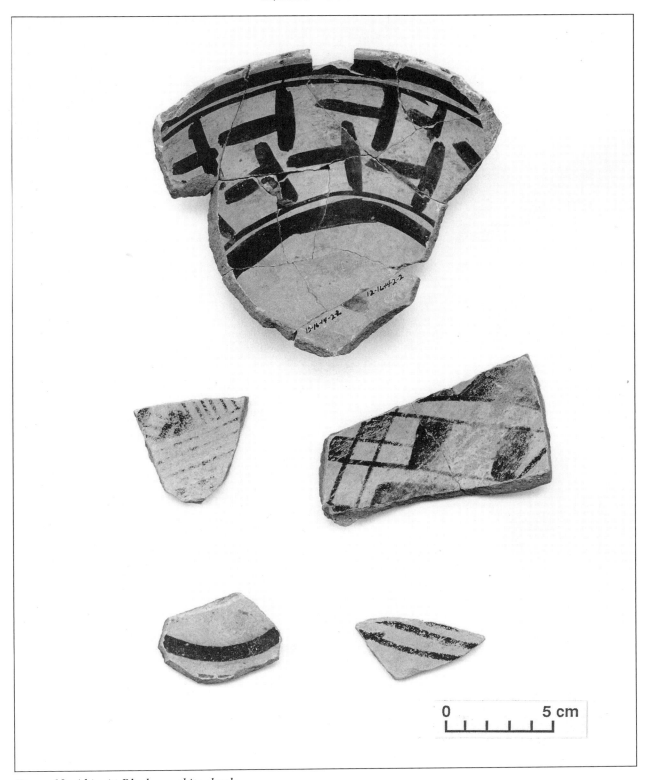

Figure 13. Abiquiú Black-on-white sherds.

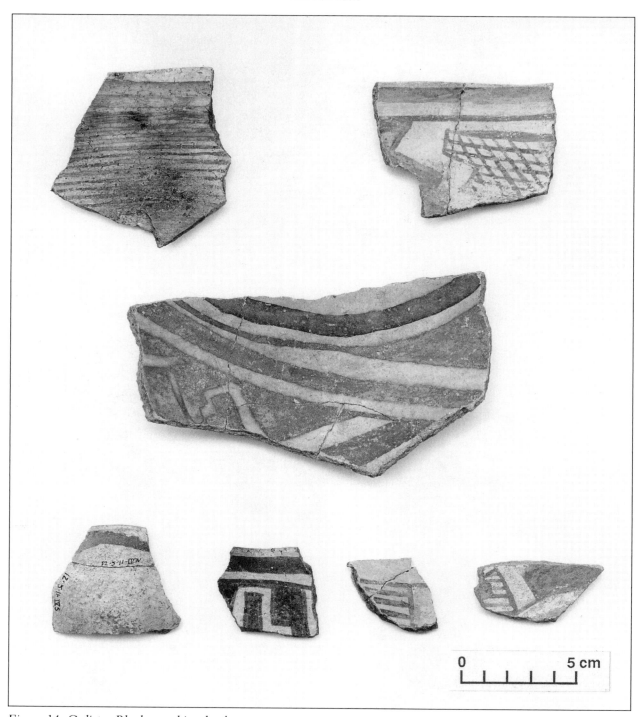

Figure 14. Galisteo Black-on-white sherds.

the mid-fourteenth century) (Kidder and Shepard 1936). Tree-ring dates associated with Poge B/W sherds at Pindi suggest that this variety was present by at least ca. A.D. 1300 and was common between 1325 and 1350. Dendrochronological and archaeomagnetic data from Arroyo Hondo indicate the continued local prominence of these ceramics well into the fifteenth century.

Although generally considered to be a late, degenerate form of Galisteo B/W (Kidder and Amsden 1931:26; Stubbs and Stallings 1953:56), the above dates clearly illustrate that Rowe B/W was a more or less contemporaneous type. Both the distribution and the physical characteristics of Rowe and its varieties suggest that they represent attempts to copy the Mesa Verde style of Galisteo B/W, using the inferior local clays and slips of the Santa Fe–Pecos district.

The *Poge* variety of Rowe B/W is the most common decorated ceramic type in the Component I assemblage from Arroyo Hondo but drops dramatically in frequency in Component II contexts (see table 5). Seriational data indicate that the variety peaked in popularity (ca. 20 to 30 percent) during a brief period between ca. A.D. 1320 and 1330 (Lang, this volume).

Poge sherds from Arroyo Hondo are characterized by soft, gray (10yr5/1 to 6/1; 7.5yr5/0 to 6/0) to light brownish gray (10yr6/2) and, occasionally, light brown (7.5yr6/4) pastes. Temper is predominantly medium to coarse lithic sand or a mixture of lithic sand and sherd. The lithic sand appears macroscopically as a heterogeneous mixture of gray and pink granite, gneiss, mica schist, pink and white feldspar, milky quartz, and mica. Coarse fragments of pumice are also common. In general, *Poge* pastes closely resemble Wiyo and *Pindi* pastes. Small or eroded fragments of all three types can be easily misidentified if close attention is not paid to temper.

Poge vessels are relatively thin walled (ca. 5 mm). As is true of all the black-on-white types from the northern Rio Grande, bowl forms predominate. Rim forms are direct to slightly inverted. A high percentage (43%) of flattened lips was recorded, reflecting the influence of the Mesa Verde style.

Considerable variation in surface treatment occurs on *Poge* vessels. Slips can be thin and streaky but are more often thick and chalky and erode easily. In many instances, virtually all of the slip and paint are gone, leaving a faint negative or ghost image of the original decoration. Remnants of slip were recorded on over 60 percent of vessel interiors and about half of the exteriors. Originally, however, bowls probably were slipped routinely on both surfaces. Slip colors are predominantly a dirty gray (10yr5, 6, or 7/1 to 2) to white (10yr8/1 to 8/2).

Poge paints are as variable as its slips. The degree to which painted designs have been retained is often directly related to the adhesion qualities of the slip underlying them. In some cases, however, the paint has been completely lost, although the slip itself has remained; whereas in others, the painted areas have withstood wear far better than adjacent slipped areas. Although densely painted examples occur, paint is normally rather thin and watery. Colors are predominantly dark gray (2.5y4/0) to gray (2.5y5/0). In some examples, the paint is only slightly darker than the slip over which it has been applied. Designs are similar to those characteristic of Galisteo B/W but are much more poorly executed (fig. 15).

ROWE BLACK-ON-WHITE, VAR. ARROYO HONDO. A small series of sherds (< 50) was identified in the decorated assemblage from Arroyo Hondo that fell within the general definition of Rowe B/W but was characterized by relatively dark (10yr4/1 to 5/1), poorly fired, coarse-textured pastes. This group of pottery appears to have been made using the same residual clays that were used to produce much of the culinary ware found at the site. These clays contain abundant coarse to very coarse, angular lithic fragments of granite, gneiss, and/or, to a lesser extent, quartz-mica schist. Coarse, platy fragments of gold or silver mica are also common. In some instances, crushed sherd has been added to the paste as temper. Bowls are generally slipped on both surfaces, with thick, chalky slips reminiscent of the *Poge* variety of Rowe. These slips, however, appear to adhere better to the coarser-textured pastes.

About three-quarters (32) of all the sherds classified as belonging to the *Arroyo Hondo* variety of Rowe B/W came from Component II contexts. More than half (18) of these sherds came from the fill of a single room (12-10-3), which yielded two tree-ring dates of 1375vv and 1385r, indicating that most of this pottery probably dates to after about A.D. 1380.

Jeddito Yellow Ware

JEDDITO SERIES

Jeddito Black-on-yellow. One fragment identified as Jeddito Black-on-yellow was recovered from the fill of a second component kiva in plaza C. One of a series of fine, yellow pottery types from the Hopi region of northern Arizona, Jeddito B/Y originated about A.D. 1350 and was still in existence as late as 1450 (Haury and Hargrave 1931; Hargrave 1932; Kidder and Shepard 1936; Smith 1971). Although it was widely traded, stratigraphic tests at Pecos Pueblo indicate that Jeddito Yellow Ware was not common in the northern Rio Grande until early

Figure 15. Rowe Black-on-white, vars. Poge *and* Arroyo Hondo, *sherds.*

Glaze II times (Kidder and Shepard 1936:368), or toward the end of the second component occupation at Arroyo Hondo, thus accounting for its extreme rarity at the site.

The sherd from Arroyo Hondo is characterized by a thick yellow slip (10yr8/6) over a pale yellow (10yr8/3), fine-textured paste. Both the interior and exterior are well polished. The interior of the bowl sherd is covered with a complex, repetitive design consisting of stepped line elements executed in a dark brown matte paint.

White Mountain Red Ware

ZUNI SERIES

ST. JOHNS POLYCHROME. Fifteen fragments of St. Johns Polychrome were identified in the ceramic assemblage from Arroyo Hondo. Most of these fragments came from Component I contexts. This type has been associated with dates ranging from A.D. 1175 to 1300 (Carlson 1970:39). Its presence at Arroyo Hondo suggests that it may have continued to be produced into the early decades of the fourteenth century.

The core area of the type's distribution is the Cibola area of west-central New Mexico, but it has long been known to be one of the most widespread pottery types in the Southwest. Small quantities of St. Johns Polychrome have been found from Mesa Verde on the north, east to the Pecos River, south to around Casas Grandes in Mexico, and west to the Chino Valley in Arizona (Carlson 1970:37). Along with the small number of Socorro B/W and Chupadero B/W sherds found at Arroyo Hondo, the St. Johns Polychrome sherds may reflect early, low-level contacts between the site's inhabitants and peoples living to the south and west of the northern Rio Grande valley.

The author examined 8 of the 15 St. Johns sherds from the site. Paste colors fall within the typical range for the type, from creamy white (10yr8/2) to light gray (10yr7/2), very pale brown (10yr7/3), or reddish yellow (5yr6/6). A gray (7.5yr5/0 to 6/0) carbon streak is common. Temper is medium, angular, crushed, black or red sherd. A thick, even, red (2.5yr5/6, 10r5/6) to reddish brown (2.5yr5/4) slip covers the interior and exterior of bowl fragments. Both surfaces are generally well polished.

Bowl interiors are painted with a dark gray (2.5yr4/0) to very dark gray (2.5yr3/0), matte mineral to matte glaze paint. A soft, chalky, white paint was used to decorate exteriors. Exterior decorations are generally heavy, with medium to wide linework. Designs are either contiguous bands or repeated unit elements. In many cases, the exterior decoration is highly eroded.

HESHOTAUTHLA POLYCHROME. Sixteen fragments of pottery from Arroyo Hondo were classified as Heshotauthla Polychrome. Heshotauthla is poorly dated but has been estimated to have been produced between A.D. 1275 and 1400 (Woodbury and Woodbury 1966). Heshotauthla evolved from St. Johns Polychrome in the Zuni area of west-central New Mexico. The major distinction between the two types is in decoration. Heshotauthla paints more often achieve a true glaze, although poorly vitrified examples were noted. Interior glaze-painted designs are simpler and more open than on St. Johns. Banded designs, with narrow banding lines and large, repeating elements laid out obliquely, predominate. Common elements include parallel lines and pendent dots. The exterior white-line decoration consists of a narrow band of either contiguous or paneled designs. Exterior linework is much finer than on St. Johns vessels (Carlson 1970) (fig. 16).

Rio Grande Glaze Ware

EARLY GLAZE RED

Indigenous copies of the Heshotauthla style have been found on sites in the Rio Grande valley (Warren 1976: B10) and are seen as the precursors of the Rio Grande Glaze Ware tradition. Local variations of this style are generally lumped into a loosely defined category referred to as Los Padillas Polychrome. Twenty-five glaze polychrome fragments from Arroyo Hondo were identified as belonging to this local northern Rio Grande variant of the Heshotauthla style. Most were tempered with either schist-temper sherd or black basalt, indicating a source of production in the Albuquerque or Zia–Santo Domingo districts (see fig. 11).

Although red ware vessels with glaze-painted designs may have been produced along the southern and western peripheries of the northern Rio Grande valley as early as A.D. 1300, glaze wares do not appear in significant quantities on sites outside the Albuquerque and Zia–Santo Domingo districts until after 1340–50 (Mera 1940:3; Stubbs and Stallings 1953:56; Schaafsma 1969). Even after this period, however, Arroyo Hondo appears to have been at the northern edge of the distribution of early glazes (fig. 17), remaining a predominantly black-on-white site throughout its occupation. Stratigraphic and seriational data (Lang, this volume) indicate that glaze ware, although present as early as ca. 1330–50, was not common at the site until after 1370 and that it never represented more than about 20 to 35 percent of the decorated assemblage, even in Component II. During a similar period at Las Madres, to the south

Figure 16. Heshotauthla Polychrome sherds.

in the Galisteo Basin, Glaze A Red represented between 40 and 50 percent of the decorated assemblage (Schaafsma 1969).

Almost 80 percent of all the analyzed glaze-on-red sherds from Arroyo Hondo are undecorated body sherds of indeterminate type. All of these sherds are characterized by light red (2.5yr6/6–8), red (2.5yr5/6), or reddish yellow (5yr5/6) pastes. Gray (2.5yr5/0 to 6/0) carbon streaks were recorded in over half of the specimens analyzed by the author. Pastes are generally fine textured. Three types of temper dominate the assemblage: gray

sherd, a fine-grained black basalt, and white or gray intermediate volcanic rock (i.e., latite). Mixtures of sherd and crushed rock were also noted.

Bowls continue to dominate the assemblage; however, unlike the black-on-white types, where jars are extremely rare (see table 6), nearly one-third of the glaze-on-red sherd fragments analyzed are from jars. Vessel walls are uniformly thin, averaging 4.5 mm in thickness. Interior and exterior surfaces are covered with a thick, even, light red (2.5yr6/6), red (2.5yr5/6), or reddish brown (2.5yr5/4; 5yr5/4) slip.

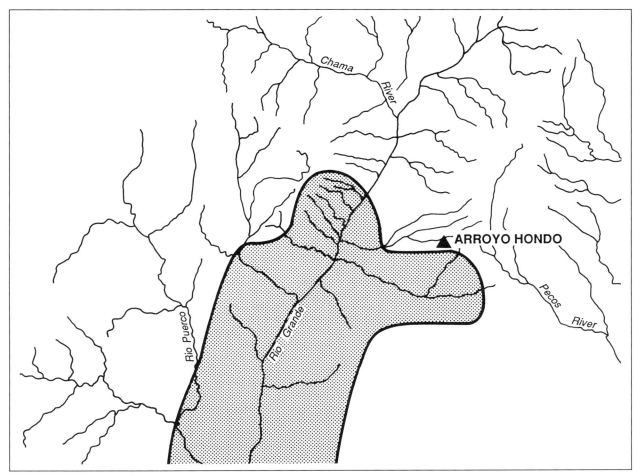

Figure 17. Distribution of early glaze ware production in the northern Rio Grande region, ca. A.D. *1350 to 1450.*

Early researchers (Kidder and Shepard 1936; Mera 1940) recognized that glaze ware vessels from the northern Rio Grande could be arranged in a temporal sequence from early to late based on differences in the rim forms of bowls. Most of the glaze-painted sherds from Arroyo Hondo belong to the earliest, or Glaze A, group. Bowls in this group have parallel sides, direct rims, and flattened lips (fig. 18a). Mera (1933) referred to the red ware version of Glaze A as Agua Fria Glaze-on-red (fig. 19). This simple bichrome pottery is the most common and widely distributed of the Glaze A types.

Mera (1933) also identified a rarer polychrome variant of Agua Fria, called San Clemente, that is characterized by a band of light gray (10yr7/2–3), tan (10yr8/3 to 6/3), or pinkish white slip (7.5yr8/2) on the interior of bowls or (rarely) exterior of jars that acted as a background for the application of a geometric band of glaze-painted decoration (fig. 19). The earliest dates for San Clemente cluster around A.D. 1325–50 (Honea 1973). Most (62) of the San Clemente Polychrome sherds recovered from excavations at Arroyo Hondo came from Component II contexts, thus supporting a mid- to late fourteenth-century date for the type.

Glaze A paints range from dull to glossy. Paint colors are generally dark to very dark gray (2.5yr3/0 to 4/0), with a hint of reddish brown. Designs differ from the black-on-white types, with a decreased emphasis on paneled bands and an increased emphasis on pendent triangular, rectangular, and lunar zones arranged to produce a pattern of overall bilateral, trilateral, or quadrilateral symmetry. Such designs are reminiscent of the so-called Pinedale style that characterized contemporaneous western polychromes from the upper and middle Little Colorado River valley (Carlson 1970).

35

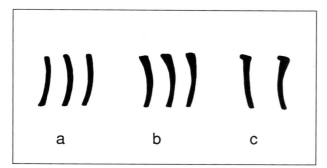

Figure 18. Early glaze ware rim forms.

Three sherds of a very rare early glaze type, known as Sanchez Glaze-on-red, were identified in the Arroyo Hondo collection. This type first appears in the northern Rio Grande around A.D. 1400 and differs from other early glazes primarily in bowl rim form. Rims are all of the low angular everted type, with a sharp inflection point near the lip (see fig. 18c). First occurring late in the Glaze A period, this rim form becomes the dominant type in the later Glaze C period (Honea 1973).

Forty-nine glaze-on-red sherds were found that had thickened rims characteristic of the Glaze B group (see fig. 18b). Almost all (45) of these sherds came from Component II contexts. Following Mera's (1933) classification, these sherds were categorized as Largo Glaze-on-red. Body sherds of Largo G/R, however, are generally indistinguishable from sherds of Agua Fria, and both were classified in this analysis as Indeterminate Early Glaze-on-red. Although the red version of Glaze B is very rare and poorly studied, it is probably contemporaneous with the better-known yellow version, dating to after A.D. 1425 (Hawley 1950:82; Honea 1973). The rare presence of Glaze B sherds places the terminal occupation of Arroyo Hondo during the third decade of the fifteenth century.

EARLY GLAZE YELLOW

Light-slipped, glaze-painted ceramics make up less than one percent (127 sherds) of the decorated assemblage from Arroyo Hondo. The relative rarity of glaze-on-yellow (G/Y) pottery at Arroyo Hondo is somewhat surprising, given the site's proximity to the type's presumed center of production in the Galisteo Basin. At Las Madres, Glaze A Yellow pottery, also known as Cieneguilla Glaze-on-yellow, first appears in contexts dated to between A.D. 1370 and 1380 (Schaafsma 1969), and potters in the Cochiti area began producing their own version of the type between 1380 and 1400 (Warren 1979:190).

The Cieneguilla pastes from Arroyo Hondo were predominantly light gray (10yr7/1–2; 7.5yr7/0) to gray (2.5yr6/0) or pink (5yr7/3–4 or 8/3) to light red (2.5yr6/6–8). Temper is generally either an intermediate volcanic rock (latite) or a fine-grained black basalt. Crushed sherd was also added in over half of the samples analyzed.

The majority (88%) of the sherds analyzed are from bowls. Bowl rims are mostly typical of the Glaze A group, being direct with parallel sides and flat to beveled lips. Two bowl rims with expanded rims characteristic of Glaze B (Largo Glaze-on-yellow), however, were also identified in the collection. Both interiors and exteriors are well slipped, although glaze-on-yellow slips tend to be softer and more chalky than their red counterparts. Colors range from a dirty white (10yr8/1–2) to very pale brown (10yr8/3–4 or 7/3–4) or yellow (10yr8/6).

The glaze paint is generally well vitrified and ranges in color from dark gray to black (10yr4/1 to 2/1), with a tendency toward brown (10yr4–5/2–3).

Form and Function

Among the Eastern Pueblos of the northern Rio Grande valley, ceramic vessels functioned primarily as containers for the processing, cooking, storing, and serving of food. Specialized vessels were also used in a variety of religious or ceremonial contexts. The unique physical properties of ceramic materials offer certain advantages for their use in a variety of different activities. For example, the types of raw materials selected and the ways in which these materials are manipulated during the manufacturing process can impart very specific physical properties to ceramic vessels that, in turn, can affect the suitability of these vessels to perform certain tasks. Furthermore, the plasticity of clay makes possible the creation of an almost infinite variety of forms that can be adapted to the particular needs of any task (Arnold 1985:138). Vessel shape, in fact, is one of the most behaviorally significant of all ceramic attributes. The adoption of a new form into the ceramic inventory of a culture may reflect the introduction of some new activity of economic or social importance to that society.

Most of the pottery from Arroyo Hondo can be divided roughly into three groups, or wares, based on fundamental differences in the use of raw materials, manufacturing techniques, and inventory of vessel forms. These groups are the gray wares, the white wares, and the glaze wares. Each ceramic group occupied a position of differing economic and social significance within northern Rio Grande society.

Figure 19. Agua Fria Glaze-on-red and San Clemente Polychrome sherds.

Gray Wares

The Southwestern gray wares are often referred to as utility wares or culinary wares. Ethnographic, as well as archaeological, evidence suggests that this pottery was, in fact, used primarily for the cooking and storage of food (fig. 20). This function is also substantiated by the thick, sooty, carbon deposits that coat and permeate the surface and paste of most sherds and vessels.

Cooking places a great many constraints on the range of acceptable physical and formal properties of ceramic vessels. The most critical physical attribute for cooking vessels is, of course, that they be resistant to thermal shock, or the stresses of repeated heating and cooling.

37

Figure 20. Depiction of a gray ware jar being used for cooking, from a kiva mural at Pottery Mound. (Courtesy The Maxwell Museum of Anthropology, University of New Mexico)

The principal variables affecting resistance to thermal shock are (1) the number, size, composition, and distribution of pores and aplastic inclusions (e.g., temper); (2) thermal expansion, or the extent to which the clay matrix and aplastic inclusions expand on heating; and (3) the shape of the vessel (Rye 1981:27).

Most aplastic inclusions have coefficients of thermal expansion greater than that of the surrounding fired clay and, thus, will expand differentially when the vessel is heated. Under repeated cycles of heating and cooling, differences in thermal expansion will result in fracture. The greater the average size of aplastic inclusions, the greater will be the stresses leading to fracture. Temper, however, also increases the elasticity of ceramic materials and acts to arrest crack propagation. Thus, a fine-textured ceramic paste would have a high initial strength but would lose a large proportion of that strength if subjected to repeated thermal shock. A coarser, densely tempered vessel, however, would probably be more resilient and longer lasting as a cooking vessel. The coarse-textured residual pastes that characterize the gray ware ceramics from Arroyo Hondo appear to have been well suited to maximize these physical properties.

Vessel shape can also affect its resistance to thermal shock. Thermal gradients that cause cracking are minimized by uniform wall thickness and the absence of sharp angles or corner points. Utility ware pottery at Arroyo Hondo occurs almost exclusively in the form of medium to large jars (fig. 21). These jars have nearly spherical to more elongated, ovaloid bodies. The more spherical forms tend to have angularly everted rims which meet the body of the pot at a sharp corner point, whereas the more ovaloid forms have gently inflected, everted rims. Vessel heights range from 7 cm to 36 cm, with both the mean and the median height falling at 22 cm. Mouth diameters range from 11 cm to 32 cm (mean = 19 cm), and maximum diameters range from 14 cm to 43 cm (mean = 26 cm). Vessel walls are relatively thin and even, averaging around 5.6 mm. One small, crudely made, smeared indented bowl is represented in the assemblage of whole culinary vessels from Arroyo Hondo (fig. 21f). The rim is slightly inverted, mouth diameter measures 13 cm, maximum diameter is 13.8 cm, and height is 6.5 mm.

As the above discussion indicates, the diagnostic physical and morphological attributes that characterize the Rio Grande Gray wares from Arroyo Hondo clearly indicate that these pots represent well-designed and highly

Figure 21. Gray ware vessel forms.

TABLE 6

Summary of morphological characteristics derived from white ware sherds from Arroyo Hondo Pueblo.

Type	Mean Thickness (mm)	Mouth Diameter			Rim Profile			Lip Form		Vessel Form		
		Range (cm)	Mean (cm)	Median (cm)	Invert %	Direct %	Evert %	Flat %	Round %	Bowl %	Jar %	Other
Santa Fe: Component I	4.9	12–34	22	22	58	40	2	41	59	96.8	3.2	–
Santa Fe: Component II	4.9	12–38	21	22	45	52	3	27	73	97.3	2.6	1 ladle
SF-Pindi: Component I	5.2	12–38	21	22	53	38	9	38	62	98.5	1.0	2 ladles
SF-Pindi: Component II	4.8	14–34	19	18	56	39	5	27	73	98.2	1.8	–
Wiyo: Component I	5.4	12–34	23	22	55	38	7	36	64	98.6	1.4	–
Wiyo: Component II	5.2	14–38	22	22	38	54	8	39	61	95.7	4.3	–
Abiquiú: Component I	6.1	(34)	(34)	(34)	–	33	37	33	67	100	–	–
Abiquiú: Component II	6.7	18–26	22	22	31	54	15	62	38	98.6	1.4	–
Galisteo: Component I	5.1	12–34	22	22	49	47	4	59	41	97.5	2.5	–
Galisteo: Component II	4.9	12–34	22	18	33	64	3	62	38	96.7	3.3	–
Rowe-Poge: Component I	4.8	14–34	21	22	56	44	–	38	62	96.0	4.0	–
Rowe-Poge: Component II	4.6	10–30	20	22	43	57	–	44	56	96.2	3.8	–

specialized cooking vessels. Storage may have been another important function of the corrugated ceramics. With the exception of a few imported Chupadero B/W vessels, there are no other large-capacity jars in the ceramic assemblages from the northern Rio Grande prior to the introduction of the glaze wares during the mid- to late fourteenth century.

White Wares

Bowl forms clearly dominate the black-on-white assemblage from Arroyo Hondo, with jars and other vessel forms represented by less than 4 percent of the sherds from each of the major types. The overall uniformity in size and shape of the black-on-white bowls in the Arroyo Hondo assemblage suggests that there was little or no functional distinction made between similar vessels from each of the local ceramic styles. These decorated bowls make up the bulk of the northern Rio Grande pueblos' "service ware" during the fourteenth century, being used in a variety of food processing and serving activities. They also may have played an important role in ceremonial activities as containers for offerings.

Such activities generally require vessels with fairly open, nonrestricted contours, and the bowls from Arroyo Hondo fulfill these requirements. The major morphological characteristics of these bowls are summarized in tables 6 and 7. The majority of these bowls appear to be ellipsoidal, with their diameter being as much as 2 to 2½ times greater than their height. Bases are generally rounded to slightly flattened (fig. 22). Inverted rim forms with the point of greatest diameter lying just below the lip predominate in Component I contexts. By Component II, however, the ratios have shifted in favor of more direct forms, with the point of greatest diameter at the lip. There is also a gradual trend among the Pajarito White Ware types toward an increase through time in the number of vessels with inflected contours and everted rims (from 2% to 15%). This variant is relatively rare among the Galisteo and Pecos series types, however, being represented by only 3 to 4 percent of the Galisteo rim sherds and none of the Rowe, var. Poge, sherds. Rounded lips outnumber flattened lips as much as 3 to 2, except among Galisteo B/W, where this ratio is reversed. The high frequency of flattened rims in Galisteo probably reflects the type's close stylistic relationship to Mesa Verde White Ware ceramic types, where such lip treatments predominate.

The range in vessel diameters (from 12 to 38 cm) is roughly the same for all the black-on-white types. The majority of bowls fall within a medium size category (20 to 30 cm). Vessel walls are uniformly thin (ca. 5 cm) within the Galisteo and Pecos series. There is a gradual temporal trend toward increasing wall thickness, however, among types in the Pajarito Series. In fact, sherd thickness is an important diagnostic attribute among the types in this series.

Although rare, a number of nonbowl forms were represented in the white ware collection from Arroyo Hondo. Detailed information on jar forms is difficult to determine, given the fragmentary nature of the specimens. Most were probably small to medium-sized (< 20 cm in height), spherical to ellipsoidal jars with short, raised, constricted necks (2–4 cm in diameter) and direct or slightly everted rims with contracting, rounded lips (fig. 23). Two small Santa Fe jar fragments in the Arroyo Hondo collection show the addition of small loop handles placed horizontally between the shoulder and the base of the neck. Isolated loop and strap handle fragments in the collection also may be from small to medium-sized canteen-style jars. Similar jars are illustrated by Stubbs and Stallings (1953: fig. 36h–1) from Pindi. These jars were probably used primarily to collect, transport, and store water.

A small number of ladles and ladle fragments also were identified among the black-on-white ceramic assemblage from Arroyo Hondo (fig. 24). Several other unusual forms are represented in the sample of whole or partially reconstructed vessels. One is a small (9.5 cm × 8.5 cm), spherical, simple restricted Galisteo vessel of the form often referred to as a seed jar (fig. 25a). Another is a medium-sized Galisteo jar with inflected contours and gently everted rim (fig. 25b). The most unusual feature of this vessel is its footed base. Strap handles are attached at either side of the jar from just below the inflection point to the point of vertical tangency. A paneled band design decorates the exterior, and a contiguous row of nested triangles is painted along the interior of the rim. The third specimen is a double-spherical, or gourd-shaped, vessel (fig. 25c). A contiguous band design decorates the interior of the upper lobe of the vessel, and a geometric cross is painted on the interior of the base. The function of these unusual vessel forms is unknown.

Finally, seven whole or nearly whole miniature jars are present in the decorated ceramic assemblage from Arroyo Hondo. Three of these vessels are illustrated in figure 26. All of the jars range between 4 cm and 7 cm in height. Four of the seven have spherical bodies with short, constricted necks. The other three are beaker shaped with distinctly flattened bases. Five specimens had small loop handles attached. One beaker-shaped vessel is decorated with a representation of a human

41

TABLE 7
Morphological characteristics of whole and partially reconstructed decorated vessels from Arroyo Hondo Pueblo.

Type	Form	Height (cm)	Mouth Diameter (cm)	Maximum Diameter (cm)	Mean Thickness (mm)
Santa Fe B/W	Bowl	14	35	–	6.0
Santa Fe B/W	Bowl	14	30	–	5.9
Santa Fe B/W	Bowl	13	28	–	6.1
Santa Fe B/W	Bowl	13	34	–	7.3
Santa Fe B/W	Bowl	8	18	–	6.5
SF-Pindi B/W	Bowl	14	30	–	5.9
SF-Pindi B/W	Bowl	13	32	–	5.7
SF-Pindi B/W	Bowl	11	22	–	6.3
SF-Pindi B/W	Bowl	11	32	–	4.9
SF-Pindi B/W	Bowl	?	26	–	6.2
Wiyo B/W	Bowl	13	22	–	4.5
Wiyo B/W	Bowl	11	27	–	6.8
Wiyo B/W	Bowl	?	34	–	6.7
Wiyo B/W	Bowl	15	33	–	5.0
Wiyo B/W	Bowl	13	32	–	6.4
Wiyo B/W	Bowl	12	25	–	6.7
Wiyo B/W	Bowl	13	29	–	6.1
Wiyo B/W	Bowl	13	29	–	6.2
Wiyo B/W	Bowl	9	20	–	6.9
Wiyo B/W	Bowl	11	28	–	5.5
Wiyo B/W	Bowl	13	30	–	9.1
Wiyo B/W	Bowl	?	26	–	5.8
Abiquiú B/W	Bowl	8	20	–	8.2
Galisteo B/W	Bowl	15	33	–	5.5
Galisteo B/W	Bowl	13	27	–	6.4
Galisteo B/W	Bowl	11	26	–	5.7
Galisteo B/W	Bowl	8	27	–	5.0
Galisteo B/W	Bowl	11	29	–	6.0
Galisteo B/W	Bowl	?	27	–	5.3
Galisteo B/W	Seed jar	9	9	10	7.2
Galisteo B/W	Jar	13	?	16	7.0
Galisteo B/W	Gourd jar	11	?	13	4.7
Galisteo B/W	Kiva jar	5	2	6	3.2
Galisteo B/W	Kiva jar	6	?	8	5.5
Rowe-Poge	Bowl	14	30	–	5.3
Rowe-Poge	Bowl	10	19	–	4.6
Rowe-Poge	Bowl	12	28	–	6.0
Rowe-Poge	Bowl	13	28	–	6.6
Rowe-Poge	Kiva jar	6	2	6	4.7
Heshotauthla Poly	Bowl	?	?	–	5.0
St. Johns Poly	Bowl	9	24	–	7.2
Agua Fria G/R	Bowl	?	30	–	6.1
Agua Fria G/R	Bowl	?	27	–	7.0

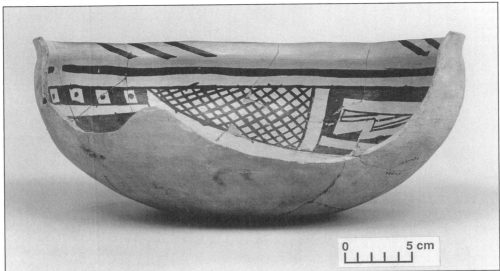

Figure 22. White ware bowl forms.

43

Figure 23. White ware jars.

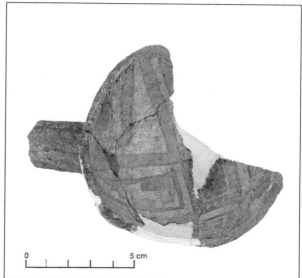

Figure 24. White ware ladles.

figure similar to that often depicted in rock art in the area. Another vessel exhibits a band with pendent lines and overall dots that may be meant to symbolize clouds and rain. The remaining five vessels are decorated with simple geometric band designs.

Miniature jars of this sort are commonly referred to as kiva jars. One was, in fact, recovered from the fill of a plaza kiva (12-C-2), and another came from the roof of what may have been a ceremonial room (12-5-11). The depiction of a human (deity?) figure and possible water symbols on two of these jars also indicates that they probably served some ritual function. Miniature pottery vessels, resembling full-sized water jars or canteens, have been reported ethnographically as part of Rio Grande Pueblo ceremonialism (Parsons 1925:119–21; Kidder 1958:333; Hewett 1930:83; Stevenson 1904:pl. 35). In particular, they are said to have been used to collect water from sacred springs and were placed on altars or shrines as part of prayer offerings. Like so much of Pueblo ceremonialism, they appear to be closely associated

Figure 25. Eccentric white ware forms.

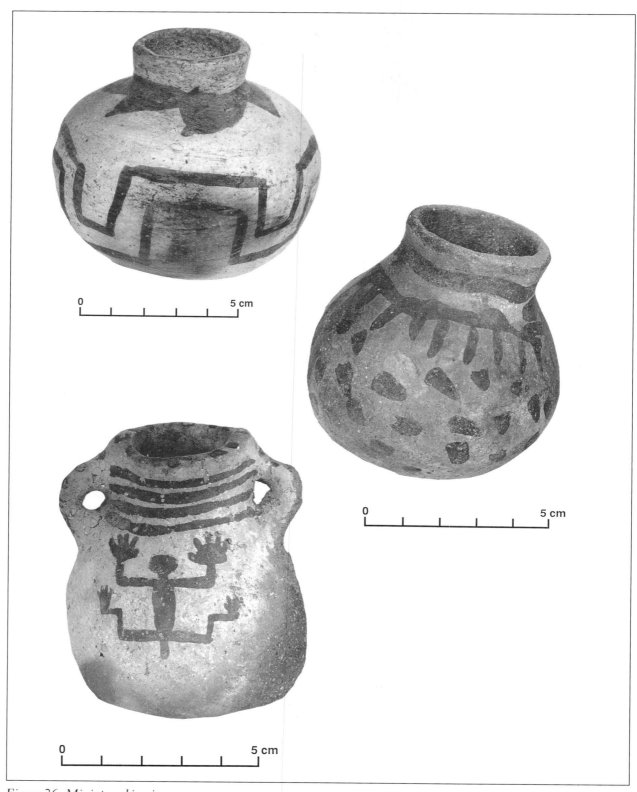

Figure 26. Miniature kiva jars.

with water and rainmaking. Miniature jars also are depicted in ritual contexts, such as kiva murals, usually spouting water or rain (e.g., Hibben 1975) (fig. 27).

Glaze Wares

No whole or nearly whole glaze ware vessels were recovered from excavations at Arroyo Hondo. This is probably due in part to the overall paucity of this material at the site and in part to the fact that these ceramics were rarely, if ever, included in burial offerings at Arroyo Hondo.

The glaze wares occurred in two forms: bowls and widemouthed jars, or "ollas." As both Kidder (Kidder and Shepard 1936:3–5) and Lambert (1954:66) have pointed out, Glaze A Red vessels are characterized by an exceptionally high degree of uniformity and fine craftsmanship. Most of the bowls from Arroyo Hondo fall into Kidder and Lambert's "small" category, ranging primarily between 18 and 22 cm, or 7 to 8¾ inches in diameter. Most of the Glaze A Yellow bowls from the site, although not so well made, also fall within this same general size range. Glaze A bowl rims are either direct or slightly inverted and are always parallel sided, exhibiting no contraction or expansion of the vessel wall toward the lip. Lips are either flattened or slightly rounded. Glaze B bowl rims exhibit a noticeable expansion toward the lip, which is usually either slightly rounded or flattened (see fig. 18).

One of the most distinctive characteristics of the glaze ware tradition is the introduction of the olla form, which is virtually unknown in the earlier white ware tradition of the northern Rio Grande valley. Nearly 30 percent of the Early Glaze Red sherds from Arroyo Hondo came from ollas. Although fragmentary, rim sherds indicate that these ollas were similar in form to contemporaneous vessels found at other sites, such as Pecos (LA 625) (Kidder and Shepard 1936:5) and Paa-ko (LA 162) (Lambert 1954:66). Early glaze ware ollas were generally large jars, measuring roughly 20 to 23 cm in height and around 32 cm at their greatest diameter. Orifice diameters at Arroyo Hondo averaged 17 cm, which is comparable to specimens from other sites. Olla bodies tend to be low in proportion to their height. Shoulders are full and rounded; necks tend toward vertical. Rims are direct, and lips are either rounded or flattened.

This basic olla form, with minor modification, continued to be produced in the northern Rio Grande area up to the modern period. Ethnographically, it is often associated with the transport and storage of water, but this widemouthed jar form is equally well suited to the transport and storage of virtually any sort of dry good.

Figure 27. Depiction of miniature kiva jars being used in a Kachina ritual, from a kiva mural at Pottery Mound. (Courtesy The Maxwell Museum of Anthropology, University of New Mexico)

The sudden appearance and widespread distribution of glaze ware ollas throughout the northern Rio Grande during the mid-fourteenth century may reflect an increasing need for durable and portable storage containers in the area. It is interesting to note that the introduction of the olla form corresponds temporally with evidence for increasing contact and trade between the various pueblos of the northern Rio Grande (see chap. 4). These vessels may have played an important role not only as trade goods themselves but also as containers for the exchange of foodstuffs and exotic raw materials throughout the area.

Decoration
White Wares

The majority of the black-on-white ceramics from Arroyo Hondo belong to a single, local ceramic tradition referred to here as Pajarito White Ware. The design systems used on the various local styles of this ware, which

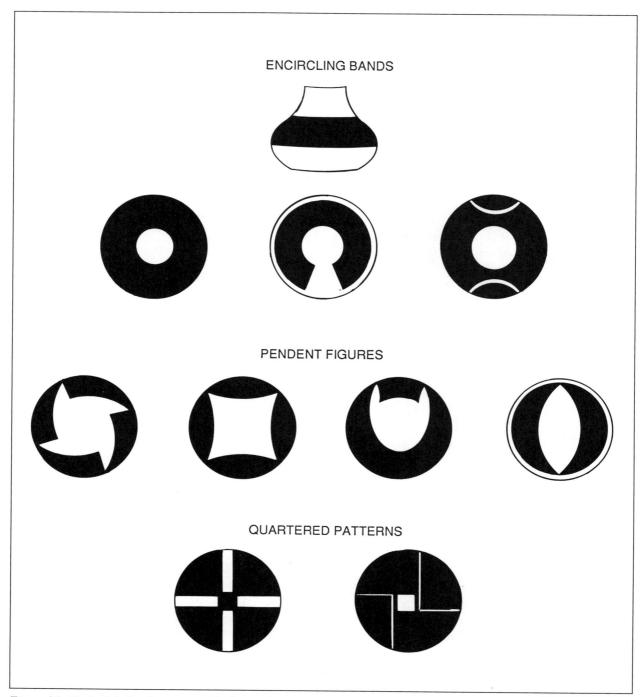

Figure 28. Typical design layouts on black-on-white pottery from Arroyo Hondo.

proliferated during the fourteenth century, are so similar that they are most easily discussed as a single group. Certain features that are distinctive of specific types or series were noted, and these are highlighted in the general discussion below. Distinctive, yet minor, temporal trends in design structure and content are also summarized.

Excellent and comprehensive analyses of the design systems of the black-on-white ceramics from this region have been published by Amsden (Kidder and Amsden 1931) and Stubbs and Stallings (1953). The present analysis is not meant to replace or revise these studies but merely to add the design data from Arroyo Hondo to the existing corpus of published material.

DESIGN LAYOUT

ZONES OF DECORATION. As noted previously, the overwhelming majority of white ware vessels from Arroyo Hondo were in the form of bowls. Painted decoration was usually limited to the interior of these bowls. Rarely, a simple, narrow band of decoration was added to the exterior surface, just below the rim. Direct rims were sometimes painted black or ticked. Everted rims were commonly ticked or decorated with a narrow continuous band pattern. Jars were usually decorated over the upper two-thirds of their exteriors. A secondary band sometimes adorned the neck. Lips and handles were commonly ticked or striped.

Four distinct design layouts are represented in the sample of whole and partially reconstructed white ware vessels examined from Arroyo Hondo. These layouts are encircling bands (28), pendent figures (7), quartered patterns (2) (fig. 28), and overall patterns (2).

ENCIRCLING BANDS. This layout overwhelmingly dominates the black-on-white ceramics produced during the fourteenth century in the northern Rio Grande. Within this general category, however, there exists a wide range of variability in both structure and composition. The basic structure of these bands consists of the band proper outlined by two "banding lines." In addition, one or more parallel "framing lines" are commonly added above and below the band. Occasionally, the top framing line is broken and not continuous around the entire vessel (see fig. 36e). The band proper can be divided into a number of smaller design fields. The most common band structures at Arroyo Hondo are continuous bands (6), simple sectioned bands (5), and paneled bands (13).

Continuous Bands. Of the six vessels decorated with continuous band designs, three consist of checkered bands or alternating sections of checkered and lined bands (fig. 29a–c). One of these has a half-band of pendent right triangles below the primary band in place of a

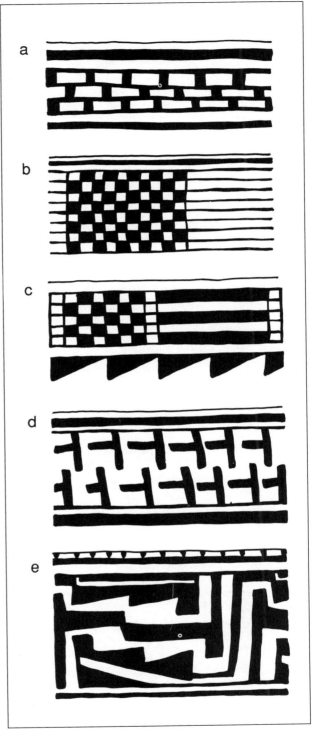

Figure 29. Examples of continuous band designs: a, 12-G-2-4-3 (Galisteo); b, 12-18-15-1 (Wiyo); c, 12-18-15-1,1,2 (Rowe, var. Poge); d, 12-16-14-2-2 (Abiquiú); e, 12-6-6-III-10 (Wiyo).

49

Figure 30. Examples of simple sectional band designs: a, 12-18-15-2,II (Santa Fe, var. Pindi); b, 12-11-9-2 (Santa Fe); c, 12-11-9-1 (Santa Fe, var. Pindi); d, 12-18-15-1 (Santa Fe, var. Pindi); e, 12-11-9-1,7-4 (Galisteo; jar).

lower framing line. One small Abiquiú B/W bowl was crudely painted with a simplified, abstract variant of opposed unstalked keys suspended from the two banding lines (fig. 29d). A continuous band of dense black, interlocking stalked key elements adorned a Wiyo bowl with an outcurved, ticked rim (fig. 29e). Finally, the interior of the upper lobe of the gourd-shaped Galisteo vessel was decorated with a band composed of opposed triangular elements.

Simple Sectioned Bands. Bands in this category are subdivided into secondary design fields by a series of lines drawn from one banding line to the other (Stubbs and Stallings 1953:64). The design fields are generally small, simple, and repetitive. There is not the same emphasis on elaboration of the section lines themselves or the individual design fields seen in formal paneled bands. Three types of sectioning were recorded in the Arroyo Hondo sample: X or double X (2), triangular (1), and diagonal (2). An example of each of these categories is illustrated in figure 30.

Paneled Bands. Paneling of the band is accomplished by isolating each design field by means of vertical lines, bars, or spaces (fig. 31). The most common method of panel separation recorded at Arroyo Hondo is a space with one bar. The number of panels per vessel varies with the overall proportions of the vessel, but the usual range is between three and seven. Each panel is further subdivided by means of layout lines or figures, and, rarely, these smaller fields are in turn subdivided into secondary design units.

The methods of panel subdivision are potentially endless, but, in practice, a limited number of popular conventions and variants were used consistently by northern Rio Grande potters. The resulting design layouts were almost exclusively rectilinear and blocky. The most common types of panel subdivisions in the sample from Arroyo Hondo are diagonal (9) (fig. 32), horizontal (3) (fig. 33), opposed keys on two banding lines (1) (fig. 34a), double-ended interlocking stalked keys (1) (fig. 34b), triple X (1) (fig. 34c), and cross (1) (fig. 35b).

On most vessels the same design was repeated in each panel. On three specimens in the Arroyo Hondo collection, however, different designs were placed in alternating panels to create an *abab* rhythm in the overall pattern (fig. 35).

Although most potters followed the basic conventions outlined above, there appears to have been some experimentation with more unusual methods of band division and decoration. One unique example, using pendent triangles in place of the upper banding line and band divisions, was recorded on a Rowe, *var. Poge,* vessel from Arroyo Hondo (see fig. 34d).

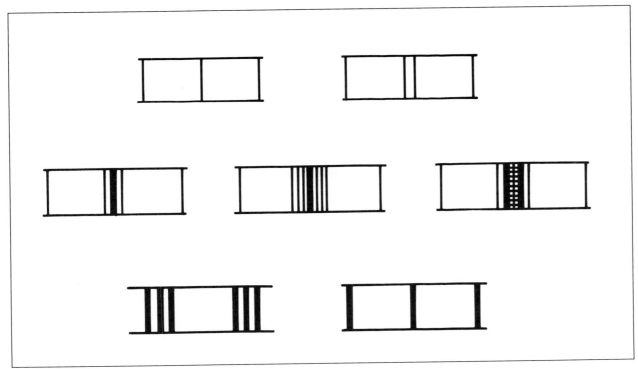

Figure 31. Examples of section lines from paneled bands.

PENDENT FIGURES. Another common design layout on black-on-white ceramics from Arroyo Hondo consists of large pendent figures (triangles, lunes, or rhombs) suspended from a single upper band line (fig. 36). The pendent figures act as independent design fields, more or less equivalent to the panels in a paneled band. Such layouts are most common on Wiyo B/W and, less frequently, on Galisteo B/W vessels, and they appear to be relatively late (four of the six examples from Arroyo Hondo are from Component II contexts). They share a definite relationship with early glaze ware designs (Kidder and Shepard 1936:10, 24–25), which, in turn, were influenced by the sweeping, rotational symmetry of early White Mountain Red Ware from the Cibola region (Woodbury and Woodbury 1966:figs. 39, 40; Carlson 1970). These designs mark a distinct departure from the segmental symmetry of traditional paneled bands.

One exceptionally beautiful and well-made Wiyo bowl falls into this category (fig. 36d). The vessel walls are unusually thin (5 mm) and even. The interior is self-slipped and polished, and the paint is a dense, dark, even black against the off-white paste. The design consists of a pendent rhomb and curvilinear design field arranged such that the undecorated interior space resembles a feline face or mask. Whether this effect was intentional or not is unclear, but the overall design is very effec-tive, elegant, and well executed. This piece is by far the most finely crafted black-on-white vessel recovered from Arroyo Hondo. It stands in stark contrast to the generally poor workmanship that characterizes most of the fourteenth-century white wares from the northern Rio Grande valley.

One unique Wiyo B/W bowl fragment (fig. 36g) in this category has a stylized bird motif suspended from the end of a triangular pendent design field. Such motifs are far more characteristic of early glaze ware and biscuit ware designs and emphasize the "late" feel of many of the Wiyo designs recorded from Arroyo Hondo. Another interesting and well-made Wiyo bowl appears to combine both the encircling band and pendent figure concepts of design layout (fig. 36e). The encircling band is cut in two opposing areas by a lune-shaped design field. Again, the use of oblique and curvilinear layout lines, fine parallel line elements, and secondary pendent dot elements are all reminiscent of the Pinedale-style characteristics of Heshotauthla Polychrome and other fourteenth-century western polychromes (Carlson 1970).

QUARTERED. Quartered bowls are extremely rare and appear to be limited largely to the *Pindi* variety of Santa Fe B/W (Stubbs and Stallings 1953:84). One example of this type of design layout illustrated from Arroyo

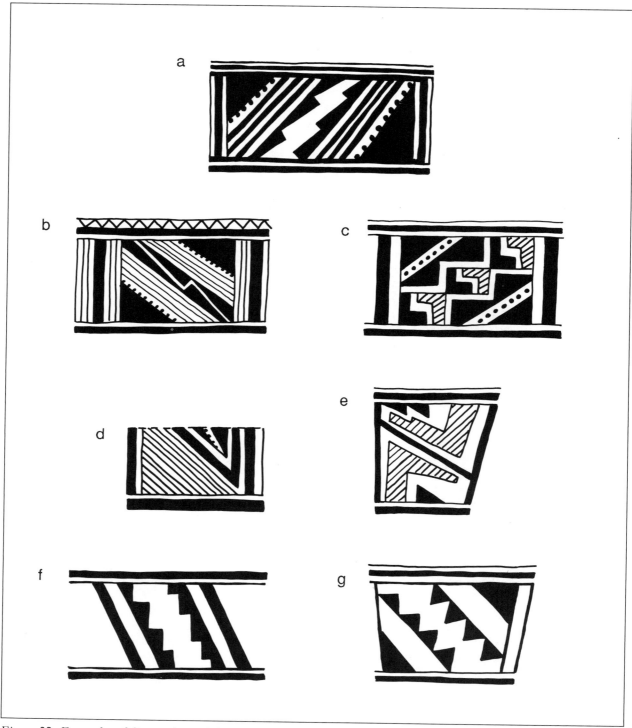

Figure 32. Examples of diagonal panel divisions: a, 12-16-37-1 *(Santa Fe,* var. Pindi); b, 12-12-4-2-1 *(Santa Fe);* c, 12-5-4-7-28 *(Santa Fe);* d, 12-5-10-Vw-1 *(Galisteo; puki);* e, 12-11-XI-3-3 *(Rowe,* var. Poge); f, 12-14-5-III *(Wiyo);* g, 12-16-34-1 *(Wiyo).*

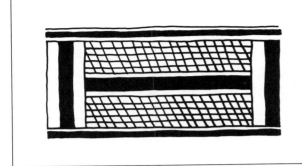

Figure 33. Example of horizontal panel division: 12-14-5-III (Santa Fe).

Hondo (fig. 37b) is of the offset quartered variety and also comes from a *Pindi* vessel. Another unusual variant of the quartered layout was recorded for a Santa Fe B/W bowl from the site (fig. 37a). The main design field is divided into eight sections by a double cross. The sections are filled with two alternating designs: the open space at the bottom is embellished by a rectangular framing line, and a secondary continuous band of opposed keys is placed just below the rim.

OVERALL PATTERN. An example of an overall design layout with bilateral symmetry is illustrated in figure 37c. The use of curvilinear design fields is reminiscent of some of the pendent figure layouts discussed above. As in those cases, this design layout, from a small Wiyo bowl, probably represents a relatively late development in the prebiscuit black-on-white design sequence and was probably influenced by emerging trends in glaze ware design. The center of one of these bowls is filled by a depiction of a lizard. Such animal representations are extremely rare on fourteenth-century white ware sherds from the northern Rio Grande.

SPACE FILLERS. Space fillers used in the bottom of bowls are relatively rare at Arroyo Hondo but occur in a variety of forms. Some examples are illustrated in figure 38.

Glaze Wares

Glaze ware sherds with large identifiable and analyzable sections of design are relatively rare at Arroyo Hondo. Those that do exist suggest that the pendent figure design layouts predominated. Rectangular sections are often segmented, using many of the same conventions seen on encircling bands on white ware vessels. Fragmentary sections of such designs are illustrated in figure 39.

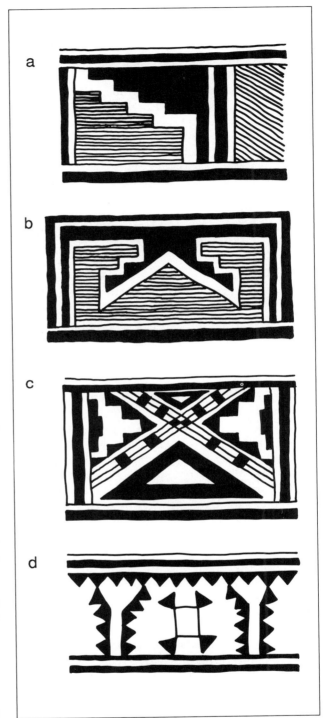

Figure 34. Examples of miscellaneous panel divisions: a, opposed keys, 12-5-6-III (Galisteo); b, double-ended interlocking keys, 12-20-6-3 (Galisteo); c, triple X, 12-16-38-II (Wiyo); d, miscellaneous, 12-14-5-III (Rowe, var. Poge).

Summary

The pottery from Arroyo Hondo is a microcosm of the broad regional trends that swept Rio Grande ceramics during the fourteenth and early fifteenth centuries. At the same time, there is a distinctly local character to the collection that links Arroyo Hondo, materially and culturally, to its nearest neighbors along the Santa Fe and upper Pecos drainages. This local patterning is most clearly seen in the relative frequencies of decorated ceramic types at the site, which closely parallel those recorded from other sites in the area, including Pindi (Stubbs and Stallings 1953), Agua Fria Schoolhouse (Lang and Scheick 1989), Rowe (Douglass 1985), and Pecos (Kidder and Amsden 1931; Kidder and Shepard 1936).

The earliest levels at Arroyo Hondo are dominated by Santa Fe B/W, the diagnostic decorated ceramic of the late Coalition period in the northern Rio Grande. By A.D. 1320 or so, Santa Fe B/W is surpassed in frequency by Galisteo B/W, whose center of distribution lies to the south of Arroyo Hondo in the Galisteo Basin. The rapid spread and popularity of Galisteo B/W reflect the strong influence of the Mesa Verde style on Rio Grande ceramics during the early fourteenth century.

Wiyo B/W is present in small to moderate amounts throughout Component I deposits at Arroyo Hondo. Although it is the most common decorated white ware in Component II deposits when analyzed as a whole (see table 5), seriational studies show that there was no time when Wiyo B/W clearly dominated the assemblage at the site. In general, inhabitants at Arroyo Hondo continued to prefer the more archaic style of Santa Fe B/W, which rises from a period of relatively low frequency toward the end of the first component to renewed popularity at the beginning of the second component.

For a short time, between A.D. 1320 and 1350, two local ceramic types, Santa Fe, var. *Pindi*, and Rowe, var. *Poge*, gained prominence at the site. This episode spans the period of population maximum and initial decline in the Component I town. The appearance of *Pindi* pottery in the Santa Fe–Pecos area may reflect influence from the Española-Chama district to the north, where potters had long favored the use of ash and pumice tempers. Rowe B/W and its varieties, however, appear to be crude attempts to imitate the thick, crackled slips and complex designs of the Mesa Verde style, as best exemplified by Galisteo B/W.

The distribution of both Rowe and *Pindi* is highly circumscribed and serves as an important indicator of strong material and cultural links between the people of the Santa Fe drainage and those of the upper Pecos. In regard to ceramics, the towns of the Santa Fe drainage (i.e., Pindi, Agua Fria Schoolhouse, Arroyo Hondo, etc.) are closer to those in the upper Pecos (i.e., Forked Lightning, Rowe, Pecos, etc.) than to sites in the adjacent Galisteo, Zia–Santo Domingo, or Española-Chama districts, each of which was characterized at the time by the local production of its own distinct decorated ceramic types. The socioeconomic and cultural significance of this localization of pottery styles and other aspects of material culture in the northern Rio Grande during the early fourteenth century will be discussed in greater detail in chapter 4.

Figure 35. Examples of abab *rhythm: a, 12-21-6-2 (Santa Fe); b, 12-5-4-1 (Wiyo); c, 12-5-14-4 (Wiyo).*

Figure 36. Examples of pendent figures: a, *12-11-9-1 (Galisteo);* b, *12-20-6-3 (Galisteo);* c, *12-16-1-7-3 (Wiyo);* d, *12-16-17-3-2 (Wiyo);* e, *12-14-5-III,4,6 (Wiyo);* f, *12-C-2-2 (Wiyo);* g, *12-C-8 (Wiyo).*

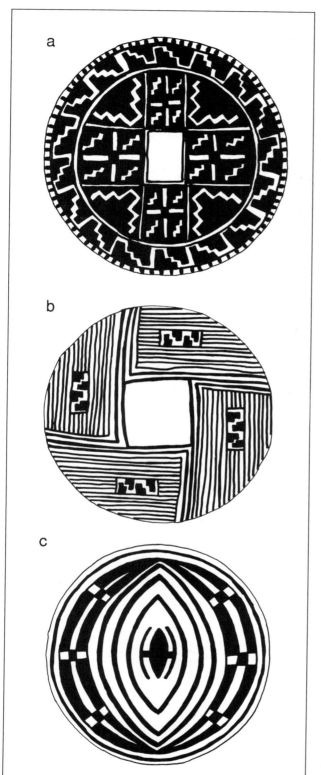

Glaze ware ceramics are present at Arroyo Hondo in trace amounts prior to A.D. 1350, but it is not until after about 1370 that they form a significant part of the ceramic assemblage. By approximately 1400 to 1410, Agua Fria G/R is the most common decorated ceramic type at the site. Taken together, however, the white wares continue to dominate the assemblage up through the abandonment of the second component village (Lang, this volume).

The pottery from Arroyo Hondo was used primarily in domestic foodway activities such as storage, cooking, and serving. Ceremonially, decorated forms functioned as containers for ritual offerings, such as food or sacred spring water. These domestic and ritual functions are reflected in the range of sizes and shapes recorded for the vessels from the sites, including large corrugated jars, decorated bowls and ollas, ladles, miniature kiva jars, and a smattering of more eccentric forms. The spread of the glaze ware olla form after A.D. 1350 may reflect a new need for transport and storage containers associated with increasing trade between the towns and provinces of the northern Rio Grande during the Classic period.

Ceramic decoration at Arroyo Hondo follows trends seen throughout the northern Rio Grande. Gray ware jars are characterized by a wide variety of textured surface treatments, including various combinations of smeared indented corrugations, smeared corrugations, ribbing, and banding. These surface treatments occur in association with a variety of paste types throughout the northern Rio Grande during the fourteenth and fifteenth centuries. The examples from Arroyo Hondo were produced using two varieties of micaceous residual clay.

Encircling bands dominate the repertoire of painted designs from the site. The most common design layout on all types of fourteenth-century white ware is the paneled band. Solid opposed elements and parallel lines were manipulated to form relatively simple to more complex patterns. Secondary elements such as pendent dots are also common. Rim ticking and other embellishments are present but not common. Nonband design layouts, such as pendent triangle, rectangle, and lune divisions, are most common on late Wiyo B/W and early glaze ware vessels and foreshadow changes in design layout and structure that would become prevalent during the fifteenth century.

Figure 37. Examples of quartered layouts and overall designs: a, 12-18-15-1 (Santa Fe); b, 12-11-9-2 (Pindi); c, 12-16-38-II (Wiyo).

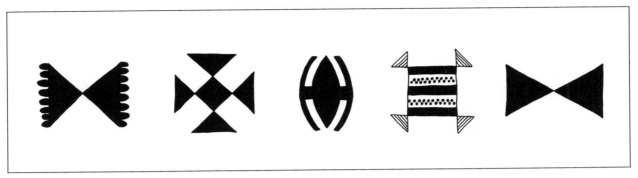

Figure 38. Examples of space fillers.

Figure 39. Examples of red ware and glaze ware designs: a, 12-18-15-1 *(Los Padillas)* (left: *interior, black-on-red;* right: *exterior, white-on-red);* b, 12-18-15-1 *(Heshotauthla)* (left: *interior, black-on-red;* right: *exterior, white-on-red);* c, 12-K-6-II-5 *(Agua Fria);* d, 12-11-7-4-1 *(Agua Fria).*

Chapter 3

Pottery Manufacture and Trade at Arroyo Hondo Pueblo

As we have seen in the preceding chapter, the pottery from Arroyo Hondo Pueblo consists of three technologically and functionally distinct wares—the gray, white, and glaze wares—that are commonly found on contemporaneous early Classic period sites throughout the northern Rio Grande. Unlike the gray ware or culinary pottery, which shows very little stylistic change or change in relative frequency through time, the decorated ceramics from the site exhibit marked and patterned changes in the relative popularity of specific styles or types within each ware category and between the white wares and glaze wares, in general, over the entire period of the site's occupation (see Lang, this volume).

For example, the earliest trash deposits at Arroyo Hondo are characterized by a high percentage of Santa Fe Black-on-white. Throughout much of Component I, however, the relative frequency of the classic variety of Santa Fe B/W dropped in favor of a number of local styles of Pajarito White Ware, including Galisteo B/W, Wiyo B/W, Rowe, *var. Poge*, and Santa Fe, *var. Pindi*. This differentiation and localization of decorated ceramic styles is a diagnostic feature of the late Coalition–early Classic transition in the northern Rio Grande.

Glaze-painted ceramics first appeared toward the end of the first component (ca. 1340), and the relative frequency of glaze ware pottery increased dramatically during the second occupation of the site. By the end of the fourteenth century, glaze-painted pottery may have accounted for as much as 35 percent of the decorated ceramics in use at the site, but at no time did it outnumber the combined Pajarito White Ware types that continued to dominate the assemblage (see Lang, this volume).

The earliest locally produced, glaze-painted pottery in the northern Rio Grande appears at sites near Albuquerque and in the Zia–Santo Domingo district dating to around the turn of the fourteenth century. By the end of the century, however, glaze-painted ceramics are found in significant quantities on sites located throughout the northern Rio Grande area. The widespread distribution of glaze ware represents the most extensive and best-documented archaeological evidence we have for the emergence of a regional network of local craft or resource specialization and regional trade during the Rio Grande Classic period (Snow 1981; Wilcox 1981, 1984; Cordell 1984:330). The pioneering research of Anna Shepard (1942) and more recent studies by Helene Warren (1969, 1970, 1976, 1981) indicate that after about 1350, local centers of glaze ware production emerged that can be identified on the basis of distinct differences in mineralogical composition. At any one time, it appears that specific regions may have controlled the manufacture and trade of glaze-painted ceramics over large areas of the northern Rio Grande. During the late fifteenth and early sixteenth centuries, for example, sites in the Galisteo Basin are believed to have specialized in the production of light-slipped, glaze-painted pottery that was widely traded throughout the Rio Grande valley and beyond (Shepard 1942; Snow 1981:363; Cordell 1984:340).

The specialized production and widespread trade of glaze-painted ceramics is generally contrasted with the supposedly more localized production and limited distribution of the various white ware types (Snow 1981:363). As a result, the introduction and spread of glaze-painted pottery is often viewed as a reflection of a major restructuring of economic and social networks among the northern Rio Grande Pueblos. This assumption is made despite the fact that there is very little comparable data for the black-on-white ceramics—certainly none of the technical detail and regional scope of Shepard's work on the glazes. A detailed compositional analysis of the various white ware types from Arroyo Hondo will, it is hoped, help to redress this deficiency to some extent.

The pottery collections from Arroyo Hondo Pueblo provide us with an excellent data base for addressing the question of whether or not the spread of glaze-painted pottery throughout the northern Rio Grande reflects a fundamental shift in the organization of local pottery manufacture and regional trade during the early Classic period. First, the collection spans the period of the initial introduction and spread of the early glazes during the fourteenth century. Although Arroyo Hondo remained predominantly a white ware site throughout its occupation, there is a dramatic increase in the number of glaze ware ceramics recovered from second component contexts, compared to those from the first component. Second, the upper Santa Fe drainage, where the site is located, is bordered on the west and south by the Santo Domingo and Galisteo basins, two areas that are believed to have been important centers of early glaze ware production and trade. By tracing the decorated ceramics from Arroyo Hondo, both the white ware and glaze ware, to their origins of manufacture, we hope to gain a better understanding of changing patterns of trade relations in the region and of the changing economic and social roles that pottery played in evolving local and regional alliances.

Methods of Analysis

Since the 1930s, the major technique for determining where Rio Grande ceramics were manufactured has been mineralogical analysis (Kidder and Shepard 1936). The rationale behind this technique is that ceramics produced in different localities using regionally distinct raw materials should differ from each other mineralogically and that, in turn, these differences should directly reflect the geologic source of the raw materials used.

This logic, of course, assumes that raw materials are not being transported over large distances. Ethnographic studies of modern nonindustrialized potters tend to support this assumption. Arnold (1985:39–49), in a survey of 110 ethnographic cases, showed that although the distance potters regularly travel to obtain raw materials varies greatly, 85 percent of the reported resources were obtained within seven kilometers of a potter's work area.

Temper is the least likely of the major ceramic materials to be transported over long distances because its technological requirements are so broad that something suitable is generally available in the general vicinity (Shepard 1980:165). Temper and other aplastic inclusions are also usually the most conspicuous component of ceramic pastes and the easiest to analyze directly. Crystalline fragments, such as crushed rock or sand grains, are particularly useful for identifying ceramics produced in different localities or regions because such inclusions often directly reflect their geologic origins (Ferring and Perttula 1987; Peacock 1970:379).

Convenience and proximity are not the only criteria for selecting a temper source, however. Modern Rio Grande potters often overlook suitable temper sources immediately available near a village for a more distant source that is considered technologically or aesthetically superior. Furthermore, highly regarded temper sources are often used by potters from a number of surrounding villages. As a result, although it is possible to identify the general locality of pottery manufacture through the mineralogical analysis of temper, it is often difficult to pin down the point of origin to a specific community within that locality.

The most accurate and efficient means of optically identifying mineral inclusions in ceramics is through petrographic analysis. The basic principle of petrography is that an unknown mineral can be identified by observing the way in which that mineral affects the transmission of light with known characteristics of vibration (i.e., wave length and direction). The various optical properties, which can be identified and measured with a polarizing microscope, provide very accurate and precise criteria for identifying transparent minerals.

Because of the accuracy and breadth of this technique (Peacock 1970:379; Shepard 1980:157; Rice 1987:379), petrography was chosen as the primary method of mineralogical analysis in this study. Sherds from each of the major pottery types at Arroyo Hondo were sorted into discrete categories based on recognizable differences in paste composition and texture using a low-power stereo microscope. For each of the decorated types, one sherd from each of the major paste categories was selected for petrographic analysis. A total of 83 sherds was sent to Mann Petrographics in Los Alamos, New Mexico, for sample preparation. The resulting thin sections were examined and analyzed by the author using a polarizing microscope provided by the Geology/Geochemistry Group at Los Alamos National Laboratory. Summary tables of the mineralogical data recorded for each section are presented in appendix B.

Based on these petrographic data, each sherd in the sample was reexamined using a low-power stereo microscope to form new, more inclusive temper categories for each type. The mineralogical characteristics of each of these temper categories were then compared with the known surface geology at Arroyo Hondo and its immediate vicinity. A field trip was made to the site by the author and Dr. W. Scott Baldridge of Los Alamos National Laboratory. During this trip, lithic samples from potential local temper sources were collected (see fig. 63). These samples were then thin-sectioned and compared petrographically with the ceramic sections from the site in order to determine which groups of ceramics may have been produced locally. Comparisons were also made with type sherds at the Laboratory of Anthropology in Santa Fe and with published reports on previous petrographic studies and on the surface geology of other areas of northern New Mexico in order to determine likely sources for some of the nonlocal ceramics.

There are several reasons why petrographic analysis is particularly well suited for the study of Rio Grande ceramics. First, the northern Rio Grande region is characterized by a broad range of local geologic diversity. This diversity is due, in large part, to relatively recent volcanic activity in the region that deposited a series of highly distinctive lavas, magmas, and ash deposits over well-defined and reasonably restricted areas. Second, Rio Grande potters from any one pueblo or region have tended to use a very specific suite of locally available raw materials. In fact, what a pot is made of appears to be at least as important as vessel form and design in defining the work of a particular pueblo or ethnic group. For example, the Tewa potters of the Española district have used the same fine volcanic ash temper in their pottery for nearly eight hundred years. This extreme conservatism in raw material selection is the enduring and defining hallmark of the Tewa style of ceramic manufacture and contrasts markedly with the many changes in slip, paint, design, form, and firing technology that have taken place within the Tewa ceramic tradition during this same period.

Despite these advantages, petrographic analysis has had certain limitations as well. Even with careful analysis and a detailed knowledge of local field geology, it is often difficult to distinguish between raw materials from closely related geologic sources. For example, it would be nearly impossible to distinguish optically between volcanic ash from a variety of different sources within the Española Basin purely on the basis of mineralogical composition. Similarly, intermediate volcanic rocks of virtually identical composition outcrop in the Ortiz Mountains, the Cerrillos Hills, the La Cienega area, and even at Arroyo Hondo (Stearns 1953).

This problem is particularly acute for a site such as Arroyo Hondo, which sits astride the boundary between several major geologic areas—the Sangre de Cristo Mountains to the east, the Caja del Rio and Pajarito Plateau to the west, the Española Basin to the north, and the Galisteo Basin to the south. Without a detailed understanding of the local geology of the site, it would be quite easy to label as "trade ware" pottery that may, in fact, have been produced locally. Merely identifying potential geologic sources of raw materials is often not enough to identify the place where certain pottery types were manufactured. The mineralogical evidence must be interpreted in light of our full knowledge of the structure of ceramic production and distribution, as well as other evidence of trade and social interaction between communities in the region.

Chemical analyses hold the promise of making more fine-grained distinctions possible. Methods such as x-ray fluorescence and neutron activation analysis provide information on the ratio or actual amounts of major, minor, and trace elements in a substance. Different techniques are more or less sensitive to a different number and range of elements, making them suitable to different problems and materials.

Major elements, present in pottery in amounts of 2 percent or more, include silica, alumina, and oxygen. Minor elements, present in amounts of between 0.1 percent and 2 percent, may include any or all of the following: calcium, iron, potassium, titanium, magnesium, manganese, sodium, chromium, and nickel. Trace and ultra-trace elements (less than 0.1%) include geochemically rare elements such as cesium, rubidium, vanadium, uranium, tantalum, scandium, lithium, gold, selenium, antimony, strontium, zirconium, yttrium, niobium, cobalt, and the rare earth or lanthanide series (atomic numbers 57–71). The kinds and amounts of trace elements present uniquely characterize ceramic materials from different geologic sources. For this reason, they, together with the minor elements, traditionally form the basis of most provenience studies of pottery (Rice 1987:390).

Because one is dealing on the level of elements, the potential exists to make much finer distinctions between groups of material than is possible with mineralogical analysis alone. It should be emphasized, however, that techniques such as x-ray fluorescence are bulk analyses, which means that the chemical signature they produce combines all the compositional elements of a ceramic, including clay, temper, slip, and paint. It is impossible to determine from the chemical data alone what aspects of the signature are due to which component. As a result, chemical analyses of pottery are best if performed in conjunction with petrographic studies, which provide a mineralogical and geologic context for interpreting the chemical data (Rice 1987:375, 390).

Chemical analysis of the Arroyo Hondo ceramics was conducted using x-ray fluorescence (XRF). XRF was chosen because Dr. Bart Olinger of Los Alamos National Laboratory offered to run samples using the laboratory's analytic equipment free of charge and because previous research had shown this technique to be useful in distinguishing pottery from different vicinities in the Rio Grande area (Bower and Snow 1984; Olinger 1987a, 1987b).

At least 15 sherds from each of the major decorated types and approximately 30 culinary sherds from each component were selected for analysis. All of the black-on-white sherds sampled were from bowls, and all of the gray ware sherds were from jars. The glaze ware samples represent a mix of bowls and jars, with jar forms predominating. An attempt was made to sample a broad range of temper classes, although not necessarily in relation to their relative proportions in the assemblage as a whole; thus, rare temper types tend to be overrepresented in the XRF samples. Petrographic control of these data, however, should prevent any misinterpretation of the significance of chemical signatures based on rare or isolated cases.

Also submitted for XRF analysis were approximately a dozen clay samples from Arroyo Hondo that were found in contexts that suggested to the excavators that they may represent the remains of potter's clay. Also, five clay samples collected by Richard Lang and four lithic samples collected by the author from sources in the canyon adjacent to the site were analyzed. It was hoped that these samples would provide data on pottery manufacture at the site and on potential local sources of raw materials.

The elements in Rio Grande pottery that have been shown to emit the greatest number of x-ray counts for the energy range available (20 kv) are iron (Fe), zirconium (Zr), and strontium (Sr). The relative numbers of x-ray counts, given as percentages, detected from these three elements were considered the XRF signature for the pottery in this analysis. Other trace elements, such as rubidium (Rb), niobium (Nb), and yttrium (Y), were used to discriminate between groups of data with similar Fe, Sr, and Zr counts (Olinger 1987a:1). The relative frequencies of x-ray counts for the eight elements with the consistently highest x-ray counts in each of the samples are presented in appendix C.

In the following discussion, these chemical data are presented graphically by plots of Zr percent versus Sr percent—the Fe value being estimated by the other two using the following formulas:

$$Zr\% = (Zr/Fe + Zr + Sr) \times 100$$
$$Sr\% = (Sr/Fe + Zr + Sr) \times 100$$

Visually distinct clusters on these plots were interpreted as representing pottery from chemically distinct sources. By referring back to the mineralogical characterization of the sherds in each cluster, the probable geologic source of the pottery in that cluster could often be determined.

It should be emphasized that the numbers reported in appendix C and in the scatter plots presented in this chapter are of percentage x-ray counts and not actual compositional ratios. No attempt was made to convert the data from this raw form because no standards were used during analysis, making accurate quantitative comparisons between analytical runs impossible. The resulting chemical data are thus very qualitative and should be interpreted as such.

A second limitation of the chemical data is that the XRF technique used in this study detects relatively few elements. As a result, it is not as sensitive to differences between actual sources as are other, more sophisticated forms of chemical analysis, such as neutron activation. In those instances where distinct clusters of sherds are visually distinguishable on the scatter plots, those differences are probably significant. In those cases where the XRF plots show an undifferentiated cluster, however, it is impossible to conclude on the basis of the chemical data alone whether all the pottery in that cluster came from a single source or whether the XRF analysis was unable to differentiate significant differences in paste composition. Despite these serious limitations, the XRF data, when used cautiously and interpreted within the context of the mineralogical data, provide interesting and important information on the structure of ceramic manufacture and trade at Arroyo Hondo Pueblo.

Summary of Mineralogical and Chemical Analyses
Cibola White Ware

One sherd each of Kwahe'e Black-on-white and Chupadero Black-on-white was examined petrographically. The Kwahe'e sherd was characterized by a dark gray, fine-textured clay with fine to medium subrounded to subangular quartz, plagioclase, and microcline feldspar, and coarse subrounded to subangular pellets of unprocessed clay. Although similar in composition and texture to Santa Fe B/W pastes, the Kwahe'e sherds lacked the calcareous siltstone and calcium carbonate lumps so characteristic of Santa Fe B/W. The Chupadero B/W sherd was tempered with coarse to very coarse angular fragments of dark brown to black sherd with quartz-mica schist temper. Mineral inclusions consisted of fine to medium subangular quartz and alkali feldspar and fine platy mica. Coarse lithic fragments included quartz-mica schist and quartzite.

Pajarito White Ware

PAJARITO SERIES

SANTA FE BLACK-ON-WHITE, VAR. SANTA FE. In general, it appears that the makers of the Santa Fe B/W pottery recovered from Arroyo Hondo favored the use of silty to sandy, sedimentary clays, to which fine-textured volcanic ash was often, although not always, added (fig. 40). The silt/sand fraction of these pastes is composed primarily of fine to medium subangular grains of quartz and feldspar. Characteristic accessory minerals include muscovite, biotite, hornblende, and magnetite. Coarse fragments of granular calcium carbonate are common, as are fragments of siltstone with a fine calcareous cement (fig. 41a). Coarse to very coarse lumps of dark, dense, unprocessed clay occur in most sherds and are conspicuous, even macroscopically, in some (about 11% of the sample). These silty/sandy paste categories appear to correspond to Shepard's (Kidder and Shepard 1936) "untempered" subtype of Santa Fe B/W (Blue-Gray Type).

In over half (50.5%) of the Santa Fe B/W sherds sampled from Arroyo Hondo, fine volcanic ash temper was added to the naturally silty/sandy clays (fig. 41b). The principal components of this ash are very fine, sharp, irregular fragments of clear and pinkish brown volcanic glass. Larger flakes of pumice, showing flow lines and vesicles, are also present in most sherds. Differences in the number and variety of accessory minerals and in the sorting and texture of nonplastic inclusions occurred within both the ash-tempered and untempered silty/sandy paste categories. But this variability was not consistent enough to suggest distinct geologic sources for this material. Warren (1976:B133) lumped similarly diverse samples of Santa Fe B/W from other sites into a single paste category (i.e., "vitric tuff, grading to siltstone, sandstone or pumiceous sandstone").

The chemical signatures of the major paste groups characteristic of Santa Fe B/W ceramics from Arroyo Hondo tended to overlap within a single analytic cluster on the XRF plot (fig. 42). (Note that solid symbols in these scatter plots represent sherds from Component I contexts, whereas open symbols represent Component II sherds.) The variability recorded by petrographic analysis suggests that the XRF technique used in this study may not have been sensitive enough to detect subtle differences between distinct, yet geologically similar, sources of clay and temper. As many as three to five secondary sources, however, may be distinguishable on the XRF plot. These peripheral sources appear to have been more important during the first component and are all char-

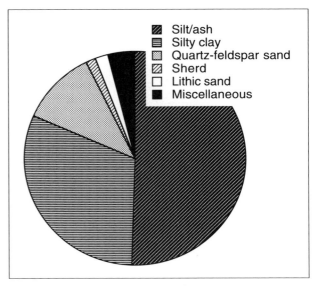

Figure 40. Santa Fe Black-on-white temper categories.

acterized by generally higher strontium counts, while exhibiting a broad range of zirconium counts. A similar pattern characterizes most of the Wiyo B/W ceramics from Arroyo Hondo (see fig. 48), suggesting that these peripheral sources may be associated with those areas of the Española-Chama district where Wiyo B/W became the dominant ceramic type after ca. A.D. 1300.

SANTA FE BLACK-ON-WHITE, VAR. PINDI. The single most diagnostic attribute of the *Pindi* variety of Santa Fe B/W is the presence of coarse pumiceous ash temper. It is, therefore, not surprising that the sample of *Pindi* pottery analyzed from the Arroyo Hondo collection should display a high degree of mineralogical and chemical homogeneity (figs. 43, 44). All of the sherds analyzed petrographically were tempered with medium to coarse vesicular pumice and subhedral crystals of alkali feldspar (microcline, sanidine, and oligoclase). Minor accessories included biotite, green hornblende, augite, magnetite, and cryptocrystalline quartz (fig. 45a).

Distinct analytic sources are not distinguishable on the XRF plot (see fig. 44), supporting the conclusion, based on mineralogical analysis, that the potters who produced the *Pindi* pottery recovered from Arroyo Hondo probably used raw materials from closely related and relatively homogeneous geologic sources.

WIYO BLACK-ON-WHITE. Ninety-two percent of the Wiyo pottery fragments examined from Arroyo Hondo were tempered with volcanic ash (fig. 46). In only 10 percent

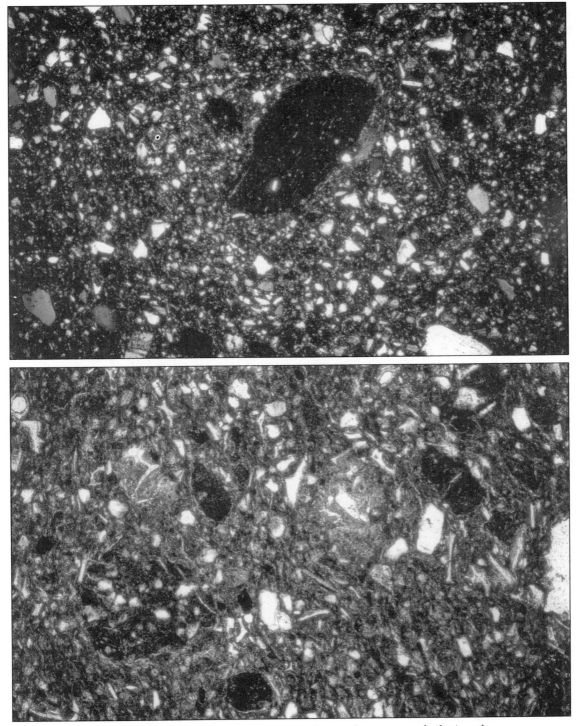

Figure 41. Photomicrographs: top, *Santa Fe Black-on-white with untempered silty/sandy paste (field = 2.4 mm);* bottom, *Santa Fe B/W with volcanic ash temper (field = 2.4 mm).*

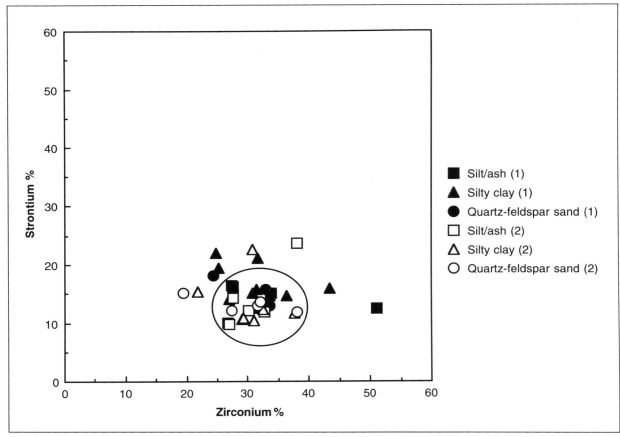

Figure 42. Santa Fe Black-on-white x-ray fluorescence analysis. (Note: Solid symbols represent sherds from Component I contexts; open symbols represent Component II context sherds.)

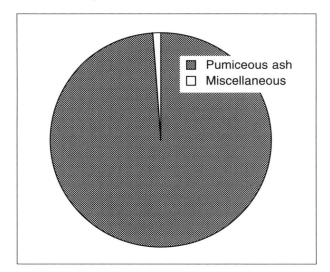

Figure 43. Santa Fe Black-on-white, var. Pindi, temper categories.

of the sherds, however, was ash temper added to silty/sandy clays resembling those used to produce most of the Santa Fe B/W ceramics from the site. In the remainder of the cases, the paste clays appeared to have been extremely fine textured and largely free of any naturally occurring aplastic inclusions. The ash itself is very similar to that described for the Santa Fe B/W examples; however, there is a tendency for Wiyo pastes to be finer and more glassy, with a lower frequency of coarse pumice and mineral inclusions (fig. 47). Granular calcium carbonate and coarse lumps of unprocessed clay are present but not nearly as common as in the Santa Fe B/W sample.

Slight differences in paste texture and composition suggest the presence of several distinct sources for the ash temper and/or clays used in the Wiyo B/W assemblage from Arroyo Hondo. This deduction is supported by the diffuse patterning of the chemical data (fig. 48). It is interesting to note that the Wiyo scatter plot forms almost

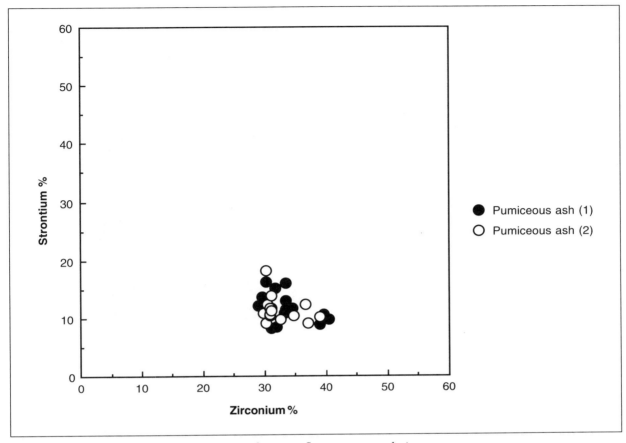

Figure 44. Santa Fe Black-on-white, var. Pindi, *x-ray fluorescence analysis.*

the reverse image of the Santa Fe plot, with most of the Wiyo values forming a halo around the area where the densest cluster of Santa Fe values is centered. This diffuse band of chemical values may represent a variety of production areas that shifted from the manufacture of the Santa Fe style to the Wiyo style of black-on-white pottery after A.D. 1300, whereas the dense cluster of chemical values that characterize the Santa Fe plot probably represents areas that continued producing the classic style of Santa Fe B/W up through the first quarter of the fifteenth century.

ABIQUIÚ BLACK-ON-WHITE. Biscuit wares were never very popular at Arroyo Hondo, suggesting that they were a relatively minor trade ware at the site. All of the biscuit ware sherds from Arroyo Hondo examined petrographically were tempered with volcanic ash. As with the Wiyo pottery from the site, minor differences in mineral content and texture indicate that several different ash beds and/or clay sources were being used in the production of

this ware. Most (62%) of the sherds analyzed were tempered with fine-textured, glassy volcanic ash similar to that which characterized the Wiyo B/W assemblage, although a small fraction (3%) had a siltier/sandier texture more reminiscent of Santa Fe B/W pastes. Eleven of the Abiquiú sherds examined were tempered with a coarse pumiceous ash, similar in texture to *Pindi* temper. Unique to the biscuit wares, however, was a distinct fine-textured ash with a relatively high proportion of fine platy biotite.

GALISTEO SERIES

GALISTEO BLACK-ON-WHITE, VAR. GALISTEO. The classic variety of Galisteo B/W is characterized by the addition of sherd temper. In hand section this temper shows up as angular, dull, opaque, gray and black fragments against the dense, compact, whitish clay of the paste. Both culinary and painted pottery appear to have been used as temper by Galisteo potters. Culinary pot fragments are characterized by their dense black paste and

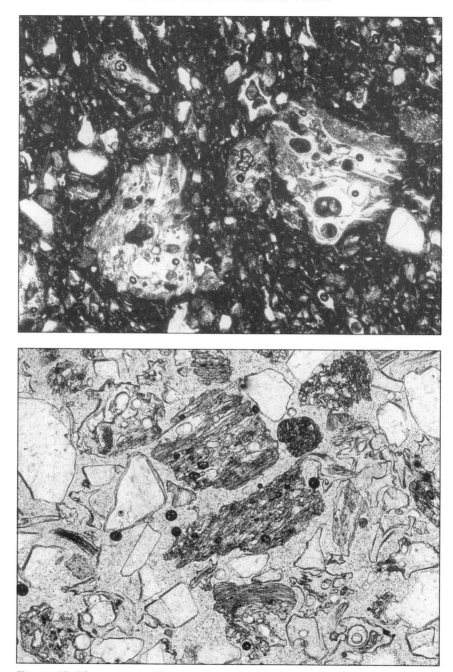

Figure 45. Photomicrographs: top, *Santa Fe Black-on-white, var. Pindi, with coarse pumiceous ash temper (field = 2.4 mm)*; bottom, *coarse pumiceous ash collected near Arroyo Hondo Pueblo (field = 2.4 mm).*

coarse, angular lithic inclusions, and painted ware fragments are identified by their more translucent gray or brown pastes and finer textures (fig. 49). Shepard (Kidder and Shepard 1936:465) noted, however, that in the sample of Galisteo B/W (Crackle Type) from Pecos no sherd-tempered sherd (i.e., ground Galisteo B/W) was

used, and this appears to have been the case with the sample from Arroyo Hondo as well. Mineral inclusions consist primarily of fine to medium subangular quartz-feldspar sand, with occasional flakes of muscovite mica. Coarse lithic fragments of quartz, quartzite, and granite are rarely present. These lithic inclusions are probably

66

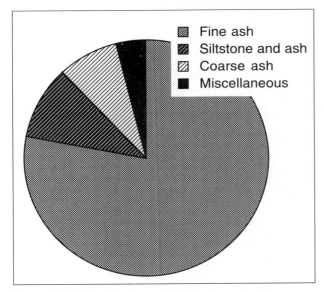

Figure 46. Wiyo Black-on-white temper categories.

derived from the coarsely tempered ground culinary sherds. The diffuse x-ray signature of the classic variety of Galisteo B/W from Arroyo Hondo suggests that this pottery came from at least three distinct analytic sources (fig. 50). Both the mineralogical and chemical data support the conclusion that no one source monopolized production and trade of this black-on-white pottery style during the fourteenth century.

GALISTEO BLACK-ON WHITE, VAR. KENDI. This variety of Galisteo pottery shares most of the diagnostic attributes of the classic variety of the type, with the exception of sherd temper. Instead, the *Kendi* variety is characterized by crushed rock temper of intermediate volcanic composition. This temper generally appears macroscopically as an opaque, white crystalline matrix flecked with black laths. Petrographically, two classes of volcanic rock have been identified. The first can be described as an augite latite/monzonite, composed of tabular, zoned, and weathered plagioclase, euhedral to subhedral pale green augite, hornblende (less common), and anhedral patches of magnetite (fig. 51). The second is a highly weathered volcanic porphyry composed of phenocrysts of tabular plagioclase and alkali feldspar with rare hornblende and magnetite. The volcanic rock–tempered variety of Galisteo B/W displays a distinct chemical signature (fig. 52) characterized by relatively high strontium and correspondingly low zirconium x-ray counts. A similar pattern was recorded for latite-tempered sherds of Glaze A Red (see fig. 59). As a result, this distinction between the *Kendi* and classic varieties of Galisteo B/W

may be due largely to differences in temper, although both varieties may have been manufactured in the same region of the northern Rio Grande.

PECOS SERIES

ROWE BLACK-ON-WHITE, VAR. POGE. The *Poge* variety of Rowe B/W is quite common at Arroyo Hondo, making up 24 percent of the Component I and 15 percent of the Component II decorated ceramic assemblage from the site. The distribution of Rowe B/W and its variants is limited primarily to a crescent-shaped area extending from the upper Pecos River, around the southern and western flanks of the Sangre de Cristos, and up the Santa Fe drainage to the vicinity of the city of Santa Fe.

Poge variety pastes are composed of soft tan, buff, olive, or pinkish firing clays, containing abundant medium to coarse fragments of lithic sand, to which ground sherd was usually added as temper. Mineral inclusions consist primarily of fine to medium subangular grains of quartz, alkali feldspars (including microcline), and plagioclase. Common accessories include biotite and muscovite mica, hornblende, and (rarely) augite. Coarse subangular fragments of granite, quartz-mica schist, quartzite, and rare micaceous sandstone are diagnostic (fig. 53). Over 85 percent of the *Poge* sherds examined were also tempered with medium to coarse angular fragments of black, brown, or gray sherd. Fragments of ground sherds containing volcanic ash temper, typical of Santa Fe–Wiyo pottery, were clearly identified, as were fragments of sherd-tempered sherd. The XRF data present a relatively well defined analytic cluster, again supporting the mineralogical evidence that suggests that much of the *Poge* pottery at Arroyo Hondo may have been manufactured in the same general area using relatively homogeneous raw materials (fig. 54).

ROWE BLACK-ON-WHITE, VAR. ARROYO HONDO. This newly defined variety of Rowe B/W is extremely rare. It is so distinctive, however, that it warrants separate discussion. The *Arroyo Hondo* variety is characterized by silty/sandy dark brown to black pastes, containing coarse to very coarse fragments of pink granite or, less commonly, a combination of pink granite, gneiss, and quartz-mica schist (fig. 55). The silty fraction of the paste consists of fine grains of quartz, feldspar, and platy muscovite mica. There appears to be a great deal of variability in both the texture and composition of the paste in this group of ceramics. In particular, the density and texture of mica seems to fluctuate significantly from one sherd to another. This variability is clearly reflected in the chemical data that suggest at least two distinct analytic sources for this variety (fig. 56).

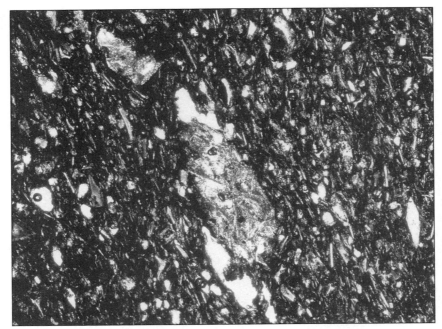

Figure 47. Photomicrograph: Wiyo Black-on-white with very fine volcanic ash temper (field = 1.2 mm).

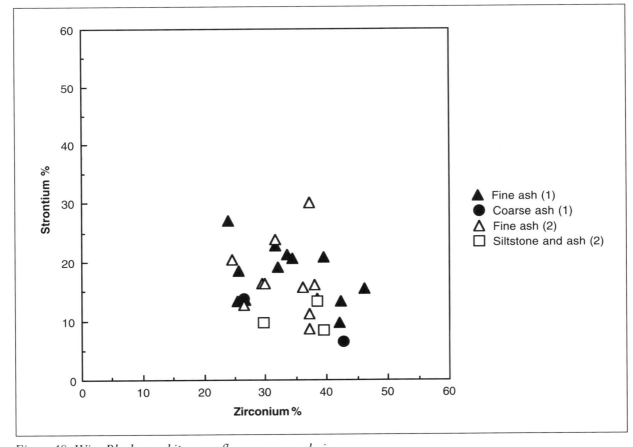

Figure 48. Wiyo Black-on-white x-ray fluorescence analysis.

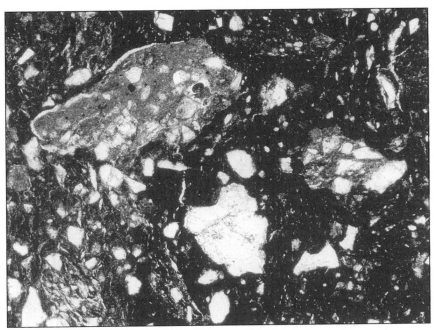

Figure 49. Photomicrograph: Galisteo Black-on-white with coarse sherd temper (field = 1.2 mm).

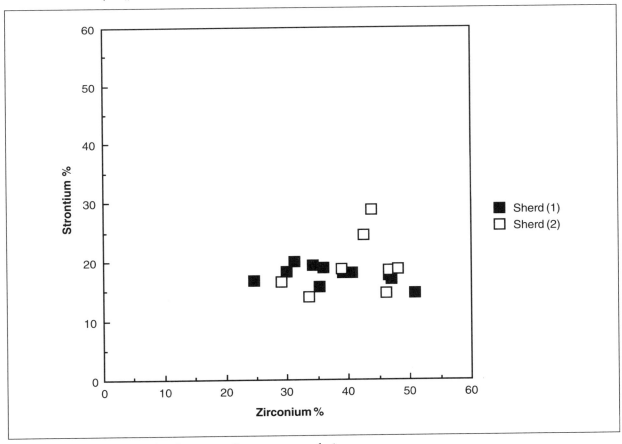

Figure 50. Galisteo Black-on-white x-ray fluorescence analysis.

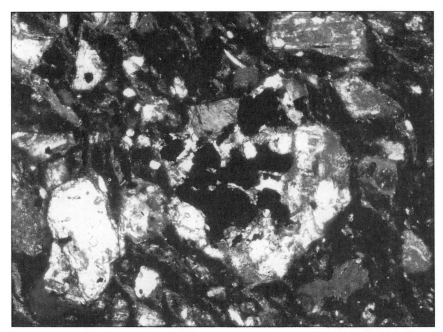

Figure 51. Photomicrograph: Galisteo Black-on-white, var. Kendi, *with augite monzonite temper (field = 1.2 mm).*

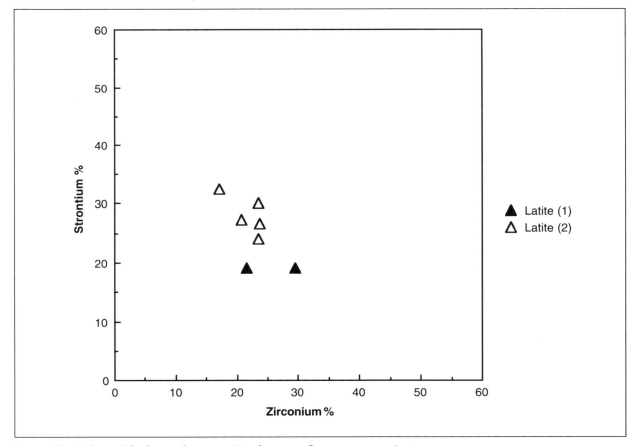

Figure 52. Galisteo Black-on-white, var. Kendi, *x-ray fluorescence analysis.*

70

Figure 53. Photomicrograph: Rowe Black-on-white, var. Poge, *with coarse lithic sand temper (field = 1.2 mm).*

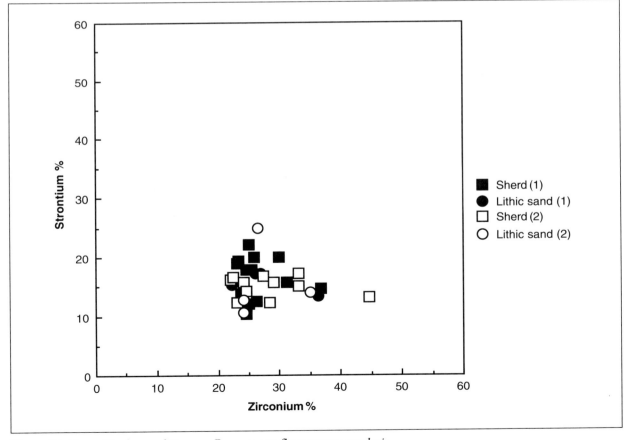

Figure 54. Rowe Black-on-white, var. Poge, *x-ray fluorescence analysis.*

71

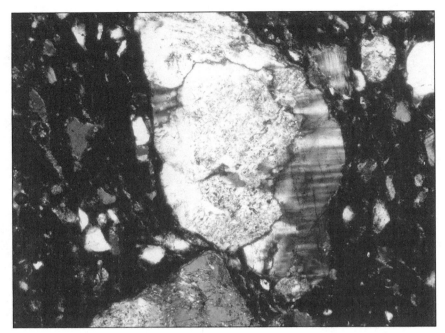

Figure 55. Photomicrograph: Rowe Black-on-white, var. Arroyo Hondo, with coarse granitic/gneissic clay (field = 1.2 mm).

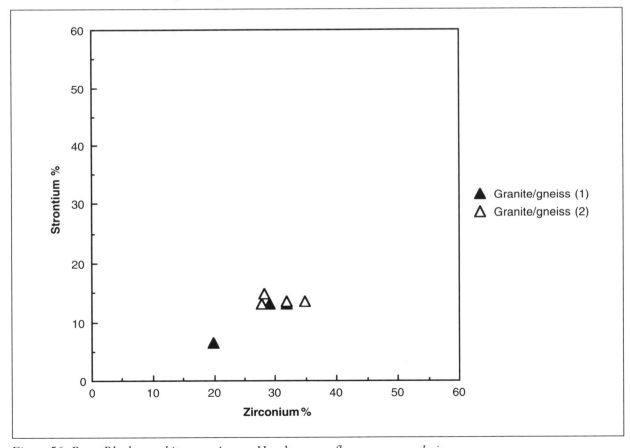

Figure 56. Rowe Black-on-white, var. Arroyo Hondo, x-ray fluorescence analysis.

JEMEZ SERIES

The Vallecitos and Jemez Black-on-white sherds found at Arroyo Hondo were tempered with fine to very coarse pumiceous ash. Inclusions consisted of fine angular glass fragments, coarse to very coarse vesicular pumice, quartz, plagioclase and alkali feldspar phenocrysts, augite, and hematite. The presence of plagioclase phenocrysts and mafic and opaque accessories indicates a more dacitic or andesitic composition for these ashes, as compared to the ashes found in Pajarito Series types, such as Wiyo B/W, Abiquiú B/W, or Santa Fe, *var. Pindi.*

Rio Grande Glaze Ware

GLAZE A RED. The Agua Fria Glaze-on-red, San Clemente Polychrome, and Sanchez Polychrome pottery from Arroyo Hondo is dominated by two distinct paste categories (fig. 57). The more common paste category is characterized by crystalline basalt and sherd temper (51%). In hand section these sherds contain angular dull black or red lithic clasts mixed with varying amounts of light brown and gray sherd fragments. Petrographically (fig. 58a), these crystalline basalts can be seen to be composed of fine tabular plagioclase microlites and intergranular augite, magnetite, red basaltic hornblende, and rare olivine. A number of different pottery types appear to have been ground for temper, including black culinary sherds, light brown ash-tempered sherds, and other gray- and red-paste painted types. Mineral inclusions consist of quartz, feldspar, and rare mica, augite, and altered hornblende. Rarely, lithic clasts of coarse pumice and latite are present, probably derived from the ground sherds.

About 43 percent of the Glaze A Red sherds from Arroyo Hondo are tempered with clasts of intermediate volcanic rock. Two distinct varieties were identified. The more common is a fine-textured augite latite/monzonite identical to that described for the *Kendi* variety of Galisteo B/W. The other rock type can be described as a hornblende latite porphyry (fig. 58b). It is composed of tabular phenocrysts of acid plagioclase (probably andesine or oligoclase) that are more or less altered to calcite in a crystalline to microcrystalline ground mass. Augite and brown hornblende are the most common mafic minerals. The hornblende is often entirely replaced by opaque minerals such as magnetite.

As can be seen from the XRF plot (fig. 59), these two major temper categories are clearly distinguishable, both chemically and mineralogically. The latite-tempered sherds are characterized by relatively high strontium counts and correspondingly low zirconium

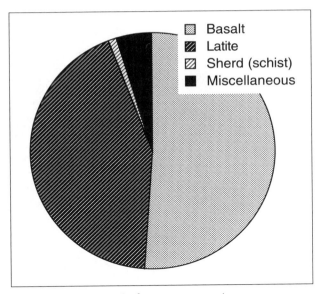

Figure 57. Glaze A Red temper categories.

counts, whereas the basalt-tempered sherds are marked by more intermediate values for both strontium and zirconium.

All of the Los Padillas Polychrome sherds examined were tempered with ground schist-tempered sherd. Pastes include fine to medium fragments of angular quartz, plagioclase, and mica; medium to coarse subangular clasts of quartzite, mica schist, and gneiss; and medium to coarse angular dark brown schist-tempered sherd. Rarely, fine clasts of crystalline basalt are also present. The sherds in this paste group show up as a distinct cluster in the lower right-hand corner of the Glaze A Red scatter plot (fig. 59). These types are characterized by their relatively high zirconium counts and low strontium counts.

GLAZE B RED. Twenty-one out of 27 (78%) of the Largo Glaze-on-red sherds analyzed from Arroyo Hondo were tempered with schist-tempered sherd similar to that described for Los Padillas Polychrome. The remaining six Largo sherds from the site contained lithic clasts that resembled the latite/monzonite temper reported for Galisteo B/W, *var. Kendi,* and Agua Fria G/R.

GLAZE A YELLOW. Fifty-two percent of the Cieneguilla Glaze-on-yellow sherds examined were tempered with altered latite and sherd, and 44 percent were tempered with crushed augite latite identical to that described for Agua Fria G/R and the *Kendi* variety of Galisteo B/W

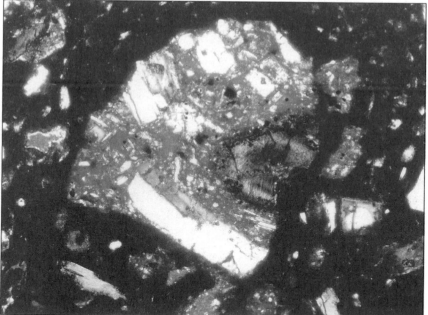

Figure 58. Photomicrographs: top, *Agua Fria Glaze-on-red with sherd and basalt temper (field = 1.2 mm);* bottom, *Agua Fria G/R with porphyritic hornblende-latite temper (field = 1.2 mm).*

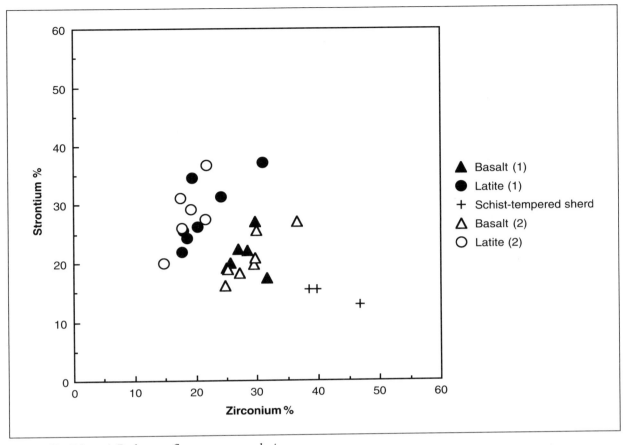

Figure 59. Glaze A Red x-ray fluorescence analysis.

(fig. 60). These two temper groups form two clearly distinct clusters on the XRF scatter plot (fig. 61). The remaining 4 percent of the Cieneguilla sherds analyzed were tempered with basalt-tempered sherd. This temper group also shows up as a distinct cluster on the x-ray scatter plot.

Rio Grande Gray Ware

As noted previously, the culinary ware from Arroyo Hondo was not subjected to the same degree of technical analysis as the painted wares. During the sorting process, however, it was noted that Tesuque Gray sherds could be separated into two broad paste categories. Both paste types appear to have been derived from coarse-textured primary clays, the inclusions being naturally occurring rock fragments in the clay, making the addition of temper unnecessary. The more common paste type is characterized by the conspicuous inclusion of coarse to very coarse angular clasts of pink granite and/or gneiss. In addition, medium to coarse platy bundles of muscovite mica are moderately to highly abundant. This variation in the density of mica in the pastes suggests some natural variation in the original source of the clay.

The second group of culinary ceramics common at the site is composed of a very distinctive, highly micaceous residual clay. The paste is reminiscent of the clay used by potters at Nambe, San Juan, Taos, and Picuris to produce their traditional micaceous ware. These clays are derived from deposits of decomposed and altered Precambrian schists found in various locations throughout the Sangre de Cristo Mountains. This paste type is considerably more common in the Component II assemblage, indicating a gradual shift in the source of culinary pottery at the site after A.D. 1370.

The XRF signatures for both these general classes of culinary ware overlap considerably, despite the mineralogical differences noted above (fig. 62). These data suggest that the XRF technique used in this analysis was not sensitive to the particular chemical differences that potentially distinguish these mineralogically distinct categories of culinary ceramics.

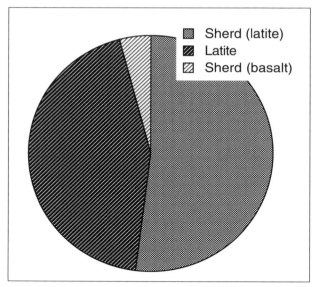

Figure 60. Glaze A Yellow temper categories.

Interpretations

In order to determine where the various ceramics from Arroyo Hondo were being manufactured, it is necessary to have a clear understanding of the distribution of geologic resources, both in the immediate vicinity of the site and throughout the northern Rio Grande as a whole (fig. 63). Arroyo Hondo Pueblo is located above the southwest bank of Arroyo Hondo canyon at a point where the eastern edge of the piedmont plain meets the foothills of the Sangre de Cristo Mountains. The surface of the plain is covered by several hundred feet of recently deposited alluvial sand, silt, and gravel of the Ancha formation. These gravels consist primarily of metamorphic and igneous rocks washed down from the adjacent mountains (Spiegel and Baldwin 1963:35). Exposed within the Ancha formation for about 0.2 miles along the upper bank of the arroyo immediately adjacent to the site is a narrow but prominent lens of coarse, white, pumiceous ash. These ash deposits consist of an unconsolidated

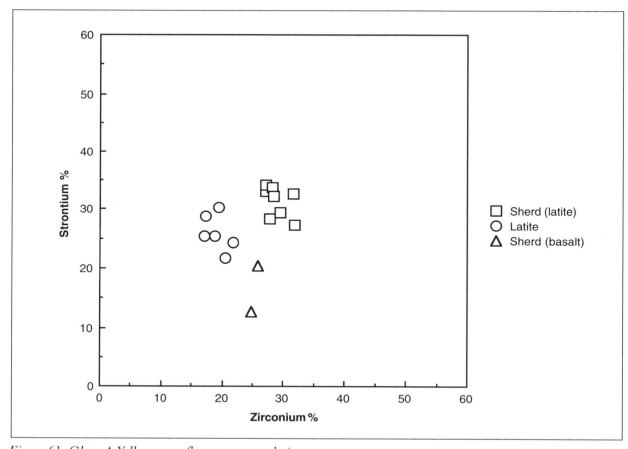

Figure 61. Glaze A Yellow x-ray fluorescence analysis.

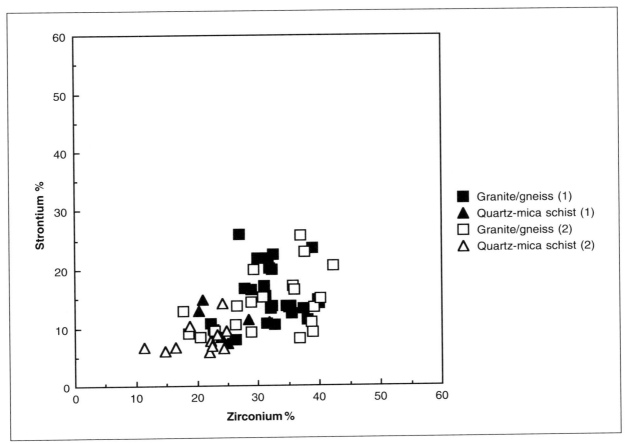

Figure 62. Tesuque Gray x-ray fluorescence analysis.

mixture of vesicular pumice, crystalline alkali feldspar and quartz, and rare black specks of augite and mica.

North and east of the site, massive deposits of volcanic latite form the upper walls of the adjacent canyon. The latite is composed of two distinct components. The upper component consists of a porphyritic gray latite with abundant coarse, tabular phenocrysts of white plagioclase. The lower component is a porphyritic dark gray-brown latite with abundant coarse phenocrysts of black augite and white tabular plagioclase. The two components are separated by a layer of baked soil (Spiegel and Baldwin 1963:35–36; Stearns 1953:430–31). These latites are similar in both composition and origin to the Espinaso volcanics that outcrop to the south along the Arroyo San Marcos and Galisteo Creek, in the Tonque Valley, Cerrillos Hills, and Ortiz Mountains, and to the west near La Cienega (Stearns 1953).

The lower walls of the arroyo consist of deep deposits of reddish siltstone, sandstone, and conglomerate with inclusions of volcanic conglomerate and andesitic tuff.

These deposits are known collectively as the Galisteo formation (Spiegel and Baldwin 1963:33).

The foothills and mountains to the east of the site are composed of Precambrian pink and gray granite, gneiss, and schist. Gneiss makes up the bulk of the high peaks in the immediate vicinity of the site, whereas pink granite forms the foothills that separate the piedmont from the higher gneissic mountains. Scattered outcrops of schist and amphibolite also occur in the mountains (Kelley 1980:16). The floor of Arroyo Hondo canyon is covered by recent stream wash consisting of sand and gravel washed down from the mountains.

As the preceding summary indicates, potters at Arroyo Hondo could have used clays and tempers from a wide variety of geologically distinct local sources. For example, the deposits of pumiceous ash near the site are virtually identical in composition and texture to the temper used in the *Pindi* variety of Santa Fe B/W (see fig. 45b). Similarly, as noted above, the augite latites from Arroyo Hondo are very similar mineralogically to

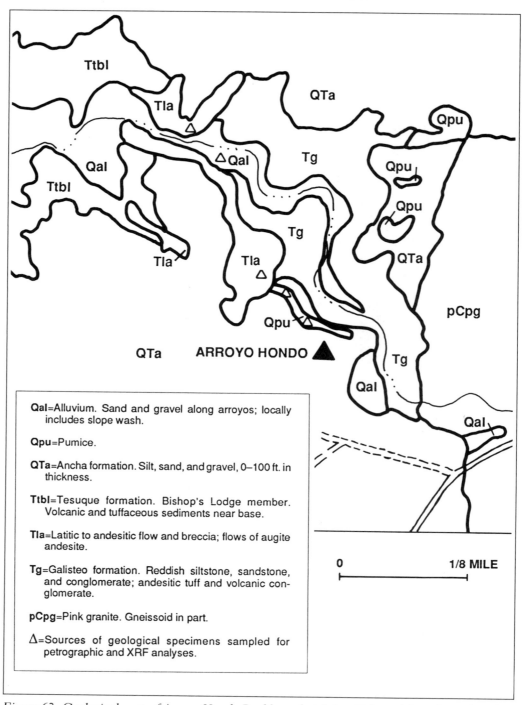

Figure 63. Geological map of Arroyo Hondo Pueblo and vicinity. (Adapted from Spiegel and Baldwin 1963)

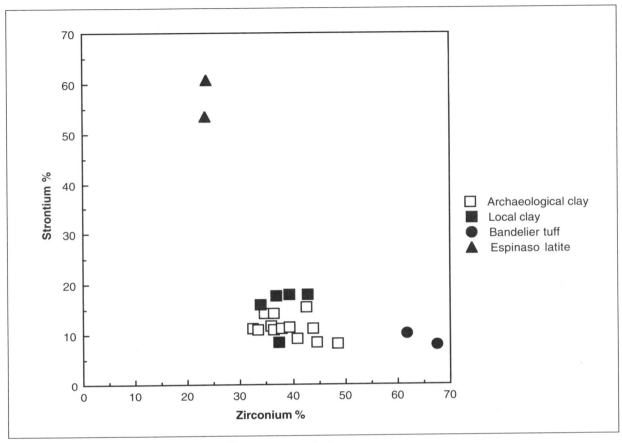

Figure 64. Clay and rock samples, x-ray fluorescence analysis.

the augite latites used as temper in both the glaze wares and the *Kendi* variety of Galisteo B/W. Petrographically, however, certain textural differences were noted. The latites from Arroyo Hondo had a distinctly porphyritic texture with phenocrysts of plagioclase and augite in a fine-grained microcrystalline ground mass, whereas the augite latites/monzonites seen in the sherds from the site had a more holocrystalline texture indicative of an intrusive magma rather than an extrusive flow origin. The Precambrian deposits of the adjacent foothills and mountains are a likely place to search for sources of the primary clays used in the production of the culinary wares, as well as the *Poge* and *Arroyo Hondo* varieties of Rowe B/W.

Showing that the inhabitants of Arroyo Hondo had access to these lithic resources is not enough to prove that any or all of these pottery types were actually manufactured at the site. Chemical analyses of clays found in the excavations and of clay and lithic samples collected near the site were conducted to help resolve this issue.

Richard Lang collected clay from five different locations near the site. All of the clays were red to reddish brown in color and contained moderate to abundant fine silty or sandy inclusions. These clays were similar in color, texture, and composition to a series of clays found in room deposits during the excavation of the pueblo. It was presumed by the excavators that they represented the remains of potter's clay used by the inhabitants of the pueblo to make ceramic vessels.

Figure 64 illustrates the results of the analysis of 13 of the clay samples excavated from Component II contexts and the 5 clay samples collected from sources in the arroyo. The strontium and zirconium values for these clays overlap the values for Santa Fe, *var. Pindi*, Rowe, *vars. Poge* and *Arroyo Hondo*, and Tesuque Gray—the most likely types to have been locally produced, based on mineralogical evidence.

A look at the rubidium values, however, reveals a striking contrast. The mean rubidium count for the excavated clay samples is 30.3 percent, with individual counts ranging from 19.7 percent to 38.1 percent. The mean value for four of the five clay samples collected from the arroyo is 16.8 percent; individual counts range from 12.7 percent to 21 percent. The fifth sample has a rubidium value of 46.4 percent, well out of the range of even the excavated samples. For the most part, these unusually high rubidium values fall outside the range recorded for the potentially local ceramic types cited above, although the rubidium counts for several of the *Pindi* and Tesuque Gray samples overlap the lowest values recorded for the geologic samples. It is unclear, however, what effect the addition of various types of temper would have on diluting these values; nor is it possible, without additional experimentation and replication studies, to determine the effects of firing on chemical composition. Given these limitations and the relative insensitivity of the particular XRF technique used in this analysis, it is impossible to conclude whether or not the local red clays from the Galisteo formation near Arroyo Hondo were ever used to produce any of the pottery recovered from the site.

There is archaeological evidence, however, to suggest that at least some pottery was in fact manufactured at the site. The most convincing of this evidence is the recovery of *pukis*, or "turnpots," in the excavations at the site. The pukis are constructed from broken pots that have been specially ground to form shallow saucers. Pueblo potters would start a pot by either molding the base directly in the puki or by pressing the first series of coils into the saucer; the walls of the vessel were then built up by the addition of successive coils (Guthe 1925). The curved base of the puki allowed the potter to turn the pot while building and thinning the walls of the vessel. Some of the pukis from Arroyo Hondo have a thick, gritty coating of what appears to be dried clay and cornmeal on the interior. This coating probably acted as a parting medium so that the pot being constructed did not stick to the turnpot.

In lieu of the immediately local red clay sources of the Galisteo formation, Arroyo Hondo potters also may have sought clays in the adjacent foothills of the Sangre de Cristo Mountains. The clays in this area are principally residual clays derived from the erosion of the local pink granite and gneiss that form the mountains here. This is certainly the source of the coarse granitic/gneissic pastes used in much of the culinary ware pottery at the site, strongly suggesting, on mineralogical grounds, that these pots were produced locally—at either Arroyo Hondo or other contemporaneous sites located along the western and southern edges of the Sangre de Cristo Mountains. For example, compositionally similar culinary wares have been described from Pecos Pueblo (Kidder and Shepard

1936). The relatively diffuse chemical signature for this variant of Tesuque Gray indicates a high degree of variability in the granitic/gneissic clay sources used by culinary ware potters in this general region. The more micaceous, schisty variety of culinary ware pottery from the site, however, was probably not produced locally. Most likely, it came from sources farther north in the mountains where schist outcroppings and the residual clays derived from such sources are more common.

Coarse-textured granitic clays were also used in the production of the rare *Arroyo Hondo* variety of Galisteo B/W. This variety is represented by literally only a handful of sherds from the site. The poor technical quality of the ware suggests that it was made by potters who were generally unfamiliar with the techniques of painted ware production. The coarse-textured, low-fired pastes appear to be more suitable to cooking pots than decorative serving bowls and may represent the results of experimentation by potters who usually specialized in the production of corrugated ceramics.

Medium-textured lithic sand of granitic and gneissic composition also characterizes the *Poge* variety of Rowe B/W. These lithic inclusions may represent local stream sand that was added to the clay as temper, but the addition of sherd temper to most of the pastes suggests that these lithic clasts may have occurred naturally in the clay. Thus, the mineralogical evidence clearly indicates a local origin for *Poge* pottery. The relative abundance of the variety at the site also supports this hypothesis. *Poge* is the most common painted pottery in Component I, making up almost 24 percent of the decorated assemblage. In Component II, its frequency drops to only 15 percent, largely due to the increasing popularity of Wiyo B/W and the glaze wares. As was discussed in chapter 2, the distribution of the *Poge* variety of Rowe B/W is generally limited to sites in the Santa Fe–Pecos district, suggesting it is a local product of that region. Of the four major Classic period sites in the area—Pecos (LA 625), Pindi (LA 1), Agua Fria Schoolhouse (LA 2), and Arroyo Hondo (LA 12)—Arroyo Hondo appears to be the most likely source of this variety, both because of the relatively high proportion of *Poge* recovered from the site and because of the site's proximity to clay and temper sources most likely used in its manufacture. In summary, the *Poge* variety of Rowe B/W probably represents *the* diagnostic local pottery from Arroyo Hondo.

The case for the local production of *Pindi* pottery at Arroyo Hondo is also compelling. Traditionally, the Pajarito Plateau, with its thick deposits of airborne ash exposed below the massive consolidated tuffs of the Bandelier formation, has been cited as the most probable source of the coarse, pumiceous, ash-tempered *Pindi* variety of Santa Fe B/W (Kidder and Shepard 1936:483). Contrary to this assumption, however, *Pindi* pottery is rarely encountered on Pajarito sites. Like *Poge*, its distribution appears to be limited largely to the Santa Fe–Pecos district (Stubbs and Stallings 1953). The presence of local deposits of pumiceous ash of the same composition and texture as the *Pindi* temper indicates that there is no geological reason why all the *Pindi* recovered from Arroyo Hondo could not have been made there. Furthermore, the tight, well-defined chemical signature for the type supports a common, local origin for the variety.

Coarse ash temper also characterizes the 10 sherds of Vallecitos and Jemez B/W examined from Arroyo Hondo. Inclusions of plagioclase, augite, and hornblende reflect the more andesitic composition of tuffs and ashes from the north and west sides of the Jemez Mountains, from which these ceramics were probably manufactured.

The other volcanic ash-tempered ceramics from Arroyo Hondo, including Santa Fe B/W, Wiyo B/W, and Abiquiú B/W, were probably all manufactured at sites located north of Santa Fe in the Española Basin. The silty untempered and sand-tempered pastes of Kwahe'e B/W and Santa Fe B/W are also traceable to this region. Here the rolling piedmont gives way to a higher, more dissected area that forms the divide between the Santa Fe River and the more northerly drainage of Tesuque and Pojoaque creeks. The latter drainages have caused intricate dissection and strong local relief, including some badlands (Spiegel and Baldwin 1963:8). This rough area, which descends northward into the Española Valley of the Rio Grande, represents the traditional homeland of the northern Tewa Pueblos (Peckham 1984:275).

The predominant geologic deposit in this region, the Tesuque formation, consists of several thousand feet of pinkish tan, loosely consolidated sandstone, siltstone, and conglomerate. The Tesuque formation is well exposed in the badlands between the villages of Tesuque and Pojoaque. The deposits are composed predominantly of fragments of Precambrian rocks (i.e., red feldspar [microcline], granite, quartz, schist, gneiss, and quartzite) cemented by calcium carbonate, derived from the solution of limestone. Clay is present only in very small amounts, but silt and very fine sand form a large proportion of the unit (Spiegel and Baldwin 1963:39–40).

Interbedded with these sedimentary deposits are numerous layers of fine white volcanic ash (Galusha and Blick 1971). These ash beds are exposed throughout the basin and have been a favorite source of tempering material for the Pueblo potters of the area for some eight hundred years. Modern San Ildefonso potter Alice Martinez still uses the silty local clays and ash deposits near

Pojoaque Pueblo in her pottery (Bart Olinger, personal communication, 1989). A thin section made from one of her polished black ware vessels reveals a paste that is very similar in both texture and composition to early Abiquiú B/W vessels from Arroyo Hondo (fig. 65).

The classic sherd-tempered variety of Galisteo pottery offers few mineralogical clues to its origin. As we have seen, Galisteo B/W has a far more limited distribution than the ubiquitous Santa Fe B/W. It is generally found in varying proportions on sites located south of the Santa Fe River, from the Rio Grande valley on the west to Pecos on the east. The center of this distribution is the Galisteo Basin, where Galisteo B/W is the principal ceramic type on sites dating to the late Coalition and early Classic, and this area has generally been regarded as its source of manufacture (Kidder and Shepard 1936:485). Shepard noted that the distinctive dense, white clays of classic Galisteo B/W ceramics are more characteristic of the carbonaceous, buff-burning, Cretaceous clays of the Galisteo Basin than of the red-burning, sedimentary clays that predominate to the north and west (Kidder and Shepard 1936:481; Shepard 1965:65).

The *Kendi* variety of Galisteo B/W can also trace its origins to sites in the Galisteo Basin. During the Tertiary period, extensive volcanic activity resulted in massive amounts of molten lava and tuff being spread over vast areas of north-central New Mexico (Talmage and Wootton 1937:37). At the same time, the Paleozoic and Mesozoic sediments in this area were intruded by magmas of largely intermediate composition (Atkinson 1961; Disbrow and Stoll 1957). The sequence of extrusive and intrusive igneous rocks associated with this period of volcanism are referred to as the Espinaso volcanics. Extensive exposures of these volcanics can be found in the Tonque Valley, the Ortiz Mountains, and the Cerrillos Hills; along the upper drainages of Galisteo Creek, Arroyo San Marcos, and Arroyo Hondo; and along the Santa Fe River and Cienega Creek between Cieneguilla and La Bajada (Stearns 1953:420). These rocks are almost entirely latites, quartz latites, or monzonites. Large phenocrysts of hornblende and/or augite are usually conspicuous, although biotite occurs as the primary dark mineral in some varieties. Despite these generalities, there is a high degree of variability in composition, structure, and texture in these rocks.

The most common lithic temper in the *Kendi* pottery from Arroyo Hondo is a white holocrystalline augite latite/monzonite. Although very similar in composition, the Espinaso volcanics exposed near Arroyo Hondo are dark gray augite latite porphyries. The dense, white to buff clays of the *Kendi* variety appear to be similar to those used in sherd-tempered Galisteo, suggesting that

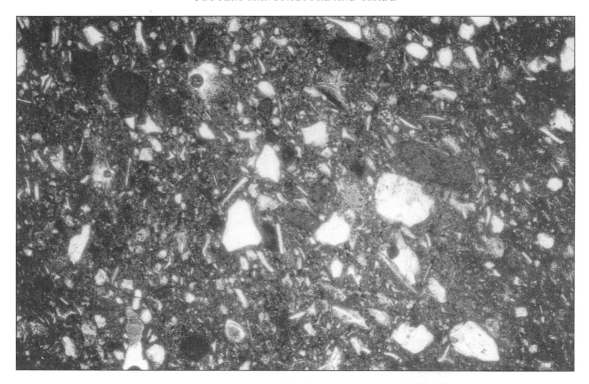

Figure 65. Photomicrographs: top, *modern San Ildefonso polished black ware with fine volcanic ash temper (field = 1.7 mm);* bottom, *Abiquiú Black-on-white with fine volcanic ash temper (field = 2.4 mm).*

both varieties were manufactured in the same basic region. As noted above, these light-firing clays appear to be diagnostic of the Cretaceous deposits of the Galisteo Basin.

Forty-three percent of the Glaze A Red and all of the Glaze A Yellow sherds from Arroyo Hondo are tempered with some type of intermediate volcanic rock. This temper is not as common in the first component, where it was identified in only 4 of the 17 Glaze A Red sherds examined. In the second component, however, it characterized nearly half of the sample. Latite temper has long been considered a diagnostic feature of glaze-painted pottery produced in the Galisteo Basin (Kidder and Shepard 1936; Shepard 1942; Warren 1970, 1976, 1981; Schaafsma 1969, 1979). This area is known to have been a prominent center of glaze ware production, exporting more pottery than any other glaze-producing district. Its importance probably stemmed from the fact that the only known source of lead, essential for the manufacturing of glaze paint, in the northern Rio Grande was in this district (Shepard 1942:187–88).

Although the preeminence of the Galisteo Basin glaze ware trade came primarily during the Intermediate (Glaze C and D) period, villages in this district were already supplying large quantities of glaze-on-red and glaze-on-yellow ceramics to adjacent areas by the end of the Early Glaze period. For example, 72 percent of the Glaze A [I] Red pottery from Pecos had intermediate volcanic temper (Shepard 1942:152).

As noted previously, two major and several minor varieties of intermediate volcanic rock temper were identified petrographically in the glaze ware assemblage from Arroyo Hondo. The most common variety is an augite latite/monzonite, which appears to correspond to what Warren (1976, 1981) calls San Marcos latite because 60 to 100 percent of the glaze-painted ceramics she examined from all periods at San Marcos contained this temper. Petrographic studies of Rio Grande Striated culinary sherds from the site also indicated that augite latite/monzonite was the tempering material favored by local potters at San Marcos (Habicht-Mauche 1988a). This material is also diagnostic of the *Kendi* variety of Galisteo B/W. One possible source of this temper is the latitic flows and monzonitic intrusions that outcrop in the vicinity of San Marcos Pueblo (Warren 1976:B98; Habicht-Mauche 1988a), although compositionally similar material would have been available in other areas along Galisteo Creek and in the Cerrillos Hills (Disbrow and Stoll 1957).

The second most common variety of intermediate rock temper identified in the glazes from Arroyo Hondo

was a fine-textured hornblende latite porphyry. Warren (1976:B99) suggests that the source of this variety of latite is the tuff-breccia units of the Espinaso formation that outcrop throughout the Galisteo Basin and Tonque Valley. It is particularly characteristic of the glazes from Tonque Pueblo but was probably used by potters from other villages in the area as well.

Over half (51%) of the Glaze A Red sherds from Arroyo Hondo are tempered with fine crystalline basalt or basalt-tempered sherd. Extensive basalt flows occur all along the northern Rio Grande, making sourcing of this material extremely complex. Shepard (1942:150), however, demonstrated that the distribution of this fine crystalline variety of basalt temper clearly centered in the Zia–Santo Domingo district, being well represented in adjacent areas but relatively unimportant in others. Warren's (1968, 1976, 1979) more recent work on ceramics from the Cochiti area has served to refine our understanding of the distribution and use of basalt sources. The basalt temper that dominates the Glaze A Red pottery from Arroyo Hondo corresponds most closely to what Warren calls San Felipe basalt. Shepard's (1942:243) intergranular basalt can probably be identified, in part, with this same material. The source of this temper is most likely the fine-grained Quaternary basalts of Santa Ana Mesa in the Santo Domingo Valley near San Felipe Pueblo. This area appears to have been an important early center of glaze ware production, but by Glaze C times production and trade had virtually ceased (Warren 1976:B94, 1979:208–209).

Contacts with the Zia–Santo Domingo district are not demonstrated for any of the earlier black-on-white pottery. The predominance at Arroyo Hondo of glaze-painted pottery from this district may reflect an expansion of trade networks beyond the immediately adjacent Española-Chama and Galisteo districts to include more distant communities toward the end of Component I and continuing throughout Component II.

Two minor yet distinctive temper types were also identified in the Glaze A Red sample. Each represented only about 1 percent of the sample. Nine sherds examined were tempered with well-sorted stream sand. This temper is characteristic of glaze-painted ceramics produced at Pecos, located just southeast of Arroyo Hondo on the other side of the mountains (Kidder and Shepard 1936). Eleven sherds containing mica schist-tempered sherd also were examined. Schist-tempered sherd is diagnostic of early glaze-painted ceramics from the Albuquerque and Bernalillo districts (Shepard 1942:189). Outcrops of schist are reported in the Tijeras Canyon area (Warren 1980), which is one possible source of this material.

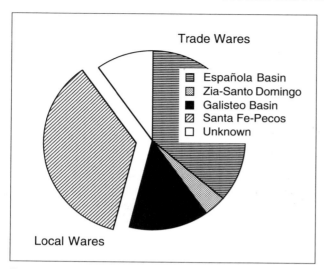
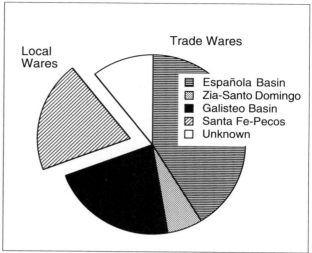

Figure 66. Sources of pottery from Arroyo Hondo Pueblo: left, *Component I;* right, *Component II.*

The Albuquerque district was an important center for early glaze ware production, and potters in this area appear to have played a significant part in the earliest development of glaze ware technology in the Rio Grande region. All of the Los Padillas Glaze Polychrome ceramics from Arroyo Hondo also contain schist-tempered sherd, as do the Socorro and Chupadero Black-on-white pots from the site. This evidence suggests that minor yet long-standing contacts existed between Arroyo Hondo and sites to the south.

One of the reasons often cited for the Albuquerque district's prominence in the early development and spread of the Rio Grande glazes is its close proximity to, and long-standing contacts with, the Little Colorado region, where glaze ware technology was first invented. In this respect, it is interesting to note that all of the ceramics identified on stylistic criteria as being Little Colorado red wares (i.e., St. Johns and Heshotauthla polychromes) were tempered with the identical mica schist-tempered sherd seen in the early Rio Grande glazes and black-on-white ceramics from the Albuquerque district. This mineralogical evidence, although based on a relatively small sample, suggests that prior to the full-blown development of a local glaze ware tradition, copies of Little Colorado red wares were being produced at sites along the Rio Grande. Local copies of glaze polychromes from west of the Rio Grande were also identified in the ceramic assemblage from Pueblo del Encierro (LA 70) (Snow 1976:B172).

Summary

Although some culinary and decorated pottery was clearly manufactured at Arroyo Hondo, it appears that a significant portion of the culinary wares and a majority of the decorated wares at the site were obtained in trade with pueblos outside the local Santa Fe–Pecos district (table 8). *Poge,* the diagnostic local pottery at the site, makes up about one-quarter of the decorated assemblage from Component I but drops to only 15 percent of Component II collections. *Pindi,* the other demonstrably local type, also drops in popularity from 12 percent to only 4 percent between the earlier and later occupations at the site. Conversely, the clearly imported mica schist variant of Tesuque Gray is more common in second component assemblages. This drop in frequency of locally produced pottery indicates that the inhabitants of Arroyo Hondo were becoming more and more dependent on trade for their domestic ceramic vessels as time went on (fig. 66).

The *Poge* variety of Rowe B/W appears to have had a fairly limited distribution that does not seem to have extended much beyond the immediate Santa Fe–Pecos district. This distribution would seem to indicate that *Poge* was produced for local consumption and was not exchanged in large quantities for the painted pottery of other districts. For a brief period during the middle of the fourteenth century, a local coarse-tempered variety

TABLE 8
Probable sources of pottery from Arroyo Hondo Pueblo.

Ware	Type	Probable Source
Cibola White Ware	Kwahe'e B/W	Española-Chama district
	Chupadero B/W	Albuquerque district
Pajarito White Ware		
Pajarito Series	Santa Fe, *var. Santa Fe*	Española-Chama district
	Santa Fe, *var. Pindi*	Santa Fe–Pecos district
	Wiyo B/W	Española-Chama district
	Abiquiú B/W	Española-Chama district
Galisteo Series	Galisteo, *var. Galisteo*	Galisteo district
	Galisteo, *var. Kendi*	Galisteo district
Pecos Series	Rowe, *var. Poge*	Santa Fe–Pecos district
	Rowe, *var. Arroyo Hondo*	Santa Fe–Pecos district
Jemez Series	Vallecitos and Jemez B/W	Jemez district
Rio Grande Glaze Ware		
Glaze A Red	Los Padillas G/P	Albuquerque district
	Agua Fria G/R, San Clemente G/P, etc.	Zia–Santo Domingo district
		Galisteo district
		Albuquerque district
		Santa Fe–Pecos district (rare)
Glaze A Yellow	Cieneguilla G/Y	Galisteo district
		Zia–Santo Domingo district
Glaze B Red	Largo G/R	Albuquerque district
		Galisteo district
Rio Grande Gray Ware	Tesuque Gray	Santa Fe–Pecos district
		Española-Chama district

of Santa Fe B/W became popular with Arroyo Hondo potters. *Pindi* pottery may reflect a short-lived period of experimentation, wherein local potters attempted to emulate the popular ash-tempered ceramic tradition of their neighbors to the north. Its presence at the site may also signal the presence of potters from the Española-Chama district at Arroyo Hondo, who continued their own distinct potting tradition using the most appropriate local materials. Suggestive of the second alternative is the fact that high incidences of *Pindi* pottery appear to be spatially restricted to a few roomblocks along the southern and western periphery of the Component I ruin and are not widespread throughout the site, even in deposits dating to the peak of the type's popularity during the 1340s (see Lang, this volume).

For the most part, the people of Arroyo Hondo appear to have obtained most of their decorated pottery from their immediate neighbors to the north and south (table 8; fig. 66). Pottery manufactured at sites in the Española-Chama district make up 36 percent of the Component I decorated assemblage and 41 percent of Component II. Most of this increase is due to the rise in popularity of Wiyo B/W in the later assemblage. The highly micaceous, schisty variant of Tesuque Gray probably also was produced in this district, particularly at sites along the western edge of the mountains.

The Galisteo Basin was the next most common source of decorated ceramics, contributing up to 14 percent of the painted pots from Component I. The Galisteo district's growing importance as a center for glaze ware production is reflected in the increase of 8 percent in the relative frequency of decorated sherds from this area in Component II.

Glaze ware ceramics from the Zia–Santo Domingo district make up a rather consistent 4 percent and 6 percent of the Component I and Component II decorated assemblages, respectively. Less than one percent of the entire decorated pottery from the site can be traced to other areas, such as the Jemez, Albuquerque, or Little Colorado districts.

The black-on-white ceramics from Arroyo Hondo present a pattern of ceramic manufacture and trade that stands in marked contrast to that which has been proposed for the Rio Grande glazes. During the late Coalition and early Classic (ca. A.D. 1250–1350), distinct regional styles of the generic black-on-white bowl form were being developed throughout the northern Rio Grande (see fig. 11). The primary difference between these regional traditions was in paste composition, which, in large part, was mitigated by the distribution and variability of local resources. As noted in chapter 2, however, stylistic differences among these types also have been recorded in slip, surface finish, paint, and, to a much lesser extent, design.

The relative distribution of these regional styles at Arroyo Hondo and at other contemporaneous sites indicates that large quantities of black-on-white ceramics were being exchanged between adjacent villages and districts, but there is little evidence of extensive long-distance trade. Although some large pueblos—Arroyo Hondo and Pecos, for example—appear to have produced few of their own black-on-white ceramics, there are no data to indicate that one village or district ever controlled or dominated trade in the early Classic white wares. For the most part, black-on-white bowls appear to have changed hands as part of fairly generalized reciprocal exchanges between neighboring communities.

The mineralogical and chemical data recorded for glaze-painted ceramics from Arroyo Hondo reflect a fundamental change in the organization of pottery manufacture and trade in the northern Rio Grande valley. In contrast to the black-on-white assemblage, where each imported type is marked by a diffuse pattern of mineralogical and chemical variability, the chemical signature for the glaze ware is characterized by distinct analytical sources that correlate with each of the three geologically defined regions of production—the Galisteo Basin, Zia–Santo Domingo, and Albuquerque districts—identified petrographically. Within each analytic cluster, however,

the chemical signature appears to be relatively homogeneous. This pattern may be indicative of a greater degree of standardization in resource selection and use than was recorded for the imported white wares, or it may simply be an artifact of the XRF analysis's inability to distinguish between closely related geologic sources of raw materials.

In either case, these data indicate that the production of early glaze-painted ceramics was limited to pueblos in a small number of districts and then widely traded from these production areas to towns located throughout the northern Rio Grande and beyond. Glaze technology is very complex and requires special resources, such as lead, that are extremely limited in their distribution. Glaze ware production appears to have flourished in those districts, such as the Galisteo Basin, where potters could control access to both the new technology and the necessary resources. Unfortunately, we do not yet possess the necessary microprovenience data that would allow us to pinpoint specific production centers within these districts or to begin to analyze the actual organization of production, in terms of the division of labor and resources among individuals or groups, within these centers (Rice 1984). In general, however, it appears that the early glazes reflect a shift in the basic mode of ceramic production in the northern Rio Grande from a level of household production, largely for local domestic consumption, to that of a household industry, with pottery being produced as a commodity specifically for trade (Rice 1987:184).

The glaze ware trade was an integral part of a regional network of social and economic interaction that linked the various local districts of the northern Rio Grande during the Classic period. The introduction of glaze technology to the northern Rio Grande may have facilitated the development of this regional system by establishing new economic links between geographically and ethnically disparate groups. What is clear from these data is that prior to the widespread distribution of glaze ware pottery during the mid-fourteenth century, even large, aggregated communities like Arroyo Hondo were engaged in much more parochial networks of economic and social interaction.

Chapter 4

Tribalization, Trade, and the
Rio Grande Classic Transition

Patterned changes have been documented in the frequency of various decorated pottery types recovered from excavations at Arroyo Hondo Pueblo (LA 12). These patterns correspond to broader trends in ceramic style that characterized the entire Santa Fe–Pecos district and other districts of the northern Rio Grande culture area during the fourteenth and early fifteenth centuries. Compositional analyses have revealed distinct and shifting sources for much of the pottery from the site. These data indicate that with the introduction of glaze ware technology to the northern Rio Grande, a fundamental change took place both in the structure of ceramic production and exchange and in the role that pottery played in economic and social interactions between communities in this area.

In this chapter, changes in both ceramic style and the nature of ceramic production and exchange, recorded in the Arroyo Hondo pottery assemblage, will be examined in the context of a broader regional perspective. The occupation of Arroyo Hondo Pueblo spans the transition between the so-called late Coalition and early Classic periods, which was characterized by fundamental transformations in the structure and integration of Rio Grande society. Documented patterns of stylistic diversity, recorded for the decorated white ware ceramics from Arroyo Hondo, will be correlated with structural changes in cultural and ethnic diversity in the northern Rio Grande during the fourteenth century. This transformation of the social landscape can be interpreted as an organizational response to increasing population density and an intensification of intergroup competition for essential productive resources, especially prime agricultural land. The intensive localized production and widespread trade of glaze ware pottery after about A.D. 1350 are seen as reflections of the emergence of a regional tribal network of social and economic integration that brought interdependence and stability to interethnic re-

lations in the region. The ultimate goal of this study is to examine the role of material culture and technology in restructuring social and economic relations during this critical transitional period in the development of Eastern Pueblo society.

The Early Coalition Period
(A.D. 1200–1250)

Prior to the end of the twelfth century, the population density of the northern Rio Grande appears to have remained relatively low. It has been estimated, however, that sometime between A.D. 1150 and 1250 the area experienced as much as a tenfold increase in population. This figure is based on an increase in both the total number and the average size of early Coalition sites (Stuart and Gauthier 1981:51; Cordell 1989:314–15).

The rapidity and scale of this population increase has been interpreted as evidence for a migration of people into the area during the thirteenth century (Cordell 1989). The archaeological record of abandonment in the San Juan Basin and Mesa Verde regions of the Colorado Plateau during this same period suggests that these areas were likely sources of this new population (Cordell 1984: 333). Alternatively, the movement of people off the plateau may have put pressure on groups living along the northwestern periphery of the northern Rio Grande, creating a ripple effect that resulted in an increasing concentration of people within the core area of the upper Rio Grande valley. Other potential sources of population include the upper Little Colorado region of west-central New Mexico and east-central Arizona (Adams 1991).

Nevertheless, not a single site has ever been identified in the northern Rio Grande that contains an assemblage of features or artifacts that can be interpreted as evidence of a wholly immigrant community (Cordell 1979b: 144, 1984:333). The overall continuity of northern Rio

Grande culture has been cited as evidence for the local development of early Coalition culture without substantial migration. The magnitude of population changes reflected in the settlement data, however, cannot be explained readily by biological models of in situ population growth. As a result, the continuity of local material culture reflected in the archaeological record may indicate that the processes of population movement, social integration, and the emergence of the various historic ethnic groups of the area may have been much more complicated and harder to read "on the ground" than most archaeologists have imagined.

As Upham (1984) and Cordell (1979a:103) have pointed out, mass migrations of entire villages are extremely rare ethnographically. It is more likely that throughout the Coalition, families leaving the San Juan Basin and Mesa Verde areas traveled south and east to join local Rio Grande communities with whom they had existing economic or kin-based relationships (Cordell 1979a:103, 1979b:150, 1984:334). In societies like those of the Eastern Pueblos, agricultural land and other productive resources are not the property of individuals but are held in common by a community or kinship group and distributed to members on the basis of need or status. As a result, there is a strong impetus for newcomers to develop cultural and familial ties with the recipient community in order to gain access to these resources (Barth 1969). This process would act to sustain the general homogeneity and continuity of local material culture by selecting against the persistence of those cultural traits that marked newcomers as "foreigners" or "outsiders." From this perspective, then, the continuity of local cultural development in the northern Rio Grande is not inherently antithetical to the proposed model of population growth and settlement expansion due, in part, to population movement into the area during the thirteenth century.

As population density increased, groups spread out and established farmsteads and villages in previously unoccupied areas. At first, there was a preference for areas at lower elevations near prime agricultural lands. As these areas filled up, groups began to occupy increasingly marginal highland zones (Dickson 1979). This pattern of broadly dispersed, small- to medium-sized settlements, located in a variety of topographic and climatic settings, characterized the Coalition period (ca. A.D. 1200–1300) throughout much of the northern Rio Grande (Collins 1975; Cordell 1979a).

Diversity of settlement type and location both supported and encouraged the development of a wide variety of subsistence strategies and agricultural techniques.

For example, the distribution of water conservation features, such as stone grids, waffle gardens, terraces, check dams, and bordered gardens with gravel mulch (Lang 1977; Cordell et al. 1984; Woosley 1986), indicate that dry farming was practiced in a number of topographic settings, including the edges of the Jemez Mountains, the Pajarito Plateau, the Taos Valley, the Galisteo Basin, and the foothills of the Sangre de Cristo Mountains. The use of canal irrigation also has been hypothesized for this period. Analysis of the tree-ring record from Arroyo Hondo indicates that between A.D. 990 and 1430, the northern Rio Grande climate, although generally favorable for agriculture, was characterized by both high frequency and high amplitude variability in seasonal precipitation (Rose et al. 1981). By diversifying field locations and agricultural strategies, groups could buffer the effects of periodic crop loss in any one setting.

Hunting and gathering also appears to have remained an important aspect of the subsistence strategy of the northern Rio Grande Pueblos (Anschuetz 1987:153; Cordell 1979a:7; Wetterstrom 1986). For example, communal deer drives, rabbit hunts, and the collection of wild piñon nuts were important elements of Eastern Pueblo subsistence that continued well into the historic period (Ford 1972a:24). Although it is not clear from the archaeological remains what percentage of total dietary calories was derived, on average, from foraged resources, such foods would have provided a critical supplement to the largely agricultural subsistence base during periods of drought and crop shortage (Anderson and Oakes 1980; Wetterstrom 1986).

Such a diversified subsistence strategy would have required that individual groups maintain access to a broad range of territory in order to compensate for spatial, seasonal, and annual variability in the availability of wild resources and the productivity of farmland. Given the patchiness of the northern Rio Grande environment, however, it would have been extremely difficult, if not impossible, for small, dispersed, early Coalition communities to establish and maintain exclusive use rights to areas distant from their main villages (Anschuetz 1987:154). Rather, a fairly broad, open network of social relations would have been required in order to insure groups' mutual access to neighboring foraging territories and to information about the availability and distribution of food resources outside their home ranges (Cordell 1979b:148).

The widespread homogeneity of material culture that characterizes the early Coalition may be a reflection of just such a broad, open network of economic and social relations. The diagnostic ceramic type of the period is

Santa Fe Black-on-white. As noted in chapter 2, Santa Fe B/W was the earliest widely distributed carbon-painted pottery in the northern Rio Grande. Stylistically, there is a strong connection between Santa Fe and its Cibola-influenced predecessor, Kwahe'e Black-on-white, but the type also bears a noticeable resemblance to contemporary Mesa Verde pottery styles (Lang 1982, 1989). Nevertheless, Santa Fe B/W represents a uniquely local ceramic development, and with its production the northern Rio Grande ceramic tradition is born.

During the early decades of the thirteenth century, Santa Fe B/W was the dominant decorated ceramic type on sites ranging from the Taos Valley to below Albuquerque and from the Jemez Mountains to the eastern flank of the Sangre de Cristos (see fig. 8). The type is characterized by a broad, regional uniformity of style, contrasting with a high degree of local compositional and technological variability. Warren (1976) has identified at least 35 distinct temper varieties for Santa Fe B/W, indicating that throughout the northern Rio Grande, potters were producing these ceramic vessels using locally available resources while at the same time adhering to widely accepted regional canons of ceramic style. The widespread distribution of these temper varieties further indicates that relations between local groups were extensive and largely reciprocal (Snow 1976).

The Late Coalition–Early Classic Transition (A.D. 1250–1350)

The last half of the thirteenth century was characterized by drought throughout much of the American Southwest (Rose, Dean, and Robinson 1981:94; Jorde 1977). These deteriorating climatic conditions may have been a key factor in the final abandonment of much of the northern San Juan–Mesa Verde region between 1260 and 1300. Some portion of the population from those areas probably came to join related groups already settled in the northern Rio Grande. Evidence cited to support this migration theory includes the local production, beginning around the turn of the fourteenth century, of Mesa Verde–influenced ceramic types, such as Galisteo Black-on-white, Rowe Black-on-white (including *var. Poge*), and early Jemez Black-on-white (Mera 1935; Wendorf and Reed 1955; Ford, Schroeder, and Peckham 1972; Lang 1982; Sundt 1987); an increase in the number and size of late Coalition sites; the increasing use of masonry architecture; the construction of aboveground kivas with deflectors and south-oriented floor features; and the modification of several circular kivas in the region into kivas with southern keyhole-shaped re-

cesses (Snow 1974; Traylor et al. 1977; Cordell 1989).

None of these traits co-occur in a context that can clearly be identified as a "site unit intrusion." As noted above, the need of migrants to gain access to critical productive resources through full participation in the economic and social life of existing Rio Grande communities would have mitigated against the retention of cultural traits that would have marked individuals as "outsiders." Foreign styles, technologies, and ideologies might have been adopted by host communities, however, either when the efficacy or functional superiority of such traits was generally recognized or as a means of creating cultural diversity and enhancing community identity in the increasingly crowded and ethnically complex social landscape of the northern Rio Grande during the late thirteenth and early fourteenth centuries.

Immigrants were probably drawn to the northern Rio Grande by the promise of potentially rich farmland along permanent rivers and streams. But the continued influx of population into the area during an episode of deteriorating climatic conditions would have placed increasing stress on the limited agricultural resources of the area. Toward the end of the thirteenth, and continuing throughout the fourteenth, century, there was a dramatic shift in settlement pattern in the northern Rio Grande, as many of the smaller sites, especially those in the more marginal upland areas, were abandoned. This period was also marked by the first appearance of very large aggregated towns, consisting of over several hundred rooms each, arranged in multistory roomblocks around multiple plazas. These two processes of abandonment and aggregation are closely related and can be seen as a direct result of continued population expansion in the region and the concomitant competition for increasingly limited arable land and natural resources (Hunter-Anderson 1979; Cordell, Earls, and Binford 1984).

Large consolidated towns and settlement clusters were established on land of relatively high agricultural potential along primary drainages. These aggregated settlements were occupied at the expense of previously more dispersed sites located along secondary streams and in a variety of other upland zones (Dickson 1979). A decrease in seasonal precipitation during the late thirteenth century may have reduced streamflow in upper drainages during agriculturally critical times of the year, forcing farmers to concentrate settlements closer to more reliable sources of water. Thus, at the same time that population was increasing, the amount of agriculturally productive land in the northern Rio Grande may have been decreasing. The agricultural productivity of the remaining land could have been intensified through the construction and maintenance of water diversion and conservation facilities or the more efficient organization of the increased labor pool from these larger aggregated settlements (Stone, Netting, and Stone 1990). Aggregation also may have promoted and facilitated the development of more formalized systems of food sharing, land tenure, and territorial boundary maintenance (Hunter-Anderson 1979; Kohler 1989).

Increased territorial circumscription would have intensified competition and conflict over limited and widely dispersed land and other natural resources. The presence of conflict among the Classic period residents of the northern Rio Grande is reflected in the depiction of shield- and weapon-bearing figures in the rock art of the time (Schaafsma 1990; Adams 1991) and in the defensive layout of many villages and settlement clusters (Mera 1934; Peckham 1984). Further evidence of the endemic nature of intergroup conflict among the Eastern Pueblos is the central focus on war themes in their mythology and the traditionally high status of war chiefs and warrior societies in most Rio Grande communities. War and warrior society symbolism is also a common theme in northern Rio Grande kiva murals dated to the fourteenth and fifteenth centuries (Adams 1991).

Large aggregated settlements may have provided inhabitants with greater security and protection against raids, while at the same time abandoned upland areas may have acted as buffer zones, physically separating competing local groups. The political importance of these buffer zones in stabilizing intergroup relations may explain why large areas of the northern Rio Grande that were abandoned during the late Coalition were never reoccupied, even after climatic conditions improved during the early fourteenth century. These upland zones also may have represented important hunting and foraging territories. Access to these areas may have been critical, especially during periodic crop losses or seasonal food shortages. As a result, competition for territorial control of such areas may have been intense.

Despite the labor investment in constructing large aggregated towns, a high degree of settlement instability is clearly reflected in the archaeological record of the northern Rio Grande during the early Classic (Mera 1940), indicating that these people were far more mobile than their architecture would lead us to suspect. Much of the northern Rio Grande is only marginally suited to agriculture. Precipitation is meager, and annual variability in the length of the growing season and frost-free period characterizes the entire region (Wendorf and Reed 1955; Cordell 1979a, 1979b). These climatic factors can

affect agricultural productivity from one area to another and from one season to the next (Ford 1972b). Furthermore, problems such as flooding, salinization, stream entrenchment, crop disease, and insect pests may have severely limited the long-term productivity and viability of intensive agricultural strategies in any one area. As a result, individuals and whole settlements may have had to move periodically to compensate for these changing conditions.

Abandonment followed by reoccupation is a common pattern at most large sites in the region. The history of settlement in the Santa Fe area exemplifies this pattern. Toward the end of the thirteenth century a large aggregated settlement was founded along the banks of the Santa Fe River about six miles west of the city of Santa Fe, as is evidenced by the remains of the twin sites of Pindi (LA 1) and Agua Fria Schoolhouse (LA 2) (Kidder 1915; Stubbs and Stallings 1953; Lang and Scheick 1989) (see fig. 5). Widespread finds of late Coalition and early Classic trash suggest that a third settlement in this cluster may have been located within the modern town of Santa Fe (LA 930, 1051, etc.) (Mera 1934; Dickson 1979:120–23). Due to historic occupation in the area, however, evidence for this site remains tenuous.

The years 1295 to 1335 were characterized by episodes of consistently above-average precipitation, especially during the spring and early summer (Rose, Dean, and Robinson 1981). At the peak of this postdrought maximum, between 1315 and 1320, both Pindi and Agua Fria Schoolhouse show signs of partial abandonment in the form of collapsed, trash-filled rooms (Stubbs and Stallings 1953; Lang and Scheick 1989). This same episode, however, witnessed the rapid growth and expansion of Arroyo Hondo Pueblo (LA 12), located just ten miles to the west at the edge of the Sangre de Cristo foothills and along a secondary tributary of the Santa Fe River. Increased moisture would have allowed crops to mature despite the shortened growing season and cooler temperatures characteristic of this piedmont setting. Under conditions of above-average annual precipitation, it is also possible that certain floodplain settings, such as the location of Pindi–Agua Fria along the low terraces of the Santa Fe River, would have remained inundated well into the late spring, thus making the relocation of villages to peripheral highland locations necessary (Anschuetz 1987:157; Lang and Scheick 1989:197).

Several small to medium-sized sites, located in the foothills south and west of Santa Fe, also appear to have been abandoned during the first few decades of the fourteenth century. These sites include Upper Arroyo Hondo

90

(LA 76), Chamisa Locita (LA 4), and Pueblo Alamo (LA 8) (Allen 1971; Dickson 1979) (see fig. 5). Former inhabitants of these upland settlements, along with people from the Santa Fe River villages, probably account for the bulk of the Component I population at Arroyo Hondo Pueblo.

This large aggregated village of nearly one thousand rooms may have been more defensible and less prone to raiding and attack than the earlier scattered hamlets and farmsteads of the area. Both its setting and its construction suggest a somewhat defensive posture. The site fronts the Sangre de Cristo Mountains and is accessible from the east only through Pecos and the Glorieta Pass; its back is toward the open but forbidding and sparsely inhabited Caja del Rio Plain. Perched at the edge of a steep arroyo, the village's main entrance consisted of a narrow gateway between two roomblocks, allowing access to a steep trail that led to a spring (the village's main source of drinking water) and rich farmland along the arroyo bottom. The first component village consisted of two-story roomblocks arranged around closed plazas. Exterior walls lacked windows or doorways, access to roomblocks being limited to those rooms that fronted the plazas, and many of these could only be entered with the use of ladders through rooftop entryways (Creamer 1993).

Decreased precipitation and increased arroyo cutting between 1330 and 1345 may have drastically reduced the agricultural productivity of farmland in the vicinity of Arroyo Hondo (Rose, Dean, and Robinson 1981:104). Scattered tree-ring dates and isolated evidence of rebuilding, particularly in Roomblock 16, indicate that at least a small, remnant population lived at the site during the 1340s through 1370s. The thick layer of overburden separating the first and second construction sequences at the site, however, suggests that much of the village was abandoned at this time (Creamer 1993; Lang, this volume). Inhabitants of the Santa Fe area probably retreated to older villages, such as Pindi–Agua Fria, and new villages, such as Cieneguilla (LA 16), founded around A.D. 1350 (Creamer and Haas 1989), with access to the more reliable water supply of the Santa Fe River.

As the above example from the Santa Fe area illustrates, settlement during the late Coalition–early Classic transition was characterized by the presence of discrete clusters of large aggregated villages within each of the major tributary drainages along the northern Rio Grande. Village aggregation was probably an organizational response to increasing demographic and climatic stress during the late thirteenth century. These large communities also may have provided their inhabitants with greater security and defense in the face of increasing competition and conflict for arable land. Population movements between villages within clusters occurred throughout the fourteenth century and appear to have been triggered by microclimatic changes within each area and subsequent shifts in the agricultural productivity of different topographic settings in each area.

Village clusters such as those recorded for the Santa Fe area may represent emerging ethnic alliances bound by loose networks of kinship ties and reciprocal social obligations. These family, sodality, and ritual networks would have facilitated the movement of individuals and families from one settlement to another when crops failed, food shortages developed, or some other disaster occurred (i.e., fire, flood, or disease). Such ties also would have promoted cooperation between ethnically allied settlements in the face of competition and conflict with neighboring groups. Intergroup competition would have also fostered an increasing emphasis on social and territorial boundary maintenance as a means of strengthening intragroup identity and solidarity and of structuring and regulating intergroup relations.

Cultural and stylistic diversity can be an effective means of marking and maintaining social and territorial boundaries. In this context, the emergence of clearly identifiable archaeological districts within the northern Rio Grande during the fourteenth century may reflect a process of increasing social differentiation and territorial boundary maintenance. These districts are distinguished from one another on the basis of local patterning in material culture, architecture, and settlement. In particular, around the turn of the fourteenth century, there appears to have been a dramatic proliferation of local decorated black-on-white pottery styles throughout the northern Rio Grande. The area of manufacture of each of these local pottery styles or types corresponds, more or less, with the boundaries established for each of the archaeological districts in the area on the basis of similarities in other aspects of material culture and settlement pattern (compare figs. 4 and 11).

Many of these new types share a number of traits that are generally believed to have been derived from a common Mesa Verde style (Mera 1935; Stubbs and Stallings 1953; Lambert 1954; Wendorf and Reed 1955; Lang 1982; Douglass 1985; Sundt 1987). For example, a late, degenerate version of Chaco-McElmo, called San Ignacio Black-on-white, is common on Rio Puerco sites dating as early as the mid-thirteenth century (Bice and Sundt 1972; Lang 1982:179; Sundt 1987:128). By the end of the century local varieties of Mesa Verde Black-on-white appear on sites in the northern Rio Grande, especially in the Jemez district and southern Pajarito area near Cochiti (Lang 1982:179; Sundt 1984, 1987:128). Mesa Verde attributes incorporated into the local ceramics of the Jemez district (i.e., Vallecitos and Jemez B/W), include thick white slips and designs consisting of solids with large pendent dots, chevron-filled panels, bands of parallel horizontal lines, and dotted lips (Lang 1982:178). In general, traits diagnostic of Mesa Verde–style ceramics produced in the northern Rio Grande include thick, polished, and crackled slips; rounded or flattened rims; rim ticking; paneled-band design layouts; a preference for solid design elements; use of secondary design elements such as dots, dashes, and ticks; and the use of sherd and/or crushed rock tempers (Douglass 1985; Lang 1982:178).

As noted above, the appearance of this style in the northern Rio Grande around the turn of the fourteenth century is generally cited as evidence for the arrival of Mesa Verde immigrants (Lang 1982:178; Wendorf and Reed 1955). But the adoption, modification, and spread of several variants of this style throughout the northern Rio Grande may have had more to do with the dynamics of intergroup relations within the region than with the simple presence of foreign immigrants in and of itself.

The most common of these new ceramic types was Galisteo B/W. Although production of Galisteo B/W was limited primarily to the Galisteo district, it occurred as a common trade ware on sites in the Santa Fe–Pecos, Albuquerque, and Zia–Santo Domingo districts. In fact, it was the dominant black-on-white ceramic type encountered south of the Santa Fe River during much of the fourteenth century. The earliest dates for the type are somewhat tentative, but preliminary investigations at several late Coalition sites in the Galisteo Basin (i.e., Burnt Corn [LA 135], LA 8843, LA 8844, LA 8845, etc.) indicate that production of the type may have been widespread in this district as early as the late thirteenth century (Schaafsma 1967). Galisteo B/W reached its maximum distribution and popularity, however, during the mid-fourteenth century. In the lowest levels of Las Madres (LA 25), dating between A.D. 1340 and 1350, for example, Galisteo accounts for nearly three-quarters of all the decorated pottery (Schaafsma 1969:20).

At the same time, in the Española-Chama district there is a continuation of the earlier Santa Fe B/W style, now as a more localized phenomenon. Santa Fe B/W and its associated types are distinguished from the so-called Mesa Verde types by their general lack of exterior slipping and polishing; the use of thin slips, washes, or floated surfaces; and a preference for very fine, silty,

sedimentary clays and volcanic ash tempers. Late Santa Fe B/W and its successors (i.e., Wiyo Black-on-white and the biscuit wares) do, however, emphasize a number of San Juan–derived design elements, including opposed stepped triangles or keys; terraces; ticked triangles; stalked interlocking keys; dot fillers; lip dotting and ticking; bands of horizontal lines; bold, opposed solid and hatched double-ended keys; rectangular or, more rarely, curvilinear scrolls; and rare naturalistic motifs, usually in the form of birds and geometric anthropomorphs. A wide range of new panel division techniques appear, and band framing lines become more prevalent after A.D. 1300 as well.

Because the main occupation of Arroyo Hondo dates after 1300, most of the Santa Fe B/W from the site dates to this later period of its production. In contrast to its widespread distribution throughout the Coalition period, during the fourteenth century the manufacture and use of Santa Fe B/W were more or less restricted to the Española Valley and its immediate vicinity. And although Santa Fe B/W pottery is relatively rare on most sites in the northern Rio Grande after 1325, at sites near its center of production it can be found in significant quantities in contexts dating well into the early fifteenth century.

A new yet technologically related type, Wiyo B/W, soon came to dominate ceramic assemblages north of the Santa Fe River, however. In the Chama drainage, for example, a number of medium-sized pueblos (i.e., 25+ to 100+ rooms), such as Riana (LA 920) and the Palisades site (LA 3505), are associated with virtually pure deposits of Wiyo B/W (Hibben 1937; Cordell 1979a:51). Wiyo sites in the Chama drainage are generally quadrangular with roomblocks along three sides, the fourth side being enclosed by a palisade of jacal or a line of stones, suggesting a somewhat defensive posture. Wiyo pottery also dominated the ceramic assemblages of early fourteenth-century sites in the Española Valley (Mera 1934, 1935). On the northern Pajarito Plateau the predominant ceramic type during this period is a poorly known local hybrid of Santa Fe–Wiyo B/W.

Ceramic assemblages dated to the first half of the fourteenth century in the Santa Fe–Pecos district reveal a pattern of extensive trade with adjacent districts along with the small-scale production of several distinctive local pottery types. In the upper levels of Forked Lightning (LA 672), dated by Kidder (Kidder and Shepard 1936:610) to around the turn of the fourteenth century, Galisteo and Santa Fe B/W were recovered in about equal quantities (Kidder and Shepard 1936:477). In the lowest cuts at Pecos, however, Galisteo makes up more than 80 percent of the decorated assemblage, and

Santa Fe drops to less than 20 percent. Wiyo B/W appears somewhat later in the stratigraphic tests and increases in frequency throughout the first half of the fourteenth century. At Rowe Pueblo (LA 108), another fourteenth-century site in the Pecos drainage, Galisteo B/W and Wiyo B/W compose 25 percent and 21 percent, respectively, of the decorated pottery assemblage from recent excavations (Morrison 1985).

A similar pattern has been recorded for sites in the Santa Fe area. At Agua Fria Schoolhouse, for example, Santa Fe B/W drops from a high of 89 percent of the decorated ceramic assemblage early in the first component to 34 percent by the end of that component (ca. 1320). During the same period, Galisteo increases from 2 percent to 25 percent, and Wiyo from 3 percent to 25 percent, of the assemblage (Lang and Scheick 1989: 192). At Arroyo Hondo, Santa Fe B/W accounts for more than three-quarters of the decorated pottery in the earliest deposits from the site, dated to around the turn of the fourteenth century, but quickly and steadily drops in frequency over the next few decades, until by the 1330s it represents less than 10 percent of the assemblage. At the same time, Galisteo reaches its peak in popularity, accounting for anywhere between a third and two-thirds of the decorated assemblage in deposits dated between A.D. 1330 and 1350. Wiyo B/W does not appear to have been very common at Arroyo Hondo until the end of the first component. At its peak in the 1350s, however, it represented nearly 25 percent of the decorated assemblage from the site (Lang, this volume).

Although all of the Galisteo, Santa Fe, and Wiyo B/W pottery from the Santa Fe–Pecos district appears to have been produced at a wide variety of villages in the adjacent Galisteo and Española-Chama districts, two minor yet highly distinct styles of black-on-white pottery were produced locally. Rowe B/W, like Galisteo, Jemez, and the other so-called Mesa Verde–style black-on-white ceramics from the northern Rio Grande, is characterized by the addition of thick, polished, and crackled or crazed slips. In the case of Rowe, however, this slip generally adhered quite poorly to the soft brown or gray sand-tempered pastes. Although Rowe B/W was the diagnostic local ceramic type of the Santa Fe–Pecos archaeological district during the first half of the fourteenth century, it rarely accounts for more than about 30 percent of the total decorated assemblage from any site in the region. At Arroyo Hondo, the local *Poge* variety of Rowe B/W reached its peak in popularity during the height of the Component I expansion during the 1320s. Even more restricted in its temporal and spatial distribution is the local *Pindi* variety of Santa Fe B/W. This distinctive,

pumice-tempered pottery appears to have been manufactured at Arroyo Hondo Pueblo for a short period between about 1335 and 1350 (Lang and Scheick 1989: 196; Lang, this volume). This period marks the beginning of an episode of population decline and partial abandonment at the site. The local production of a variant of the Santa Fe–Wiyo style may reflect the presence of refugees from the Española area among the remaining inhabitants at the site.

Far to the north, ceramic developments in the Taos district appear to have followed their own local trajectory from around A.D. 1300 to 1600 (Wetherington 1968; Ellis and Brody 1964; Dick 1965). Nevertheless, in many features the development of Talpa and Vadito Black-on-white mirrors the Santa Fe–Wiyo–biscuit ware sequence of the Española-Chama district (Dick 1965; Lang 1982). The addition of thick slips to Vadito vessels and the incorporation of certain design elements (i.e., solid triangles, broad parallel lines, pendent dots, etc.) also suggest influence from the Mesa Verde style reflected in Galisteo, Jemez, and Rowe B/W.

Throughout the thirteenth century, small quantities of St. Johns Polychrome and other White Mountain Red wares were imported into the northern Rio Grande from the Cibola area west of Zuni. Toward the end of the century, the frequency of imported glaze-painted and polychrome ceramics increased markedly, especially in the region south of the Santa Fe River. Responding to the popularity of such imported types as Heshotauthla Glaze Polychrome, local potters started making a variety of local imitations.

The first experiments in local glaze-on-red ceramic production occurred in the Albuquerque and Zia–Santo Domingo districts around the turn of the fourteenth century. Direct copies of western polychromes have been identified from Pueblo Quemado (LA 8943), west of Cochiti, and Chakam (LA 375), near Zia. Rio Grande copies of Heshotauthla, St. Johns, Kwakina, and Four-mile polychromes were all found at a site near San Isidro in the lower Jemez Valley (Warren 1976:B9–10). All of the St. Johns and Heshotauthla polychromes identified from Arroyo Hondo were tempered with schist-tempered sherd, indicative of manufacture in the Albuquerque district of the northern Rio Grande.

Along with these western copies are generally found a whole series of local polychrome ceramics that are subsumed under the general category of Los Padillas Glaze Polychrome. This transitional type is characterized by a high degree of variability in paste, slip, form, paint, and design. Whereas Warren (1976:B8) has interpreted this variation as reflecting newly arrived potters from the west experimenting with new clays, slips, and paints in a strange environment, Snow (1976:B179) sees the same data as representing a local technological development. During the early decades of the fourteenth century, Los Padillas Polychrome represented a regional ceramic style, diagnostic of the southwestern portion of the northern Rio Grande. It is not until after A.D. 1340–50 that glaze wares achieved widespread distribution throughout the area.

Differences in artifact style are often used to communicate differences in the nature and structure of relationships between groups (Wobst 1977; Hodder 1979). For example, in situations of intense interethnic contact and competition, stylistic differences in material culture can be an effective and efficient means of marking social and territorial boundaries and establishing group identity and ownership. Within this context, the stylistic districts, identified in the archaeological record of the early fourteenth century in the northern Rio Grande, can be interpreted as representing nodes of social interaction and cooperation that define emerging ethnic alliances within the increasingly competitive social landscape of the late Coalition–early Classic transition.

The distribution of stylistic attributes has less to do with the frequency or intensity of interactions than with the structure of relationships. Interactions between kinsmen and friends will be fundamentally different from those between outsiders and potential enemies, even though both types of contact may be frequent and necessary. Stylistic and cultural diversity helps to structure and stabilize interpersonal and intergroup interactions by identifying players and roles and by marking and maintaining social and territorial boundaries.

It is interesting to note that the boundaries between stylistic districts in the northern Rio Grande appear to lie more or less along historically documented sociolinguistic lines and that these boundaries remain remarkably stable during the succeeding centuries. The earliest Spanish explorers clearly recognized these districts as the provinces of distinct groups (Hodge 1907) that largely parallel modern ethnographic divisions in the area (fig. 67). Thus, the elaboration of discrete local ceramic styles during the early fourteenth century can be interpreted as evidence for the emergence and consolidation of these historically recognizable ethnic groups. I should emphasize that I am not trying to draw a simple correlation between specific pottery types and specific language groups (e.g., Tewa, Tiwa, Towa, etc.). Rather, I am trying to suggest that patterns of linguistic, cultural, and stylistic diversity in the region all may have been by-products of the same processes of ethnogenesis and boundary maintenance.

The Early Classic Period (A.D. 1350–1450)

The material record indicates that the northern Rio Grande during the early fourteenth century was characterized by a fragmentation of the cultural landscape, reflecting the emergence and consolidation of a number of local ethnic alliances that were in at least partial competition with one another for land and other critical resources in the region. As Barth (1969) has observed, such a situation of interethnic competition and conflict is inherently unstable and will result either in one group out-competing and displacing the others or in the self-conscious development of interethnic systems of cooperation and interdependence. During the early Classic period, a new regional system of economic and social integration emerged in response to these critical challenges to the stability of northern Rio Grande society. I refer to this type of system as a "complex tribe" and to the process by which the ethnic and interethnic alliances that supported it formed as "tribalization."

Tribes are systems of social and economic integration based on segmental alliances. These alliances are supported by formalized, reciprocal transactions based on consciously maintained patterns of complementarity and interdependence. Expansion of these segmental systems across traditional local or ethnic boundaries results in the formation of "complex tribes" (Habicht-Mauche, Hoopes, and Geselowitz 1987; Habicht-Mauche 1988b). Complex tribes are relatively stable systems of regional integration that lack the centralized political authority and redistributive economies generally associated with other complex forms of regional integration, such as chiefdoms and states.

In the northern Rio Grande, agricultural and subsistence resources, although patchy and somewhat limited, are widely dispersed. As a result, complementarity and interdependence between groups was probably established and maintained through the development of local systems of intensified craft production, resource exploitation, and regional trade. Archaeological evidence for the emergence of such a complementary network of regional integration and economic interdependence is reflected in the sudden widespread distribution of locally circumscribed raw materials, such as turquoise from the Cerrillos Hills, obsidian from the Jemez Mountains, fibrolite axes from the Sangre de Cristo Mountains, travertine from south of Albuquerque, and Pedernal chert from the Chama Valley (Snow 1981). Exotic goods, such as bison hides, marine shells, and feathers, obtained in trade with groups living outside the region, were probably also an important component of this system (Spielmann 1982; Baugh 1984; Wilcox 1984; Habicht-Mauche

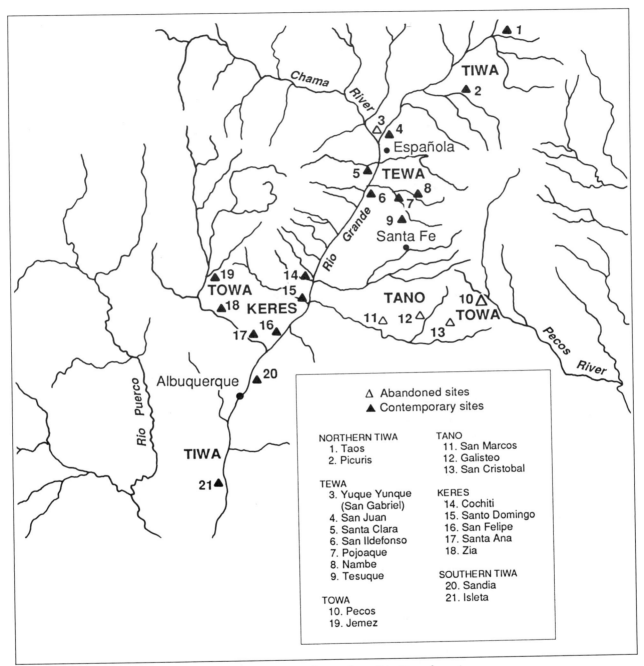

Figure 67. Historic pueblos and linguistic divisions in the northern Rio Grande region.

1988a). Historic and ethnographic evidence indicate that other districts may have specialized in the production of certain craft items such as basketry (Jemez), textiles (Southern Tiwa), or leather goods (Pecos) (Snow 1981). The growing importance of regional trade may also be reflected in the relatively large number of ollas present in glaze ware assemblages, as compared to earlier white ware assemblages. These beautiful yet versatile wide-mouthed jars may have functioned not only as trade goods themselves but as containers for the transport and exchange of other commodities as well.

This regional diversification of production can be thought of as a form of economic specialization in the sense that it involved the regulation of the manufacture, distribution, and use of raw materials and craft products by particular groups within a society via certain socially instituted mechanisms. This particular type of economic specialization was characterized by two general processes of intensification. First was the process of "localization" noted above, with different areas of the northern Rio Grande specializing in the exploitation or production of specific raw materials or craft items. Second was the process of "commodification," whereby materials that had previously been produced primarily for local domestic consumption now appear to have been produced in increasingly large quantities specifically for trade outside the local area. Both processes appear to have occurred more or less simultaneously and rather suddenly in the northern Rio Grande around the middle of the fourteenth century.

Similar large-scale regional networks in the Southwest have been interpreted as being controlled by the village leadership or a specific class of "elite" individuals (Lightfoot 1984; Upham 1982). There are several reasons why such a model does not fit the data from the northern Rio Grande. The majority of the materials exchanged between districts consists primarily of relatively utilitarian craft products and raw materials whose distribution does not appear to have been limited to any particular segment of society. There is also no archaeological evidence at Arroyo Hondo or the other large, early Classic pueblos in the northern Rio Grande of wealth accumulation, architectural differentiation, or the other status differences one would generally associate with the control of valuable commodities within a stratified society. Furthermore, no evidence of centralized workshops or storage facilities has been identified from any of these Classic period sites.

Craft production, although increasingly intensified and locally specialized, appears to have remained largely a cottage industry under the control of individual artisans and their families. The continuing control of the basic means of production by independent family units or lineages within an economic system characterized by increasing complementarity and interdependence on a regional scale is a characteristic feature of the emergence of tribal systems (Sahlins 1972; Habicht-Mauche, Hoopes, and Geselowitz 1987).

This pattern of economic specialization and regional integration is particularly well illustrated by the structural changes that occurred in ceramic production and exchange during the late fourteenth century. As noted above, around A.D. 1300 a new style and technology of pottery production, featuring vitrified glaze-painted decorations on a red-slipped background, was developing in

the Albuquerque and Zia–Santo Domingo districts of the northern Rio Grande area. The proliferation of styles and techniques that characterize the early glaze wares from this region is suggestive of an era of experimentation with a new and unfamiliar technology (Snow 1976:B179). By the middle decades of the century, however, the production of Glaze A Red pottery appears to have become highly standardized, reaching a level of craftsmanship that far surpasses that which characterized the preceding white ware tradition of the area (Kidder and Shepard 1936; Lambert 1954).

It is also at about this time that glaze ware ceramics achieve a truly widespread popularity throughout the northern Rio Grande (Mera 1940). For example, glaze wares first make their appearance in the uppermost levels of Pindi Pueblo, tree-ring dated to ca. A.D. 1348 (Stubbs and Stallings 1953). At Arroyo Hondo, small quantities of Glaze A Red sherds have been recovered from contexts dating as early as the middle of the 1330s, but the type does not exhibit any appreciable increase in frequency until the 1370s. In the lowest levels of Las Madres Pueblo, dated to approximately 1340–50, Glaze A Red makes up only 11 percent of the decorated assemblage. All of the glaze wares from these early levels are tempered with crushed sherd, diagnostic of production in the Albuquerque district. By the succeeding decade (1350–60), however, Glaze A Red frequency increases to 37 percent, and local production within the Galisteo Basin is indicated by the use of latite temper in a small percentage of sherds (Schaafsma 1969:20).

Along with the Albuquerque district, the Zia–Santo Domingo and Galisteo districts emerged as important early centers for the production and trade of this new pottery style. Shepard's (1942:156–57) analysis of surface collections from throughout the northern Rio Grande indicated that Glaze A Red pottery was dominated by sherd, basalt, and intermediate volcanic temper. The distribution of sherd temper centered around the Albuquerque district, whereas intermediate volcanics were characteristic of early glazes from the Galisteo Basin. Shepard recognized two classes of basalt temper: vitric and crystalline. Warren's (1968, 1976, 1979) more recent studies of ceramics from the Cochiti area, however, have revealed the use of a whole range of basaltic rocks whose origins can be traced to a variety of sources in the lower Jemez drainage, southern Pajarito Plateau, and Santo Domingo Basin. This same pattern is reflected in the Glaze A Red assemblage from Arroyo Hondo, which is dominated by basalt- and latite-tempered material from the Zia–Santo Domingo and Galisteo districts. Schist-tempered sherd from the Albuquerque district characterizes the White Mountain Red Ware and early, transitional Los Padillas polychromes from the site.

Around A.D. 1370 (Schaafsma 1969; Sundt 1987) a second style of glaze-painted pottery, characterized by white to yellow slips, began to be produced in the Galisteo Basin. Although the inspiration for glaze-on-yellow pottery has been traced back to certain Little Colorado types (Snow 1976:B179; Woodbury and Woodbury 1966:311–24; Adams 1991), it seems just as likely that Cieneguilla Glaze-on-yellow resulted from a local merging of the imported glaze-paint technology with the indigenous white ware tradition. Although rare at Arroyo Hondo, light-slipped, glaze-painted pottery (i.e., Cieneguilla, Largo, and Espinoso G/Y) produced primarily at sites in the Galisteo Basin appears to have dominated the glaze ware trade in the northern Rio Grande throughout much of the succeeding fifteenth century.

At first, glaze ware production may have been restricted by the complexity of the new technology and the limited distribution of resources critical to its manufacture (i.e., lead and copper ores). Early centers also may have attempted to limit access to both technology and resources in order to maintain their monopoly on both production and distribution. Not only was production of early glaze ware pottery limited to a small number of districts in the southwestern part of the region, but also fewer villages within each district may have been involved in ceramic production and trade. This trend toward increasing local intensification and specialization of production is reflected in the Arroyo Hondo glaze ware assemblage, which is characterized by increasing mineralogical and chemical homogeneity within each temper group.

Despite the widespread popularity of glaze ware ceramics, local black-on-white types continued to be produced in a number of areas in the northern Rio Grande, in particular, in the Jemez, Taos, and Española-Chama districts. In general, these Classic period black-on-white ceramics were produced for local consumption and were not traded extensively beyond their home districts. The so-called biscuit wares, produced after A.D. 1370 in the Española-Chama district, however, are a notable exception to this trend. Both Abiquiú and Bandelier B/W reflect a level of standardization and efficiency in ceramic design and technology that is generally associated with more specialized modes of production (Hagstrum 1985; Snow 1976:B177). There also appears to have been a trend toward the emergence of community specialization, similar to that recorded for the glaze wares. Biscuit wares also were traded widely throughout the northern Rio Grande, although in not nearly as great a quantity as the contemporaneous glaze wares. At Pecos, for example, biscuit ware ceramics make up between 10 and 20 percent of the pottery from early Classic period tests (Kidder and Amsden 1931:37–43), and at Arroyo Hondo they never compose more than about 2 percent of the decorated pottery from Component II (Lang, this volume).

The development of this regional exchange network would have stabilized interethnic relations and reduced competition and conflict by ameliorating the negative effects that decreasing seasonal mobility and increasing territoriality had on the subsistence base of local groups. In particular, the ceremonial networks and reciprocal obligations that sustained these economic transactions helped to forge important interdependent links between individuals, communities, and ethnic groups. In times of crop failure, food shortages, or other local crises, these networks provided an established structural context through which communities, individual families, or both could gain access to the more abundant resources or agricultural surpluses of other areas (Ford 1972a; Snow 1981).

One important social mechanism that helped to sustain this regional network of economic interdependency was the spread of a unifying religious system (Habicht-Mauche 1988b). The presence of large communal kivas at some of the larger sites of this period and the organization of these pueblos around open plazas, in which public performances could be held, seem to reflect the growing role of ceremonialism in the integration of local Rio Grande society.

The fourteenth century was also characterized by the appearance of a highly distinctive, iconographic art style throughout much of the Pueblo area (Adams 1990, 1991; Crown 1990). The most characteristic element of this style is the depiction of elaborately costumed and masked dancers. The distribution of this art style is generally believed to parallel the development and spread of the Pueblo Kachina cult. The shared symbolism, ritual, and ideology of the Kachina cult crosscut linguistic and cultural boundaries between competing local ethnic groups in the northern Rio Grande, providing a basis for the development of regional systems of economic interdependency and tribal alliance.

In the northern Rio Grande these motifs, referred to as the Rio Grande art style, are most often associated with elaborate kiva murals and rock art (Schaafsma and Schaafsma 1974; Crotty 1990; Adams 1991). Although pottery decoration remained largely abstract and geometric, iconographic representations of horned or plumed serpents (*Awanyus*), birds (especially parrots), butterflies, and stars are common motifs on Rio Grande glaze ware vessels (Kidder and Shepard 1936; Lambert 1954). Examples from Arroyo Hondo (see fig. 36) and Pecos (Kidder and Shepard 1936) suggest that similar representations also occur on late Wiyo B/W and biscuit ware ceramics from the Española-Chama district, dated after approximately 1350. Depictions of masked figures on pottery, although rare, have also been found on northern Rio Grande ceramics dating to the mid- to late fourteenth century (Snow 1976; Ferg 1982). These iconographic motifs are similar to those characteristic of the Pinedale and Fourmile ceramic styles that dominated fourteenth- and early fifteenth-century polychrome pottery throughout much of the Western Pueblo area (Adams 1991).

Summary

The fourteenth and early fifteenth centuries were marked by fundamental changes in the structure and scale of northern Rio Grande society. The Classic period transition was characterized by a dramatic rise in local population, settlement aggregation into large, clustered towns, increasing differentiation of local ethnic groups, and, finally, the emergence of a regional tribal network of social, ceremonial, and economic integration. These social transformations are reflected in changes in the style and technology of pottery recovered from individual transitional period sites such as Arroyo Hondo and in the structure of pottery production and distribution throughout the northern Rio Grande.

At the time of Spanish contact, the northern Rio Grande consisted of a series of clearly recognizable linguistic and ethnic provinces. These ethnic provinces consisted, for the most part, of clusters of medium to large towns, separated by peripheral highland zones that were used on a seasonal and short-term basis for dry farming and food gathering and as a buffer zone for settlement during periods of environmental or sociopolitical crisis. This essentially single-tier settlement structure probably reflects the formation of local ethnic alliances as a result of increasing competition for the limited arable land and natural resources of the northern Rio Grande, following an influx of population from abandoned areas to the north and west during the late Coalition period. The emergence and consolidation of these new social groups is reflected in the proliferation of regional ceramic styles throughout the northern Rio Grande at the turn of the fourteenth century. During the first half of the century, social and economic interactions between communities, although intensive, were largely parochial and locally restricted.

By mid-century, however, the whole structure and scale of regional interaction had changed. Indicative of this change was the development of local centers of craft or resource specialization and networks of long-distance trade. The earlier pattern of ceramic distribution, characterized largely by local production and consumption, was replaced by one characterized by regional production centers dedicated to the intensive manufacture of pottery specifically for trade. The role of pottery in economic and social interactions shifted from that of generalized reciprocal gift item to that of specialized economic commodity. The proliferation of local ceramic styles that marked the emergence of competing ethnic groups during the late Coalition period was superseded in the early Classic period by the development of a uniform ceramic style, whose distribution signaled incorporation into a highly integrated economic system that formed the basis of a regional tribal alliance.

Summary of Decorated Ceramic Frequencies by Excavated Provenience

The following tables were compiled by Anthony Thibodeau, archaeology laboratory coordinator at the School of American Research, based on data assembled by Theodore Reinhart (1970), Michael Marshall (1971), and Richard Lang (1972–74) at the end of each of the five field seasons at Arroyo Hondo Pueblo (LA 12).

Sherds identified as coming from the same vessel were only counted once. Type names have been modified to conform with the classificatory system outlined in chapter 2. Occasionally, type identifications were changed after reexamination by the author.

KEY TO TABLE A.1

Indet. = Indeterminate White Ware
SF = Santa Fe B/W, *var. Santa Fe*
SF,P = Santa Fe B/W, *var. Pindi*
WY = Wiyo B/W
ABQ = Abiquiú B/W
JMZ = Jemez B/W
VLL = Vallecitos B/W
GAL = Galisteo B/W (incl. *var. Kendi*)
RW = Rowe B/W (incl. *vars. Poge* and *Arroyo Hondo*)
RM = Red Mesa B/W
KWH = Kwahe'e B/W
CHP = Chupadero B/W
SCR = Socorro B/W

KEY TO TABLE A.2

WMR = White Mountain Red Ware
SJP = St. Johns Polychrome
HSH = Heshotauthla Polychrome
JDT = Jeddito B/Y
EGR = Early G/R
LPP = Los Padillas G-P
AGR = Agua Fria G/R
SCP = San Clemente G-P
SZP = Sanchez G-P
LGR = Largo G/R
CGY = Cieneguilla G/Y
LGY = Largo G/Y

TABLE A.1
Frequency of white ware ceramics by excavated provenience.

Provenience	Indet.	SF	SF,P	WY	ABQ	JMZ	VLL	GAL	RW	RM	KWH	CHP	SCR
Plaza Tests:													
12-C-A-0				1				1					
12-C-A-1		8						3					
12-C-A-2		4		6				4					
12-C-A-3		7		4	5			7					
12-C-A-4				8	35			14					
12-C-A-5		45	9	22	78			47					
12-C-A-6		32	2	18	25			32					
12-C-A-7		14	1	15	7			11					
12-C-A-8		3		4				4					
12-C-A-9		1		2				1					
12-C-B-general		4	4	3	2			12					
12-C-B-1		2		2				7					
12-C-B-2		3		3	7			17					
12-C-B-3		11	1	3	7			8					
12-C-B-4		2		8	2			2					
12-C-B-5				1				5					
12-C-B-6		3		2	2			3					
12-C-B-7				2				1					
12-C-B-8		8		14	29	6		15					
12-C-B-9		5	4	13	26	8		10					
12-C-B-10		1	4		4			9					
12-C-B-11		1	2	1				1					
12-G-36A-2		7	40	15				29	58				
12-11-0		7	3	1	2			8					
12-11-1 (backfill)		4	3	14	1			3	7				
12-11-N2 (backfill)		5	3	1									
12-11-N4 (backfill)		7	5	1									
12-11-T.S.3A-II	14	21	1	10				14			1		
12-11-T.S.3B-2	2	4		4	1			4	1				
12-11-T.S.3B-3	2	4		6	1			2	1				
12-T.T.A (backfill of 12-16-1)		11		7				7					
12-21-0				1									
Subtotal:	18	224	83	191	234	14	0	281	67	0	1	0	0
Component I:													
12-4-2-I								1	1				
12-4-2-1	4	1		9				2					
12-4-2-II	11	3		7				3	1				
12-4-2-2	4	8		12	1			10	6				
12-4-2-3/III		1						3					
12-4-2-4	2							3	1				
12-4-2-5	29	9		18		2		23	10				
12-5-4-I	11		2	10				12	4				
12-5-4-1	4		1	8				2	3				
12-5-4-II	3			1				2					
12-5-4-2	9	2	5	5				6	3				
12-5-4-III	4		1	4				5					
12-5-4-3	5	2	2	6				5					
12-5-4-7	11	4	2	2				10					

TABLE A.1 (*continued*)

Provenience	Indet.	SF	SF,P	WY	ABQ	JMZ	VLL	GAL	RW	RM	KWH	CHP	SCR
12-5-4-10-1								5					
12-5-5-I	7	4		7				5	3				
12-5-5-II	3	1		9				10	5				
12-5-5-2	1							3	2				
12-5-5-3	2	1		1					1				
12-5-5-III	7	3		8				5	2				
12-5-5-IV	3	2		2				3	1				
12-5-5-4	4	1		1				4	2				
12-5-5-V	1	3		1									
12-5-5-5				1				2					
12-5-5-22		1		3				1					
12-5-5-23	4	1						1					
12-5-6-I			1	2				1					
12-5-6-II	1			3				3	1			3	
12-5-6-III			3	2				2					
12-5-7-0,I,II		1		2				4	2				
12-5-7-III				2				1	1				
12-5-7-IV,3,4,5		2	5	5				4	14				
12-5-7-V,6		2	1	3				4	7				
12-5-7-VI		1		1				3					
12-5-7-VII		2											
12-5(6)-8-I,II,1,2				4				3	3				
12-5(6)-8-III,3			1	4					8				
12-5(6)-8-IV,4		4	2	3				4	10				
12-5(6)-8-V,5		1		4				2	2				
12-5(6)-8-VI,6				6				1	1				
12-5-9-I		2							4				
12-5-9-III			2					2	2				
12-5-9-IV			9					2	1				
12-5-9-V			2	1					3				
12-5-9-VI								1					
12-5-9-2		9	1	4			1	4	39				
12-5-9-3		7	1	5				7	50				
12-5-9-5		2						1	4				
12-5-9-14-1		4		1					5				
12-5-9-14-2				1				1	3				
12-5(6)-10-III,3			2	5				1	3				
12-5(6)-10-V-1								1					
12-5(6)-10-IV,V,VI,4			1	11				2	12				
12-5-11-I,II,2		1	8	6		1		8	12				
12-4-11-III,3			2	1				8	9				
12-5-11-IV,V,VI,4		1	3	2				6	21				
12-5-11-5			1										
12-5(6)-13-I,II,2			1					1	2				
12-5(6)-13-III				1									
12-5(6)-13-IV				2				1	1				
12-5(6)-13-V								2	2				
12-5(6)-14-I,II			1					1	1				
12-5(6)-14-III,3		2	6	14				42	31				
12-5(6)-14-4		7	3	21				34	23				
12-5(6)-14-5			1	4				6	4				

TABLE A.1 (continued)

Provenience	Indet.	SF	SF,P	WY	ABQ	JMZ	VLL	GAL	RW	RM	KWH	CHP	SCR
12-6-6-I				1				1					
12-6-6-1	4		2	4				5	2				
12-6-6-II	3	1		10				1	4				
12-6-6-2	1			3					2				
12-6-6-III-10								2	11				
12-6-6-3									1				
12-6-6-IV				3				2	2				
12-6-6-V	1			1				3					
12-7-7-I	5			3	1			1					
12-7-7-2	1	1		1									
12-7-7-III	1												
12-7-7-3	2	1		1									
12-7-7-4	4			1									
12-7-7-IV	6		5					2	2				
12-7-7-V	2	1		3				1	1				
12-7-7-5			1	3					2				
12-7-7-6	3		1	8				5	2				
12-7-7-VI				1				1					
12-7-7-7	2		1	4				6					
12-8-5-I	3	2		2				3					
12-8-5-1	1												
12-8-5-II	1	1	8					2	2				
12-8-5-2	8	6		8				4	3				
12-8-5-3	2		1	1				1	2				
12-8-5-III			1						1				
12-8-5-4	1	1	1										
12-8-5-5				2					1				
12-8-5-12	2	3		2				3					
12-8-5-13		1		1				1	1				
12-9-7-II		2											
12-9-7-2			1	1									
12-9-7-III	1		2										
12-9-7-3		1						1					
12-9-7-IV	2	2	1	2				5					
12-9-7-4		1	1										
12-9-7-V	1	2	2	5				3	2				
12-9-7-5	4	2	1	6					2				
12-9-7-6				1				1					
12-9-7-7		1		2				3					
12-9-7-8	4		2	3				1					
12-9-7-9		2		1				2					
12-9-7-VI		1	1	3				3					
12-10-3-VIII	13	15		6	1			11	5				
12-10-3-10,12,13	6	5		6				4	1				
12-10-3-14	3	1						4	2				
12-11-xI-2			1					1					
12-11-xI-3		4											
12-11-4-1		1	1					2	10				
12-11-4-2	1	7	1	2				1	7				
12-11-4-3		3	2						4				
12-11-4-7		1		1				1	2				
12-11-5-4	1	1		3					3				

TABLE A.1 *(continued)*

Provenience	Indet.	SF	SF,P	WY	ABQ	JMZ	VLL	GAL	RW	RM	KWH	CHP	SCR
12-11-5-6		1											
12-11-5-A		2							1				
12-11-6-1		4	1	2				10	3		1		
12-11-6-2		1											
12-11-8-1	2		1	2				2	5				1
12-11-8-2		3		1								1	
12-11-8-2-1		6		4				1	5				
12-11-8-3-1-1		1											
12-11-8-4		5		2					1				
12-11-9-1	10	8		5				2	2				
12-11-9-2	3	3		3				1	5				
12-11-9-3	4	6		3				1	6				
12-11-9-4-1									1				
12-12-4-I	9	4	2	5				3	4				
12-12-4-1	11	6	2	8				6	10				
12-12-4-II	3	4	1	1				4	1				
12-12-4-2	4	3	2						3				
12-12-4-2-1		1											
12-12-4-5	8	4		11				4	3				
12-12-4-6	42	23		27				20	37				
12-12-4-7	24	2		7				5	22				
12-12-4-8	5	7		2				3	3				
12-12-4-9	59	23		43				30	40				
12-12-4-3	8	4		5				8	2				
12-12-4-4	10	6		5				1	8				
12-13-9-II		2	2					3	2				
12-13-9-2	2	4		2				4	2				
12-13-9-3	1	1						1					
12-14-5-I	1								1				
12-14-5-II				2									
12-14-5-2	2	1	1	4				3	2				
12-14-5-3	3	1		2				1					
12-14-5-4								2	1				
12-14-5-5		4		2				2					
12-14-5-6		2	1	1				3	2				
12-14-5-III	22	15		7				16	1				
12-14-5-8		2						1					
12-14-5-9	3	9		2					5				
12-14-5-10	3	19		3				11	7				
12-14-5-11	1	4		1					2				
12-15-7-I		1	3	3					2				
12-15-7-1	2	2	4	3				2	3				
12-15-7-II	2	1	3	3				3	2				
12-15-7-2	6	8	1	2				7	10				
12-15-7-3	10	7	2	6				4	5				
12-15-7-4,IV	1		1										
12-15a-9-IV		1	3	1				5					
12-15a-9-4	4		3	1				2					
12-15a-9-5	8	4	3	3				5	4				
12-15a-9-6	1	3	3	2				3	1				
12-16-8-1		4		8				2	1				
12-16-8-2		1			1			7					

TABLE A.1   (continued)

Provenience	Indet.	SF	SF,P	WY	ABQ	JMZ	VLL	GAL	RW	RM	KWH	CHP	SCR
12-16-8-3		1						7					
12-16-8-4		3							1				
12-16-8-5		2						2					
12-16-24-1		2		2					4				
12-16-24-2	12	2	1	22				3	8				
12-16-24-3				7				2	16				
12-16-24-4	3	22	7	21				4	22				
12-16-26-1	4	15	1	12				3	5				
12-16-26-2		1		7					11				
12-16-26-3	5	6	2	14				3	34				
12-16-26-subfloor 1				2									
12-16-27-1		1		2									
12-16-27-2			4						2				
12-16-27-3		7	4	3					8				
12-16-27-3-2			8										
12-16-27-4		1	6	5					6				
12-16-28-1	3	9	3	9					19				
12-16-28-2	3	3		8				1	7				
12-16-28-3	2	7	2	1					7				
12-16-29-0		3		1									
12-16-29-1	6	26	26	38				8	55				
12-16-29-2		3							5				
12-16-29-3									1				
12-16-29-4		2							1				
12-16-29-5		2		1				1	5				
12-16-29-6		5	1	5					10				
12-16-29-8									2				
12-16-29-?		1		2					3				
12-16-30-4(I)				1					1				
12-16-30-4(II)				3					1				
12-16-30-4(IV)				2									
12-16-30-4(V)		2	3	1				1	2				
12-16-30-4(VII)									2				
12-16-30-4(VIII)									3				
12-16-30-1	7	23	2	20				9	21				
12-16-30-1,2		3	1	2									
12-16-30-2		21	9	19				2	48				
12-16-30-3		1											
12-16-31-I		4		2					6				
12-16-31-2		4	3	1					15				
12-16-31-2-3		1											
12-16-31-3		11		5				1	7				
12-16-31-4		8	5	2					7				
12-16-31-11		11		3				2	4				
12-16-31-test pit		1							1				
12-16-32-I	2	1		3					3				
12-16-32-1	6	18	22	70				16	73				
12-16-32-II			1	1				1					
12-16-32-2	2	4	1	10					9				
12-16-32-3			15	2					4				
12-16-32-4		2	16	2				6	2				
12-16-32-10				2									

TABLE A.1   (continued)

Provenience	Indet.	SF	SF,P	WY	ABQ	JMZ	VLL	GAL	RW	RM	KWH	CHP	SCR
12-16-33-5	1	1							6				
12-16-33-7		12		2				3	2				
12-16-33-8		8		3					2				
12-16-33-9		1											
12-16-34-1	6	9	2	65				7	34				
12-16-34-2		3		3					10				
12-16-34-3								3	5				
12-16-34-test pit		23		8				2	9				
12-16-35-1	2	5		4				2	1				
12-16-35-3	2	1											
12-16-35-4		1		1					1				
12-16-36-1	21	20	1	85	3			1	28				
12-16-36-2	4	31	4	59				9	66				
12-16-36-3		2											
12-16-36-4		4							1				
12-16-36-5		2	12						2				
12-16-36-6									1				
12-16-36-7		1											
12-16-36-8	1	12	1	5				2	6				
12-16-36-9		4							2				
12-16-36-11									1				
12-16-36-12		2							3				
12-16-36-13		4		5					3				
12-16-37-1		19	14	3				3	14				
12-16-37-2		4	13	4				3	8				
12-16-37-4-2, 4-3,2-2			32						12				
12-18-5-I,1		1	6	2				4	6			2	
12-18-5-II,2		4	7	5				6	9			1	
12-18-5-III,3		2	1	4				3	6				
12-18-5-3		5	2					3					
12-18-5-5		10		4				2	6				
12-18-6-I,1			4	4				2	2				
12-18-6-II,III,2		6	7	5				3	21				
12-18-6-IV,3		1							1				
12-18-7-I	1			1				1	1				
12-18-7-II	4							1	2				
12-18-7-2			2	1				3	2				
12-18-7-III	2		1	1					2				
12-18-7-3	3		2					3	7				
12-18-7-IV	3		2	1				4	1				
12-18-7-4		2	2					2					
12-18-7-V				1				1	4				
12-18-7-5	28	57		59				44	22				1
12-18-7-6	7	25		16				18	14				
12-18-8-1		3	1	2					4			1	
12-18-8-2		4	2					1	4				
12-18-8-III,3,IV		6	3	2				2	4			1	
12-18-8-V,4		10	3					1	6				
12-18-8-7-2		3							1				
12-18-9-I,1			2	2					6				
12-18-9-II,III,2		7	6	4				3	15				

TABLE A.1 *(continued)*

Provenience	Indet.	SF	SF,P	WY	ABQ	JMZ	VLL	GAL	RW	RM	KWH	CHP	SCR
12-18-14-I,1		1	10	3				7	8				
12-18-14-II,2		5	12	1				8	15				
12-18-14-III,3		3	14	5	1			6	7				
12-18-14-IV,4			4	1				1	1				
12-18-14-V									1				
12-18-15-1		7	168	16	2			26	109				
12-18-15-2		6	123	6				11	38				
12-18-32-1		2	2	1				2	1				
12-18-32-II,2		2	4	2					3				
12-18-32-III,3		1	7	3				3	5				
12-18-32-4			1										
12-18-32-5		42		7				19	16				
12-18-37-I		1	1	1				1					
12-18-37-II,2				2									
12-18-37-III			1					1					
12-18-37-4,5	1	14	2	6				7	9				
12-18-38-I,1		2	5					2	7				
12-18-38-II,2		2	16	1					2				
12-18-38-III,3		1	4	2				1	7				
12-18-39-I,1		7	3	4				7	2				
12-18-39-II,2,III,3		10	8	10				13	5				
12-18-39-IV,4		1	4	3				3	4				
12-18-39-5-1		4						1					
12-18-39-5		1											
12-18-39-6		2							1				
12-18-42-II,2		2	1	2				1	2				
12-18-42-III,3		2	2					2	2				
12-18-42-IV,4				1				1					
12-18-42-5		2	1					1	1				
12-18-48-1,I		6	14	6				7	9				
12-18-48-2		1	1					1	2				
12-18-49-I		3	4	1				2	5				
12-18-49-1		3	7	5				4	8				
12-18-49-2			2						2				
12-18-49-II		5	2	2				3	12				
12-18-49-3		3	1					1	2				
12-18-49-4		5	3	1				4	8				
12-18-49-5		2		1				1					
12-18-49-6		24	1	8				4	18				
12-18-49-7		4		2				2	3				
12-18-49-8		32		5				3	7				
12-19-1-I		1		4				1	1				
12-19-1-III				1				5					
12-19-1-3	1	1	2					1	3				
12-19-1-V	1	1											
12-20-6-I		1		2					4				
12-20-6-1		2		1				1					
12-20-6-II			1										
12-20-6-2	1	1		1				4	6				
12-20-6-III			1	1					1				
12-20-6-III-7								1					
12-20-6-3	2		1	2				1	2				

TABLE A.1   (continued)

Provenience	Indet.	SF	SF,P	WY	ABQ	JMZ	VLL	GAL	RW	RM	KWH	CHP	SCR
12-20-6-7		4						1					
12-21-6-0	8		1	5					1				
12-21-6-I			7	1									
12-21-6-1			2					2					
12-21-6-II	2		1	2					1				
12-21-6-2		1	2	1									
12-21-6-6				1					1				
12-23-4-II				3					2				
12-23-4-2				1					1				
12-23-4-3				2									
12-23-4-5	22	1	2	13				11	2				
12-23-4-6		1		4					8				
12-24-3-I			2						5				
12-24-3-1				1				1					
12-24-3-II				1					1				
12-24-3-2		1	2										
12-24-3-3								1					
12-24-3-4	1		1	1				1					
12-24-3-6	6	3	1	7				1	2				
12-24-3-IV	2												
12-C-3-11	15	15	5	11				34	14				
12-C-3-12	7	25		4				21					
12-D-3-1		12	8	13				3	9				
12-D-3-2-A		4	5	5	1			6	3				
12-D-3-1-1-1			1	4				3					
12-D-3-2-B		101	83	26				64	71			1	
12-D-3-3		10	33	10				17	23				
12-D-3-4									1				
12-D-3-5		3	5	1									
12-D-3-10			1										
12-D-3-8				1				1					
12-D-3-11		1	1	2				2	2				
12-D-2		16		7				10	5				
12-D-2-1		3	1					3	5				
12-D-2-2-A		5	1					1	2				
12-D-2-2		52	1	11	1			24	24				
12-D-2-A		1		3				1					
12-D-2-3								1					
12-G-36B-2		13	13	6				12	29				
Subtotal:	702	1,429	1,033	1,475	12	3	1	1,169	1,973	0	1	10	2
Component II:													
12-7-6-I	17	1		2				5	4				
12-7-6-1	15		1	4				12	5				
12-7-6-II	1			2				6	2				
12-7-6-2	5	1		3	1			3	1			1	
12-7-6-III		1		3	2			4	2				
12-7-8		1	9	10				6	18				
12-7-9-1,I		17	13	34				44	32				
12-7-10-1,I		11	6	19				31	24				
12-8-4-I	25	2	5	12				23	5				

TABLE A.1 (continued)

Provenience	Indet.	SF	SF,P	WY	ABQ	JMZ	VLL	GAL	RW	RM	KWH	CHP	SCR
12-8-4-1	13		1	21				15	7				
12-8-4-2	10	1		6				12	2				
12-8-4-II								2					
12-8-4-3	3			5									
12-8-4-IV				1									
12-8-6-I,1		9	14	21	2			16	34				
12-8-6-2			6	4				4	3				
12-8-6-II		4		3									
12-8-6-3			5	4	2			2	6				
12-9-6-I	6	1	1	9				7	5				
12-9-6-1	29	10	3	15				33	7				
12-9-6-II	21	8	3	26				28	5				
12-9-6-2	16	8	3	16				20	6				
12-9-6-III	5	3	1	7				5	3				
12-9-6-3				2									
12-9-6-4		1	1	2				2					
12-9-6-5								1	3				
12-9-8-I	12	4	2	3				1	1				
12-9-8-1	4	1		1				1					
12-9-8-2	1	2		3									
12-9-8-II	10	5		4					3				
12-9-8-III	12	6		4				8	3				
12-9-8-3	3	1	1	5				2	1				
12-9-8-IV	25	18	2	21				12	15				
12-9-8-5	5	3	1	4	1			1	1				
12-9-8-6	11	11	8	5				9	5				
12-9-8-7	30	15	3	18	3			12	8				
12-9-9-1		6	12	26				28	35				
12-9-9-2		22	18	37	2			43	39				
12-10-3-1,2	30	21	7	24	1			20	10				
12-10-3-I	29	16	1	10	4			16	9				
12-10-3-3,4,5	44	32	4	17				21	14				
12-10-3-II		4	3	12				12	7				
12-10-3-III	13	12	4	17				12	3				
12-10-3-VII	3	1	1	1									
12-10-3-6	2	1		1					1				
12-11-2-1		11		8					20				
12-11-2-2		12	2	6				3	16				
12-11-2-3	3	28	2	20				5	25				
12-11-2-4		5		6					8				
12-11-3-1		1											
12-11-3-2		7	1	5			3	3	9				
12-11-3-3	4	33	5	4	2			3	28				
12-11-3-4	5	6	4	16	2			1	11				
12-11-3-5	1	10	3	19	2			1	7				
12-11-3-6	1	8	2	8				1	17				
12-11-3-7		3		4					2				
12-11-3-8		4	1	3				1					
12-11-3-9		10		1			1	2	11				
12-11-5-1	4	6	1	13				2	14				
12-11-5-2	5	7	4	7				1	7				
12-11-5-3	8	24	8	19				5	13			1	

TABLE A.1 (continued)

Provenience	Indet.	SF	SF,P	WY	ABQ	JMZ	VLL	GAL	RW	RM	KWH	CHP	SCR
12-11-7-1	10	31	5	24				6	23				
12-11-7-2	4	21	4	23	1			1	22			1	
12-11-7-2-1	2	11	2	5				4	3				
12-11-7-3		4		7					2				
12-11-7-3		1											
12-11-7-4		2	1	6					3				
12-15-6-1	48	15	3	16				12	16				
12-15-6-2		1											
12-15-6-6	13	4	1	4				2	5				
12-15-6-7	7	2	1					2	3				
12-15a-7-1	16	4	2	32				15	5				
12-15a-7-2	4	1	2	5				6	2				
12-15a-8-1	24	25	7	16				13	9				
12-15a-8-4		2	1	3				1					
12-15a-8-6	1												
12-15a-8-7				1					2				
12-15a-8-9				1				1	2				
12-15a-8-10	7	1	1						4				
12-15a-9-I	2	5	3	2				1					
12-15a-9-1	5	9	1	7	3			3	3	1			
12-15a-9-II	1	1	1	1				1	1				
12-15a-9-2	2	6	1	2				1					
12-15a-9-III	20	5	3	6				12	5				
12-15a-9-3	11	2	4					1	1				
12-15a-9-3-7									1				
12-16-1-1		5											
12-16-1-14		1											
12-16-1-2		6	1	2				3					
12-16-1-3		27		4	4			4					
12-16-1-4		8		5									
12-16-1-5		8		4	2			1					
12-16-1-6		16	1	3	1			2					
12-16-1-7		35	2	14	3			1					
12-16-1-9		3	1	1				1					
12-16-2-1		15		1	1			8	2				
12-16-3-0								1					
12-16-3-1		5			2			4					
12-16-4-1		26		4	1			14	1				
12-16-5-1		8		1					3				
12-16-5-2		2		2				2					
12-16-5-3		3		1				1	1				
12-16-5-4		10							3				
12-16-5-5		5		1				2	2				
12-16-5-6		44		7	2			17					
12-16-5-7		25						6	2				
12-16-5-8				2					1				
12-16-5-14									1				
12-16-5-17		3		1				1	1				
12-16-5-17-3		1			1			1	1				
12-16-6-1		8		2				5	1				
12-16-6-2		13		3				2	3				
12-16-6-3		1											

TABLE A.1 (continued)

Provenience	Indet.	SF	SF,P	WY	ABQ	JMZ	VLL	GAL	RW	RM	KWH	CHP	SCR
12-16-6-4		2						2					
12-16-6-5		6		1				2					
12-16-6-6		1		1				1	1				
12-16-6-7				1	1			1					
12-16-6-8	1								1				
12-16-6-10		3						1	1				
12-16-7-1(A)		79		19	1			34	14				
12-16-7-1(B)		18		3	13			2	4				
12-16-7-1(C)		5		2	2			6	1				
12-16-7-2		5		5				1	2				
12-16-7-3								1					
12-16-9-1		12		8				6	7				
12-16-10-1		7		1				3					
12-16-10-2		1		6				1					
12-16-11-1		7		5	1			8	4				
12-16-11-2		2							1				
12-16-11-2,3		4		5					6				
12-16-11-4		4		1				4	1				
12-16-11-4,5		10		5	2			4	4				
12-16-11-5		40		13	1	1		14	19				
12-16-11-6		16		7				13	4				
12-16-11-7		6		3		1		6	6				
12-16-11-8		2		2					2				
12-16-11-9		1						1					
12-16-11-9(A)		5		2				2					
12-16-11-12		1						1	1				
12-16-11-13		12						3	1				
12-16-12-1		9						3	1				
12-16-13-1		20		3	1			3	6				
12-16-13-2	1	22		7	1			13	4				
12-16-13-3		16		11	3			9	3				
12-16-13-6		1		2									
12-16-14-1		6		1	1			7					
12-16-14-2		25		6	2			13	2				
12-16-14-2-2					16			1					
12-16-14-4				1				1					
12-16-15-0									1				
12-16-15-1		14		22	1			11	17				
12-16-15-2			1	15	7				9				
12-16-16-1 (upper)		8	2	4					2				
12-16-16-1 (lower)		4	4	48				16	3				
12-16-17-1	10	5	1	13					2				
12-16-17-2	8	3	3	23					24				
12-16-17-3				10					4				
12-16-17-3-2				26									
12-16-18-1		2	2	30				1	18				
12-16-18-2	7	9	2	18					58				
12-16-18-3				3					7				
12-16-18-4				1									
12-16-18-5				1									
12-16-19-1				3					2				
12-16-19-2	6	1		4					3				

TABLE A.1   (*continued*)

Provenience	Indet.	SF	SF,P	WY	ABQ	JMZ	VLL	GAL	RW	RM	KWH	CHP	SCR
12-16-19-3		1	1	13					11				
12-16-19-11									1				
12-16-19-15		1		5					2				
12-16-20-1		4	1	8				4	5				
12-16-20-2		11	6	33				18	12				
12-16-20-3		29		28				24	24				
12-16-20-4		22	4	15	2			14	11				
12-16-20-5		1											
12-16-20-7				1									
12-16-21-1	17	17		49				4	27				
12-16-21-2		5	1	24	4			2	16				
12-16-21-3		1	1	9					6				
12-16-22-1	8	18	1	16				1	9				
12-16-22-2	8	14	2	27	1			3	26				
12-16-22-3		2		6					3				
12-16-22-4		1		5				1	2				
12-16-23-1		3	4	40					18				
12-16-25-1	5	8	1	1				3					
12-16-25-2				2									
12-16-25-4				1									
12-16-33-1	4	10	2	23				2	16				
12-16-33-2	10	8	6	22				7	29				
12-16-33-3	6	13	11	3					16				
12-16-33-4	10	43	27	10				2	9				
12-16-38-I				1									
12-16-38-1	6	5	1	14				3	1				
12-16-38-II	16	13	1	35	2			17	5				
12-16-38-2	21	4	1	15				10	5				
12-16-38-III	6	1		3				4	2				
12-16-38-3		1		1				1	2				
12-16-38-4	4	2	2	4	2			4					
12-16-38-5,IV	176	42	20	104				85	136				
12-16-38-V	5	3	1	9				7	8				
12-20-4-1	1								1				
12-20-4-2		1	1	1									
12-20-4-3	3			4				2					
12-20-5-1				3				1	5				
12-21-3-I	3	1	1	4				5	5				
12-21-3-1	2	1						1	4				
12-21-3-II	6	1	1	6				3	8				
12-21-3-2								1	1				
12-21-3-II-1								1					
12-21-3-4	1	2		4				1					
12-21-3-5				3					2				
12-21-3-6		4	2	5				3	5				
12-21-3-8		5		3				4	3				
12-21-3-11	1	3		3				3	4				
12-21-3-13		1											
12-21-4-1	1	1	1	1				1	2				
12-C-2-1		34	11	9	3			46	24				
12-C-2-2		75	43	161	30			98	108			1	
12-C-2-3		21	13	25	5			19	29				

TABLE A.1 (continued)

Provenience	Indet.	SF	SF,P	WY	ABQ	JMZ	VLL	GAL	RW	RM	KWH	CHP	SCR
12-C-2-sub. feature 3-4		3		7	1			6	2				
12-C-2-sub. feature 3-1								1					
12-C-2-sub. feature 3-27		1											
12-C-2-I			1		1								
12-C-2-II		2	1	2				1					
12-C-2-III	2	9	1	5				8	7				
12-C-2-IV		3	2	1				4	5				
12-C-2-V,VI		5		3	1			2	5				
12-11-1-1		2		4	1								
12-11-1-2		1	5										
12-11-1-3		1	3										
12-11-1-4		1											
12-11-1-6		1											
12-11-1-7		1						1					
Subtotal:	962	1,723	415	1,925	151	2	4	1,288	1,519	1	0	4	0
TOTAL:	1,682	3,376	1,531	3,591	397	19	5	2,738	3,559	1	2	14	2

TABLE A.2
Frequency of red, yellow, and glaze ware ceramics by excavated provenience.

Provenience	WMR	SJP	HSH	JDT	EGR	LPP	AGR	SCP	SZP	LGR	CGY	LGY
Plaza Tests:												
12-C-A-0					2							
12-C-A-1					2							
12-C-A-2					3							
12-C-A-3					3						2	
12-C-A-4					5							
12-C-A-5					82						11	
12-C-A-6					48						4	
12-C-A-7					14							
12-C-A-8					2			1				
12-C-A-9					1							
12-C-B-general							8				1	
12-C-B-1							2				2	
12-C-B-2							26				3	
12-C-B-3						1	23					
12-C-B-4							11	1			1	
12-C-B-5							4					
12-C-B-6							4				2	
12-C-B-7							4				1	
12-C-B-8							85				3	
12-C-B-9							27					
12-C-B-10					2		3					
12-G-34A-2					3							

TABLE A.2   (continued)

Provenience	WMR	SJP	HSH	JDT	EGR	LPP	AGR	SCP	SZP	LGR	CGY	LGY
12-11-0							13	1			1	
12-11-1-backfill					9		2	1			3	
12-11-N2-backfill							8					
12-11-N4-backfill							1					
12-11-T.S.3A-II					8							
12-11-T.S.3B-2					1		1					
12-11-T.S.3B-3					5		1					
12-T.T.A (backfill of 12-16-1)							5					
Subtotal:	0	0	0	0	185	6	228	4	0	0	34	0

Component I:

Provenience	WMR	SJP	HSH	JDT	EGR	LPP	AGR	SCP	SZP	LGR	CGY	LGY
12-4-2-1		1										
12-4-2-2		1			1							
12-5(6)-8-V,5					1							
12-5(6)-9-2		1										
12-5(6)-9-3						1						
12-5(6)-14-4					1							
12-6-6-II					1							
12-7-7-I					1							
12-7-7-2					1							
12-7-7-3					1							
12-7-7-4							1					
12-7-7-5					1							
12-8-5-II		1										
12-8-5-2					2							
12-8-5-3		1				1						
12-8-5-5						1						
12-9-7-5		1										
12-10-3-VIII					2							
12-11-5-4					1							
12-11-9-3					1							
12-12-4-3					1							
12-14-5-I					1							
12-14-5-II					1							
12-16-24-2					2							
12-16-26-1					2							
12-16-26-2					2							
12-16-26-3					1							
12-16-28-5							1					
12-16-29-1			1		10		1			1	3	
12-16-29-4					1							
12-16-29-6							1					
12-16-30-4(I)					1							
12-16-30-1			1		1						2	
12-16-31-2							1					
12-16-32-I					3							
12-16-32-1					36		10	1		1	4	
12-16-32-2					1							
12-16-32-10					1							
12-16-34-1					9				1	1		

113

TABLE A.2 *(continued)*

Provenience	WMR	SJP	HSH	JDT	EGR	LPP	AGR	SCP	SZP	LGR	CGY	LGY
12-16-34-test pit		1										
12-16-35-1					1							
12-16-36-1			1		62		8	1			11	1
12-16-36-2					42		7	2			9	1
12-16-37-1					5		1					
12-18-6-I,1						1						
12-18-6-II,III,2			1			1	1					
12-18-6-IV,3						1						
12-18-7-3					1							
12-18-7-IV							1					
12-18-7-5		1										
12-18-8-III,3,IV						2						
12-18-14-II,2		1										
12-18-14-III,3					1							
12-18-15-1						5						
12-18-15-2						1						
12-18-32-1					1							
12-18-38-I,1					1							
12-18-38-II,2					2							
12-18-39-II, 2,III,3			1		1							
12-18-48-1,I			2		1	1						
12-21-6-0					6							
12-21-6-I					1							
12-23-4-5			1									
12-24-3-I		1										
12-D-3-1					5		2	2			1	
12-D-3-2-A					2					1	1	
12-D-3-2-B					4	3	1					
12-D-2							1					
12-D-2-1					1							
12-D-2-2-A							1					
12-D-2-2											1	
12-G-36B-2					1	1						
Subtotal:	0	10	8	0	225	19	38	6	1	4	32	2

Component II:

Provenience	WMR	SJP	HSH	JDT	EGR	LPP	AGR	SCP	SZP	LGR	CGY	LGY
12-7-6-I					6	1					1	
12-7-6-1					4							
12-7-6-II					2							
12-7-6-2					5							
12-7-6-III					2							
12-7-8					13						2	
12-7-9-1,I			1		6			1		1		
12-7-10-1,I					12		1	1			1	
12-8-4-I					7		2				3	
12-8-4-1					5			1				
12-8-4-2					1							
12-8-4-II					2							
12-8-6-I,1					7		1	2		1	2	
12-8-6-2								1				

TABLE A.2   (continued)

Provenience	WMR	SJP	HSH	JDT	EGR	LPP	AGR	SCP	SZP	LGR	CGY	LGY
12-8-6-II					2			1			2	
12-8-6-3					5						1	
12-9-6-I					2							
12-9-6-1					6							
12-9-6-II		1			5					1		
12-9-6-2					12		1	1				
12-9-6-III					5		3			2		
12-9-6-3					1							
12-9-6-4					2							
12-9-8-I					6			1			1	
12-9-8-2	1				7			1		1		
12-9-8-II					4		1					
12-9-8-III					6			1			2	
12-9-8-3					1							
12-9-8-IV					16	1	3	1				
12-9-8-5					2							
12-9-8-6					2							
12-9-8-7					13		2	1				
12-9-9-1					7		1					
12-9-9-2					8		2	1			1	
12-10-3-1,2					7			1			1	
12-10-3-I					2					1		
12-10-3-3,4,5					4			2				
12-10-3-II					5						1	
12-10-3-III					10							
12-10-3-VII					1							
12-11-2-1					1		1	1				
12-11-2-2					1							
12-11-2-3					12		2					
12-11-2-4					3		1					
12-11-3-2					20		1			1	1	
12-11-3-3					39		1				4	
12-11-3-4					14						1	
12-11-3-5					15		1				2	
12-11-3-6					7		1					
12-11-3-7					3							
12-11-5-1					8		1			1		
12-11-5-2					1							
12-11-5-3											1	
12-11-7-1					10		2					
12-11-7-2					16	2				1		
12-11-7-2-1					1						1	
12-11-7-3					7		1					
12-11-7-3-1					1							
12-11-7-4-1							3					
12-15-6-1					2		1			2	2	
12-15-6-1-5							1					
12-15-6-6							2				1	
12-15a-7-1	2				7		1			1	1	
12-15a-7-2					1							
12-15a-7-3					1							

115

APPENDIX A

TABLE A.2   (continued)

Provenience	WMR	SJP	HSH	JDT	EGR	LPP	AGR	SCP	SZP	LGR	CGY	LGY
12-15a-7-7					1							
12-15a-8-1					9		1				1	
12-15a-8-4					2							
12-15a-8-6					1							
12-15a-8-7					2							
12-15a-8-9					3							
12-15a-9-I					1		1					
12-15a-9-1					3		2					
12-15a-9-II							1					
12-15a-9-2					1							
12-16-1-1					2							
12-16-1-2					5							
12-16-1-3					5						1	
12-16-1-4					2							
12-16-1-5					6							
12-16-1-6					5						2	
12-16-1-7					4						1	
12-16-2-1							1					
12-16-3-1					2							
12-16-4-0					1							
12-16-4-1					3							
12-16-5-1							1					
12-16-5-3					2		2					
12-16-5-4											1	
12-16-5-5					2							
12-16-5-6					4			1			1	
12-16-5-7											2	
12-16-5-8											1	
12-16-5-17					2							
12-16-6-1					2	2					2	
12-16-6-2					1							
12-16-6-3					1		1					
12-16-6-5					1							
12-16-6-7					1							
12-16-6-10							1					
12-16-6-11							2					
12-16-7-1(A)					11		16				1	
12-16-7-1(B)					3		5				1	
12-16-7-1(C)					5		2				1	
12-16-7-2					1							
12-16-9-1					2		2					
12-16-10-1					1							
12-16-11-1									1			
12-16-11-2,3	1		1									
12-16-11-5			1		6		1	1				
12-16-11-6					6		2					
12-16-11-7							2					
12-16-11-8					1							
12-16-11-9(A)					1		1				1	
12-16-11-13					3	1	2	2				
12-16-12-1					3		2					

116

TABLE A.2   (continued)

Provenience	WMR	SJP	HSH	JDT	EGR	LPP	AGR	SCP	SZP	LGR	CGY	LGY
12-16-13-1					1							
12-16-13-2					1		4					
12-16-13-3					10	2		2				
12-16-13-6					1		10					
12-16-14-1					1							
12-16-14-2					2		1					
12-16-15-0							1					
12-16-15-1					4		2					
12-16-15-2					6		2	1		2	3	
12-16-16-1 (upper)					5							
12-16-16-1 (lower)					36		2	1		4	2	
12-16-17-1					2		1					
12-16-17-2					8							
12-16-17-3							1					
12-16-17-4A							1					
12-16-17-4B					1							
12-16-18-1					4			1			1	
12-16-18-2					11						1	
12-16-18-3					1							
12-16-18-4											1	
12-16-19-2							1	1				
12-16-19-3					13			1				
12-16-19-15							1					
12-16-20-1					2					2	1	
12-16-20-2		1			10					1	4	
12-16-20-3					15		2				2	
12-16-20-4			1		9		2					
12-16-21-1					7			3			2	
12-16-21-2					18	1	4	1		1	2	
12-16-21-3					8		1	1			2	
12-16-21-4					1						1	
12-16-21-5					1						1	
12-16-22-1					2		1				1	
12-16-22-2					8		2					
12-16-22-3					2				1			
12-16-22-4					1							
12-16-23-1					16		1	3		1	3	
12-16-25-1					1							
12-16-25-2					2		1					
12-16-33-1					15		5	4			5	
12-16-33-2					6						1	
12-16-38-1	1				9		1					
12-16-38-II					17		2	2			1	
12-16-38-2					10		2				1	
12-16-38-III					5							
12-16-38-3					4		1					
12-16-38-4					6							
12-16-38-5,IV		1	4		16		3	1		1		
12-20-4-1							1					
12-20-5-1					4						1	
12-20-5-2					1						1	

117

TABLE A.2 *(continued)*

Provenience	WMR	SJP	HSH	JDT	EGR	LPP	AGR	SCP	SZP	LGR	CGY	LGY
12-21-3-1					2							
12-21-3-4					4							
12-21-3-11					2							
12-C-2-1					88		13	2		11	3	
12-C-2-2		1		1	165		33	12	2	6	1	
12-C-2-3		1			51		5	1		2	4	
12-C-2-sub. feature 3-4					11		2	1				
12-C-2-II					2						1	
12-C-2-III					6		1					
12-C-2-IV					2							
12-C-2-V,VI					3		1					
12-11-1-1							4					
12-11-1-4							1					
12-11-1							18	1			1	
Subtotal:	5	5	8	1	1,139	10	219	62	2	45	95	0
TOTAL:	5	15	16	1	1,549	35	485	72	3	49	161	2

Appendix B

Summary of Point Counts of Petrographic Thin Sections

Ia. Galisteo Black-on-white, var. Galisteo

Sherd 12-18-15-II/211/03-1. Temper VIIIa

	No.	%	% Nonplastics
Matrix	53	53	–
Nonplastics	40	40	–
Voids	7	7	–
Quartz	24	24	60
Plagioclase	1	1	2.5
Alkali feldspar	3	3	7.5
Mica	*	*	*
Quartzite	1	1	2.5
Sherd	11	11	27.5

* Present but not sampled.

Grain size
  Mean: 0.24 mm
  Range: 0.01–1.5 mm

Note: Dense, gray clay tempered with medium to coarse, subangular, gray and black sherd.

Ib. Galisteo Black-on-white, var. Kendi

Sherd 12-C-2-2/211/05-2. Temper IIIa

	No.	%	% Nonplastics
Matrix	44	44	–
Nonplastics	44	44	–
Voids	12	12	–
Quartz	5	5	11
Alkali feldspar	5	5	11
Augite	3	3	7
Augite monzonite	31	31	71

Grain size
  Mean: 0.27 mm
  Range: > 0.01–0.9 mm

Note: Dense, slightly silty, dark gray paste tempered with moderate amounts of medium subangular to angular augite monzonite (holocrystalline rock with weathered laths of zoned plagioclase, augite, rare hornblende, and opaques).

Sherd 12-C-2-2/211/26-5. Temper IIIa

	No.	%	% Nonplastics
Matrix	57	57	—
Nonplastics	41	41	—
Voids	2	2	—
Quartz	7	7	17
Plagioclase	2	2	5
Alkali feldspar	4	4	10
Augite	6	6	15
Hornblende	3	3	7
Hematite	4	4	10
Granite	1	1	2
Augite monzonite	14	14	34

Grain size
   Mean: 0.38 mm
   Range: 0.01–1.8 mm

Note: Dense, slightly silty, gray clay tempered with medium, subangular to angular, augite monzonite (holocrystalline with weathered, zoned plagioclase, alkali feldspar, augite, altered hornblende, and opaques).

Sherd 12-10-3-II/[212]/05-10. Temper IIIa

	No.	%	% Nonplastics
Matrix	44	44	—
Nonplastics	54	54	—
Voids	2	2	—
Quartz	12	12	22
Plagioclase	6	6	11
Alkali feldspar	3	3	5.5
Muscovite	1	1	2
Augite	7	7	13
Opaques	3	3	5.5
Augite monzonite	22	22	41

Grain size
   Mean: 0.29 mm
   Range: 0.03–1 mm

Note: Silty, brown paste tempered with medium to coarse, angular augite monzonite (holocrystalline with weathered, zoned laths of plagioclase, alkali feldspar, augite, and opaque minerals).

Sherd 12-C-2-2/211/21-3. Temper IIIe

	No.	%	% Nonplastics
Matrix	58	58	—
Nonplastics	38	38	—
Voids	4	4	—
Quartz	12	12	32
Plagioclase	5	5	13
Perthite	1	1	3
Alkali feldspar	4	4	10
Microcline	1	1	3
Hornblende	2	2	5
Opaques	4	4	10
Hematite	1	1	3

Sherd 12-C-2-2/211/21-3 (*continued*)

	No.	%	% Nonplastics
Highly altered volcanic	8	8	21

Grain size
  Mean: 0.29 mm
  Range: < 0.01–1.3 mm

Note: Fine-textured, silty clay tempered with medium, subangular, highly altered volcanic rock (porphyrytic with feldspar ground and phenocrysts of plagioclase, quartz, alkali feldspar, and opaques).

Sherd 12-16-20-2/211/42-6. Temper IIIe

	No.	%	% Nonplastics
Matrix	50	50	–
Nonplastics	47	47	–
Voids	3	3	–
Quartz	25	25	53
Cristobalite	1	1	2
Plagioclase	4	4	9
Perthite	1	1	2
Alkali feldspar	7	7	15
Hornblende	1	1	2
Opaques	5	5	11
Highly altered volcanic	3	3	6

Grain size
  Mean: 0.18 mm
  Range: < 0.01–1.2 mm

Note: Fine, silty, gray clay tempered with medium, subrounded to subangular highly altered volcanic rock (porphyrytic, feldspar ground with medium euhedral to subhedral phenocrysts of weathered plagioclase, alkali feldspar, and rare opaque minerals).

Sherd 12-C-2-2/[212]/20-12. Temper IIIf

	No.	%	% Nonplastics
Matrix	45	45	–
Nonplastics	52	52	–
Voids	3	3	–
Quartz	7	7	13
Plagioclase	4	4	8
Alkali feldspar	3	3	6
Biotite	4	4	8
Augite	3	3	6
Hornblende	7	7	13
Opaques	1	1	2
Hematite	2	2	4
Intermediate volcanic	21	21	40

Grain size
  Mean: 0.47 mm
  Range: 0.03–1.5 mm

Note: Fine-textured, silty clay tempered with coarse to very coarse, subangular, intermediate volcanic rock (porphyrytic with coarse tabular phenocrysts of plagioclase, alkali feldspar, hornblende, and biotite).

IIa. Rowe Black-on-white, var. Poge

Sherd 12-7-6-1/212/07-8. Temper Vb

	No.	%	% Nonplastics
Matrix	36	36	–
Nonplastics	52	52	–
Voids	12	12	–
Quartz	24	24	46
Plagioclase	3	3	6
Perthite	4	4	8
Alkali feldspar	1	1	2
Microcline	1	1	2
Muscovite	2	2	4
Biotite	4	4	8
Augite	*	*	*
Hornblende	2	2	4
Granite	9	9	17
Sandstone	2	2	4

* Present but not sampled.

Grain size
 Mean: 0.48 mm
 Range: 0.03–1.5 mm

Note: Well-sorted, medium-textured paste consisting of dense, black, slightly silty clay tempered with lithic sand consisting of medium to coarse, subangular granite and lesser amounts of fine to medium quartz, plagioclase, alkali feldspar, hornblende, and coarse, platy muscovite and biotite mica.

Sherd 12-7-6-1/212/11-11. Temper Vb

	No.	%	% Nonplastics
Matrix	40	40	–
Nonplastics	46	46	–
Voids	14	14	–
Quartz	26	26	56
Plagioclase	4	4	9
Alkali feldspar	6	6	13.5
Microcline	3	3	6.5
Opaques	1	1	2
Granite	4	4	9
Rhyolite	1	1	2
Quartzite	1	1	2

Grain size
 Mean: 0.55 mm
 Range: 0.05–2.3 mm

Note: Medium-textured, well-sorted paste consisting of dense, black, silty clay tempered with medium to coarse, angular lithic sand.

Sherd 12-9-6-2/212/33-13. Temper VIIIa

	No.	%	% Nonplastics
Matrix	45	45	–
Nonplastics	49	49	–
Voids	6	6	–
Quartz	7	7	14
Plagioclase	4	4	8
Alkali feldspar	8	8	16
Microcline	1	1	2
Glass	1	1	2
Muscovite	1	1	2
Biotite	1	1	2
Hornblende	*	*	*
Calcite	4	4	8
Hematite	1	1	2
Granite	1	1	2
Quartzite	2	2	4
Quartz-mica schist	*	*	*
Argillite	1	1	2
Sandstone	*	*	*
Sherd	17	17	35

* Present but not sampled.

Grain size
   Mean: 0.54 mm
   Range: 0.05–2 mm

Note: Fine-textured, brown clay tempered with lithic sand, consisting of medium to coarse alkali feldspar, plagioclase, quartz, mica, granular calcium carbonate, quartzite, granite, quartz-mica schist, and micaceous sandstone; and medium, subangular, black, brown, and gray sherd.

Sherd 12-C-2-2/212/29-14. Temper Vs

	No.	%	% Nonplastics
Matrix	46	46	–
Nonplastics	47	47	–
Voids	7	7	–
Quartz	18	18	38
Plagioclase	4	4	9
Alkali feldspar	3	3	6
Microcline	2	2	4.25
Muscovite	1	1	2
Augite	1	1	2
Hornblende	2	2	4.25
Opaques	2	2	4.25
Granite	2	2	4.25
Gneiss	1	1	2
Sherd	11	11	23

Grain size
   Mean: 0.43 mm
   Range: 0.03–1.3 mm

Note: Fine-textured, brown clay tempered with medium, subangular, dark brown sherd and medium, subangular and angular lithic sand.

Sherd 12-16-20-4/212/21-9. Temper VIIsb

	No.	%	% Nonplastics
Matrix	51	51	–
Nonplastics	46	46	–
Voids	3	3	–
Quartz	1	1	2
Plagioclase	3	3	7
Alkali feldspar	22	22	48
Muscovite	4	4	9
Pyroxene	*	*	*
Hornblende	1	1	2
Opaques	1	1	2
Sherd	14	14	30

* Present but not sampled.

Grain size
    Mean: 0.21 mm
    Range: 0.03 – 1 mm

Note: Fine-textured, silty clay with abundant very fine and medium, angular alkali feldspar and plagioclase, lesser amounts of quartz and fine, platy muscovite, and rare hornblende and fine pyroxene. Tempered with abundant fine to medium, subangular, black sherd.

Sherd 12-7-6-I/212/03-7. Temper XVII

	No.	%	% Nonplastics
Matrix	50	50	–
Nonplastics	37	37	–
Voids	13	13	–
Quartz	1	1	3
Plagioclase	2	2	5
Alkali feldspar	15	15	40.5
Muscovite	1	1	3
Biotite	2	2	5
Opaques	1	1	3
Quartzite	*	*	*
Sherd	15	15	40.5

* Present but not sampled.

Grain size
    Mean: 0.50 mm
    Range: 0.05 – 1.6 mm

Note: Fine-textured, dark, metamorphic, brown clay tempered with coarse to very coarse, brown and black sherd.

IIb. Rowe Black-on-white, var. Arroyo Hondo

Sherd 12-18-15-2/211/16-4. Temper Va

	No.	%	% Nonplastics
Matrix	52	52	–
Nonplastics	39	39	–
Voids	9	9	–
Quartz	16	16	41
Plagioclase	2	2	5
Perthite	2	2	5
Alkali feldspar	4	4	10
Microcline	*	*	*
Hornblende	3	3	8

Sherd 12-18-15-2/211/16-4 (*continued*)

	No.	%	% Nonplastics
Granite	12	12	31

* Present but not sampled.

Grain size
    Mean: 0.64 mm
    Range: 0.05–2.5 mm

Note: Very silty, brown, primary clay with abundant fine to very fine, angular quartz, plagioclase, and muscovite/sericite; medium to very coarse, subangular granite (holocrystalline with quartz, plagioclase, microcline, perthite, micrographic quartz-feldspar, muscovite, hornblende, and opaques); and lesser amounts of medium, subangular quartz, feldspar, alkali feldspar, and hornblende.

III. Vallecitos Black-on-white

Sherd 12-D-2/311/31-15. Temper Ia

	No.	%	% Nonplastics
Matrix	43	43	–
Nonplastics	50	50	–
Voids	7	7	–
Quartz	1	1	2
Plagioclase	1	1	2
Alkali feldspar	8	8	16
Glass shards	23	23	46
Opaques	14	14	28
Vesicular pumice	3	3	6

Grain size
    Mean: 0.1 mm
    Range: 0.03–0.4 mm

Note: Fine-textured, tan clay tempered with fine volcanic ash.

IV. Jemez Black-on-white

Sherd 12-4-2-5/[312]/06-16. Temper VIIIa (Poge ?)

	No.	%	% Nonplastics
Matrix	51	51	–
Nonplastics	45	45	–
Voids	4	4	–
Quartz	4	4	9
Plagioclase	2	2	4
Alkali feldspar	15	15	33
Microcline	1	1	2
Glass	5	5	11
Muscovite	4	4	9
Biotite	2	2	4
Opaques	4	4	9
Granite	1	1	2
Sherd	6	6	13
Quartz-mica schist	1	1	2

Grain size
    Mean: 0.23 mm
    Range: 0.01–1.1 mm

Note: Fine-textured, silty clay tempered with lithic sand and medium, subrounded to subangular, gray and brown, ash-tempered sherd.

Sherd 12-4-2-5/312/13-17. Temper IIa

	No.	%	% Nonplastics
Matrix	53	53	–
Nonplastics	42	42	–
Voids	5	5	–
Quartz	1	1	2
Alkali feldspar	12	12	29
Glass shards	9	9	21
Pyroxene	1	1	2
Opaques	2	2	5
Hematite	1	1	2
Vesicular pumice	15	15	36
Quartz-mica schist	1	1	2

Grain size
   Mean: 0.26 mm
   Range: 0.03–1.2 mm

Note: Fine-textured, silty, dark brown clay tempered with coarse pumiceous ash.

Va. Santa Fe Black-on-white, var. Santa Fe

Sherd 12-D-2/321/01-18. Temper Ib

	No.	%	% Nonplastics
Matrix	39	39	–
Nonplastics	51	51	–
Voids	10	10	–
Quartz	16	16	31
Plagioclase	1	1	2
Alkali feldspar	3	3	6
Glass shards	8	8	16
Muscovite	2	2	4
Biotite	1	1	2
Calcite	1	1	2
Opaques	9	9	18
Pumice	7	7	14
Sandstone/siltstone	1	1	2
Clay pellets	2	2	4

Grain size
   Mean: 0.14 mm
   Range: 0.02–0.9 mm

Note: Light brown, silty clay tempered with fine volcanic ash and micaceous siltstone/sandstone with accessory clay pellets and granular calcium carbonate.

Sherd 12-16-18-2/321/12-21. Temper IXc

	No.	%	% Nonplastics
Matrix	68	68	–
Nonplastics	31	31	–
Voids	1	1	–
Quartz	16	16	52
Plagioclase	2	2	7
Alkali feldspar	3	3	10
Microcline	1	1	3
Muscovite	1	1	3
Biotite	1	1	3
Calcite	*	*	*
Opaques	5	5	16
Quartzite	1	1	3
Clay pellets	1	1	3

* Present but not sampled.

Grain size
    Mean: 0.26 mm
    Range: 0.01–1.8 mm

Note: Very fine-textured, untempered, gray clay with abundant very fine to fine quartz-feldspar silt, quartzite, and clay pellets.

Sherd 12-16-20-3/321/25-25. Temper IXa

	No.	%	% Nonplastics
Matrix	34	34	–
Nonplastics	65	65	–
Voids	1	1	–
Quartz	27	27	42
Cristobalite	2	2	3
Perthite	1	1	1.5
Plagioclase	6	6	9
Alkali feldspar	4	4	6
Sericite	2	2	3
Muscovite	1	1	1.5
Biotite	3	3	5
Hornblende	2	2	3
Calcite	4	4	6
Opaques	4	4	6
Quartzite	1	1	1.5
Calcareous sandstone	1	1	1.5
Clay pellets	7	7	11

Grain size
    Mean: 0.26 mm
    Range: 0.02–3.1 mm

Note: Silty/sandy, dense, untempered, gray clay with accessory quartzite, calcareous sandstone, and clay pellets.

Sherd 12-D-2/321/09-19. Temper X

	No.	%	% Nonplastics
Matrix	41	41	–
Nonplastics	52	52	–
Voids	7	7	–
Quartz	30	30	58
Plagioclase	5	5	10
Alkali feldspar	6	6	11
Microcline	3	3	6
Muscovite	2	2	4
Calcite	*	*	*
Quartzite	1	1	2
Sandstone/siltstone	5	5	10

* Present but not sampled.

Grain size
    Mean: 0.18 mm
    Range: 0.03–0.55 mm

Note: Medium-textured, black clay tempered with fine quartz-feldspar silt/sand and calcareous sandstone.

Sherd 12-C-2-2/321/11-20. Temper IXa

	No.	%	% Nonplastics
Matrix	41	41	–
Nonplastics	56	56	–
Voids	3	3	–
Quartz	27	27	48
Plagioclase	7	7	13
Alkali feldspar	5	5	9
Microcline	2	2	3.5
Muscovite	4	4	7
Biotite	1	1	2
Calcite	*	*	*
Opaques	6	6	11
Rhyolite	1	1	2
Sandstone/siltstone	1	1	2
Clay pellets	2	2	3.5

* Present but not sampled.

Grain size
    Mean: 0.32 mm
    Range: 0.04–2 mm

Note: Fine, silty, dense, gray clay with abundant fine to medium quartz-feldspar silt/sand and calcareous sandstone with accessory clay pellets and granular calcium carbonate.

Sherd 12-16-13-1/321/18-24. Temper X

	No.	%	% Nonplastics
Matrix	37	37	–
Nonplastics	55	55	–
Voids	8	8	–
Quartz	25	25	45
Cristobalite	2	2	4
Plagioclase	2	2	4
Alkali feldspar	1	1	2
Microcline	2	2	4
Muscovite	4	4	7
Biotite	1	1	2
Calcite	10	10	18
Calcareous sandstone	8	8	14
Clay pellets	*	*	*

* Present but not sampled.

Grain size
    Mean: 0.14 mm
    Range: 0.03–0.4 mm

Note: Medium-textured, brown, silty/sandy clay tempered with calcareous sandstone.

Sherd 12-9-6-1/321/17-22. Temper VIIIb (Rowe B/W, *var. Poge* ?)

	No.	%	% Nonplastics
Matrix	38	38	–
Nonplastics	59	59	–
Voids	3	3	–
Quartz	7	7	12
Plagioclase	3	3	5
Alkali feldspar	17	17	29
Microcline	2	2	3
Glass shards	1	1	2
Muscovite	7	7	12
Biotite	3	3	5
Augite	2	2	3
Hornblende	4	4	7
Calcite	*	*	*
Opaques	1	1	2
Granite	6	6	10
Quartzite	2	2	3
Sandstone	3	3	5
Clay pellets	1	1	2

* Present but not sampled.

Grain size
    Mean: 0.25 mm
    Range: 0.05–1.4 mm

Note: Dense, medium-textured, sandy, gray clay with fine to medium, angular alkali feldspar, plagioclase, quartz, mica, fine hornblende, and pyroxene and medium to coarse lithic fragments of quartzite, granite, and calcareous sandstone.

129

Sherd 12-5-4-1/321/15-26. Temper Xs

	No.	%	% Nonplastics
Matrix	47	47	–
Nonplastics	47	47	–
Voids	6	6	–
Quartz	19	19	40
Cristobalite	2	2	4.25
Plagioclase	4	4	9
Alkali feldspar	1	1	2
Microcline	1	1	2
Muscovite	3	3	6
Biotite	1	1	2
Calcite	8	8	17
Opaques	1	1	2
Granite	2	2	4.25
Quartzite	1	1	2
Calcareous sandstone	2	2	4.25
Sherd	2	2	4.25

Grain size
    Mean: 0.38 mm
    Range: 0.03–1.7 mm

Note: Fine-textured, brown, silty clay tempered with medium to coarse, subrounded to subangular, quartz-feldspar sand, calcareous sandstone, granite, quartzite, and subangular to angular, brown and black sherd.

Sherd 12-15a-7-1/321/03-23. Temper VIIsb

	No.	%	% Nonplastics
Matrix	46	46	–
Nonplastics	45	45	–
Voids	9	9	–
Quartz	15	15	33
Plagioclase	2	2	4
Alkali feldspar	5	5	11
Microcline	*	*	*
Muscovite	1	1	2
Biotite	*	*	*
Augite	2	2	4
Basaltic hornblende	1	1	2
Opaques	1	1	2
Sherd	18	18	41

* Present but not sampled.

Grain size
    Mean: 0.21 mm
    Range: 0.01–0.9 mm

Note: Medium-textured, sandy, gray clay tempered with fine to medium, subrounded, black sherd.

Vb. Santa Fe Black-on-white, var. Pindi

Sherd 12-18-15-1/331/02-40. Temper IIb

	No.	%	% Nonplastics
Matrix	44	44	–
Nonplastics	49	49	–
Voids	7	7	–
Quartz	16	16	33
Cristobalite	2	2	4
Plagioclase	4	4	8
Alkali feldspar	2	2	4
Glass shards	2	2	4
Muscovite	1	1	2
Augite	2	2	4
Calcite	3	3	6
Opaques	2	2	4
Pumice	15	15	31

Grain size
    Mean: 0.26 mm
    Range: 0.04–1.5 mm

Note: Fine-textured, brown clay tempered with medium to coarse pumiceous ash. Accessories include muscovite, augite, and opaque minerals.

Sherd 12-7-6-II/331/19-41. Temper IIb

	No.	%	% Nonplastics
Matrix	37	37	–
Nonplastics	52	52	–
Voids	11	11	–
Quartz	15	15	29
Perthite	1	1	2
Alkali feldspar	4	4	8
Glass shards	3	3	6
Muscovite	3	3	6
Biotite	1	1	2
Hornblende	1	1	2
Rhyolite	2	2	4
Pumice	22	22	42

Grain size
    Mean: 0.34 mm
    Range: 0.02–1.3 mm

Note: Dense, dark brown clay tempered with medium pumiceous ash with lesser amounts of muscovite, biotite, hornblende, and lithic rhyolite.

Sherd 12-C-2-2/331/35-43. Temper IIb

	No.	%	% Nonplastics
Matrix	36	36	–
Nonplastics	59	59	–
Voids	5	5	–
Quartz	21	21	35
Alkali feldspar	6	6	10
Glass shards	4	4	7

(Continued on next page)

131

Sherd 12-C-2-2/331/35-43 (*continued*)

	No.	%	% Nonplastics
Muscovite	1	1	2
Augite	4	4	7
Hornblende	1	1	2
Opaques	1	1	2
Rhyolite	1	1	2
Pumice	20	20	34

Grain size
    Mean: 0.40 mm
    Range: 0.02–1.4 mm

Note: Fine, silty, brown clay tempered with coarse pumiceous ash. Accessories include augite, muscovite, and hornblende.

Sherd 12-C-2-2/331/19-42. Temper IIc

	No.	%	% Nonplastics
Matrix	53	53	–
Nonplastics	40	40	–
Voids	7	7	–
Quartz	6	6	15
Alkali feldspar	2	2	5
Glass shards	12	12	30
Biotite	2	2	5
Rhyolite	2	2	5
Pumice	16	16	40

Grain size
    Mean: 0.21 mm
    Range: 0.02–1.3 mm

Note: Brown, silty clay tempered with medium to coarse pumiceous ash.

VI. *Wiyo Black-on-white*

Sherd 12-18-15-1/322/01-27. Temper Ia

	No.	%	% Nonplastics
Matrix	57	57	–
Nonplastics	40	40	–
Voids	3	3	–
Alkali feldspar	12	12	30
Glass shards	22	22	55
Biotite	1	1	2.5
Hematite	1	1	2.5
Pumice	4	4	10

Grain size
    Mean: 0.14 mm
    Range: 0.03–1.2 mm

Note: Fine-textured, brown clay tempered with fine volcanic ash consisting of abundant angular, clear and pink glass shards and fine, subrounded to subangular quartz with lesser amounts of medium, subrounded, vesicular pumice. Minor accessories include biotite and hematite.

Sherd 12-C-2-2/322/36-32. Temper Ia

	No.	%	% Nonplastics
Matrix	53	53	–
Nonplastics	40	40	–
Voids	7	7	–
Quartz	11	11	27.5
Plagioclase	2	2	5
Alkali feldspar	1	1	2.5
Glass shards	18	18	45
Hematite	2	2	5
Pumice	6	6	15

Grain size
    Mean: 0.12 mm
    Range: 0.03–0.5 mm

Note: Fine-textured, silty, brown clay tempered with fine volcanic ash.

Sherd 12-9-10-2N/322/09-29. Temper Ic

	No.	%	% Nonplastics
Matrix	60	60	–
Nonplastics	36	36	–
Voids	4	4	–
Quartz	3	3	8
Plagioclase	1	1	3
Glass shards	26	26	72
Pumice	6	6	17

Grain size
    Mean: 0.11 mm
    Range: 0.02–0.7 mm

Note: Fine-textured, light brown clay tempered with fine volcanic ash and medium to coarse, vesicular pumice.

Sherd 12-C-2-2/322/31-33. Temper Ic

	No.	%	% Nonplastics
Matrix	58	58	–
Nonplastics	39	39	–
Voids	3	3	–
Quartz	1	1	3
Glass shards	27	27	69
Hematite	*	*	*
Pumice	9	9	23
Clay pellets	2	2	5

* Present but not sampled.

Grain size
    Mean: 0.17 mm
    Range: 0.02–1.4 mm

Note: Fine-textured, brown clay tempered with fine volcanic ash with lesser amounts of medium to coarse pumice, fine, subrounded to sub-angular quartz, and medium, subrounded, clay pellets.

Sherd 12-16-20-4/322/12-30. Temper Id

	No.	%	% Nonplastics
Matrix	61	61	–
Nonplastics	39	39	–
Voids	0	0	–
Quartz	3	3	8
Plagioclase	2	2	5
Glass shards	22	22	56
Calcite	1	1	2.5
Hematite	1	1	2.5
Pumice	8	8	21
Clay pellets	2	2	5

Grain size
  Mean: 0.25 mm
  Range: 0.02–1.2 mm

Note: Fine-textured, brown clay tempered with fine volcanic ash with coarse, vesicular pumice, granular calcium carbonate, and clay pellets.

Sherd 12-9-10-2N/322/11-31. Temper IIb

	No.	%	% Nonplastics
Matrix	53	53	–
Nonplastics	43	43	–
Voids	4	4	–
Quartz	21	21	49
Alkali feldspar	2	2	5
Glass shards	4	4	9
Opaques	2	2	5
Pumice	14	14	32

Grain size
  Mean: 0.17 mm
  Range: 0.03–0.5 mm

Note: Fine-textured, brown clay tempered with moderate amounts of subrounded to subangular, vesicular pumice and medium, subangular to angular quartz. Accessories include alkali feldspar, glass shards, and opaques.

Sherd 12-10-3-3,4,5/322/03-34. Temper IVsb

	No.	%	% Nonplastics
Matrix	42	42	–
Nonplastics	54	54	–
Voids	4	4	–
Quartz	11	11	20
Cristobalite	1	1	2
Myrmekite	1	1	2
Perthite	1	1	2
Plagioclase	5	5	9
Alkali feldspar	2	2	4
Muscovite	2	2	4
Augite	1	1	2
Opaques	3	3	5.5
Rhyolite	12	12	22
Calcareous sandstone	3	3	5.5
Sherd	12	12	22

Sherd 12-10-3-3/4, 5/322/04-34 (*continued*)

	No.	%	% Nonplastics

Grain size
    Mean: 0.62 mm
    Range: 0.01–5.3 mm

Note: Fine-textured, silty, brown clay tempered with coarse to very coarse, subangular to angular, dark brown sherd and medium, subangular to angular rhyolite and pumice.

Sherd 12-C-2-2/322/09-28. Temper X

	No.	%	% Nonplastics
Matrix	43	43	–
Nonplastics	57	57	–
Voids	0	0	–
Quartz	27	27	47
Cristobalite	3	3	5
Perthite	1	1	2
Plagioclase	5	5	9
Alkali feldspar	1	1	2
Microcline	2	2	4
Muscovite	3	3	5
Biotite	2	2	4
Calcite	7	7	12
Granite	1	1	2
Quartzite	2	2	4
Calcareous sandstone	3	3	5

Grain size
    Mean: 0.23 mm
    Range: 0.02–1.1 mm

Note: Medium-textured, dark brown clay tempered with medium to coarse, subrounded to subangular quartz-feldspar sand with accessory mica, quartzite, granite, and calcareous sandstone.

VII. *Abiquiú Black-on-white*

Sherd 12-C-2-3/323/01-35. Temper Ia

	No.	%	% Nonplastics
Matrix	51	51	–
Nonplastics	44	44	–
Voids	5	5	–
Quartz	15	15	34
Cristobalite	1	1	2
Plagioclase	2	2	5
Alkali feldspar	1	1	2
Glass shards	16	16	36
Muscovite	1	1	2
Biotite	1	1	2
Hematite	*	*	*
Pumice	7	7	16

* Present but not sampled.

Grain size
    Mean: 0.1 mm
    Range: 0.01–0.45 mm

Note: Fine-textured, tan clay tempered with fine volcanic ash and vesicular pumice.

Sherd 12-16-30-1,2/323/19-36. Temper IIc

	No.	%	% Nonplastics
Matrix	46	46	–
Nonplastics	49	49	–
Voids	5	5	–
Quartz	1	1	2
Plagioclase	2	2	4
Alkali feldspar	21	21	43
Glass shards	12	12	24
Muscovite	1	1	2
Augite	1	1	2
Hornblende	1	1	2
Opaques	1	1	2
Hematite	1	1	2
Pumice	8	8	16

Grain size
    Mean: 0.15 mm
    Range: 0.02–0.9 mm

Note: Fine-textured, brown clay tempered with abundant fine, angular volcanic ash with medium to coarse, subrounded to subangular, vesicular pumice and subrounded to angular alkali feldspar. Minor accessories include plagioclase, quartz, muscovite, augite, hornblende, opaque minerals, and hematite.

Sherd 12-7-6-2/323/12-37. Temper Ie

	No.	%	% Nonplastics
Matrix	53	53	–
Nonplastics	43	43	–
Voids	4	4	–
Quartz	1	1	2
Cristobalite	2	2	5
Plagioclase	2	2	5
Alkali feldspar	11	11	26
Microcline	1	1	2
Glass shards	11	11	26
Biotite	8	8	19
Hornblende	1	1	2
Clay pellets	2	2	5
Rhyolite	1	1	2
Pumice	3	3	7

Grain size
    Mean: 0.08 mm
    Range: 0.01–0.8 mm

Note: Fine-textured, brown clay tempered with fine volcanic ash with abundant fine, angular, clear, pink glass shards and fine, subangular to subrounded alkali feldspar and lesser amounts of pumice and very fine, platy biotite mica.

Sherd 12-C-2-2/323/42-38. Temper If

	No.	%	% Nonplastics
Matrix	48	48	–
Nonplastics	45	45	–
Voids	7	7	–
Quartz	1	1	2
Cristobalite	2	2	4.4
Plagioclase	4	4	9
Alkali feldspar	12	12	27
Microcline	2	2	4.4
Glass shards	16	16	36
Biotite	2	2	4.4
Hornblende	2	2	4.4
Calcite	1	1	2
Rhyolite	2	2	4.4
Pumice	1	1	2

Grain size
    Mean: 0.15 mm
    Range: 0.02–0.45 mm

Note: Fine-textured, brown clay tempered with fine volcanic ash with abundant fine, angular shards of clear glass and fine to medium, subrounded to subangular alkali feldspar and quartz. Accessories include cristobalite, plagioclase, microcline, biotite, hornblende, rhyolite, and pumice.

Sherd 12-9-10-2N/323/09-39. Temper Ic

	No.	%	% Nonplastics
Matrix	52	52	–
Nonplastics	48	48	–
Voids	0	0	–
Quartz	1	1	2
Cristobalite	1	1	2
Plagioclase	1	1	2
Alkali feldspar	2	2	4
Glass shards	27	27	56
Muscovite	2	2	4
Augite	2	2	4
Rhyolite	2	2	4
Pumice	5	5	10
Clay pellets	5	5	10

Grain size
    Mean: 0.15 mm
    Range: 0.02–0.8 mm

Note: Fine-textured, brown clay tempered with fine volcanic ash with abundant fine, angular glass fragments and lesser amounts of medium, subrounded pumice, clay pellets, and fine, subrounded quartz and alkali feldspar. Minor accessories include plagioclase, cristobalite, muscovite, augite, and rhyolite.

VIII. *Kwahe'e Black-on-white*

Sherd 12-11-8-1/431/03-44. Temper XVI

	No.	%	% Nonplastics
Matrix	66	66	–
Nonplastics	28	28	–
Voids	6	6	–
Quartz	9	9	32
Cristobalite	1	1	4
Micrographic quartz-feldspar	1	1	4
Plagioclase	1	1	4
Microcline	*	*	*
Sandstone	*	*	*
Clay pellets	16	16	57

* Present but not sampled.

Grain size
    Mean: 0.47 mm
    Range: 0.01–1.3 mm

Note: Fine-textured, dark gray clay tempered with fine to medium, subrounded quartz-feldspar sand, medium to coarse, subangular clay pellets, and argillaceous sandstone.

IX. *Chupadero Black-on-white*

Sherd 12-15-6-1,2/422/03-45. Temper XIIs

	No.	%	% Nonplastics
Matrix	61	61	–
Nonplastics	37	37	–
Voids	2	2	–
Quartz	12	12	32
Alkali feldspar	*	*	*
Sericite	2	2	5
Calcite	1	1	3
Opaques	3	3	8
Volcanic rock	1	3	1
Quartz-sericite schist	2	2	5
Quartzite	1	1	3
Phyllite	1	1	3
Sherd	14	14	38

* Present but not sampled.

Grain size
    Mean: 0.45 mm
    Range: 0.01–1.7 mm

Note: Fine-textured, tannish brown clay tempered with coarse to very coarse, angular, dark brown and black sherd with quartz-sericite schist temper.

X. *Early Glaze-on-red*

Sherd 12-C-2-3/510/03-46. Temper VIsa

	No.	%	% Nonplastics
Matrix	41	41	–
Nonplastics	48	48	–
Voids	11	11	–
Quartz	3	3	6
Plagioclase	3	3	6
Alkali feldspar	14	14	29
Muscovite	2	2	4
Pyroxene	3	3	6
Hornblende	1	1	2
Basaltic hornblende	1	1	2
Opaques	2	2	4
Basalt	9	9	19
Sherd	10	10	21

Grain size
   Mean: 0.22 mm
   Range: 0.02–1.4 mm

Note: Fine-textured, red clay with abundant fine to medium, angular quartz, alkali feldspar, and plagioclase with lesser amounts of pyroxene and brown amphibole. Tempered with medium, subangular, crystalline basalt and brown sherd.

Sherd 12-11-7-2/510/21-49. Temper VIsb

	No.	%	% Nonplastics
Matrix	52	52	–
Nonplastics	42	42	–
Voids	6	6	–
Quartz	12	12	29
Cristobalite	1	1	2
Perthite	1	1	2
Plagioclase	1	1	2
Augite	1	1	2
Hornblende	1	1	2
Opaques	2	2	5
Hematite	1	1	2
Basalt	4	4	10
Sherd	18	18	43

Grain size
   Mean: 0.43 mm
   Range: 0.03–1.7 mm

Note: Fine-textured, brownish red clay tempered with medium, subangular, crystalline basalt and brown, ash-tempered sherd.

139

Sherd 12-11-7-1/510/07-55. Temper VIsd

	No.	%	% Nonplastics
Matrix	49	49	–
Nonplastics	46	46	–
Voids	5	5	–
Quartz	1	1	2
Cristobalite	1	1	2
Plagioclase	4	4	9
Micrographic quartz-feldspar	1	1	2
Alkali feldspar	16	16	35
Muscovite/sericite	5	5	11
Biotite	*	*	*
Pyroxene	1	1	2
Hornblende	1	1	2
Opaques	1	1	2
Basalt	3	3	6
Sherd	12	12	26

* Present but not sampled.

Grain size
    Mean: 0.21 mm
    Range: 0.02–0.8 mm

Note: Fine-textured, silty, micaceous, brown clay tempered with crystalline basalt (fine plagioclase microlites with abundant intergranular opaque minerals, pyroxene, and basaltic hornblende; or very fine feldspar and opaque mineral crystallites in glassy matrix with phenocrysts of feldspar and opaque minerals) and medium, subrounded to subangular, red sherd.

Sherd 12-20-3/510/41-51. Temper VIsc

	No.	%	% Nonplastics
Matrix	49	49	–
Nonplastics	47	47	–
Voids	4	4	–
Quartz	2	2	4
Cristobalite	2	2	4
Plagioclase	4	4	9
Alkali feldspar	12	12	26
Olivine	1	1	2
Muscovite/sericite	3	3	6
Augite	1	1	2
Hornblende	1	1	2
Opaques	1	1	2
Hematite	2	2	4
Basalt	4	4	9
Augite latite/monzonite	3	3	6
Sherd	11	11	23

Grain size
    Mean: 0.23 mm
    Range: 0.01–1.2 mm

Note: Dense, red, volcanic clay with very fine to medium, angular alkali feldspar, plagioclase, and quartz, medium, subangular basalt, augite latite, and rare mica and fine pyroxene. Tempered with fine to medium, gray, red, and black sherd.

Sherd 12-11-7-1/510/42-52. Temper VIc

	No.	%	% Nonplastics
Matrix	50	50	–
Nonplastics	48	48	–
Voids	2	2	–
Quartz	15	15	31
Perthite	1	1	2
Plagioclase	7	7	15
Alkali feldspar	2	2	4
Augite	4	4	8
Hornblende	3	3	6
Calcite	1	1	2
Hematite	3	3	6
Basalt	4	4	8
Hornblende latite porphyry	8	8	17

Grain size
    Mean: 0.23 mm
    Range: 0.04–1.1 mm

Note: Fine-textured, brown clay tempered with medium, subrounded hornblende latite porphyry and crystalline basalt.

Sherd 12-C-2-3-4/510/45-54. Temper VIb

	No.	%	% Nonplastics
Matrix	38	38	–
Nonplastics	57	57	–
Voids	5	5	–
Quartz	10	10	17
Plagioclase	4	4	7
Muscovite	2	2	3
Biotite	1	1	2
Augite	3	3	5
Hornblende	1	1	2
Hematite	3	3	5
Granite	1	1	2
Basalt	8	8	14
Rhyolite	5	5	9
Pumice	19	19	33

Grain size
    Mean: 0.27 mm
    Range: 0.01–0.95 mm

Note: Fine-textured, brown clay tempered with medium to coarse, vesicular pumice, rhyolite (glass matrix with phenocrysts of quartz, tabular feldspar, fine muscovite/sericite, and, rarely, hornblende); and basalt (microlites of clear plagioclase, augite, basaltic hornblende, and black, opaque minerals).

141

Sherd 12-7-6-I/510/05-47. Temper IIIa

	No.	%	% Nonplastics
Matrix	37	37	–
Nonplastics	57	57	–
Voids	6	6	–
Quartz	15	15	26
Plagioclase	5	5	9
Micrographic quartz-feldspar	1	1	2
Alkali feldspar	2	2	3.5
Muscovite	2	2	3.5
Augite	6	6	10
Hornblende	1	1	2
Hematite	3	3	5
Latite/monzonite	20	20	35
Quartzite	1	1	2
Clay pellets	1	1	2

Grain size
    Mean: 0.26 mm
    Range: 0.03–0.8 mm

Note: Silty, red clay tempered with fine to medium fragments of subangular to angular augite monzonite with minor augite, hematite, muscovite, and hornblende.

Sherd 12-C-2-3/510/26-48. Temper IIIa

	No.	%	% Nonplastics
Matrix	58	58	–
Nonplastics	38	38	–
Voids	4	4	–
Quartz	7	7	18
Plagioclase	5	5	13
Alkali feldspar	1	1	3
Glass shards	1	1	3
Augite	3	3	8
Hornblende	1	1	3
Hematite	5	5	13
Latite/monzonite	14	14	37
Sherd	1	1	3

Grain size
    Mean: 0.23 mm
    Range: 0.03–1 mm

Note: Dense, red clay tempered with medium, angular augite monzonite.

Sherd 12-9-6-2/510/09-50. Temper IXb

	No.	%	% Nonplastics
Matrix	39	39	–
Nonplastics	42	42	–
Voids	19	19	–
Quartz	28	28	67
Plagioclase	5	5	12
Alkali feldspar	3	3	7
Microcline	1	1	2

Sherd 12-9-6-2/510/09-50 (*continued*)

	No.	%	% Nonplastics
Muscovite	2	2	5
Biotite	1	1	2
Clay pellets	2	2	5

Grain size
 Mean: 0.21 mm
 Range: 0.02–2 mm

Note: Dense, medium-textured, black clay tempered with fine to medium, subrounded, quartz-feldspar sand with mica.

Sherd 12-9-10-IIN/510/28-53. Temper XIIIs

	No.	%	% Nonplastics
Matrix	45	45	–
Nonplastics	50	50	–
Voids	5	5	–
Quartz	14	14	28
Perthite	2	2	4
Plagioclase	3	3	6
Alkali feldspar	3	3	6
Muscovite	7	7	14
Augite	5	5	10
Hornblende	2	2	4
Opaques	1	1	2
Granite	1	1	2
Quartzite	1	1	2
Sherd	11	11	22

Grain size
 Mean: 0.29 mm
 Range: 0.02–2.1 mm

Note: Dense, black, metamorphic clay tempered with gray, pumiceous, ash-tempered sherd.

XI. Agua Fria Glaze-on-red

Sherd 12-C-2-2/511/03-56. Temper VIa

	No.	%	% Nonplastics
Matrix	51	51	–
Nonplastics	46	46	–
Voids	3	3	–
Quartz	7	7	15
Plagioclase	6	6	13
Alkali feldspar	3	3	7
Augite	6	6	13
Basaltic hornblende	2	2	4
Opaques	5	5	11
Basalt	17	17	37

Grain size
 Mean: 0.19 mm
 Range: 0.01–0.95 mm

Note: Dense, red, silty clay tempered with crystalline basalt (very fine microlites of tabular plagioclase with intergranular opaque minerals, augite, and basaltic hornblende).

143

Sherd 12-7-6-1/511/05-57. Temper IIIb

	No.	%	% Nonplastics
Matrix	52	52	–
Nonplastics	40	40	–
Voids	8	8	–
Quartz	3	3	7.5
Plagioclase	1	1	2.5
Alkali feldspar	1	1	2.5
Augite	1	1	2.5
Hornblende	2	2	5
Granite	1	1	2.5
Hornblende latite porphyry	31	31	77.5

Grain size
    Mean: 0.36 mm
    Range: 0.03–1.2 mm

Note: Dense, slightly silty, red clay tempered with medium to coarse, subangular, crushed hornblende latite porphyry (feldspar matrix with phenocrysts of zoned plagioclase, alkali feldspar, hornblende, euhedral augite, and opaque minerals).

Sherd 12-C-2-2/511/26-58. Temper IIIsa

	No.	%	% Nonplastics
Matrix	50	50	–
Nonplastics	45	45	–
Voids	5	5	–
Quartz	12	12	27
Myrmekite	1	1	2
Alkali feldspar	1	1	2
Muscovite	2	2	4.5
Augite	3	3	7
Hornblende	1	1	2
Opaques	2	2	4.5
Hornblende latite porphyry	19	19	42
Sherd	4	4	9

Grain size
    Mean: 0.25 mm
    Range: 0.04–0.75 mm

Note: Dense, slightly silty, red clay tempered with medium, subangular hornblende latite (fine, feldspathic ground with phenocrysts of tabular, zoned plagioclase, alkali feldspar, hornblende [with heavy reaction rims], and euhedral, zoned augite), and medium, micaceous, black sherd.

XII. Los Padillas Glaze Polychrome

Sherd 12-15a-7-1/515/03-59. Temper XVs

	No.	%	% Nonplastics
Matrix	49	49	–
Nonplastics	47	47	–
Voids	4	4	–
Quartz	5	5	11
Alkali feldspar	1	1	2
Muscovite	1	1	2
Opaques	6	6	13
Sherd	34	34	72

Sherd 12-15a-7-1/515/03-59 (*continued*)

	No.	%	% Nonplastics

Grain size
 Mean: 0.41 mm
 Range: 0.02–1.8 mm

Note: Dense, gray paste with red margins tempered with medium to very coarse, dark brown to gray, sherd-tempered sherd.

Sherd 12-16-30-1/516/03-65. Temper XIa

	No.	%	% Nonplastics
Matrix	49	49	–
Nonplastics	46	46	–
Voids	5	5	–
Quartz	12	12	26
Plagioclase	3	3	7
Muscovite	5	5	11
Augite	1	1	2
Hornblende	1	1	2
Opaques	1	1	2
Basalt	1	1	2
Quartz-mica schist	2	2	4
Argillite	4	4	9
Quartzite	4	4	9
Gneiss	*	*	*
Sherd	12	12	26

* Present but not sampled.

Grain size
 Mean: 0.32 mm
 Range: 0.01–1.5 mm

Note: Medium-textured, silty, dark brown, metamorphic clay tempered with medium to coarse, subangular, brown, shist-tempered sherd.

Sherd 12-11-7-2/516-39-66. Temper XIb

	No.	%	% Nonplastics
Matrix	30	30	–
Nonplastics	66	66	–
Voids	4	4	–
Quartz	26	26	39
Plagioclase	2	2	4
Muscovite	4	4	6
Biotite	3	3	3
Opaques	1	1	2
Argillite	2	2	3
Quartz-mica schist	5	5	8
Quartzite	2	2	3
Sherd	21	21	32

Grain size
 Mean: 0.18 mm
 Range: 0.02–0.95 mm

Note: Fine-textured, silty, metamorphic, brown clay with red margins tempered with medium, subangular, reddish brown and black, schist-tempered sherd.

XIII. *Sanchez Glaze-on-red*

Sherd 12-C-2-2/512/05-60. Temper IIIc

	No.	%	% Nonplastics
Matrix	42	42	–
Nonplastics	57	57	–
Voids	1	1	–
Quartz	24	24	42
Cristobalite	1	1	2
Plagioclase	5	5	9
Microcline	1	1	2
Augite	2	2	3.5
Opaques	2	2	3.5
Granite	1	1	2
Hornblende latite porphyry	20	20	35
Quartzite	1	1	2

Grain size
    Mean: 0.25 mm
    Range: 0.01–0.9 mm

Note: Fine-textured, silty, red clay tempered with hornblende latite porphyry and medium, subrounded, quartz-feldspar sand.

XIV. *Largo Glaze-on-red*

Sherd 12-C-2-2/513/03-61. Temper XIIIs

	No.	%	% Nonplastics
Matrix	50	50	–
Nonplastics	45	45	–
Voids	5	5	–
Quartz	15	15	33
Cristobalite	1	1	2
Plagioclase	3	3	7
Microcline	1	1	2
Sericite	2	2	4
Muscovite	4	4	9
Biotite	2	2	4
Opaques	1	1	2
Granite	3	3	7
Rhyolite	3	3	7
Argillite	*	*	*
Quartzite	2	2	4
Sherd	8	8	18

* Present but not sampled.

Grain size
    Mean: 0.27 mm
    Range: 0.01–1.1 mm

Note: Dense, black clay with red margins tempered with medium, subangular, crushed, brown sherd and angular, lithic sand.

Sherd 12-C-2-2/513/05-62. Temper IIIsa

	No.	%	% Nonplastics
Matrix	40	40	–
Nonplastics	49	49	–
Voids	11	11	–
Quartz	2	2	4
Perthite	1	1	2
Plagioclase	5	5	10
Sericite/muscovite	4	4	8
Biotite	2	2	4
Augite	4	4	8
Hornblende	5	5	10
Opaques	3	3	6
Granite	1	1	2
Quartzite	1	1	2
Hornblende latite porphyry	16	16	33
Sherd	5	5	10

Grain size
  Mean: 0.25 mm
  Range: 0.04–0.65 mm

Note: Dense, brownish red clay tempered with medium, subangular hornblende latite porphyry (fine, feldspathic to glassy ground with phenocrysts of tabular, zoned plagioclase, alkali feldspar, altered hornblende, opaque minerals, and fine, angular augite) and dense, black, micaceous sherd.

Sherd 12-16-20-1/513/26-63. Temper VIIsa

	No.	%	% Nonplastics
Matrix	45	45	–
Nonplastics	50	50	–
Voids	5	5	–
Alkali feldspar	12	12	24
Cristobalite	2	2	4
Plagioclase	2	2	4
Glass	1	1	2
Muscovite	2	2	4
Hornblende	2	2	4
Opaques	3	3	6
Hematite	1	1	2
Latite	4	4	8
Sherd	21	21	42

Grain size
  Mean: 0.25 mm
  Range: 0.02–0.95 mm

Note: Fine-textured, silty, grayish brown clay tempered with latite (fine, plagioclase microlites and crystallites in feldspathic ground with tabular feldspar and opaque mineral phenocrysts) and medium, subrounded to subangular, dense, gray sherd.

Sherd 12-9-6-III/513/23-64. Temper VIIsa

	No.	%	% Nonplastics
Matrix	55	55	–
Nonplastics	43	43	–
Voids	2	2	–
Quartz	4	4	9
Cristobalite	1	1	2
Plagioclase	5	5	12
Alkali feldspar	12	12	28
Microcline	1	1	2
Muscovite	2	2	5
Biotite	1	1	2
Augite	2	2	5
Hornblende	2	2	5
Opaques	2	2	5
Hematite	1	1	2
Basalt	2	2	5
Latite	1	1	2
Sherd	7	7	16

Grain size
    Mean: 0.18 mm
    Range: 0.03–1.0 mm

Note: Dense, gray, silty clay with fine, volcanic sand tempered with medium, subrounded, gray and black sherd.

XV. San Clemente Glaze Polychrome

Sherd 12-16-1-6/517/03-67. Temper IIIsc

	No.	%	% Nonplastics
Matrix	49	49	–
Nonplastics	49	49	–
Voids	2	2	–
Quartz	13	13	27
Weathered plagioclase	7	7	14
Alkali feldspar	1	1	2
Augite	3	3	6
Hornblende	1	1	2
Opaques	3	3	6
Clay pellets	1	1	2
Hornblende latite porphyry	19	19	39
Quartzite	1	1	2

Grain size
    Mean: 0.37 mm
    Range: 0.01–1.6 mm

Note: Fine-textured, brown, silty clay tempered with medium, subangular, highly weathered hornblende latite porphyry (fine, feldspathic matrix with phenocrysts of tabular, zoned plagioclase, alkali feldspar, altered hornblende, muscovite, and opaque minerals).

Sherd 12-C-2-1/517/05-68. Temper IIIb

	No.	%	% Nonplastics
Matrix	44	44	–
Nonplastics	55	55	–
Voids	1	1	–
Quartz	10	10	18
Plagioclase	6	6	11
Alkali feldspar	3	3	5
Biotite	1	1	2
Augite	3	3	5
Hornblende	5	5	9
Opaques	2	2	4
Granite	1	1	2
Hornblende latite porphyry	24	24	44

Grain size
  Mean: 0.33 mm
  Range: 0.02–1.5 mm

Note: Dense, silty, red clay tempered with medium, angular hornblende latite porphyry (glassy to feldspathic matrix with phenocrysts of tabular, zoned plagioclase, alkali feldspar, euhedral to subhedral hornblende, euhedral augite, and opaque minerals).

Sherd 12-9-6-2/517/26-69. Temper IIIb

	No.	%	% Nonplastics
Matrix	42	42	–
Nonplastics	52	52	–
Voids	6	6	–
Quartz	8	8	15
Plagioclase	6	6	11.5
Alkali feldspar	6	6	11.5
Pyroxene	7	7	13
Hornblende	4	4	8
Opaques	1	1	2
Hornblende latite porphyry	19	19	37
Sherd	1	1	2

Grain size
  Mean: 0.24 mm
  Range: 0.01–0.95 mm

Note: Fine, silty, red clay tempered with medium, subangular hornblende latite (porphyritic with feldspathic ground and phenocrysts of tabular, zoned plagioclase, alkali feldspar, hornblende, augite, and opaque minerals).

XVI. Cieneguilla Glaze-on-yellow

Sherd 12-7-6-1/520/03-70. Temper VIsc

	No.	%	% Nonplastics
Matrix	46	46	–
Nonplastics	45	45	–
Voids	9	9	–
Quartz	1	1	2
Cristobalite	1	1	2
Plagioclase	7	7	16
Alkali feldspar	14	14	31

(Continued on next page)

149

Sherd 12-7-6-1/520/03-70 (*continued*)

	No.	%	% Nonplastics
Muscovite	1	1	2
Biotite	1	1	2
Augite	2	2	4
Hornblende	2	2	4
Opaques	1	1	2
Basalt	5	5	11
Quartzite	1	1	2
Sherd	9	9	20

Grain size
    Mean: 0.16 mm
    Range: 0.05–0.4 mm

Note: Dense, tannish brown, silty clay with fine, angular fragments of crystalline basalt tempered with coarse, gray and black sherd.

Sherd 12-7-6-III/520/05-71. Temper IIIa

	No.	%	% Nonplastics
Matrix	52	52	–
Nonplastics	45	45	–
Voids	3	3	–
Quartz	8	8	18
Perthite	2	2	4
Plagioclase	8	8	18
Alkali feldspar	2	2	4
Augite	8	8	18
Opaques	1	1	2
Augite latite/monzonite	16	16	36

Grain size
    Mean: 0.32 mm
    Range: 0.03–1.1 mm

Note: Dense, slightly silty, red clay tempered with medium to coarse, subangular to angular augite latite/monzonite (holocrystalline with microlites of weathered, zoned plagioclase, alkali feldspar, and intergranular augite and opaques).

Sherd 12-7-6-III/521/05-75. Temper IIIa

	No.	%	% Nonplastics
Matrix	21	42	–
Nonplastics	3	6	–
Voids	26	52	–
Quartz	5	10	19
Plagioclase	6	12	23
Microcline	2	4	8
Muscovite	1	2	4
Augite	4	8	15
Granite	1	2	4
Augite latite/monzonite	7	14	27

Grain size
    Mean: 0.31 mm
    Range: 0.03–1.7 mm

Note: Dense, slightly silty, black clay with red margins tempered with medium, angular augite latite/monzonite (holocrystalline with laths of weathered, zoned, plagioclase, alkali feldspar, augite, and opaques).

Sherd 12-C-2-2/520/41-73. Temper IIId

	No.	%	% Nonplastics
Matrix	47	47	–
Nonplastics	46	46	–
Voids	7	7	–
Quartz	14	14	31
Cristobalite	1	1	2
Plagioclase	2	2	4
Alkali feldspar	1	1	2
Muscovite	1	1	2
Augite	5	5	11
Hypersthene	1	1	2
Opaques	1	1	2
Augite latite/monzonite	17	17	37
Quartzite	1	1	2
Calcareous sandstone	2	2	4

Grain size
    Mean: 0.33 mm
    Range: 0.02–1.1 mm

Note: Fine-textured, slightly silty, black clay with red margins tempered with medium, subangular to angular augite latite/monzonite (porphyrytic with phenocrysts of plagioclase, alkali feldspar, hypersthene, and basaltic hornblende in fine-textured ground with microlites of feldspar and intergranular pyroxene).

Sherd 12-16-30-1/521/26-76. Temper IIIa

	No.	%	% Nonplastics
Matrix	40	40	–
Nonplastics	57	57	–
Voids	3	3	–
Quartz	3	3	5
Perthite	2	2	4
Plagioclase	8	8	14
Alkali feldspar	3	3	5
Glass	2	2	4
Augite	7	7	12
Calcite	3	3	5
Opaques	2	2	4
Augite latite/monzonite	26	26	45
Clay pellets	1	1	2

Grain size
    Mean: 0.37 mm
    Range: 0.04–1.4 mm

Note: Fine-textured, slightly silty, brownish red clay tempered with medium, angular augite latite/monzonite.

151

Sherd 12-9-3N/520/26-72. Temper IIIsb

	No.	%	% Nonplastics
Matrix	55	55	–
Nonplastics	43	43	–
Voids	2	2	–
Quartz	11	11	26
Cristobalite	1	1	2
Plagioclase	9	9	21
Alkali feldspar	2	2	5
Microcline	*	*	*
Augite	*	*	*
Opaques	1	1	2
Granite	*	*	*
Augite latite/monzonite	14	14	33
Sherd	5	5	12

* Present but not sampled.

Grain size
    Mean: 0.33 mm
    Range: 0.02–1.3 mm

Note: Fine-textured, brownish red clay sparsely tempered with medium, angular augite latite/monzonite (laths of zoned, weathered plagioclase, alkali feldspar, and subhedral augite phenocrysts in glassy matrix) and medium, subangular, latite-tempered sherd.

Sherd 12-9-10-2N/521/03-74. Temper IIIsc

	No.	%	% Nonplastics
Matrix	47	47	–
Nonplastics	50	50	–
Voids	3	3	–
Quartz	16	16	32
Plagioclase	2	2	4
Alkali feldspar	2	2	4
Sericite/muscovite	1	1	2
Augite	1	1	2
Hypersthene	1	1	2
Hornblende	2	2	4
Opaques	1	1	2
Pumice	1	1	2
Hornblende latite	23	23	46

Grain size
    Mean: 0.26 mm
    Range: 0.01–0.95 mm

Note: Dense, silty, grayish brown clay tempered with medium, subangular, weathered hornblende latite porphyry (feldspathic to glassy ground with phenocrysts of tabular, weathered, zoned plagioclase and hornblende with heavy reaction rims).

XVII. White Mountain Red Ware

Sherd 12-C-2-3/620/03-77. Temper XIa

	No.	%	% Nonplastics
Matrix	18	36	–
Nonplastics	27	54	–
Voids	5	10	–
Quartz	5	10	19
Plagioclase	1	2	4
Muscovite	5	10	19
Basalt	1	2	4
Quartz-mica schist	1	2	4
Argillite	1	2	4
Quartzite	*	*	*
Sherd	13	26	48

* Present but not sampled.

Grain size
    Mean: 0.30 mm
    Range: 0.02–0.95 mm

Note: Fine-textured, slightly silty, brown metamorphic clay tempered with medium to coarse, subangular, dark brown, schist-tempered sherd.

Sherd 12-C-2-2/620/39-78. Temper XIb

	No.	%	% Nonplastics
Matrix	49	49	–
Nonplastics	51	51	–
Voids	0	0	–
Quartz	11	11	22
Plagioclase	2	2	4
Alkali feldspar	1	1	2
Muscovite	1	1	2
Augite	1	1	2
Opaques	1	1	2
Basalt	2	2	4
Argillite	1	1	2
Quartz-mica schist	2	2	4
Quartzite	1	1	2
Sherd	28	28	55

Grain size
    Mean: 0.41 mm
    Range: 0.02–2 mm

Note: Fine-textured, metamorphic, brown clay with red margins tempered with medium to coarse, subangular, red and gray, schist-tempered sherd.

153

XVIII. St. Johns Polychrome

Sherd 12-9-7-5/621/03-79. Temper XIb

	No.	%	% Nonplastics
Matrix	40	40	–
Nonplastics	59	59	–
Voids	1	1	–
Quartz	18	18	30.5
Plagioclase	3	3	5
Alkali feldspar	3	3	5
Muscovite	5	5	8
Biotite	1	1	2
Augite	1	1	2
Hornblende	1	1	2
Quartz-mica schist	3	3	5
Quartzite	2	2	3
Sherd	22	22	37.5

Grain size
    Mean: 0.22 mm
    Range: 0.02–1 mm

Note: Fine-textured, silty, metamorphic, brown clay tempered with medium to coarse, subangular, red and black, schist-tempered sherd.

XIX. Heshotauthla Polychrome

Sherd 12-16-20-4/622/33-80. Temper IVa

	No.	%	% Nonplastics
Matrix	47	47	–
Nonplastics	51	51	–
Voids	2	2	–
Quartz	8	8	16
Perthite	2	2	4
Plagioclase	3	3	6
Muscovite	4	4	8
Biotite	1	1	2
Augite	1	1	2
Rhyolite	17	17	33
Basalt	2	2	4
Argillite	*	*	*
Quartzite	1	1	2
Sherd	12	12	23

* Present but not sampled.

Grain size
    Mean: 0.39 mm
    Range: 0.02–1.1 mm

Note: Dense, reddish brown, silty clay tempered with medium, angular rhyolite (glassy matrix with angular quartz phenocrysts, tabular alkali feldspar, and very fine sericite mica) and dense red and silty brown sherd.

Sherd 12-16-13-3/631/03-81. Temper XIa

	No.	%	% Nonplastics
Matrix	94	47	–
Nonplastics	105	52.5	–
Voids	1	0.5	–
Quartz	17	8.5	16
Cristobalite	1	0.5	1
Plagioclase	9	4.5	9
Microcline	2	1	2
Muscovite	2	1	2
Pyroxene	1	0.5	1
Opaques	1	0.5	1
Rhyolite	10	5	9
Quartz-mica schist	10	5	9
Quartzite	9	4.5	9
Phyllite	1	0.5	1
Argillite	1	0.5	1
Sherd	41	20.5	39

Grain size
    Mean: 0.35 mm
    Range: 0.02–1.5 mm

Note: Dense, gray, silty clay tempered with medium to coarse, subangular, gray and black, schist-tempered sherd.

XX. *Tesuque Gray*

Sherd 12-5-4-7/C1-82. Temper XIVa

	No.	%	% Nonplastics
Matrix	35	35	–
Nonplastics	62	62	–
Voids	3	3	–
Quartz	23	23	37
Plagioclase	1	1	2
Muscovite	8	8	13
Biotite	6	6	10
Pyroxene	1	1	2
Opaques	3	3	5
Granite	9	9	14
Quartz-mica schist	3	3	5
Quartzite	3	3	5
Gneiss	5	5	8

Grain size
    Mean: 0.85 mm
    Range: 0.02–3 mm

Note: Coarse-textured, primary clay with fine to medium, subangular quartz, feldspar, mica, and very coarse, subangular granite, quartz-mica schist, quartzite, and gneiss.

Sherd 12-5-6-1,2/C2-83. Temper XIVb

	No.	%	% Nonplastics
Matrix	30	30	–
Nonplastics	64	64	–
Voids	6	6	–
Quartz	24	24	38
Micrographic quartz-feldspar	2	2	3
Muscovite	16	16	25
Biotite	8	8	12
Granite	12	12	19
Quartzite	*	*	*
Gneiss	2	2	3

* Present but not sampled.

Grain size
    Mean: 1.1 mm
    Range: 0.02–5.1 mm

Note: Coarse-textured, dense, brown, primary clay with abundant medium to very coarse, subrounded to subangular quartz, feldspar, platy muscovite, biotite, granite, quartzite, and gneiss.

Appendix C

Summary of X-Ray Fluorescence Analysis

Bart Olinger

Approximately 30 sherds from each decorated ceramic type and 60 culinary sherds from Arroyo Hondo Pueblo (LA 12) were submitted for x-ray fluorescence analysis (XRF). A total of 270 sherds was analyzed. Thirteen archaeological clay samples found during excavations, along with 11 geological clay and lithic samples collected in the vicinity of the site, also were examined. Each lithic and sherd sample was ground along one edge to expose a clean, flat surface. This technique was used because it was relatively nondestructive to the sample. Since no attempt was made to standardize sample size, only relative rather than absolute quantities were obtained.

Each sample was irradiated with monochromatic x-rays from a ^{109}Cd source that have an energy of 22 kev. The constituent chemical elements in each sample excited by the x-rays emitted secondary x-rays, whose energies are characteristic of their sources and whose intensities are proportional to the elements' concentrations.

The relative frequency of x-ray counts associated with eight different elements are recorded in table C. X-ray counts were recorded in windows bracketing the characteristic energies for each element. The largest numbers of detected x-rays for each sample were associated with iron (Fe), strontium (Sr), and zirconium (Zr). The raw counts for each of the three elements were divided by their sum to yield the percentages used to define the characteristic x-ray signature for each sample recorded on the scatter plots in chapter 3. The x-ray counts associated with the remaining five elements were also divided by the same sum (Fe + Sr + Zr), thus preserving their relative quantities. The relative counts for these elements, as determined by the ratio of Fe, Sr, and Zr counts, were used to enhance distinctions between samples when necessary.

KEY TO TABLE

Pottery Type	Code
Galisteo B/W	GAL
Galisteo B/W, *var. Kendi*	KEN
Galisteo B/W, *var. Arroyo Hondo*	AH
Rowe B/W, *var. Poge*	POG
Santa Fe B/W	SFE
Wiyo B/W	WYO
Santa Fe, *var. Pindi*	PDI
Glaze A Red	GZR
Glaze A Yellow	GZY
Tesuque Gray	CUL
Clay	CLY
Lithic sample	MIN

Occupations	Code
Component I	C1
Component II	C2

Temper Category	Code
Fine volcanic ash	FA
Silty clay with ash	SA
Quartz-feldspar sand	QS
Latite	LA
Lithic sand	LI
Very coarse granite/gneiss	GN
Schist-tempered sherd	ST
Coarse pumiceous ash	PA
Silty clay	SC
Sherd	SH
Latite and sherd	LS
Lithic sand and sherd	LH
Very coarse mica schist	MS
Basalt	BA
Basalt and sherd	BS

APPENDIX C

TABLE C
Relative frequency of x-ray counts for eight elements in pottery samples from Arroyo Hondo Pueblo and a sample of local clay and lithic sources.

Sherd	Type	Fe	Zr	Sr	Rb	Nb	Ca	Y	Pb	Occupation/Temper
LA12-00001	SFE	36.5	51.1	12.5	08.4	06.6	02.2	05.7	01.3	C1/SA
LA12-00002	SFE	47.4	31.5	21.1	08.2	08.6	09.3	04.9	01.1	C1/SC
LA12-00003	SFE	57.6	24.3	18.0	08.8	11.6	11.3	04.6	01.7	C1/QS
LA12-00004	SFE	50.7	24.6	14.7	06.3	09.3	04.8	05.1	01.5	C1/SA
LA12-00005	SFE	63.5	26.7	09.8	09.0	08.9	03.4	05.8	02.4	C1/SA
LA12-00006	SFE	54.2	30.7	15.1	08.1	05.4	02.7	04.8	00.7	C1/SC
LA12-00007	SFE	40.8	43.3	15.9	06.3	06.0	03.0	03.8	01.2	C1/SC
LA12-00008	SFE	51.1	33.8	15.1	07.0	06.9	03.2	05.0	01.0	C1/SA
LA12-00009	SFE	53.6	33.6	12.8	08.8	09.9	03.1	07.6	01.7	C1/QS
LA12-00010	SFE	49.2	36.2	14.6	07.7	05.3	05.1	05.2	02.0	C1/SC
LA12-00011	SFE	55.7	31.8	12.5	09.4	05.8	03.7	04.3	01.8	C1/SC
LA12-00012	SFE	55.5	25.2	19.3	09.2	05.4	04.4	04.1	01.7	C1/SC
LA12-00013	SFE	53.3	24.8	22.0	07.5	06.3	10.5	04.5	02.3	C1/SC
LA12-00014	SFE	53.1	31.3	15.6	07.3	06.5	04.3	06.6	01.0	C1/SC
LA12-00015	SFE	56.5	27.5	16.1	06.8	03.9	03.9	04.7	00.5	C1/SC
LA12-00016	SFE	59.2	26.9	14.0	10.7	05.6	02.7	04.3	01.3	C1/SC
LA12-00017	SFE	51.6	32.8	15.6	10.0	06.7	02.8	06.6	01.1	C1/QS
LA12-00018	SFE	51.9	33.5	14.6	07.6	06.0	02.9	04.0	01.4	C1/SC
LA12-00019	GZY	38.6	27.2	34.2	04.8	04.4	03.4	03.1	00.9	C1/LS
LA12-00020	GAL	45.2	35.8	19.0	05.6	07.4	03.9	04.4	00.8	C1/SH
LA12-00021	GAL	51.7	30.0	18.3	07.9	06.7	04.2	05.5	01.4	C1/SH
LA12-00022	GAL	58.7	24.5	16.8	08.1	05.1	02.9	04.9	00.6	C1/SH
LA12-00023	AH	55.1	31.8	13.1	04.8	07.1	03.6	04.6	00.7	C1/GN
LA12-00024	GAL	35.4	47.0	17.7	12.1	08.7	03.1	09.3	02.7	C1/SH
LA12-00025	GAL	48.9	31.1	20.0	07.0	06.6	02.7	03.7	01.7	C1/SH
LA12-00026	GAL	34.4	50.9	14.6	10.5	16.8	05.3	08.8	01.8	C1/SH
LA12-00027	GAL	42.8	39.0	18.1	11.5	11.6	03.8	07.5	01.2	C1/SH
LA12-00028	AH	57.8	29.0	13.2	09.3	10.2	05.0	07.0	00.8	C1/GN
LA12-00029	KEN	51.4	29.4	19.2	07.5	07.7	05.1	04.6	00.9	C1/LA
LA12-00030	KEN	59.2	21.6	19.2	08.2	07.2	03.5	03.8	01.2	C1/LA
LA12-00031	GAL	41.4	40.5	18.1	09.9	07.3	04.0	06.4	01.3	C1/SH
LA12-00032	GAL	49.2	35.2	15.6	09.8	09.7	02.6	04.6	01.7	C1/SH
LA12-00033	GAL	36.0	47.0	17.0	10.8	08.6	03.4	05.1	00.9	C1/SH
LA12-00034	AH	73.6	19.9	06.5	14.8	07.0	02.8	07.5	01.5	C1/GN
LA12-00035	GAL	46.4	34.1	19.4	07.5	05.4	02.3	06.5	02.7	C1/SH
LA12-00036	GAL	35.7	46.6	17.7	09.8	10.5	03.7	07.7	01.7	C1/SH
LA12-00037	PDI	53.7	34.5	11.8	11.9	10.6	03.7	08.5	02.2	C1/PA
LA12-00038	PDI	49.7	39.6	10.7	12.8	18.7	04.0	09.6	01.2	C1/PA
LA12-00039	PDI	53.7	33.3	13.0	09.8	14.9	03.7	06.8	01.2	C1/PA
LA12-00040	PDI	58.9	28.9	12.2	11.3	12.0	04.1	07.1	01.4	C1/PA
LA12-00041	PDI	59.5	32.0	08.5	12.2	13.5	04.3	07.4	01.4	C1/PA
LA12-00042	PDI	53.2	31.7	15.1	08.3	08.0	05.0	06.8	01.8	C1/PA
LA12-00043	PDI	57.3	31.0	11.7	11.0	11.2	04.5	06.0	01.5	C1/PA
LA12-00044	PDI	49.7	40.5	09.8	11.4	16.9	03.2	12.3	02.0	C1/PA
LA12-00045	PDI	55.2	33.4	11.4	11.2	12.3	04.4	07.2	01.2	C1/PA
LA12-00046	PDI	56.1	33.1	10.8	11.3	10.2	03.4	06.9	01.1	C1/PA
LA12-00047	PDI	50.4	33.5	16.1	11.0	11.4	03.4	06.4	01.3	C1/PA
LA12-00048	PDI	52.2	38.9	08.8	11.9	15.0	02.7	10.9	01.7	C1/PA
LA12-00049	PDI	60.6	31.2	08.3	10.8	13.1	03.1	07.3	01.0	C1/PA

TABLE C (*continued*)

Sherd	Type	Fe	Zr	Sr	Rb	Nb	Ca	Y	Pb	Occupation/Temper
LA12-00050	PDI	56.8	29.6	13.6	09.8	11.2	03.3	05.9	01.7	C1/PA
LA12-00051	PDI	53.6	30.2	16.2	08.8	08.8	03.0	07.7	02.2	C1/PA
LA12-00052	POG	54.3	25.9	19.9	07.6	07.7	03.2	05.6	00.8	C1/LH
LA12-00053	POG	57.4	23.3	19.3	06.2	04.6	02.4	03.4	00.7	C1/LH
LA12-00054	POG	49.9	30.0	20.1	09.3	08.0	04.4	05.9	00.9	C1/LH
LA12-00055	POG	58.0	23.0	18.9	05.8	07.0	03.9	05.2	01.5	C1/LH
LA12-00056	POG	53.0	24.9	22.1	05.2	04.1	02.9	04.6	01.3	C1/LH
LA12-00057	POG	65.0	24.6	10.4	06.6	07.8	02.8	04.6	00.8	C1/LH
LA12-00058	POG	56.6	25.5	17.9	05.9	06.5	03.3	04.8	01.0	C1/LH
LA12-00059	POG	48.7	36.7	14.6	08.0	07.0	03.1	03.7	01.6	C1/LI
LA12-00060	POG	62.4	22.3	15.3	06.9	06.7	03.1	03.7	01.0	C1/LH
LA12-00061	POG	62.6	23.7	13.7	05.6	06.0	03.7	05.4	01.0	C1/LH
LA12-00062	POG	53.2	31.3	15.6	07.3	07.1	04.0	05.7	00.5	C1/LI
LA12-00063	POG	50.4	36.2	13.4	04.7	06.1	02.0	03.4	00.6	C1/LI
LA12-00064	POG	55.8	26.9	17.3	07.8	08.0	04.5	06.2	01.3	C1/LI
LA12-00065	POG	56.8	26.1	17.1	06.5	05.7	03.8	04.2	00.9	C1/LI
LA12-00066	POG	61.3	26.3	12.5	07.1	07.4	03.8	05.5	01.0	C1/LH
LA12-00067	POG	63.1	24.9	12.1	08.8	06.9	02.9	03.6	00.8	C1/LH
LA12-00068	POG	57.6	24.6	17.8	06.4	05.8	03.1	04.5	01.4	C1/LH
LA12-00069	WYO	59.9	26.6	13.5	13.0	07.7	04.3	05.9	01.2	C1/FA
LA12-00070	WYO	44.2	42.3	13.4	16.1	19.8	02.3	13.2	00.4	C1/FA
LA12-00071	WYO	48.8	32.0	19.1	12.7	07.3	03.0	06.5	00.8	C1/FA
LA12-00072	WYO	38.4	46.1	15.5	06.6	06.0	02.2	04.8	00.6	C1/FA
LA12-00073	WYO	55.9	25.7	18.4	12.7	05.7	01.6	04.2	01.4	C1/FA
LA12-00074	WYO	44.9	34.4	20.6	09.5	07.1	04.4	04.7	02.8	C1/FA
LA12-00075	WYO	48.7	24.0	27.2	11.5	05.6	02.9	02.8	02.0	C1/FA
LA12-00076	WYO	59.6	26.5	13.8	07.7	05.9	08.8	03.6	02.4	C1/PA
LA12-00077	WYO	48.4	42.0	09.6	09.7	09.2	03.5	07.0	01.2	C1/FA
LA12-00078	PDI	58.0	29.9	12.1	10.2	10.4	03.5	06.6	01.2	C1/PA
LA12-00079	WYO	61.2	25.5	13.4	14.4	10.1	04.0	06.3	02.3	C1/FA
LA12-00080	WYO	45.6	31.5	22.9	10.9	08.5	02.9	04.4	01.1	C1/FA
LA12-00081	WYO	54.3	37.1	08.6	08.5	07.4	02.3	07.1	01.2	C1/FA
LA12-00082	WYO	45.2	33.5	21.3	07.6	06.4	02.5	04.8	00.8	C1/FA
LA12-00083	WYO	50.9	42.6	06.5	18.6	22.8	02.9	15.3	01.2	C1/PA
LA12-00084	WYO	39.6	39.6	20.9	13.0	19.7	04.8	09.8	00.5	C1/FA
LA12-00085	GZR	56.4	18.0	25.6	04.4	03.1	02.7	05.6	14.2	C1/LA
LA12-00086	GZR	31.9	30.9	37.2	06.1	05.6	01.7	04.5	00.5	C1/LS
LA12-00087	GZR	44.3	24.2	31.5	04.2	04.9	02.6	05.4	08.8	C1/LS
LA12-00088	GZR	50.8	31.7	17.5	06.1	06.2	04.7	04.8	02.4	C1/BS
LA12-00089	GZR	46.0	19.4	34.6	03.6	02.1	02.5	06.0	25.3	C1/LA
LA12-00090	GZR	54.4	25.7	19.9	05.0	06.4	04.1	03.1	01.0	C1/BS
LA12-00091	GZR	50.7	26.9	22.4	07.8	08.3	04.0	04.6	02.2	C1/BS
LA12-00092	GZR	43.1	29.7	27.2	04.1	04.1	03.2	05.2	04.3	C1/BS
LA12-00093	GZR	46.1	38.4	15.5	07.2	06.5	03.2	08.4	17.1	C1/ST
LA12-00094	GZR	53.4	20.3	26.2	05.1	05.2	04.6	04.1	01.1	C1/LA
LA12-00095	GZR	56.0	25.0	19.1	07.9	05.7	02.7	05.6	03.2	C1/BS
LA12-00096	GZR	49.4	28.4	22.2	08.2	05.5	01.9	03.6	01.6	C1/BS
LA12-00097	GZR	57.2	18.6	24.2	04.1	02.0	03.5	07.3	24.8	C1/LA
LA12-00098	GZR	60.3	17.8	21.9	03.2	03.9	03.8	02.8	00.5	C1/BS
LA12-00099	SFE	57.8	30.1	12.1	07.8	07.6	02.1	04.6	01.3	C2/SA
LA12-00100	SFE	46.6	30.8	22.6	07.1	05.3	03.8	05.0	00.6	C2/SC

(*Continued on next page*)

TABLE C (*continued*)

Sherd	Type	Fe	Zr	Sr	Rb	Nb	Ca	Y	Pb	Occupation/Temper
LA12-00101	SFE	65.4	19.5	15.0	06.0	05.4	01.8	04.3	00.4	C2/QS
LA12-00102	SFE	38.4	37.9	23.6	12.5	13.2	04.2	09.9	01.7	C2/SA
LA12-00103	SFE	55.4	31.7	12.9	09.9	12.6	05.8	09.0	01.0	C2/QS
LA12-00104	SFE	55.3	32.5	12.2	08.7	07.2	03.7	05.5	02.1	C2/SC
LA12-00105	SFE	50.1	38.0	11.9	08.1	07.4	03.9	06.4	01.3	C2/QS
LA12-00106	SFE	54.4	32.0	13.6	13.0	13.6	02.8	08.6	01.0	C2/QS
LA12-00107	SFE	50.7	37.6	11.7	10.5	09.2	02.6	06.6	01.0	C2/SC
LA12-00108	SFE	55.6	32.6	11.8	06.8	05.6	02.8	05.6	00.6	C2/SA
LA12-00109	SFE	62.9	21.8	15.2	06.1	05.5	02.3	03.7	00.6	C2/SC
LA12-00110	SFE	63.4	26.9	09.7	09.3	07.0	03.8	04.7	01.2	C2/SA
LA12-00111	SFE	59.9	29.3	10.8	09.3	05.7	03.0	05.0	01.0	C2/SC
LA12-00112	SFE	60.4	29.0	10.5	08.1	04.6	03.1	04.1	01.2	C2/SC
LA12-00113	SFE	60.7	27.4	12.0	12.1	13.8	03.2	07.5	00.9	C2/QS
LA12-00114	SFE	58.6	31.0	10.3	06.9	08.1	07.1	05.5	01.5	C2/SC
LA12-00115	SFE	58.2	27.5	14.3	07.2	07.2	06.8	06.2	01.1	C2/SA
LA12-00116	GAL	42.4	38.8	18.8	10.4	05.1	03.4	05.9	01.2	C2/SH
LA12-00117	AH	57.1	28.1	14.9	05.1	06.1	02.4	07.4	00.5	C2/GN
LA12-00118	GAL	27.4	43.7	28.9	07.8	09.0	02.8	04.9	01.9	C2/SH
LA12-00119	GAL	34.9	46.6	18.5	10.0	10.5	03.0	08.1	01.1	C2/SH
LA12-00120	KEN	51.9	20.8	27.3	05.9	06.4	02.1	04.0	01.0	C2/LA
LA12-00121	GAL	39.2	46.1	14.7	11.1	12.1	04.4	08.9	01.9	C2/SH
LA12-00122	GAL	32.9	42.5	24.6	05.4	06.2	02.9	03.7	00.8	C2/SH
LA12-00123	GAL	54.4	29.1	16.5	07.4	05.5	03.0	04.3	00.5	C2/SH
LA12-00124	AH	51.6	34.9	13.5	09.7	08.0	02.5	06.2	01.0	C2/MS
LA12-00125	GAL	33.1	48.1	18.8	11.2	12.9	04.5	08.3	01.5	C2/SH
LA12-00126	KEN	49.6	23.7	26.7	04.6	05.2	03.6	02.8	00.8	C2/LA
LA12-00127	AH	59.0	27.8	13.2	05.8	07.8	04.0	04.9	01.0	C2/MS
LA12-00128	KEN	50.6	17.0	32.5	04.2	03.9	02.0	02.1	01.1	C2/LA
LA12-00129	AH	54.7	31.8	13.5	06.7	06.1	01.9	08.2	00.7	C2/GN
LA12-00130	KEN	52.4	23.5	24.1	04.5	03.8	03.6	03.1	00.7	C2/LS
LA12-00131	KEN	46.5	23.5	30.0	04.6	03.9	03.2	02.6	01.1	C2/LA
LA12-00132	GAL	52.5	33.5	14.0	10.2	05.7	03.6	04.6	00.5	C2/SH
LA12-00133	PDI	57.3	30.4	12.3	11.4	10.3	02.2	07.6	01.0	C2/PA
LA12-00134	PDI	54.9	34.7	10.4	09.1	10.5	03.2	05.4	01.8	C2/PA
LA12-00135	PDI	58.6	30.8	10.6	10.7	10.4	02.7	05.5	00.7	C2/PA
LA12-00136	PDI	58.9	30.8	10.4	13.8	12.5	02.4	06.9	01.3	C2/PA
LA12-00137	PDI	59.4	29.8	10.8	10.7	08.7	03.2	06.4	01.0	C2/PA
LA12-00138	PDI	51.1	36.6	12.4	10.8	09.5	03.8	06.6	01.1	C2/PA
LA12-00139	PDI	57.6	31.0	11.3	11.0	09.3	02.3	07.2	00.2	C2/PA
LA12-00140	PDI	55.0	31.2	13.9	12.5	13.9	04.0	07.8	00.9	C2/PA
LA12-00141	PDI	53.9	37.0	09.0	10.3	11.9	04.1	07.4	00.8	C2/PA
LA12-00142	PDI	57.7	32.5	09.8	12.5	10.2	03.4	08.3	01.1	C2/PA
LA12-00143	PDI	60.7	30.3	09.0	09.7	08.6	04.1	07.7	00.4	C2/PA
LA12-00144	PDI	51.5	30.3	18.2	11.3	12.2	03.2	07.2	01.0	C2/PA
LA12-00145	PDI	51.0	38.9	10.1	12.1	14.3	03.7	08.3	01.2	C2/PA
LA12-00146	PDI	57.7	30.8	11.6	10.9	13.8	02.0	07.1	01.2	C2/PA
LA12-00147	POG	64.7	23.1	12.3	08.6	08.9	03.9	04.7	01.1	C2/LH
LA12-00148	POG	51.0	35.1	14.0	05.0	04.4	01.9	03.4	00.4	C2/LI
LA12-00149	POG	42.1	44.7	13.2	09.9	07.6	03.7	06.6	00.8	C2/LH
LA12-00150	POG	59.5	28.3	12.2	07.6	08.4	03.4	04.5	00.5	C2/LH
LA12-00151	POG	65.2	24.2	10.6	08.3	13.8	04.5	05.3	01.4	C2/LI

TABLE C (continued)

Sherd	Type	Fe	Zr	Sr	Rb	Nb	Ca	Y	Pb	Occupation/Temper
LA12-00152	POG	55.4	29.0	15.6	06.2	05.3	02.7	04.8	00.5	C2/LH
LA12-00153	POG	49.6	33.2	17.2	07.3	05.8	03.1	04.5	01.0	C2/LH
LA12-00154	POG	60.9	22.5	16.6	06.6	06.6	02.5	04.9	00.9	C2/LH
LA12-00155	POG	48.5	26.5	25.0	08.0	05.2	02.3	04.0	01.1	C2/LI
LA12-00156	POG	56.1	27.3	16.7	10.0	08.1	04.0	04.6	01.9	C2/LH
LA12-00157	POG	60.2	24.1	15.6	08.1	05.7	04.7	04.1	01.8	C2/LH
LA12-00158	POG	63.2	24.2	12.7	07.2	07.4	03.5	07.5	00.6	C2/LI
LA12-00159	POG	61.4	24.5	14.1	07.4	04.7	02.1	02.3	00.9	C2/LH
LA12-00160	POG	51.9	33.1	15.0	09.5	05.3	01.9	04.3	02.0	C2/LH
LA12-00161	POG	61.8	22.0	16.2	08.0	04.8	02.9	03.8	01.5	C2/LH
LA12-00162	WYO	44.6	31.5	23.9	12.6	08.2	04.7	06.5	00.7	C2/FA
LA12-00163	WYO	52.5	42.3	15.2	14.0	15.0	03.3	07.7	01.3	C2/FA
LA12-00164	WYO	32.5	36.9	30.6	16.1	07.7	03.4	05.9	00.7	C2/FA
LA12-00165	WYO	60.7	29.7	09.6	08.7	07.8	02.8	05.7	00.9	C2/SA
LA12-00166	WYO	53.4	32.4	14.1	27.2	12.5	03.5	07.6	01.1	C2/FA
LA12-00167	WYO	55.4	30.4	14.2	13.2	07.8	04.5	05.3	01.4	C2/PA
LA12-00168	WYO	52.0	39.6	08.4	19.4	22.4	03.5	11.7	01.4	C2/SA
LA12-00169	WYO	51.7	37.2	11.1	15.1	17.8	03.1	12.0	01.5	C2/FA
LA12-00170	WYO	55.0	24.5	20.5	11.0	08.4	04.0	05.0	01.2	C2/FA
LA12-00171	WYO	48.1	38.5	13.3	11.9	13.5	03.3	09.6	01.2	C2/SA
LA12-00172	WYO	54.2	37.2	08.6	08.6	07.5	02.5	07.4	01.1	C2/FA
LA12-00173	WYO	45.8	38.0	16.2	07.4	06.1	04.2	05.4	00.8	C2/FA
LA12-00174	WYO	61.0	26.4	12.6	06.7	04.6	03.5	04.7	01.2	C2/FA
LA12-00175	WYO	53.7	30.0	16.4	14.6	10.3	04.7	07.1	02.1	C2/FA
LA12-00176	WYO	54.1	29.5	16.3	14.7	07.0	04.7	06.2	01.5	C2/FA
LA12-00177	GZR	58.7	24.6	16.0	08.1	06.8	03.5	05.3	04.2	C2/BS
LA12-00178	GZR	51.4	19.3	29.3	04.5	03.5	02.8	02.1	01.1	C2/LA
LA12-00179	GZR	51.0	21.6	27.5	05.5	04.0	03.0	03.3	05.3	C2/LA
LA12-00180	GZR	36.3	36.6	27.1	05.5	06.2	02.7	03.3	00.8	C2/BA
LA12-00181	GZR	65.4	14.7	19.9	02.5	04.1	02.8	02.7	08.2	C2/LA
LA12-00182	GZR	54.7	27.1	18.2	06.9	06.3	03.1	07.2	19.8	C2/BS
LA12-00183	GZR	56.3	17.7	26.1	04.5	03.7	02.5	05.6	11.4	C2/LA
LA12-00184	GZR	55.9	25.2	19.0	08.0	05.8	03.7	04.7	04.0	C2/BA
LA12-00185	GZR	40.5	46.7	12.8	04.6	05.6	03.2	06.1	05.7	C2/ST
LA12-00186	GZR	50.8	29.5	19.7	10.0	08.2	03.5	06.2	03.0	C2/BS
LA12-00187	GZR	51.3	17.5	31.2	03.4	03.1	03.1	02.2	01.0	C2/LA
LA12-00188	GZR	44.6	29.9	25.5	04.5	04.5	03.9	07.2	27.9	C2/BS
LA12-00189	GZR	44.7	39.8	15.5	06.6	06.7	01.6	03.9	01.3	C2/ST
LA12-00190	GZR	49.6	29.6	20.8	08.8	05.7	03.2	02.8	03.0	C2/BS
LA12-00191	GZR	41.5	21.7	36.8	03.5	03.7	03.3	04.0	03.9	C2/LS
LA12-00192	GZY	44.0	27.7	28.4	05.9	08.2	03.9	05.6	03.3	C2/LS
LA12-00193	GZY	35.8	31.5	32.7	04.2	04.2	03.3	03.6	01.7	C2/LA
LA12-00194	GZY	40.9	31.8	27.3	08.7	07.8	04.2	06.4	12.0	C2/LS
LA12-00195	GZY	38.0	28.2	33.7	05.1	03.8	04.2	07.6	08.1	C2/LS
LA12-00196	GZY	53.9	17.3	28.8	04.4	05.5	04.8	02.6	01.3	C2/LA
LA12-00197	GZY	53.8	21.7	24.4	05.1	03.9	04.1	03.3	01.6	C2/LA
LA12-00198	GZY	57.7	20.6	21.7	05.4	05.7	03.0	03.7	00.4	C2/LA
LA12-00199	GZY	53.7	25.8	20.5	07.0	06.1	04.0	04.4	03.8	C2/BS
LA12-00200	GZY	57.6	17.1	25.3	03.9	03.4	02.4	03.4	05.0	C2/LA
LA12-00201	GZY	55.8	18.8	25.4	04.9	07.4	03.6	04.8	10.3	C2/LS
LA12-00202	GZY	39.2	28.5	32.3	06.7	05.9	02.4	03.5	03.4	C2/LS

(Continued on next page)

TABLE C (*continued*)

Sherd	Type	Fe	Zr	Sr	Rb	Nb	Ca	Y	Pb	Occupation/ Temper
LA12-00203	GZY	39.6	27.1	33.2	05.8	05.8	04.4	04.3	03.6	C2/LS
LA12-00204	GZY	62.7	24.7	12.7	08.1	06.9	04.2	04.5	00.7	C2/BA
LA12-00205	GZY	50.2	19.5	30.3	04.2	05.2	02.9	03.3	01.0	C2/LA
LA12-00206	GZY	41.2	29.4	29.4	05.4	05.4	05.2	07.4	11.0	C2/LA
LA12-00207	CUL	37.6	38.8	23.7	05.1	05.9	02.6	03.2	01.0	C1/GN
LA12-00208	CUL	50.5	38.0	11.5	06.4	05.9	02.2	05.4	01.1	C1/GN
LA12-00209	CUL	67.0	20.2	12.8	05.3	05.7	01.7	04.2	01.3	C1/MS
LA12-00210	CUL	53.9	32.3	13.8	06.5	03.8	02.6	04.7	01.8	C1/GN
LA12-00211	CUL	57.2	31.8	11.0	06.5	08.0	05.3	04.7	02.3	C1/MS
LA12-00212	CUL	48.1	31.8	20.2	06.1	06.9	03.1	06.1	00.8	C1/GN
LA12-00213	CUL	51.7	30.9	17.3	05.9	06.1	02.7	05.3	01.0	C1/GN
LA12-00214	CUL	45.4	39.7	14.9	05.0	06.9	03.7	03.6	01.2	C1/GN
LA12-00215	CUL	51.6	34.6	13.7	06.8	06.7	02.3	05.6	00.9	C1/GN
LA12-00216	CUL	67.9	23.9	08.3	08.6	06.5	02.0	04.8	00.8	C1/MS
LA12-00217	CUL	51.1	35.2	13.7	06.2	06.9	03.0	06.5	01.6	C1/GN
LA12-00218	CUL	44.8	32.5	22.6	06.0	07.5	03.7	04.9	01.4	C1/GN
LA12-00219	CUL	55.4	27.8	16.8	06.6	06.6	02.9	05.1	01.0	C1/GN
LA12-00220	CUL	51.6	35.0	13.5	07.6	06.8	03.6	04.2	01.6	C1/MS
LA12-00221	CUL	48.1	29.9	22.0	05.9	05.9	03.5	03.6	01.1	C1/GN
LA12-00222	CUL	60.0	28.5	11.5	09.2	08.2	02.4	05.6	01.1	C1/MS
LA12-00223	CUL	67.7	25.0	07.3	09.0	05.7	01.6	06.8	01.3	C1/MS
LA12-00224	CUL	53.6	31.1	15.4	07.7	05.9	03.0	04.2	00.8	C1/GN
LA12-00225	CUL	47.8	32.2	20.0	04.2	06.5	03.9	05.5	01.5	C1/GN
LA12-00226	CUL	52.0	35.5	12.5	08.9	08.2	03.9	05.2	01.0	C1/GN
LA12-00227	CUL	45.9	39.9	14.2	06.2	06.2	01.2	04.0	01.1	C1/GN
LA12-00228	CUL	65.8	26.3	07.9	09.7	07.2	04.6	07.5	01.7	C1/GN
LA12-00229	CUL	56.8	32.6	10.6	04.7	06.0	04.0	04.7	00.9	C1/GN
LA12-00230	CUL	66.3	25.7	08.0	07.9	09.1	02.7	04.5	01.1	C1/MS
LA12-00231	CUL	49.1	37.4	13.4	05.2	07.5	04.2	04.5	01.0	C1/GN
LA12-00232	CUL	54.6	28.9	16.5	06.5	06.2	03.0	08.9	00.9	C1/GN
LA12-00233	CUL	67.0	22.2	10.7	08.9	08.2	02.6	05.8	01.2	C1/GN
LA12-00234	CUL	64.1	21.0	14.9	03.7	05.4	03.2	03.8	01.4	C1/MS
LA12-00235	CUL	46.9	27.0	26.1	04.7	08.5	03.4	04.2	01.9	C1/GN
LA12-00236	CUL	57.8	31.4	10.8	05.2	05.6	02.3	04.4	01.2	C1/GN
LA12-00237	CUL	46.5	31.5	22.0	07.3	05.6	03.2	04.3	01.3	C1/GN
LA12-00238	CUL	54.6	32.0	13.3	05.4	10.2	02.9	05.5	01.5	C1/GN
LA12-00239	CUL	67.8	22.8	09.4	05.5	05.2	02.7	04.6	01.1	C2/GN
LA12-00240	CUL	50.4	38.6	11.0	06.4	08.1	02.4	03.8	01.7	C2/GN
LA12-00241	CUL	37.2	42.2	20.6	05.4	06.8	04.0	04.6	01.6	C2/GN
LA12-00242	CUL	72.5	18.5	09.1	03.9	06.9	03.4	04.0	01.5	C2/GN
LA12-00243	CUL	70.0	22.2	07.8	06.7	03.9	02.0	04.8	01.0	C2/MS
LA12-00244	CUL	61.7	24.1	14.2	05.6	06.4	02.1	04.2	00.8	C2/MS
LA12-00245	CUL	69.2	24.4	06.4	10.7	08.4	04.4	04.5	01.0	C2/MS
LA12-00246	CUL	71.0	18.7	10.3	04.7	06.5	02.7	04.5	01.7	C2/MS
LA12-00247	CUL	37.3	36.9	25.8	07.0	07.0	03.8	03.8	01.6	C2/GN
LA12-00248	CUL	61.9	28.8	09.3	07.7	07.6	03.6	06.5	00.9	C2/GN
LA12-00249	CUL	54.1	30.7	15.2	05.4	06.6	03.6	05.8	01.7	C2/GN
LA12-00250	CUL	39.4	37.5	23.1	05.3	06.9	03.6	03.9	01.1	C2/GN
LA12-00251	CUL	70.7	22.4	06.9	09.0	06.9	03.4	04.8	01.2	C2/MS
LA12-00252	CUL	55.0	36.7	08.2	05.4	18.1	04.1	06.0	00.9	C2/GN
LA12-00253	CUL	79.2	14.7	06.1	05.4	04.9	02.5	04.0	00.8	C2/MS

TABLE C (*continued*)

Sherd	Type	Fe	Zr	Sr	Rb	Nb	Ca	Y	Pb	Occupation/Temper
LA12-00254	CUL	68.0	23.2	08.8	08.2	08.5	03.5	04.9	00.9	C2/MS
LA12-00255	CUL	69.4	17.7	12.9	04.1	04.3	01.9	03.6	00.8	C2/GN
LA12-00255	CUL	69.4	17.7	12.9	04.1	04.3	01.9	03.6	00.8	C2/GN
LA12-00256	CUL	47.6	35.9	16.5	15.2	13.5	05.6	09.2	00.9	C2/MS
LA12-00257	CUL	50.6	29.2	20.1	05.2	06.7	04.7	03.6	00.6	C2/MS
LA12-00258	CUL	81.9	11.4	06.7	07.5	05.9	03.2	05.6	00.6	C2/GN
LA12-00259	CUL	71.2	20.4	08.4	06.1	04.4	03.3	06.2	01.1	C2/GN
LA12-00260	CUL	65.8	24.8	09.4	03.4	07.0	03.2	04.2	01.0	C2/MS
LA12-00261	CUL	51.8	38.9	09.3	05.8	08.6	02.5	04.3	00.9	C2/GN
LA12-00262	CUL	67.6	22.7	09.7	02.8	06.1	02.9	04.3	01.0	C2/GN
LA12-00263	CUL	59.8	26.5	13.7	04.6	06.2	02.3	05.1	01.4	C2/GN
LA12-00264	CUL	56.7	28.8	14.5	05.9	08.9	04.2	05.8	01.3	C2/GN
LA12-00265	CUL	47.3	35.6	17.1	05.3	12.0	04.3	05.6	02.1	C2/GN
LA12-00266	CUL	76.9	16.4	06.7	05.8	05.3	02.5	03.8	00.9	C2/MS
LA12-00267	CUL	44.8	40.2	15.1	15.3	15.1	07.1	10.1	01.6	C2/MS
LA12-00268	CUL	72.3	22.0	05.7	08.9	06.7	03.0	05.5	01.1	C2/MS
LA12-00269	CUL	63.3	26.3	10.5	07.6	06.7	03.1	05.6	00.8	C2/GN
LA12-00270	CUL	47.4	39.1	13.6	08.7	06.4	04.3	05.9	01.2	C2/GN
LA12-00271	CLY	46.8	44.7	08.5	38.1	05.4	04.9	12.2	01.0	C2/Red clay
LA12-00272	CLY	43.3	48.5	08.2	36.0	07.9	02.1	12.7	01.2	C2/Red clay
LA12-00273	CLY	55.6	33.3	11.1	31.8	06.6	03.7	09.7	01.2	C2/Red clay
LA12-00274	CLY	50.7	37.8	11.4	31.0	07.8	03.1	09.8	00.5	C2/Red clay
LA12-00275	CLY	52.6	36.3	11.1	31.3	05.3	02.5	10.2	01.0	C2/Red clay
LA12-00276	CLY	49.2	39.4	11.5	30.2	05.3	03.1	09.2	00.3	C2/Red clay
LA12-00277	CLY	56.3	32.5	11.2	33.8	05.3	03.0	10.1	00.6	C2/Red clay
LA12-00278	CLY	41.8	42.7	15.5	19.7	06.8	03.7	07.8	00.7	C2/Red clay
LA12-00279	CLY	51.1	34.7	14.2	32.4	05.8	03.8	09.3	00.5	C2/Red clay
LA12-00280	CLY	52.3	35.9	11.7	29.7	04.3	04.9	08.6	01.1	C2/Red clay
LA12-00281	CLY	44.9	43.8	11.3	31.8	03.9	03.8	10.8	00.8	C2/Red clay
LA12-00282	CLY	49.5	36.3	14.2	21.5	04.7	01.9	07.8	01.1	C2/Red clay
LA12-00283	CLY	50.0	40.8	09.2	26.8	04.9	02.6	09.0	01.5	C1/Red clay
LA12-00284	CLY	45.3	36.9	17.8	21.0	05.8	02.2	08.5	01.1	Clay 1
LA12-00285	CLY	54.1	37.4	08.6	46.4	05.2	06.2	13.8	02.3	Clay 2
LA12-00286	MIN	32.8	37.2	30.0	18.3	02.9	03.0	04.9	01.4	Sandstone W/3
LA12-00287	MIN	59.9	21.9	18.2	12.7	02.1	08.4	02.9	00.9	Sandstone W/3
LA12-00288	CLY	42.8	39.3	18.0	15.6	05.8	02.5	06.8	00.6	Clay 3
LA12-00289	CLY	50.1	33.9	16.0	17.6	04.9	02.2	07.0	01.4	Clay 4
LA12-00290	CLY	39.0	42.9	18.1	13.1	06.8	03.8	06.0	00.8	Clay 5
LA12-00291	MIN	28.0	61.7	10.3	36.0	54.9	05.3	24.9	01.8	Pumice 1
LA12-00292	MIN	24.3	67.6	08.1	20.0	26.9	04.4	13.1	01.3	Pumice 2
LA12-00293	MIN	23.2	23.3	53.5	01.9	02.4	01.8	00.8	01.0	Latite 1
LA12-00294	MIN	15.7	23.7	60.6	01.9	01.7	01.9	00.5	00.4	Latite 2

Additional Reports

I

Analysis and Seriation of Stratigraphic Ceramic Samples from Arroyo Hondo Pueblo

Richard W. Lang

The purpose of this report is to define the manner in which the relative ratio of ceramic types at Arroyo Hondo Pueblo changed through time and to correlate those changes with intrasite stratigraphic and historical events. In order to accomplish these goals, pottery samples were selected from all tested areas of the site and from both components. Within a given area, samples were chosen on the basis of their potential for: (a) contributing to a detailed relative ordering of type ratios within specific time intervals identified as "ceramic horizon groups"; and (b) dating significant events within the Arroyo Hondo continuum. The representativeness of any sample, in relationship to the actual composition of the Arroyo Hondo ceramic complex at any associated temporal horizon, was primarily dependent upon sample size and the degree to which the strata from which the sample came appeared undisturbed by later activity. In several cases, the sample from a given area, such as a plaza accumulation or a series of superimposed rooms, is a stratigraphic as well as a seriational one, and it is such samples that provide the primary framework into which more isolated samples have been placed.

In addition, the author has depended greatly upon the pattern of ceramic changes defined at the nearby site of Pindi (Stubbs and Stallings 1953) for chronologically ordering those samples that fall outside the main stratigraphic sequence at Arroyo Hondo. The Pindi data is also of substantial importance to the actual dating of some ceramic horizon groups at Arroyo Hondo because poor preservation of wood at the latter site resulted in relatively few usable dates for the Component I town. Although several of the dates obtained are quite informa-

tive and find an important place in this study, large blocks of time are not associated with tree-ring dates. Our fuller understanding of the chronology of the Santa Fe drainage is immeasurably enhanced by the combined Pindi–Arroyo Hondo tree-ring series. Although differences in the composition of ceramic horizon groups clearly exist between the two sites, the dominant features of the groups are in accord; and when dated stratigraphic sequences from both sites could be compared, the patterns were found to be basically synchronous. Parallel developments were therefore demonstrated and not simply assumed.

With the completion of the Arroyo Hondo tree-ring and faunal studies (Rose, Dean, and Robinson 1981; Lang and Harris 1984), an important means of cross-checking and refining the dates of the ceramic groups became available. To a large extent, the sequential arrangement of the faunal samples was based on their ceramic associations, although stratigraphic correlations were also of great importance to the process (Lang and Harris 1984:135–43). The faunal samples contain the remains of some species that are highly sensitive to climate. Profiles of changing species composition and relative frequencies clearly reflected alternatingly wet, dry, or variable climatic conditions (Lang and Harris 1984:25–43). These oscillations are also indicated, and in the same order, in the tree-ring growth patterns of wood specimens from the site (Rose, Dean, and Robinson 1981:91–106); thus, dry and wet intervals during the site's occupation are tightly dated. As a result, secure dates of climatic events are well correlated with both the animal remains and associated pottery.

Due to the sensitivity of the painted pottery as a dating tool, this group has been focused on here. In the tables that follow, the numbers and percentages for each painted ceramic type represent vessel rather than sherd counts. During sorting and typing, matching sherds were isolated and recorded as one vessel. All specimens thus achieved equal weight, and skewing of the relative frequencies of types within each provenience area was avoided.

It should be noted that the following ceramic chronology was built in the absence of the complete series of archaeomagnetic dates, which only became available in 1991. Also, because I treated both Pindi and Poge B/W as quasi-types in the early Arroyo Hondo pottery studies, I have continued to refer to them as types in this paper. In a more recent work, however, they have been treated as varieties of other types, namely Santa Fe and Galisteo B/W (Lang 1989:66, 196). In her analysis, Habicht-Mauche (this volume) treats Poge B/W as a variety of Rowe B/W.

Ceramic Horizon Groups
Component I

Cross-correlation of ceramic type percentages from stratigraphic contexts allows definition of nine horizon groups within the Component I assemblage from Arroyo Hondo, spanning the years from the early 1300s to the 1360s. The time intervals associated with each group vary in both their length and the reliability of absolute date assignments. Sample data from each group are provided in table 9. The ceramic characteristics of each group and the date ranges assigned to them are discussed below.

CERAMIC HORIZON GROUP I

A collection of 182 vessels composed this division. Sample proveniences that formed the source of the pottery included in this group represent the earliest known deposits in the area of roomblocks 11 and 16 and along the north-south spine of the site (see fig. 2), below roomblock 18. This later deposit appears to be associated with the construction and initial occupation of roomblock 15. The single excavated core room (12-15-7) in this block produced a single structural wood date of 1308vv.

In the archaeofaunal sequence, this horizon group corresponds with the early subsample of sample 1 (Lang and Harris 1984:16, 135–36). The subsample 1 fauna is interpreted as essentially mesic in its climate associations, but it included a xeric element believed to be residual from a preceding drought (Lang and Harris 1984: 26–33). Subsample 1 is taken to correlate with the early

years of the post–Great Drought maximum of A.D. 1295 to 1335 (Rose, Dean, and Robinson 1981:100), supporting the other indices for placement of the ceramic group at ca. A.D. 1300.

Characteristic of this horizon group is a very high (i.e., 71.4–78.8%) incidence of Santa Fe Black-on-white. Small quantities of Galisteo Black-on-white are uniformly present in all samples, as are specimens of Wiyo Black-on-white, which generally occurs in somewhat lower frequencies than Galisteo. Poge Black-on-white (Habicht-Mauche's Rowe, *var. Poge*) is present in all but one of the larger samples of the group and appears to increase slightly through time. Pindi Black-on-white (Habicht-Mauche's Sante Fe, *var. Pindi*) is absent, and the only Little Colorado Red ware type present is St. Johns Black-on-red or St. Johns Polychrome.

The ceramic profile recorded for this horizon group would fall somewhere between that of Ceramic Group I and Sample B-II in the Pindi Pueblo ceramic sequence (Stubbs and Stallings 1953). Samples from Group I plaza refuse at Pindi were associated with dates of 1275r to 1301v (Stubbs and Stallings 1953:16–17, 156–59; Robinson, Hannah, and Harrill 1972:36, 39–40) and contained 81 to 84 percent Santa Fe B/W, 9 to 15 percent Wiyo B/W, and 3 to 7 percent Galisteo—Mesa Verde—a very early variant of Galisteo B/W. The presence of dates ranging upward to 1286r and 1290r from architectural features overlaid by Group I trash at Pindi would indicate that these samples probably date into the early 1300s. Sample B-II contained 70 percent Santa Fe, 8 percent Wiyo, 1 percent Pindi, 6 percent Poge, and 15 percent Galisteo and was associated with a single tree-ring date of 1301r. Dates from overlying architectural features also suggest that the Pindi Sample B-II must date sometime prior to A.D. 1315. The placement of this sample within the first decade of the fourteenth century probably provides a good bracket for the samples assigned to Ceramic Horizon Group I at Arroyo Hondo as well.

CERAMIC HORIZON GROUP II

A much larger collection of 879 vessels represents the second horizon group, dated from post-1310 to around 1315 or slightly later. Although the time period here is of about the same duration at that of Group I, inter-sample variability is somewhat greater, suggesting that changes within the ceramic assemblage may have been occurring at a faster rate than previously.

Santa Fe B/W remains the most common type during this horizon, although it evidences a 14 to 20 percent decline in frequency from Group I. This drop is associated with an increased occurrence of Galisteo B/W. The frequencies of Wiyo and Poge remain basically stable throughout groups I and II. Pindi B/W makes its initial appearance during Group II times but is very rare. St. Johns Polychrome also continues to be present in small quantities. The deposit (lower 12-C-3C) from which the Agua Fria Glaze-on-red sherds were recovered was directly overlaid by Component II trash. This context and the anomalous nature of the occurrence suggest that the glaze-painted specimens are probably intrusive. Agua Fria does not appear again until Group VI and is absent in all but one of the eight proveniences contributing to Group II.

Proveniences associated with this horizon are from trash deposits located beneath the easternmost rooms of roomblock 8; in association with the earlier rooms of roomblocks 9 and 14; beneath and north of the core rooms of roomblock 18; beneath roomblocks 23 and 24 at the extreme southern end of the site; and beneath later room additions to roomblocks 11 and 16 (see fig. 2). Little trash was found below the floor of the only excavated Component I room in roomblock 9 (12-9-7), suggesting that accumulation closely preceded room construction, datable to post-1310 on the basis of a tree-ring date of 1310vv from the room's lower-story ceiling. The pole-walled enclosure built against the south wall of the north room alignment of roomblock 14 produced six structural dates: one each at 1317vv, 1320v, and 1321r, and three at 1321v. A date of ca. 1315 from the core alignment of roomblock 18 is acceptable on the basis of two structural wood dates of 1315vv and 1315rB from room 12-18-17. As these rooms overlay midden deposits exhibiting a much higher percentage of Wiyo B/W, a lower Santa Fe showing, and the presence of Pindi B/W, the midden outside the walls of roomblock 14's earliest identified rooms would appear to have formed long before the construction of the 1321 enclosure and probably before 1315.

Group II corresponds to faunal subsample 2 of sample 1, which contained no xeric indicators (Lang and Harris 1984:29–33, 136). This subsample, then, forms a good climatic match with the continuing moist and cool conditions of the early 1300s (Rose, Dean, and Robinson 1981:102).

CERAMIC HORIZON GROUP III

This group is represented by a collection of essentially the same size as that forming Group I (i.e., 183 vessels). The samples derive from trash deposits associated with the north wing of roomblock 16, below the middle plaza surface of plaza G and the floor of kiva 12-14-6, and from a barrow pit associated with the construction of the core of roomblock 18 (see fig. 2). The latter adobe pit was filled after about 1315, when the core rooms in this block were constructed, but prior to the formation of the middle surface of plaza G. The total body of data points to the formation of this plaza surface in the 1320s. Such placement is in accord with dates of 1320vv, 1322r, and 1325vv from plaza features associated with the middle surface and with the dates of 1324vv and 1325vv from room 12-14-5, built on an elevation corresponding stratigraphically with this surface. Both the ceramics and the tree-ring dates indicate construction of kiva 12-14-6 after 1320. Conversely, the data from plaza G support assignment of ceramic samples in Horizon Group III to a period predating that construction.

Ceramic Group III corresponds to subsample 3, sample 2, of the archaeofaunal analysis, the content of which suggests a continuation of moist conditions (Lang and Harris 1984:33–35, 137). In the tree-ring series, cool, moist conditions are indicated to have been typical up to about A.D. 1323–24 (Rose, Dean, and Robinson 1981: 96, 98, 102, 104).

Characteristic of this horizon is a continued decline in the frequency of Santa Fe B/W with a concurrent increase in the Galisteo and Poge types, with the Galisteo B/W or combined Poge-Galisteo percentages roughly equal to those of Santa Fe B/W. A minor decrease in the relative frequency of Wiyo may be indicated; alternatively, there may have been a greater variability in its occurrence. The absence of St. Johns and Pindi is likely attributable to the small sample size, but it may be assumed that if present, both remained rare. Although the samples that constitute this group are not well dated, their composition relative to that of known earlier and later samples supports their attribution to the latter half of the second decade of the fourteenth century.

CERAMIC HORIZON GROUP IV

Samples forming this group, composed of 562 vessels, are associated with the latest pre–gate 12-C-3 deposits; deposits below roomblock 6; the earliest middens of the plaza A and K areas; deposits below the west end of roomblock 12; rubbish associated with the occupation of room 12-18-6; and rubbish overlying the earliest floors of 12-12-4 and 12-23-4 (see fig. 2). Material from the upper midden beneath room 12-18-49, south of 12-18-6, and within plaza I is of particular interest, as it was clearly deposited after the construction of 12-18-6, which produced a tree-ring date of 1321v.

TABLE 9
Component I ceramic horizon group data.

Ceramic Horizon Group	Contributing Samples	Ceramic Types	Frequency %	(No.)	Sample Range %
I	Sub 12-11-5&8; lower 12-C-3; sub 12-16-31&33; sub 12-16-34&36; sub 12-18-49 (pit fill)	Santa Fe B/W	76.0	(139)	71.4–78.8
		Wiyo B/W	8.2	(15)	3.2–12.6
		Poge B/W	4.9	(9)	0–14.2
		Galisteo B/W	10.4	(19)	5.6–19.3
		St. Johns Poly	0.5	(1)	0– 1.4
II	Sub 12-8-5; sub 12-9-7; pitroom 12-11-6; lower 12-C-3C; sub 12-14-5; sub 12-18-7,8,32&42; lower midden 12-18-49; sub 12-23-4 and 12-24-3	Santa Fe B/W	56.7	(498)	53.9–64.7
		Pindi B/W	0.6	(5)	0– 1.8
		Wiyo B/W	9.9	(87)	0–15.8
		Poge B/W	5.0	(44)	0–12.7
		Galisteo B/W	27.5	(242)	12.7–40.0
		St. Johns Poly	0.1	(1)	0– 0.2
		Agua Fria G/R	0.2	(2)	0– 0.6
III	Upper 12-C-3C; sub 12-14-6; sub 12-18-37	Santa Fe B/W	46.4	(83)	41.0–46.6
		Pindi B/W	0	(0)	0
		Wiyo B/W	3.4	(6)	0–15.3
		Poge B/W	7.3	(13)	3.1–46.6
		Galisteo B/W	41.8	(75)	20.8–46.6
		Kwahe'e B/W	0.6	(1)	0– 0.7
		Socorro B/W	0.6	(1)	0– 2.5
IV	Plaza A/lower; feature J; lower plaza K; sub 12-6-9; upper 12-C-3; upper midden sub 12-18-49; sub 12-12-4; lower 12-12-4; lower 12-23-4	Santa Fe B/W	25.6	(144)	17.1–37.0
		Pindi B/W	1.3	(7)	0– 8.9
		Wiyo B/W	13.5	(76)	0–23.6
		Poge B/W	29.9	(168)	5.0–41.2
		Galisteo B/W	29.5	(166)	20.0–65.0
		St. Johns Poly	0.2	(1)	0– 3.4
V	Plaza A/lower; feature J; feature G; feature H; mid 12-12-4; sub 12-D-3	Santa Fe B/W	5.5	(6)	1.5–12.5
		Pindi B/W	4.6	(5)	0–12.5
		Wiyo B/W	8.3	(9)	0–25.0
		Poge B/W	20.2	(22)	11.1–25.0
		Galisteo B/W	59.6	(65)	25.0–68.1
		Heshotauthla Poly	1.8	(2)	0–11.1
VI	Plaza A/upper midden; fill 12-3-13; fill building E-F; fill 12-4-2; mid plaza K; fill 12-5-6; fill 12-6-15; 12-G-36B-2; 12-G-39B-2; fill 12-18-15; fill 12-18-37&38; fill 12-18-14,32, 48&49; fill 12-19-1; floor 12-D-3	Santa Fe B/W	9.4	(193)	1.7–21.9
		Pindi B/W	35.0	(718)	13.6–54.5
		Wiyo B/W	11.0	(225)	5.6–29.3
		Abiquiú B/W	0.5	(1)	0– 1.0
		Poge B/W	12.9	(264)	8.3–25.0
		Galisteo B/W	29.0	(594)	10.0–44.9
		Socorro B/W	0.05	(1)	0– 0.7
		Chupadero B/W	0.1	(3)	0– 4.2
		St. Johns Poly	0.2	(5)	0– 1.6
		Agua Fria G/R	2.2	(45)	0– 6.5
		San Clemente Poly	0.05	(1)	0– 0.7
		Cieneguilla G/Y	0.05	(1)	0– 0.7

(Continued on next page)

TABLE 9 (*continued*)

Ceramic Horizon Group	Contributing Samples	Ceramic Types	Frequency %	(No.)	Sample Range %
VII	Upper plaza K; fill	Santa Fe B/W	10.1	(58)	4.8–33.3
	12-5-11; fill 12-6-10;	Pindi B/W	6.6	(38)	0–15.0
	fill 12-6-6,12-14-5;	Wiyo B/W	24.8	(143)	12.8–50.0
	fill 12-7-7; sub 12-	Abiquiú B/W	0.5	(3)	0– 3.6
	16-38; fill 12-23-4;	Poge B/W	14.9	(86)	5.0–26.9
	fill 12-21-6	Galisteo B/W	41.1	(237)	16.6–46.5
		Chupadero B/W	0.2	(1)	0– 2.6
		Agua Fria G/R	1.6	(9)	0– 6.0
		Cieneguilla G/Y	0.2	(1)	0– 1.2
VIII	Fill 12-16-31,32&34;	Santa Fe B/W	32.0	(136)	27.7–38.8
(Probably mixed	fill 12-18-7&8; fill	Pindi B/W	16.7	(71)	14.1–27.7
samples from	12-12-4; fill 12-15-7;	Wiyo B/W	11.5	(49)	0–14.4
late Compo-	fill 12-24-3	Poge B/W	15.1	(64)	12.2–17.3
nent I contexts)		Galisteo B/W	22.8	(97)	17.7–26.8
		Chupadero B/W	0.5	(2)	0– 1.6
		Agua Fria G/R	1.4	(6)	0– 5.5
IX	Fill 12-5-5; fill 12-5-	Santa Fe B/W	39.0	(1051)	16.9–76.1
	4; fill 12-6-7,8&9;	Pindi B/W	6.5	(176)	0–12.5
	lower 12-8-5; burial	Wiyo B/W	10.9	(294)	4.0–18.5
	pit fill 12-11-8; fill	Abiquiú B/W	0.3	(8)	0– 1.8
	12-10-3; fill 12-11-	Poge B/W	12.8	(346)	3.7–25.0
	4,8&9; lower 12-11-	Galisteo B/W	28.1	(758)	12.5–46.1
	5; lower 12-15a-9;	Kwahe'e B/W	0	(1)	0– 0.7
	kiva 12-G-5; fill 12-	Socorro B/W	0	(1)	0– 1.3
	13-9; fill 12-18-5;	Chupadero B/W	0.6	(17)	0– 6.2
	kiva 12-14-6; fill 12-	Vallecitos B/W	0	(1)	0– 0.4
	14-5; fill 12-20-6;	St. Johns Poly	0.3	(7)	0– 4.1
	fill 12-16-35&37; pit	Heshotauthla Poly	0.2	(5)	0– 0.6
	fill 12-16-31; lower	Agua Fria G/R	1.2	(33)	0– 6.2
	12-16-24; upper 12-	San Clemente Poly	0	(1)	0– 0.9
	16-24; fill 12-16-	Cieneguilla G/Y	0	(2)	0– 0.5
	27,8,28&30; fill 12-				
	16-26&33				

During this horizon, Santa Fe B/W continued to undergo a steady, marked decline in frequency. Concurrently, the frequency of Galisteo and Poge B/W increased until the two types collectively reached a relative position well above that of Santa Fe B/W. In particular, Poge B/W became increasingly more common during the 1320s, apparently at the expense of Galisteo B/W, although the mean percentage of Galisteo remained higher than that of Poge. Among other types, minor increases of both Wiyo and Pindi B/W are indicated, and the frequency of St. Johns Polychrome remained stable but low.

The relative frequency of types recorded for Horizon IV at Arroyo Hondo conforms remarkably well with the pattern found in the Group III samples from Pindi Pueblo (Stubbs and Stallings 1953:16–17). The Pindi A-III and B-III samples from rooms 113 and 117 and turkey pens 8 and 12, respectively, are associated with dates of 1320rB (upper room 117) and 1320vv to 1321r (pen 8) (Robinson, Hannah, and Harrill 1972:38–39; Stubbs and Stallings 1953:158–59). These are probably structural wood dates from features predating the time of Ceramic Group III deposition. The correlation of Arroyo Hondo Ceramic Horizon Group IV with Pindi Ceramic Group III and their relationship to later groups suggest that the former samples were deposited sometime during the 1320s.

Horizon Group IV corresponds to subsample 4, sample 2, of the archaeofaunal series (Lang and Harris 1984:16, 33–35, 137). The reappearance of one xeric indicator species in this subsample suggests a renewal of drier, warmer conditions. In the tree-ring series, such conditions begin at ca. 1323–24 (Rose, Dean, and Robinson 1981:102, 104).

CERAMIC HORIZON GROUP V

Of the samples contributing to this group, only those from plaza A are well dated and make up most of the sample of 109 vessels. The most significant of these plaza A deposits is the fill from the feature H earth oven, which, in addition to a 1330v date, produced three dates of 1329rB. The 12-12-4 sample is relatively small (i.e., 26 vessels) but shows excellent correlation with the much larger plaza A sample in the percentages of all common types. The assignment of 12-D-3 to this group is provisional.

The consistent presence of Pindi B/W in the plaza A subsamples and its absence in the roomblock 12 sample could correlate with a slightly earlier dating of the latter sample, presumably within the later 1320s. Internally, Group V is best dated to around A.D. 1330 and therefore represents what may be conceived of as the upper end of the Group IV series.

In the archaeofaunal series, this ceramic horizon corresponds to subsample 5, sample 2 (Lang and Harris 1984). This subsample shows a continued occurrence of xeric indicators, suggesting a basic correlation with the low precipitation interval of about 1327–31 (Rose, Dean, and Robinson 1981).

The Group V samples evidenced a sharp decline in the frequency of Santa Fe B/W at Arroyo Hondo by the end of the second decade of the fourteenth century. Correlative with this pattern was a peak in the incidence of Poge-Galisteo at the site, with this suite of Mesa Verde–style ceramics once again being dominated by Galisteo B/W in most samples. Horizon Group V, therefore, marked not only the apogee of Galisteo B/W but also the beginning of a general decline in the relative frequency of Poge B/W from its peak in the 1320s. The status of Wiyo remained relatively stable, although a minor decline in frequency may correlate with a slight increase in Pindi B/W. Within the Little Colorado types, Heshotauthla Polychrome made its appearance in the assemblage at this time.

The appearance of Heshotauthla Polychrome at this point in the profile suggests a correlation with Pindi Pueblo's Group IV, which contained the earliest examples of Heshotauthla noted for that site. Within the Group

IV samples at Pindi, Heshotauthla occurred as one sherd out of 305 in Sample B-IV, associated with a date suite of 1330r–1331r, and as eight sherds out of 1,322 forming Sample G-IV, associated with a good date cluster of 1336v, 1337r, and 1337vv (Robinson, Hannah, and Harrill 1972:37; Stubbs and Stallings 1953:16–17, 159, 161). It is probable that the best correlation lies with the earlier portion of the span, closer in time to the last use of feature H at Arroyo Hondo, at around A.D. 1331.

CERAMIC HORIZON GROUP VI

This sample consists of 2,051 vessels and includes the latest of the Component I deposits from plazas A and G, most of the late plaza K series, and the earliest terminal Component I roomfill accumulations from roomblocks 3, 4, 5, 6, 18, 19 and kiva 12-D-3 (see fig. 2). This group is associated with a longer time span than any of the preceding groups, covering the 1330s and extending into the 1340s.

Ceramics from the fill of room 12-5-6, a burned, single-story room of the exterior south room alignment of roomblock 5, were associated with one structural wood date of 1327r. The fill of this room probably represents trash dumped here after the room had burned and so substantially postdates ca. 1330. A similar date is indicated for ceramics from the upper midden of plaza G. Wood from structures associated with the terminal surface of that plaza produced dates of 1329v and 1330v. Room 12-18-15, a trash-filled, burned room adjacent to the passageway between plazas G and J, produced one burned wood element dated at 1335+G, four at 1320r, three at 1321r, one 1321rB, two at 1322r, and one 1322B. Again, the trash that accumulated in this room must date after the latest structural date recovered (i.e., post-1335).

Ceramically, this period saw a gradual increase in the frequency of Pindi B/W until it exceeded the quantity of all other types in some proveniences. Overall, however, Galisteo B/W continued to dominate many of the samples in this horizon group. The percentage of Galisteo B/W was significantly higher than that of Pindi B/W in seven of the samples, exhibited frequencies essentially equal to that of Pindi in six, and showed an incidence significantly lower than that of Pindi B/W in only four samples. When the Galisteo totals are combined with those of Poge B/W, the frequency of the Poge-Galisteo class exceeds that of Pindi B/W in all but one sample. These data seem to indicate either a variable distribution of Pindi at Arroyo Hondo or a relatively brief period of popularity. In general, the primacy of Pindi B/W appears to be associated with the initial phase of Component I abandonment after ca. 1335–38, as indicated by tree-ring dates from both Arroyo Hondo and Pindi, and tentatively assigned to the early 1340s.

Group VI corresponds to subsamples 7–9 of samples 3 and 4 of the archaeofaunal series (Lang and Harris 1984:16, 32–40, 138–40). These are primarily associated with the early phase of Component I abandonment, during which aridity-tolerant small mammals show increase in both species and numbers. The dendroclimatic reconstruction indicates a significant drought centered on A.D. 1335–42 (Rose, Hannah, and Harrill 1981).

The relationship between Galisteo and Poge B/W underwent further alteration during this period as well, with Poge B/W becoming even less common than in the preceding Horizon Group V, although two samples exhibited higher percentages of Poge than of Galisteo B/W.

An overall increase in Wiyo B/W during the 1330s and 1340s is suggested, but Wiyo, as a particularly common type, appears to be restricted to the locus of plaza K. Socorro Black-on-white, which appears in Group III, is also present in Group VI, and St. Johns continues to occur as a rare exotic trade item.

It is during Horizon VI that Rio Grande Glaze Ware seems to appear first at Arroyo Hondo, the earliest clearly nonintrusive specimens of Agua Fria G/R being present by the 1330s or early 1340s. Thereafter, the type exhibits minor increases. Although the San Clemente Glaze Polychrome specimen from this horizon could be intrusive, the character of the vessel represented suggests a formative quality. Another type that makes its appearance in the Arroyo Hondo assemblage for the first time is Chupadero Black-on-white, found only in roomblock 5.

The best correlation for Horizon Group VI is with Pindi's Ceramic Group V. It is within this group that Pindi B/W exhibits its highest percentages, and it is also within this group that the earliest examples of Rio Grande Glaze Ware appear at Pindi Pueblo. Unfortunately, no dates were associated with this ceramic horizon at Pindi; but referring back to the latest Group IV dates from the site, it may simply be observed that Group V must fall sometime after about A.D. 1340.

Overall, the data indicate an association of Horizon Group VI with the late 1330s and early 1340s. There is no clear indication, however, of how much of the 1340s this group spanned.

CERAMIC HORIZON GROUP VII

This sample consists of 576 vessels from various proveniences in plazas C and K and roomblocks 5, 6, 7, 21, and 23 (see fig. 2). Confidence in the assignment of materials from plaza C and roomblocks 21 and 23 to this horizon is limited, unfortunately, by the small size of the contributing samples.

Collectively, Group VII shows the highest frequency of Wiyo B/W of any of the Component I horizon groups; but overall, Galisteo B/W continues to be almost twice as common as Wiyo, and the combined Poge-Galisteo vessels make up more than half of the Group VII collection. Whereas the frequency of Poge B/W remained stable, Galisteo B/W shows a percentage increase of about 11 percent over the previous group. The other salient characteristic of Group VII is the very low incidence of Pindi B/W. The frequency of Santa Fe B/W also remains constant.

Using pottery and tree-ring dates alone, the Group VII horizon can be dated only in a very general way. Based on comparison with the ceramic sequence from Pindi Pueblo (Stubbs and Stallings 1953), it would appear to fall after A.D. 1348 and prior to the late 1350s (Lang 1975b). This horizon group corresponds to the earlier proveniences of subsample 10, sample 4, of the archaeofaunal series (Lang and Harris 1984:140–41). Although xeric-adapted species are present, they show a marked decrease—a configuration that may correspond with the return to wetter conditions around 1343 (Rose, Dean, and Robinson 1981:102). These fluctuated somewhat, but between 1343 and 1349, only two years show below-average moisture. Cooler, wetter conditions continued through most of the 1350s.

CERAMIC HORIZON GROUP VIII

The material included in this sample largely represents roomfill associated with the decline and abandonment of the Component I town. One such room, 12-16-34, produced an archaeomagnetic date of 1380 ± 21. A second archaeomagnetic date of 1365 ± 10 was taken from the burned walls of room 12-18-7 (Robert L. DuBois, personal communication, ca. 1975). The dates associated with the bracketing of horizon groups VII and IX suggest that the lower end of the archaeomagnetic date ranges (ca. 1355–59), or dates very close to these, are the most acceptable. In addition, correlation with some of the later proveniences of subsample 10 of the archaeofaunal sequence offers a further zooclimatic correspondence with the 1350s (Lang and Harris 1984:140–41, 181; Rose, Dean, and Robinson 1981:102, 104), although some overlap with ceramic samples of the 1340s and 1360s is evident for Group VIII.

This group differs from the others of the series in that these samples are believed to represent mixing of ceramic materials from horizons VI through IX. Generally, they resemble Group IX samples in the relatively high percentage of Santa Fe B/W, as well as in the relative frequency of all well-represented types other than Pindi B/W. The Group VIII Pindi frequency is higher than that of any group other than Horizon Group VI. Deposition in most, if not all, of the Group VIII proveniences is believed to have begun during Group VI and continued up through Group IX times. The absence of an appreciably high percentage of Wiyo B/W in Group VIII may be related to some discontinuity in site deposition history. The dramatic increase in the relative frequency of Santa Fe B/W between groups VI and VII and groups VIII and IX also suggests that a seriational unit may be missing from the sequence.

CERAMIC HORIZON GROUP IX

Group IX is composed of 2,701 vessels derived from proveniences extending from roomblocks 5, 6, 8, 13, 14, 15a, and 18 and kiva 12-G-5 on the west side of the site, eastward through roomblocks 10, 20, and 16 to roomblock 11 and kiva 12-D-2 (see fig. 2). The time span represented by Horizon IX is difficult to establish with complete accuracy, but on the basis of stratigraphic context and associated dates, it appears to range through the 1350s and 1360s. For example, room 12-5-4 produced a wood specimen dated at 1364vv, the latest from any Component I provenience. In addition, the hearth from ceremonial room 12-11-5 produced an archaeomagnetic date of A.D. 1370 ± 22 (R. L. DuBois, personal communication, ca. 1975). Zooclimatic and dendroclimatic correlations also place Group IX in the 1350s and 1360s (Lang and Harris 1984:141–42, 182; Rose, Dean, and Robinson 1981).

The overall hallmark of the horizon group is the rather high relative frequency of Santa Fe B/W. In all but four of the contributing samples, the percentage of Santa Fe is significantly higher than that of any other type. However, Poge-Galisteo B/W was also well represented in all the samples. Of these two types, Galisteo is more common overall. The percentage of Wiyo B/W in Group IX is about the same as it was in groups VI and VIII, and the percentage of Abiquiú Black-on-white is close to that seen in Group VII. The only "exotic" types occurring with any particular frequency are Chupadero B/W and Agua Fria G/R.

Group IX is associated with the potentially longest time interval of any of the ceramic horizon groups and, logically, should be subject to finer subdivisions. Two areas of the site may hold the key to such segregation. The depositional contexts of pottery samples from room-

blocks 5, 6, and 8 are suggestive of early Group IX phases. Samples from these areas exhibited some of the lowest Santa Fe and highest Poge-Galisteo frequencies of the Group IX series, showing a close affinity with earlier Group VII samples. In a second area, roomblock 16, deposits associated with the collapsed north alignment rooms produced a sample exhibiting equal percentages of Santa Fe B/W and Poge-Galisteo. Reoccupied rooms repaired after the collapse, probably around 1357, produced a sample sequence that exhibits very high percentages of Santa Fe (50–60%) and Poge-Galisteo percentages lower than those of either of the preceding phases. Roomblock 16 samples assigned to the terminal horizon of that block's Component I history exhibit a decline of Santa Fe B/W to percentages near 40 percent, whereas the incidence of Poge-Galisteo remains largely unchanged from the preceding phase.

If the Group IX samples are divided on a seriational basis that employs the data outlined above as an index for division, four distinct subgroups can be defined. The combined subgroup samples show the configuration found in table 10. The distribution and percentages of types other than Santa Fe, Galisteo, and Poge B/W generally form the kinds of profiles that may be expected in a correctly arranged seriation table. Both St. Johns and Heshotauthla are present only in the hypothetically earliest subgroup. Agua Fria G/R exhibits its lowest percentage value in Subgroup IXa, increasing from about 1 percent to 2 percent in the supposedly latest subgroup. Likewise, Chupadero B/W, which first appeared in Horizon VI, exhibits its highest showing (1%) in the early subgroup, declining thereafter until absent in Subgroup IXd. These profiles offer a degree of verification and support for the proposed subgroup composition and ordering.

Component II

The pottery samples used to develop the seriational sequence associated with the Component II occupation of Arroyo Hondo were selected from those available on the basis of two primary considerations: (1) sample size and assumed representativeness and (2) horizontal and vertical stratigraphic context. Regarding the latter criterion, sample selections were oriented toward the development of the fullest vertical series possible for each roomblock area of the Component II village. Ideally, such a series would include a sample representative of the earliest activity in a given roomblock, samples associated with various phases of block growth, and samples representing the

173

TABLE 10
Ceramic horizon Group IX subgroups.

Ceramic Types	Subgroup IXa %	(No.)	Subgroup IXb %	(No.)	Subgroup IXc %	(No.)	Subgroup IXd %	(No.)
Santa Fe B/W	31.0	(436)	42.7	(201)	54.8	(258)	44.4	(156)
Pindi B/W	7.7	(108)	3.2	(15)	4.9	(23)	8.5	(30)
Wiyo B/W	11.1	(156)	11.7	(55)	7.9	(37)	13.1	(46)
Abiquiú B/W	0.2	(3)	0.2	(1)	0.6	(3)	0.3	(1)
Poge B/W	14.8	(208)	14.0	(66)	7.6	(36)	10.3	(36)
Galisteo B/W	32.4	(455)	26.1	(123)	22.7	(107)	20.8	(73)
Kwahe'e B/W	–		–		–		0.3	(1)
Socorro B/W	–		0.2	(1)	–		–	
Chupadero B/W	1.0	(14)	0.4	(2)	0.2	(1)	–	
Vallecitos B/W	0.1	(1)	–		–		–	
St. Johns Poly	0.5	(7)	–		–		–	
Heshotauthla Poly	0.4	(5)	–		–		–	
Agua Fria G/R	0.9	(12)	1.5	(7)	1.3	(6)	2.3	(8)

states of population decline during block abandonment. Unfortunately—due variously to the nature of sampling efforts during excavation, the small size of recovered samples, or the presence of stratigraphic discontinuities—the ideal was rarely obtainable; and even the best series lacked samples representative of all phases of block development and decline. But only in the cases of roomblocks 20 and 21 were no usable samples of any kind present. A list of the proveniences sampled for this analysis is summarized in table 11.

Correlation of the Component II ceramic samples with resulting horizon group divisions follows the same procedure as applied to the Component I assemblage. Sample data for each horizon group are provided in table 11. The characteristics of each group and its temporal relationships are summarized below, continuing the number designations begun for Component I.

CERAMIC HORIZON GROUP X

A collection of sherds representing about 847 vessels forms the first of the five Component II ceramic horizon groups. The earliest known Component II deposits from the roomblock 10, 11, 15a, and 16 area are represented by these samples (see fig. 3).

Relevant temporal data suggest that contributing samples span the period from ca. A.D. 1381 to about 1391. The occurrence of tree-ring dates in the 1370s, associated with Component II contexts, however, may indicate that the samples forming Group X may not represent the earliest Component II samples present at the site. The most important tree-ring dates in the Horizon X series

came from carbonized wood recovered from trash-filled adobe barrow pits associated with the Component II construction of roomblock 10. The easternmost of these pits (12-C-A-6) produced six usable dates, four of which clustered at 1384r. A similar pit (12-C-A-11), opposite the west end of room 12-10-4, produced a date of 1386r. Both pits were sealed by the primary activity surface of plaza C, associated with a date of 1389vv. Development of this work area is directly associated with the completion of the block 10 south room alignment. The latest structural tree-ring dates in the series from rooms in that alignment are 1386v, 1390v, and 1390 + r.

In comparison with the composition of the proposed latest Component I ceramic sample, Subgroup IXd, fairly substantial changes in relative type frequencies are evident in Group X. Precipitous declines in the popularity of Santa Fe, Pindi, and Poge B/W were recorded. Galisteo B/W also declined in frequency but less dramatically than the other types that dominated the Component I assemblage. There appears to have been a substantial increase, however, in the frequency of both Wiyo and Abiquiú B/W, with Wiyo approaching its previous rate of popularity in Horizon Group VII. The most outstanding change occurred, however, in the representation of Rio Grande Glaze Ware, where a jump in frequency of around 23 percent was recorded from its showing in the latest Component I deposits.

CERAMIC HORIZON GROUP XI

Group XI, associated with the initial Component II decline, dating to some point after A.D. 1410, is composed

TABLE 11
Component II ceramic horizon group data.

Ceramic Horizon Group	Contributing Samples	Ceramic Types	Frequency % (No.)	Sample Range %
X	12-C-A-6-1; 12-C-A-11-1; 12-C-A-35&39; lower 12-11-3; fill 12-11-1; upper 12-15a-9; lower 12-15a-8; upper 12-16-33	Santa Fe B/W	28.2 (239)	15.2–32.9
		Pindi B/W	1.9 (16)	0– 5.5
		Kwahe'e B/W	0.1 (1)	0– 2.6
		Wiyo B/W	20.5 (174)	11.1–28.9
		Abiquiú B/W	2.1 (18)	0– 5.2
		Poge B/W	6.3 (53)	2.1–16.6
		Galisteo B/W	17.1 (145)	10.5–21.7
		Cieneguilla G/Y	1.7 (15)	0– 5.2
		White Mountain Red Ware	0.1 (1)	0– 1.0
		Los Padillas Poly	0.2 (2)	0– 1.0
		Agua Fria G/R	19.8 (168)	12.2–28.2
		San Clemente Poly	1.7 (14)	0– 2.8
		Espinosa Poly	0.1 (1)	0– 0.5
XI	Lower 12-C-2; upper 12-11-3	Santa Fe B/W	23.1 (54)	22.7–25.0
		Pindi B/W	0.4 (1)	0– 2.0
		Wiyo B/W	13.3 (31)	4.1–15.6
		Abiquiú B/W	1.7 (4)	0– 2.1
		Poge B/W	6.0 (14)	4.1– 6.4
		Galisteo B/W	16.7 (39)	16.2–18.7
		Cieneguilla G/Y	3.0 (7)	2.7– 4.1
		White Mountain Red Ware	0.4 (1)	0– 0.5
		Aqua Fria G/R	34.7 (81)	41.6–32.9
		San Clemente Poly	0.4 (1)	0– 0.5
XII	Fill 12-7-6; fill 12-7-10; 12-C-A-14	Santa Fe B/W	15.6 (45)	14.8–16.2
		Pindi B/W	2.0 (6)	0– 5.0
		Wiyo B/W	19.0 (55)	12.8–28.7
		Abiquiú B/W	0.3 (1)	0– 0.9
		Poge B/W	20.1 (58)	13.7–23.7
		Galisteo B/W	24.3 (70)	12.5–29.9
		Cieneguilla G/Y	1.7 (5)	0.9– 2.8
		Los Padillas Poly	0.6 (2)	0– 2.5
		Agua Fria G/R	15.2 (44)	12.1–17.5
		San Clemente Poly	0.6 (2)	0– 1.2
XIII	Fill 12-7-9; fill 12-8-4; fill 12-8-6; fill 12-9-9; lower 12-9-6; upper 12-9-6; lower 12-9-8; middle 12-9-8; fill 12-10-3; lower 12-10-4; upper 12-10-4; fill 12-15a-7; fill 12-15-6; fill 12-16-17; fill 12-16-20	Santa Fe B/W	25.2 (748)	21.6–34.6
		Pindi B/W	1.6 (50)	0– 4.2
		Wiyo B/W	20.7 (614)	11.2–25.6
		Abiquiú B/W	0.5 (17)	0– 3.0
		Poge B/W	13.5 (401)	6.3–24.4
		Galisteo B/W	27.4 (813)	19.5–37.4
		Cieneguilla G/Y	0.9 (27)	0– 2.7
		St. Johns Poly	0 (1)	0– 0.3
		Heshotauthla Poly	0 (2)	0– 0.6
		White Mountain Red Ware	0.1 (4)	0– 0.9
		Los Padillas Poly	0.1 (3)	0– 0.9
		Agua Fria G/R	8.9 (265)	4.0–15.0
		San Clemente Poly	0.5 (15)	0– 2.1

(Continued on next page)

TABLE 11 (continued)

Ceramic Horizon Group	Contributing Samples	Ceramic Types	Frequency % (No.)		Sample Range %
XIV	Upper 12-9-8; fill 12-10-5; fill 12-11-7; lower 12-11-2; upper 12-11-2; upper 12-11-5; fill 12-16-5; fill 12-16-6	Santa Fe B/W	43.5	(459)	38.6–57.5
		Pindi B/W	1.3	(14)	0– 4.0
		Wiyo B/W	14.4	(152)	9.6–17.6
		Abiquiú B/W	0.5	(6)	0– 2.9
		Jemez B/W	0	(1)	0– 0.5
		Poge B/W	5.4	(58)	0.8–10.2
		Galisteo B/W	21.8	(230)	14.7–34.5
		Chupadero B/W	0	(1)	0– 0.3
		Cieneguilla G/Y	1.5	(16)	0– 3.5
		Los Padillas Poly	0.3	(4)	0– 1.6
		Agua Fria G/R	10.1	(107)	3.7–16.3
		San Clemente Poly	0.6	(7)	0– 2.9

of sherds from two samples representing about 233 vessels. As the type percentages recorded for individual samples are not far removed from the range of variation found among the Group X samples, the cumulative differences between the groups may be exaggerated by the smaller number of contributing samples assigned to Horizon XI. If taken as an index of actual trends, a minor decline in Santa Fe and Wiyo B/W would be indicated, along with a fairly substantial increase in the frequency of Rio Grande glazes. Otherwise, the relative type frequencies remain basically stable.

CERAMIC HORIZON GROUP XII

This group is composed of samples characterized by relatively low percentages of Santa Fe B/W and more or less equal frequencies of Poge and Galisteo B/W. The stratigraphic position of several of the contributing samples in relationship to one another is open to considerable question. The association of samples from roomblock 7 with those from plaza C (see fig. 3), which is clearly associated with the prefire Component II decline, is also problematical. There are, however, some indications in the apparent sequential relationship of groups XII and XIII that the positioning of these samples in the series is probably correct.

A continued decline in Santa Fe B/W was associated with Horizon XII. The relative frequency of the Rio Grande glazes had also declined from its peak in Horizon Group XI. A fairly major increase in the frequency of Poge-Galisteo, which continues into Horizon Group XIII times, accompanied these changes.

CERAMIC HORIZON GROUP XIII

Most of the terminal Component II samples fall within this group, which temporally brackets the burning of much of the second component village. The burned roofing deposits from room 12-16-17 produced 12 structural tree-ring dates of 1410r. The hearth in this room was sampled for archaeomagnetic dating, producing a median date of 1390 ± 20. The hearth was unsealed and had been in use up to just prior to the burning of the room. Quite clearly, a terminal hearth use twenty years prior to the room's construction is impossible. This date, however, is of great interest in placing both the terminal use of this room and the temporal position of the burning of rooms in this block and elsewhere. The burned walls of rooms 12-9-6 and 12-15-6 produced identical median archaeomagnetic dates of 1395, but these dates were considered unreliable due to poor magnetization and a correspondingly large dispersion between samples (R. L. DuBois, personal communication, ca. 1975). The upper date range for the sample from 12-9-6 was placed at 1410, the same as that proposed for the sample from the hearth in 12-16-17. Considered within this context, it seems likely that, as absolute dates, the archaeomagnetic dates are all incorrect by the same order of magnitude and that the burning of rooms in blocks 9, 15a, and 16 occurred during a single event, sometime after approximately 1410.

Some 2,960 vessels are represented in the Group XIII collection. A return of Santa Fe frequencies to Group X and XI rates is suggested, whereas Wiyo B/W and Poge-

Galisteo remained stable. The popularity of the Rio Grande glazes continued to decline. Although the Horizon XI through XIII alterations in the relative frequencies of Santa Fe and Wiyo B/W seem to have been rather minor and short-lived, the decrease in the Rio Grande glazes and concomitant increase in the frequency of Poge-Galisteo appear to be part of a more gradual, long-term trend.

CERAMIC HORIZON GROUP XIV

This latest of the Component II ceramic groups, like the very late Component I subgroups, is formed of samples clustering in the area of plaza C's roomblocks 11 and 16 and suggests that the terminal population of the pueblo was concentrated in some locality along the eastern side of the complex. The sample exhibits a rather dramatic increase in Santa Fe B/W. Although the frequency of Rio Grande glazes remains basically stable, all the other major types show declines in relative frequency. Only in the case of Galisteo B/W can this decline be classed as minor.

Ceramic horizon groups XI through XIV correspond with archaeofaunal sample 8, the composition of which "clearly indicates a major drought at the end of the Component II occupation" (Lang and Harris 1984:42, 143). In the dendroclimatic reconstruction, a drought of severe proportions occurred between 1415 and 1425 (Rose, Dean, and Robinson 1981:96, 98, 100).

Summary

The Arroyo Hondo ceramic horizon group sequence is visually summarized in figures 68 and 69, which illustrate the changing relative frequencies of the common decorated ceramic types through time. To summarize the data presented, the only truly common type during the first decade of the fourteenth century was Santa Fe B/W, which gradually declined in abundance over the years between about 1310 and the beginning of the 1330s. This continuous decrease in frequency over the 35 to 40 years represented by groups I through V is associated with a concurrent increase in the quantity of the closely related types, Galisteo and Poge B/W. These latter types are present from the initial settlement of Arroyo Hondo onward in time and reached frequencies equal to those of Santa Fe B/W sometime after A.D. 1315 but before 1320, by which time the combined frequency of Poge-Galisteo exceeds that of Santa Fe B/W. Galisteo B/W, in particular, reaches its height of popularity during the late 1320s and early 1330s—the same period that is char-

acterized by the lowest incidence of Santa Fe B/W at the site.

During this same time span, the comparative frequencies of Poge B/W and Galisteo B/W also undergo change. The former type is quite rare prior to the mid-1320s, when the Galisteo-Poge suite makes its initial gains over Santa Fe B/W in relative popularity. But by ca. 1320, some samples show nearly equal percentages of Poge and Galisteo, with Poge exceeding Galisteo in a few cases. Around ca. 1330, however, Poge B/W begins a general decline in popularity, which tends to mirror a similar decline in Galisteo B/W after its peak in Horizon Group V. Both types show a rapid decrease in frequency associated with the initial stages of the decline of the Component I town, dated to the late 1330s and early 1340s.

While the late Mesa Verde–style types, Galisteo and Poge, appear to have remained dominant over some portion of the interval to which Horizon Group VI belongs, there are indications that at some point during this span both the style and its most prominent type, Galisteo B/W, were subordinated by an intrusion of large quantities of Pindi B/W. Prior to this time, Pindi B/W is barely represented; and although slightly more common in the late Group IX samples than in those of groups II through V, the type never again even begins to approach its Group VI status. This rapid florescence of Pindi B/W may not have been as dramatic as it first appears. If the Group VI samples are examined individually, they indicate that Pindi actually saw a more normal and gradual increase beginning as early as the 1320s and becoming more marked during the 1330s. The nature of Pindi's decline in popularity is considerably more difficult to document. Whether this decline was precipitous or relatively slow is impossible to determine from the Arroyo Hondo data or by reference to that from Pindi Pueblo.

During Group VII times, which appear on the basis of the limited information available to fall no earlier than the 1340s and may include the early 1350s, Galisteo regained some measure of its former prominence, although the combined Poge-Galisteo frequency is somewhat below that recorded for the 1320s. Both the specific and general form of the discontinuity recorded between Group VI and Subgroup IXa is so radical that a real break in the sample sequence seems to be indicated. The possibility of attributing this condition to sampling error seems highly unlikely, although the potential cannot be absolutely dismissed. But independent of whether a stratigraphic unit supplying the missing element of continuity between groups VII and IX is or is not present

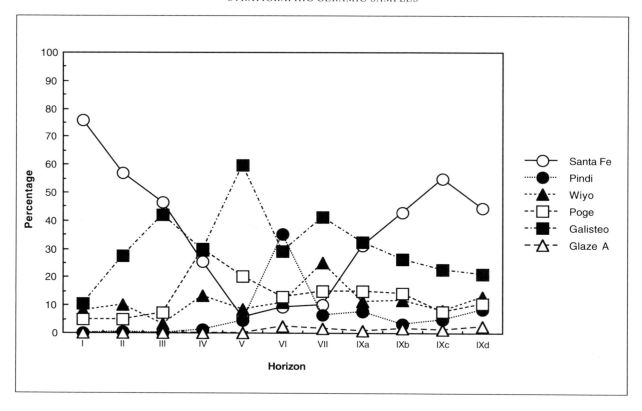

Figure 68. Summary of relative frequencies of decorated ceramic types for Component I horizon groups.

somewhere at Arroyo Hondo, the break is strongly suggestive of an extremely low population density, if not a total hiatus in occupation at some time in the 1350s.

By the time we pick up the sequence again with Subgroup IXa, the quantity of Santa Fe B/W has risen to a point relatively on a par with that of Galisteo B/W. Although Poge-Galisteo continues to dominate the ceramic spectrum into Subgroup IXb, both types are surpassed in popularity by Santa Fe B/W during the last phases of Component I activity, during the late 1350s and 1360s.

After another break in the sequence, the earliest Component II assemblages, dated to the 1380s, show a marked decrease in Santa Fe B/W along with a less dramatic drop in the other three types (i.e., Pindi, Poge, and Galisteo B/W) that dominated the Component I series. Santa Fe B/W continues to undergo a gradual decline in relative frequency during the latter decades of the fourteenth century, whereas Poge and Galisteo B/W witness a concomitant increase in frequency until both surpass Santa Fe B/W in Horizon Group XII. Although Galisteo B/W continued to be the most common decorated type in samples associated with the post-1410 burning of roomblocks 9, 15a, and 16, Santa Fe B/W rebounded in popularity until it once again dominated the decorated ceramic

collections from the latest Component II assemblages.

The dramatic increases in Santa Fe B/W toward the end of both components could easily be interpreted as being due to redeposition of earlier refuse, were it not for the substantial body of data that stands against this conclusion. There is no indication that ceramic refuse was common enough in the adobe of walls, floors, or roofs to account for a major skewing of type percentages in the architectural fill. Deposits of wall and roof/floor fall and wash containing smaller complements of pottery showed high frequencies of Santa Fe, as did contemporary intraroom trash layers. Other types common to early horizons of the sequence, such as Pindi, Poge, and Galisteo, exhibited no comparable and corresponding numeric resurgence in the later deposits.

Santa Fe B/W does not remain stylistically static over time. At both Arroyo Hondo and the Agua Fria Schoolhouse site on the Santa Fe River, it shows increasingly Wiyo-like attributes of paint, design, and surface finish (Lang 1989:64–65), and there are indications of some degree of shared geography between the production areas of Santa Fe and the derived Wiyo type. As indicated in table 12, changes in Santa Fe temper and paste characteristics appear to show a normal curve favoring an in-

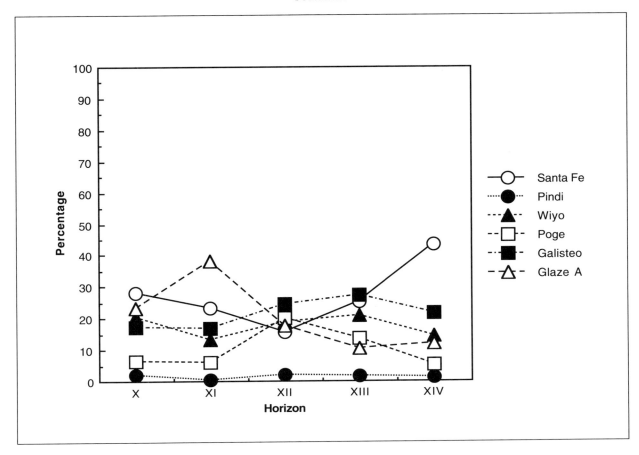

Figure 69. Summary of relative frequencies of decorated ceramic types for Component II horizon groups.

creasing use of volcanic ash temper over time. Although some earlier specimens can be expected to have intruded into later deposits through a variety of means, the data favor a low impact of this factor on the overall ceramic sequence.

Wiyo B/W exhibits considerable variation in frequency over the entire Component I occupation, showing no clear pattern beyond an overall low incidence in all but the Group VII horizon. Thereafter, the type maintains a fairly steady showing in the Group IX subgroups. Throughout Component II, Wiyo B/W is the third most popular decorated ceramic type in all ceramic horizon groups, with the exception of Group XI. In general, the relative frequency of Wiyo B/W in each of the Component II ceramic groups surpasses the frequency of the type in all but Group VII in Component I. This strong and consistent showing of Wiyo B/W is one of the most distinctive features of the Component II sequence. Although the type is present in all horizon groups from the

beginning of Arroyo Hondo's initial occupation through the very last associated with the Component II town, Wiyo never dominates group samples, and its incidence is never completely predictable.

Tree-ring date associations from other sites have suggested that Abiquiú B/W was not made until about A.D. 1375 (Breternitz 1966:70); however, the context of the type's occurrence at Arroyo Hondo contradicts that date. Although specimens of this type are rare in Component I contexts, there is no reason to believe that they are intrusive. The earliest specimen of Abiquiú B/W at Arroyo Hondo is from a deposit assigned to the Group VI horizon, and the type is thereafter present in all group and subgroup samples of the Component I occupation. The beginnings of Abiquiú production would seem, therefore, to fall minimally in the 1340s, and there can be no question that vessels of this type were being made in greater numbers by the 1350s and 1360s. Abiquiú B/W peaks in frequency at Arroyo Hondo at around 2 percent

TABLE 12

Tempers of Santa Fe Black-on-white in critical horizons of the Arroyo Hondo sequence.

	Horizon Group					
	I		IX		XIII	
Temper	No.	(%)	No.	(%)	No.	(%)
Silt	38	(76)	24	(31)	18	(26)
Silt/sand			1	(1)	1	(1)
Ash	11	(22)	45	(58)	48	(71)
Augite latite			1	(1)		
Sherd	1	(2)	6	(8)	1	(1)
Totals	50		77		68	

Note: Counts do not include Pindi B/W.

of the decorated assemblage in the earliest assemblages associated with Component II, dated to the last two decades of the fourteenth century.

Even more rare in the Arroyo Hondo ceramic assemblage are examples of Vallecitos and Jemez B/W. The two specimens from Component I assigned to Jemez B/W could not be considered classic examples and exhibit qualities suggestive of a transitional phase in the progression from Vallecitos B/W to the more characteristic expression of Jemez B/W. The depositional associations of the Jemez specimens provide no real clues regarding the potential time range associated with these types.

The rare and spotty occurrence of Kwahe'e and Socorro B/W specimens, without particular regard to the age of the deposits that produced these sherds, is not unexpected, as Kwahe'e B/W does not appear to have been produced after about A.D. 1250, and the end date suggested by Breternitz (1966:96) for Socorro is ca. A.D. 1275. The vessels representing both types, therefore, were already relics by the time the Component I settlement at Arroyo Hondo was founded.

Chupadero B/W first appears at Arroyo Hondo during the 1330s. Although the percentage changes in Chupadero B/W over the period of its Component I distribution are minimal, the cline formed by them is very regular, with the largest relative frequency of Chupadero being found in deposits believed to date to the 1350s. The quantity of this always rare type seems to have remained relatively stable in the late 1350s, declining thereafter until it is absent in the latest of the Group IX samples. Only one fragment of this type was identified

in the Component II assemblages, suggesting a continued but rare occurrence at the site well into the fifteenth century. Chupadero B/W is present at Pindi by the late thirteenth or early fourteenth century and at Forked Lightning by about A.D. 1300; but at these sites the type does not occur in later deposits (Kidder and Shepard 1936:346, 477; Stubbs and Stallings 1953). Although present at Rowe and at Pecos pueblos, it was rare at both, and no data on stratigraphic associations are available (Kidder and Shepard 1936:346). The collection of Chupadero from Arroyo Hondo is by far the largest and best provenienced from any of these sites in the Santa Fe–Pecos district.

Of the rare types, St. Johns is present earliest and continues to occur sporadically through the Subgroup IXa horizon. One vessel fragment identified as St. Johns Polychrome was also found in association with post-1410 deposits in Component II. As the latest dates associated with this type in its area of production fall within the first decade of the fourteenth century (Breternitz 1966:93–94; Carlson 1970), it may be that the type was actually extinct as an expression of the potter's art during most of the period of its occurrence at Arroyo Hondo. If this is the case, judging from the Arroyo Hondo situation and the distribution of St. Johns at Pindi Pueblo, vessels belonging to this type must have remained in circulation for as much as one hundred years after its production ceased. The relative incidence of St. Johns over comparable spans of time at both Arroyo Hondo and Pindi Pueblo (Stubbs and Stallings 1953:17, 56) is quite similar, but the higher frequency of the type in the pre–Arroyo Hondo levels of Pindi Pueblo seems supportive of a production span ending in or about the very early 1300s.

The St. Johns Polychrome derivative, Heshotauthla Polychrome, from the Zuni area may appear in the northern Rio Grande prior to the 1330s, as is suggested by its contexts at Paa-ko (Lambert 1954:42–43) and Tijeras pueblos (Judge 1974:41) in the Sandia-Manzano ranges, but there is no evidence for its presence at Arroyo Hondo prior to ca. A.D. 1331, nor do the data from Pindi support an earlier occurrence in the area. As the suggested beginning date of Heshotauthla production is A.D. 1300 (Breternitz 1966:77; Carlson 1970), this trade ware does not seem to have reached the towns and villages of the Santa Fe area until some thirty years after its initial development. Interestingly, Heshotauthla Polychrome is far more common at Pindi Pueblo than at Arroyo Hondo, although its span of occurrence embraces the same time period at both sites.

Rio Grande Glaze Ware is not unqualifiedly present

at Arroyo Hondo until ca. 1340, which date also saw its earliest presence at Pindi Pueblo (Stubbs and Stallings 1953). At the very earliest, Agua Fria G/R may have been introduced at Arroyo Hondo during the early to middle 1330s, as suggested by its initial showing in plazas G and K. If we assume these specimens are not intrusive, some support exists for recognizing the presence of Agua Fria as a rare trade item in the Santa Fe area sometime between A.D. 1330 and 1340. It does not, however, show any appreciable increase in frequency until the 1360s. By the beginning of the second component, Rio Grande glazes witnessed a dramatic increase in popularity, peaking at nearly 42 percent of the decorated assemblage during Horizon Group XI, probably dating to the last decade of the fourteenth century. The ware, however, appears to have undergone a gradual decrease in relative frequency throughout the first quarter of the fifteenth century in association with the decline and abandonment of the Component II town.

Overall, the history of painted pottery use at Arroyo Hondo is primarily one characterized by the shifting popularity of Santa Fe B/W and the suite of late Mesa Verde–style types, Poge and Galisteo B/W. For a brief period during the 1330s and early 1340s, Pindi B/W also dominated the decorated ceramic assemblage from the site. In comparing the Component I and II series, a basic continuity is expressed in the long-term importance of both Santa Fe and Galisteo B/W. The primary differences between the ceramic complexes of the two components lie in the generally lower frequencies of Wiyo B/W and Rio Grande glazes in Component I contexts. In the case of Wiyo B/W, this condition appears to reflect a generalized increase in the flow of Wiyo vessels out of the north, possibly in conjunction with the spread of Wiyo production areas southward. In the case of the Rio Grande glazes, the development of production centers in the Galisteo Basin, immediately to the south of the Santa Fe area, likely played some role in the wares' increased popularity. But the terminal Component II decline of this ware is puzzling. It could possibly be associated with a disruption in contacts with glaze production areas corresponding with the final decline and abandonment of Arroyo Hondo Pueblo during the first quarter of the fifteenth century.

II

Miscellaneous Ceramic Artifacts
from Arroyo Hondo Pueblo

Anthony Thibodeau

There were a total of 95 identifiable miscellaneous ceramic artifacts recovered at Arroyo Hondo, including pipes, effigies, balls, beads, miniature vessels, a prayer plume base, and a ring vessel (table 13). Some of the pieces of clay that could not be identified are probably fragments of handles from larger vessels, coil discard, or other forms of refuse from the manufacture of pottery (Eric Blinman, personal communication, 1991). In addition, there are a large number of utilized and worked sherds from Arroyo Hondo.

Ceramic Pipes

Forty-eight fragmentary or whole ceramic pipes were excavated from Arroyo Hondo. This sample size is comparable to other contemporary sites in the northern Rio Grande, with the exception of Pecos Pueblo (table 14), where Kidder (1932) recovered a great number of pipes with a wide variety of form and decoration. This anomaly is yet to be explained, though Pecos was probably a major trading center in the early historic period (Cordell 1984:54). It is also possible that many of these pipes are very recent productions.

Much of the Arroyo Hondo pipe collection is in fragmented condition, and usually only the mouthpiece end remains. Of the existing 32 fragments, 18 were considered probable straight conical pipes, with no visible decoration, because they closely resemble the whole examples of this type. They are not complete enough to qualify as any specific types, however. The remaining 14 fragments are simply too small to determine anything other than that they are incomplete pipes.

Sixteen of the pipes from Arroyo Hondo are complete enough to be classified according to type. Four distinct pipe types were identified at Arroyo Hondo:

1. Straight Conical Undecorated (6)
2. Straight Conical Decorated (8)
3. Acute Angle Elbow Undecorated (1)
4. Rectangular Continued Vent (1)

Derived primarily from Switzer's (1969) classification of pipes encountered archaeologically in the Southwest, based on form and general features, these types are actually elaborations on Kidder's (1932) system, in which the major types were simply too broad. In the Arroyo Hondo analysis, decoration is added as a criterion to distinguish patterns of style.

The simple straight conical pipe remains the predominant form at Pecos Pueblo and in the northern Rio Grande (Wetherington 1968:61), and this holds true at Arroyo Hondo as well. In fact, the distribution of this type extends over the entire Pueblo region, although primarily throughout New Mexico and Arizona (Ariss 1939: 54). Several of these specimens are fragmented, but most of the whole straight conical pipes have endured very well, making it easy to distinguish their characteristics. The one elbow pipe is also in very good condition, but the rectangular pipe had to be pieced and glued to recognize the form.

Description

Although there is considerable variation between specimens within types, there are also certain recognizable patterns throughout the collection, especially among the straight conical pipes. The bulk of these pipes, often described as "cloudblowers," are straight bored, tapering at

TABLE 13
Miscellaneous ceramic artifacts from Arroyo Hondo Pueblo,
by component and provenience.

	Specimen Number	Type	Comments
Component I			
Rooms	12-4-2-3-1	Straight Conical Decorated pipe	
	12-4-2-III-1	Round Body Quadruped effigy	Floor contact
	12-5-4-III-13	Straight Conical Undecorated pipe	Tree-ring date of A.D. 1364
	12-5-9-14-1	Round Body Quadruped effigy	From trash below floor
	12-5-9-14-1	Unknown animal effigy	Head fragment; from trash below floor
	12-5-9-14-2	Round Body Quadruped effigy	From trash below floor
	12-5-14-IVE	Miniature dipper or ladle	Very small, handle missing
	12-10-3-1&2	Unknown pipe	
	12-11-3-3	Miniature jar	Fat rim and restricted orifice, urn-shaped form
	12-12-4-6	Ceramic bead	
	12-12-4-6-1	Straight conical pipe	
	12-12-4-7	Miniature dipper or ladle	Shallow bowl, handle missing
	12-12-4-9	Straight conical pipe	
	12-15-7-3	Straight conical pipe	Tree-ring date of A.D. 1308; 2nd-story floor contact
	12-16-24-1	Straight conical pipe	
	12-16-24-2	Straight conical pipe	Slightly flattened form
	12-16-30-2	Ceramic ball	Lumpy, irregular surface
	12-16-31-4	Unknown miniature vessel	Squared, conelike form
	12-16-31-4-6	Straight Conical Undecorated pipe	Floor contact
	12-16-32-1	Miniature jar	Thin walls near rim
	12-16-32-2-1	Straight conical pipe	
	12-16-33-4	Straight Conical Decorated pipe	Molded "wing" on each side; 2nd-story floor contact; ceremonial storage
	12-16-35-2-1	Straight conical pipe	Floor contact
	12-18-7-V-1	Straight Conical Undecorated pipe	Floor contact
	12-18-14-IIS	Unknown pipe	Tree-ring dates of A.D. 1323 & 1325
Plazas	12-C-3-III	Straight conical pipe	From gate of plaza C
	12-C-3-9	Round Body Quadruped effigy	Pierced with small hole running length of body
	12-C-3-11	Straight conical pipe	Use-surface in plaza C
	12-C-3C-2-3	Ceramic ball	Smooth surface
	12-C-3C-4-1	Miniature ladle or dipper	
	12-E-1	Straight conical pipe	From gate between plaza D and plaza E
	12-G-1-2-1	Acute Angle Elbow Undecorated pipe	From gate of plaza G; polished surface; rounded angle
	12-G-1C-2	Ceramic ball	Slightly oval form
	12-G-2-3-22-2	Straight Conical Decorated pipe	From burial in plaza G; very long pipe; thin band of bark near mouthpiece
	12-G-8A-2	Straight conical pipe	
	12-G-14A-2	Straight Conical Decorated pipe	Etched, curved line running lengthwise; fishtail mouthpiece
	12-G-23A-2	Straight Conical Undecorated pipe	
	12-G-25C-2	Folded-Wing Bird with Base effigy	Small holes at tail and head areas, *not* pierced
	12-G-21A-2	Ceramic ball	Flattened on one side
	12-G-28A-II	Miniature bowl	Shallow depression with thick walls

(Continued on next page)

TABLE 13 (*continued*)

Specimen Number	Type	Comments
12-G-38B-2	Round Body Quadruped effigy	Long, cylindrical body
12-G-102B-2	Ceramic ball	Slightly oval form
12-G-104B-2	Ceramic bead	
12-G-106B-2	Ceramic ball	Slightly oval form
12-G-C33-3	Unknown pipe	
12-G-C35-3	Miniature ladle or dipper	Thumb-shaped depression behind bowl
12-G-C40-2	Straight conical pipe	
12-G-D12-2	Straight conical pipe	
12-G-D17-2	Straight conical pipe	
12-H-2-4	Folded-Wing Bird effigy	2 broken areas on top of head
12-H-2-9	Unknown pipe	
12-H-2-9	Unknown pipe	
12-H-3-2-3	Straight conical pipe	Straight mouthpiece protruding from tapered end of stem
12-H-3-3	Rectangular Continued Vent pipe	3 small circular imprints on each side; wide shaft
12-H-3-7	Round Body Quadruped effigy	
12-H-3-7	Unknown animal effigy	Reptile-like head fragment
12-H-3-7	Ceramic ball	Very irregular form, almost cube shape
12-F-1-1	Ceramic ball	Oval form
12-K-1-III	Miniature bowl	Most intact miniature vessel
12-K-I-III-1	Straight Conical Undecorated pipe	Very crude form
12-K-2-II-3	Straight Conical Decorated pipe	Deep incised corncob design
12-K-3	Folded-Wing Bird effigy	Small, dovelike form; most intact and intricate bird effigy
12-K-13-III-2	Ring vessel	
12-K-14-II&III	Round Body Quadruped effigy	Crude, irregular form
12-K-15-I	Folded-Wing Bird effigy	Large, flat, oval body
12-K-15-III&II	Straight conical pipe	

Kivas

12-Kiva G	Round Body Quadruped effigy	Turtlelike form
12-Kiva G	Prayer plume base or *tiponi*	
12-G-5-II	Miniature jar	Wide base and narrow orifice
12-G-5-II	Straight Conical Decorated pipe	Wide ring near mouthpiece
12-G-5-III	Unknown miniature vessel	Fat, canoe-shaped form
12-G-5-IV	Unknown pipe	
12-G-5-V	Unknown pipe	
12-G-5-V	Miniature ladle or dipper	Incomplete handle

Component II
Rooms

12-7-10-3	Unknown pipe	
12-9-8-1	Unknown pipe	
12-9-10-IIS	Ceramic ball	Conical hole extending into one end, *not* pierced
12-9-10-IIS	Ceramic ball	
12-10-3-3-4-5	Miniature jar	
12-10-3-3,4,5	Ceramic ball	
12-11-2-2	Unknown animal effigy	
12-15a-7-1	Miniature bowl	Completely intact, uneven form
12-16-7-1	Unknown pipe	
12-16-15-2	Unknown pipe	
12-16-16-2	Unknown pipe	

TABLE 13 (*continued*)

	Specimen Number	Type	Comments
Plazas			
	12-C-3C-4-1	Unknown pipe	
	12-C-9-1-9	Ceramic ball	Very irregular surface
Kivas			
	12-C-2-2	Folded-Wing Bird with Base effigy	Head broken off; V-shaped tail; 3 tree-ring dates of A.D. 1386
	12-C-2-2	Miniature bowl	
	12-D-2-1	Straight conical pipe	Component 2 fill of Component 1 kiva
Surface and Test Trenches			
	12-B-Gen	Straight Conical Decorated pipe	Test trench in plaza C; incised band of crisscross lines and perpendicular lines
	12-0-0-3	Unknown pipe	Rectangular/oval mouthpiece
	12-13-0	Straight Conical Undecorated pipe	From surface of roomblock 13
	12-15-0	Straight Conical Decorated pipe	From surface of roomblock 15; incised corncob design
	12-?-?	Straight conical pipe	

the mouthpiece and widening at the bowl. Most are similar internally, with a narrow vent enlarging at some point to form the bowl. The length of the bowl and the vent varies a great deal, however, as does the overall length of the pipe, which averages 6.55 cm and ranges from 4.80 cm to 9.80 cm. The bowl usually consumes about 40 percent of the full pipe length, but this ranges from over 50 percent to under 20 percent. A common feature on this type of pipe at Pecos Pueblo is the flattened, flaring, or fishtail mouthpiece (Kidder 1932:160), but only one such example was present at Arroyo Hondo. The mouthpieces in the Arroyo Hondo collection are usually smaller reflections of the round bowl at the other end, tapering to an average 1.21 cm in diameter. The bowl on these pipes averages 2.22 cm in diameter, and the pipe walls at the bowl average 0.44 cm thick.

STRAIGHT CONICAL UNDECORATED

The basic criterion for this type is the diagnostic tapering form of the typical conical tubular pipe in the Southwest (fig. 70). There is no decoration or ornamentation on the surface of the pipe. Pipe 12-H-3-2-3 (fig. 70a), a stem fragment, is light tan in color—the only deviance within this type from the dark gray that dominates the collection. This pipe also exhibits a straight mouthpiece protruding from the tapered end of the pipe, similar to Pecos Type IIA but with no flare (Kidder 1932:160–62). The longest pipe (7.48 cm) is pipe 12-13-0 (fig. 70b), which is also the most even in form and texture and the most aesthetically pleasing of this type. Pipe 12-5-4-III-

13 (fig. 70c), at 4.80 cm, is the shortest in this group and the entire collection of whole pipes. This pipe would be similar to Kidder's Type IC (Heavy Fat Type) because of its wide bowl and overall thick body, although the pipes from Pecos probably averaged about 13 cm in length.

Pipe 12-K-I-III-1 (fig. 70e) is interesting because it differs from any pipe in the collection by exhibiting an irregular, pitted surface texture. Almost every other sample in the collection has some surface treatment such as polishing or smoothing, suggesting that in some cases function may have prevailed over aesthetics—possibly when sufficient production time was unavailable. There is some evidence, however, that this pipe was never used: there is no dottle, or crust, remaining in the bowl, and the bowl is not blackened on the inside like many other pipes from Arroyo Hondo. Someone may have gone through with the firing, been dissatisfied with the result, and discarded the pipe.

STRAIGHT CONICAL DECORATED

These pipes are similar in form to the previous type but have added exterior decoration. Of the eight samples, five pipes are whole or nearly whole (fig. 71). The nature of the design on the fragmented samples is more or less distinguishable, but the extent is not. The primary form of embellishment consists of incised or etched lines, which range from deep incisions of nearly 0.2 cm to light scratches on the surface.

The most notable and immediately recognizable application of incised design at Arroyo Hondo is the

TABLE 14

Ceramic pipes found at Arroyo Hondo Pueblo and contemporaneous sites in the northern Rio Grande.

	Straight Conical	Elbow	Elaborated Form	Unclassified/ Fragment	Total
Arroyo Hondo	32	1	1	14	48
Pecos	227	8	323	110	668
Paa-ko	31	3	2	3	39
Unshagi	28	1	?	?	52
Pot Creek	17	0	10	0	27
Te'ewi	8	1	0	1	10
Pindi	7	0	1	0	8
Poshu	4	1	4	0	9

corncob motif on pipes 12-15-0 and 12-K-3-II-3 (fig. 71a and b). The latter has deeper incisions and "kernels" of more quadratic proportions. Pipe 12-K-3-II-3 is nearly intact and similar in form to pipe 12-5-4-III-13; it is also the shortest in total length of this type (5.64 cm). Although the designs are similar, there is considerable relief between the kernels and the mouthpiece of pipe 12-K-3-II-3 and no relief on pipe 12-15-0. A pipe with a slightly cruder corncob design was excavated by Dutton (1966:5) from Las Madres in the Galisteo Basin. It was almost identical in total length to pipe 12-K-3-II-3.

Pipe 12-B-Gen (fig. 71c) also exhibits incised design, but with less relief and in a crisscross, diamondlike pattern. The design may occupy only one side of the pipe, with straight incised lines encircling the rest of the body, but this is difficult to determine due to this specimen's fragmented condition. The only other example of incised design in the collection is a line of about 3.10 cm on pipe 12-16-33-4 (fig. 71e), extending from the top of one wing to the bottom of the opposite wing.

One curved line is lightly etched on one side of pipe 12-G-14A-2 (fig. 71d), although again the extent of this design is unknown, since only half the pipe remains. This pipe's most notable distinction, however, is not decoration but the form of the mouthpiece. It is similar to the fishtail form described by Kidder (1932:160) as Type II at Pecos, except that this mouthpiece flares only slightly from the body and then straightens, whereas the examples from Pecos generally flare at a constant angle to the end of the pipe. The purpose of this feature is unclear.

In the Arroyo Hondo collection, pipe 12-16-33-4 (fig. 71e), with its molded "wings," is most similar to an effigy pipe. The wings measure 2.11 cm in length and are scored five or six times on the crest. The precise im-age these wings represent is unknown; no doubt some sort of bird. The incised line connecting the two wings has been discussed above. This pipe is average in length and other dimensions, except for its unusually thick walls of 0.61 cm—nearly as thick as those of undecorated pipe 12-12-4-9.

Pipe 12-G-5-II (fig. 71f) bears a molded ring or collar, 0.7 cm wide and of fairly high relief, about 1.2 cm from the mouthpiece end. It is debatable, however, whether this is a form of decoration or simply serves the purpose of defining the mouthpiece. This pipe probably does not fit Switzer's type (1969:21) of Straight Collared Conical because of its much smaller collar. The body above the collar has a high polish, and the mouthpiece below the rim has been heavily worn, indicating considerable use.

Pipe 12-4-2-3-1 (fig. 71g) is only a fragment but still shows the juncture between bowl and vent. Although few measurements could be taken, the fragment plainly exhibits extremely thick walls and a wide vent entering the bowl. It also has an interesting design on the outside surface, consisting of small fingernail marks spaced about 0.4 cm apart and possibly extending around the entire body.

Pipe 12-G-2-3-22-2 (fig. 71h) is the longest in the collection and had a thin strip of bark encircling the body about 1.7 cm from the mouthpiece end, set against a slight lip. It is possible that this material could have been part of a strap for the pipe, or it may be another case of a decorative means of defining the mouthpiece.

On the pipes from Arroyo Hondo with molding, this extra amount of clay may have served a purpose other than pure decoration. When smoked, the bowls of these pipes (which in many cases make up more than half the pipe) undoubtedly became very hot and uncomfortable to hold. The molded collar—and especially the scored

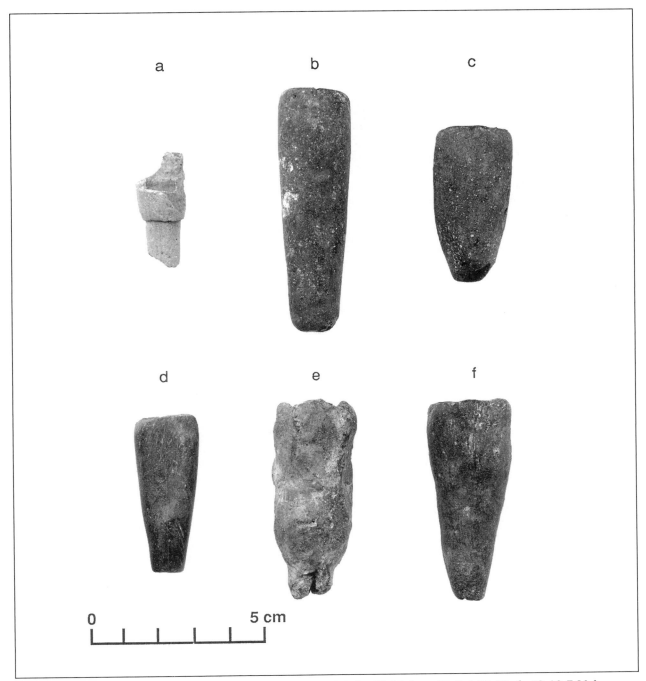

Figure 70. Straight Conical Undecorated pipes: a, *12-H-3-2-3;* b, *12-13-0;* c, *12-5-4-III-13;* d, *12-18-7-V-1;* e, *12-K-I-III-1;* f, *12-16-31-4-6.*

wings on pipes 12-16-33-4 and 12-G-5-II—may have provided a kind of handle to protect the user's fingers. West (1934:139) indicates that this was often necessary in the case of short pipes and that braided yucca fiber was also used for protection. This may be another function of the bark on pipe 12-G-2-3-22-2, although it was situated a little too far from the bowl to have been effective.

RECTANGULAR CONTINUED VENT

The Rectangular Continued Vent pipe (pipe 12-H-3-3; fig. 72a) from Arroyo Hondo is actually a variation of Switzer's Straight Tubular Collared type (1969:21). The collar form is abundant at Pecos, but this is the closest example at Arroyo Hondo. The collar is not as well defined on this pipe as on the pipes at Pecos or in Switzer's description, and is not the primary feature. The continued vent, which eliminates any bowl, seems most characteristic and warrants a more descriptive type name.

This pipe could be viewed as simply a variation of the straight conical pipe because it was probably made and used in much the same way. The differing characteristics, other than the obvious overall shape, are in this pipe's dimensions, although the total length is standard for the samples at Arroyo Hondo. There is no distinct bowl, though the vent continues to widen gradually to the pipe's end. The vent is extremely wide, measuring 1 cm—twice the diameter of some of the other pipes. The bowl end is also very wide and rectangular like the rest of the body. Because the actual smoking tube is so large, some sort of stopper probably was necessary to prevent tobacco from being sucked into the user's mouth. Some of these "tobacco stops" were recovered from Pecos in some of the larger pipes, but none were recovered from Arroyo Hondo. The Pecos stops were made of clay and sandstone and were either heavily scored or square in shape to allow smoke to pass through the passage (Kidder 1932: 156–57). Unshagi, a Pueblo site in the Jemez Mountains, has yielded several examples of this pipe type, although these are not quite as rectangular in form as the example from Arroyo Hondo. Reiter (1938:158) describes these as "undivided bore" pipes and suggests that even an unmodified pebble may have been used as a tobacco stop.

The actual body form is not truly rectangular but slightly oval. There is a distinct mouthpiece formed where the body narrows sharply at one end, and the pipe's width decreases from 3.67 cm to 2.11 cm. In external form, this pipe bears a distinct resemblance to a pipe from Poshu, a site in the Chama Valley (Jeançon 1923:pl. 34c). There is no decoration on pipe 12-H-3-3 (see fig. 72a), but there is a line of three circular indentations of about 0.7 cm each on the sides of the pipe. Their function is uncertain, but the pipe can be held quite comfortably when three fingers are placed over these marks.

ACUTE ANGLE ELBOW UNDECORATED

Although rare, elbow pipes are consistently recovered from sites in the northern Rio Grande. Otherwise, their distribution throughout the Southwest is limited primarily to the Four Corners area (Ariss 1939:56). These pipes are often attributed to some exterior influence, possibly from the eastern Plains, where such pipes are more common (Kidder 1932:170; Wendorf 1953:65). Jeançon (1923:31) believed them to be a relatively modern development among the Pueblos; however, the presence of an elbow pipe in a fourteenth-century context at Arroyo Hondo shows that this is not the case. The only elbow pipe (pipe 12-G-1-2-1; fig. 72b) from Arroyo Hondo is finely made, with a very smooth, polished surface and a bowl angle of just less than 90 degrees, pitched slightly toward the mouthpiece. This simple, undecorated pipe has a well-shaped body with a curved angle where the bowl meets the stem. The mouthpiece and bowl are both round and measure about 1 cm and 2 cm in diameter, respectively—slightly smaller but similar to most of the tubular pipes at Arroyo Hondo.

In the Southwest, most elbow pipes with angles this sharp are not this curvilinear but have a distinct joint between bowl and vent. It is common for these pipes to have been made in two parts and later cemented together, but pipe 12-G-1-2-1 was made in one piece, of the same clay as the majority of the pipes at Arroyo Hondo. Unlike many elbow pipes, this pipe did not need a separate stem but could be used much the same as the tubular pipes from Arroyo Hondo, with the obvious advantage of a more stable receptacle in which the smoking material could rest. There is a thick carbon crust on the inside of the bowl, indicating frequent use.

Manufacture

The accepted method of production of the straight conical pipe was very simple and required only two basic steps before the actual firing; production of other forms was probably quite similar. First, the stem was formed by packing the clay around a small reed, twig, or grass stem. In the collection at Pecos, Kidder (1932:157) notes plant imprints on the walls of the stem in some cases, but these were not apparent at Arroyo Hondo. Next, the bowl was probably shaped by pulling the excess clay from the stem and molding it around a finger or wooden plug (Kidder 1932:157; Lambert 1954:114; Stubbs and Stallings 1953:94; Reiter 1938:158). Most pipes have a smooth, uniform surface, sometimes polished but never slipped or painted. Several specimens exhibited a very rough, pitted surface with a crude overall form, which seems to indicate an item produced quickly. There is no distinct evidence of drilling, but it is possible that such techniques may have been used for finishing.

188

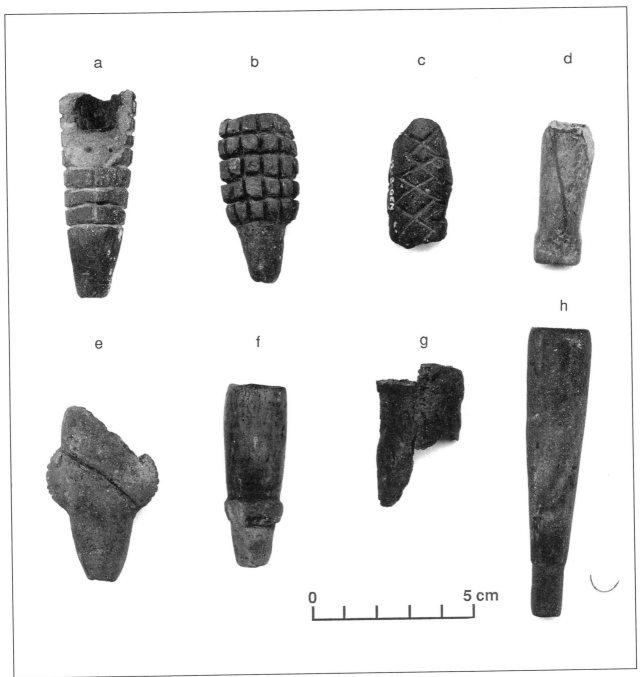

Figure 71. Straight Conical Decorated pipes: a, *12-15-0;* b, *12-K-3-II-3;* c, *12-B-Gen;* d, *12-G-14A-2;*
e, *12-16-33-4;* f, *12-G-5-II;* g, *12-4-2-3-1;* h, *12-G-2-3-22-2.*

The color ranges from shades of gray to brown in all types, a dark gray being most common. The clay resembles that of much of the culinary ware at Arroyo Hondo, which generally has a dark, gray color and coarse temper. Some pipes exhibit little or no tempering material, however, and few are as dark as most of the culinary wares. Also, very few of the pipes have any of the micaceous material common in the culinary wares. The pipes were probably fired much the same as most of the pottery, although they may have been fired separately, as

189

suggested in this account from Tschopik (1941:58–59) of the method of historic Navajo pipe making:

> The fuel is placed around the pipe, adding it in a sunwise direction, so as to form a dome-like structure. When this has been completed, wood and rabbit-brush are placed around to serve as tinder, and the kiln is lighted. The pipes are allowed to burn for from ten to twenty minutes, and no songs are sung during the firing.

Since most of the pipes are a similar shade of gray, it is probable that any differences in color are due to discrepancies in the firing technique and not to different types of clay. Kidder (1932:156) suggests that the black found on some pipes in the Pecos collection was caused by smudging.

Decoration is limited to either etched or incised lines on the surface or alterations in the basic tubular form. No definite effigy pipes were found at Arroyo Hondo, although one pipe mentioned above has molded wings on opposite sides.

Provenience

Most pipes from Arroyo Hondo Pueblo were found in the general fill of plaza areas. Pipes from plazas or kivas comprised over half the collection; many were recovered from plaza G. No pipes were recovered from plaza A. Due to these items' probable function, one would expect to see at least a few of these pipes recovered from rooms determined to have had ceremonial significance. In fact, four pipes were found in various levels of two separate kivas, although none from floor contexts. Of interest is pipe 12-16-33-4, the Straight Conical Decorated pipe with molded wings and incised lines, which was associated with the second-story floor of room 16-33. Creamer (1993) feels that this was a ceremonial room, with ceremonial storage in the room immediately below. Other artifacts found in the second story included a deflector with painted black stripes, bone awls, two ceramic vessels, a club head, a red-stained stone palette, and several pieces of ground and polished stone (Creamer 1993).

Seventeen pipes were located in storage or living rooms or a combination of both. Two pipes were found on open-air use surfaces, or work areas, and three pipes lay directly on the surface of the site, unassociated with any architectural feature. Two Straight Conical Undecorated pipes were excavated from room 12-4, a living or storage room (Creamer 1993). Pipe 12-12-4-6-1 was just below the earlier of two floors, and pipe 12-12-4-9 was found in subfloor midden #3, just above sterile soil. Room-

blocks 16 and 18 yielded three pipes in contact with the floors of rooms 16-31 and 16-35, both storage rooms, and room 18-7, a storage room converted to living space (Creamer 1993). These were all Straight Conical Undecorated pipes, and were the only three pipes in the collection found in contact with the most recent first-story floor of a Component I room.

Pipe 12-G-2-3-22-2 is the only pipe associated with a burial at Arroyo Hondo. This is the longest pipe at the site, and the one with a thin strip of bark wound close to the mouthpiece end. It was placed near the right leg of an adult male, 34 to 39 years of age, who lay flexed on the left side, with his head to the south, in plaza G (Palkovich 1980:113). Because the pipe is the only artifact associated with this burial, it is difficult to say whether its presence is a mark of ceremonial status. Kidder (1932:182) notes that pipes accompanying interments were indicative of the Glaze III and IV periods, which postdate the occupation of Arroyo Hondo.

Chronology

It is likely that the straight conical pipe form is the earliest in the Southwest, dating to around 2000 B.C. in southern Arizona (Switzer 1969:53). In the northern Rio Grande, this form also predates the more elaborate forms (Kidder 1932:181), such as the elbow pipe, which may have developed during Pueblo I (Judd 1922). There is little evidence, however, to suggest that these forms were not used contemporaneously. Given the large number of pipes recovered from Pueblo IV sites and the collection from Pecos, Switzer (1969:32) suggests that the straight conical pipes probably date to Pueblo III and that all others correlate to Pueblo IV. The flattened mouthpiece variation on straight conical pipes at sites like Pecos, Te'ewi, and Pot Creek appears between A.D. 1275 and 1350 (Wendorf 1953:65) and possibly earlier (Wetherington 1968:61). Pipe 12-16-24-2 is the closest example of this form at Arroyo Hondo, and this pipe could not be dated.

The most reliable means of dating archaeological materials in the Southwest has been the use of tree rings, which are abundant at Arroyo Hondo. Unfortunately, only three tree-ring dates are associated with pipes; two of these are with the same pipe (12-18-14-IIs), which could not be typed and was out of its original context. The two dates for pipe 12-18-14-IIS are A.D. 1323 and 1325. Pipe 12-5-4-III-13, a Straight Conical Undecorated pipe, although also recovered from fill, was dated to A.D. 1364. Pipe 12-15-7-3 is associated with the second-story floor of room 17-7, which yielded a date of A.D. 1308. Of course, these dates represent only the

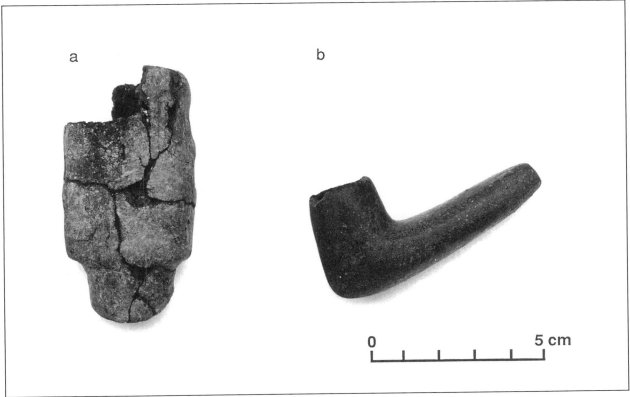

Figure 72. Pipes: a, *Rectangular Continued Vent pipe 12-H-3-3;* b, *Acute Angle Elbow Undecorated pipe 12-G-1-2-1.*

construction of the rooms and not room use or the terminal fill.

We can date these pipes relative to the occupations at Arroyo Hondo and to the established northern Rio Grande chronology. Tree rings date the Component I occupation from about A.D. 1285 to 1345 and Component II from 1353 to 1420, with a short interim of low occupation between (Creamer 1993). These dates place the two occupations of Arroyo Hondo very late in Pueblo III through Pueblo IV of the Pecos Classification (Kidder 1927:490), or Late Coalition through Early Classic of the northern Rio Grande sequence (Wendorf and Reed 1955:145–46, 149–51).

Thirty-six pipes at Arroyo Hondo occur in Component I contexts and only seven from Component II. Five pipes, including two decorated, were found on the surface of the site or in backfill where a particular occupation could not be determined. Five of the Component I pipes were typed as Straight Conical Undecorated and six as Straight Conical Decorated; 16 were considered probable straight conical pipes. Only one pipe in Component II could be recognized as a probable straight conical pipe, and the rest were untypeable, which really

limits any correlation of style and period of occupation. The Acute Angle Elbow and Undecorated Rectangular Continued Vent pipes also occurred in Component I. More undecorated than decorated pipes occur in Component I. This may simply reflect the larger sample in Component I, but it also could suggest that the Straight Conical Undecorated pipe was an earlier form in the northern Rio Grande.

Tobacco and Pipe Smoking in the Southwest

Pipe smoking of herbal materials such as tobacco and other plants has been a traditional practice both historically and prehistorically in the Southwest. Smoking was used primarily in a ritual effort to manifest improved conditions for hunting or farming. The function of the pipe here is very clear: smoking was employed in conjunction with various prayers and occasional animal effigies in specific situations to punctuate these prayers. For example, Navajos ritually used pipes in the hunting of large game animals such as elk and deer, and the prayers used with the pipe were designed either to extend good luck or to eliminate bad luck on a hunting trip

TABLE 15
Ceramic effigies found at Arroyo Hondo Pueblo and contemporaneous sites in the northern Rio Grande.

	Round Body Quadruped	Bird	Other Animal	Human	Total
Arroyo Hondo (unknown: 3)	8	5	0	0	16
Pecos	148	77	80	263	568
Paa-ko (unknown: 2)	2	1	0	2	7
Unshagi (unknown: ?)	2	4	0	0	?
Pindi	2	0	0	0	2
Poshu	0	1	0	4	5

(Tschopik 1941:63). In Hopi kiva ceremonies, smoking is an integral activity because the smoke reputedly petitions and encourages rain clouds (Stephen 1936:306, 375, 1305; Paper 1988:24). One Navajo informant stated that the clouds of smoke from the pipe *are* rain clouds, and that creating them was the main purpose of smoking (Tschopik 1941:59). The symbolism of the cloudblower pipe presumably holds true in most of the Southwest, at least where this pipe type predominates; by analogy, the primary function of these pipes prehistorically was probably to help improve the local climatic conditions.

Only commercial tobacco is smoked casually in the modern Tewa pueblos, and wild tobacco is reserved for formal and ceremonial occasions (Robbins, Harrington, and Freire-Marreco 1916:103). The most common species of wild tobacco in the Southwest seems to have been *Nicotiana attenuata* (Cordell 1980:76; Spinden 1950:94), which historically has been gathered and smoked in a mixture by Hopi and Zuni Indians, and to some extent at the pueblos of Santa Ana and Isleta (Switzer 1969:14). *Nicotiana rustica*, which may have equaled corn in its distribution in North America (Wilbert 1987:6), has been found cultivated in many modern northern Rio Grande pueblos, including Taos, Jemez, Picuris, Santo Domingo, Acoma (Castetter 1943:322), Cochiti, Santa Clara, and San Juan, as well as in the western pueblos of Hopi and Zuni (Switzer 1969:14).

The notion that the existence of these pipes in the archaeological record is evidence of extensive tobacco use in the prehistoric Southwest has been refuted to some extent by the fact that very few actual remains of tobacco have been recovered from sites, and few of these remains are believed to have been intended for smoking (Switzer 1969:14). Cordell (1980:75–78) illustrates the difficulty of recovering archaeological evidence of this plant compared with other paleobotanical material, mostly because of the very small size of *Nicotiana* seeds. *Nicotiana* is absent in the paleobotanical record at Arroyo Hondo (Wetterstrom 1986). It is widely believed that many different plants, including manzanita and mountain purslane, have been smoked in the Pueblo area, usually in a mixture, and sometimes with tobacco (Jones 1944:453–54; Scully 1970:98; Switzer 1969:14). An early analysis of pipe dottles (the remaining crust on the inside of the bowl) from Basketmaker sites in Arizona showed no trace of nicotine; that may be an indication that tobacco was not the material smoked in these pipes, although any traces of nicotine may have leached out into the soil (Dixon and Stetson 1922:245–46). Because these pipes were used ceremonially and importance was placed on the smoke being produced, the narcotic properties of tobacco probably did not play a role in choosing an appropriate smoking material (Jones 1944:454–55).

There is no mention of tobacco cultivation or smoking of any kind in the records of Coronado's expedition, and Bandelier (1890:37) claimed that tobacco was not in use in this area before the arrival of the Spanish. The bulk of the ethnographic evidence, however, indicates that cultivated tobacco and other plants were used for smoking and that wild tobacco may have been used prehistorically (White 1943:386), possibly without the knowledge of the Spanish if its use was restricted to ceremonies (Jones 1944:453). The relatively low instances of tobacco material recovered archaeologically—compared to frequent indirect evidence of smoking, such as pipes—may simply emphasize the secondary value of tobacco to other plants in ceremonial smoking. Therefore, one can only determine that the presence of ceramic pipes at Arroyo Hondo indicates that smoking of some material, probably in a ritual context, was practiced.

Ceramic Effigies

At Arroyo Hondo, 16 ceramic effigies were excavated, and 13 of these were recognizable enough to be identified as some type of animal—eight quadrupeds and five birds. The other three are also probably some part of an animal form and not human representations. This typeable percentage appears large, considering the number of fragmented specimens, but because the quadruped effigies suffered the most damage—usually in the form of missing limbs—the effigies remained in recognizable condition. The type categories used are fairly general with few criteria; this also facilitated the classification process.

Two effigy types and one subtype are present at Arroyo Hondo:

1. Round Body Quadruped (8)
2. a. Folded-Wing Bird (3)
   b. Folded-Wing Bird with Base (2)

As with many of the miscellaneous ceramic artifacts at Arroyo Hondo, the effigies resembled those collected by Kidder (1932) at Pecos Pueblo. Of course, there was a much greater abundance of these items excavated from Pecos (table 15), and Kidder (1932:133) indicates that these effigies appear no earlier than Glaze V (A.D. 1550–1650), significantly later than the occupations at Arroyo Hondo. Also, almost half of the Pecos effigies are human forms, which are completely absent at Arroyo Hondo. Although ceramic human images are present at other sites in the northern Rio Grande (Jeançon 1923; Lambert 1954; Linda Cordell, personal communication, 1990), Pecos yielded by far the greatest number and diversity in the area (table 15), most being completely aberrant to any examples from neighboring sites. This can probably be attributed, again, to external influences or a highly localized tradition (Kidder 1932:133).

All of these effigies have been formed by hand, probably by simply squeezing and working the clay between the fingers without molds or elaborate tools. Most of the clay used is an untempered potter's clay that fires to a light brown color. The clay of one of the quadrupeds and one of the birds, however, is similar to many of the culinary wares from Arroyo Hondo; the quadruped exhibits a very coarse temper, as do many of these wares. Several effigies closely resemble the majority of the ceramic pipes, which are a lighter gray than the culinary wares with either very coarse or no temper. The surface of all the effigies was given very little attention, and no decoration, beyond the conveyance of limbs, ears, and beaks, is apparent. No slip or polishing is evident, although many effigies were probably smoothed with the fingers before firing to create a more even surface and to prevent cracking.

Virtually the entire collection of ceramic effigies from Arroyo Hondo is in fragmented condition, and only effigy 12-K-3, a Folded-Wing Bird (see fig. 74), is nearly whole. Even this specimen shows slight wear on the beak area and heavy wear and cracks on the underside of the body. All the quadrupeds are fragmented, missing at least half of their limbs and usually the head or tail or both. Two of the quadrupeds consist of only half a body, two legs, and a head or tail. Only two of the five birds still have head sections. It is uncertain whether these effigies deteriorated naturally, or if they were purposefully damaged when discarded.

Description

ROUND BODY QUADRUPED

There is some variation within the group of Round Body Quadrupeds, but all of the samples follow the same pattern of a heavy, cylindrical body with four unarticulated legs, some sort of head at one end, and usually a tail at the opposite end (fig. 73). Most of the heads and tails are broken from the body, and only four legs remain intact among all eight animals. Therefore, it is very difficult to distinguish much detail from these extremities, especially the heads. In general, the legs are unfinished and thick, averaging about 1 cm in length. The tail is equally crude and averages about 0.7 cm, and in some cases the tail seems to be just a slight protrusion from the back of the body. Because most of the quadrupeds are incomplete in body length, it is not possible to calculate an average among the samples. The two complete quadrupeds average about 3.5 cm long, but some of the other body fragments are even longer. It is difficult to determine how high these effigies stood because most of the legs are broken; however, the four effigies with surviving legs suggest that these animals measured an average of 2.32 cm from the top of the back to the bottom of where the foot would be.

Although generally cylindrical, most of the quadruped bodies are slightly wider in the middle than at the ends. Effigy 12-G-38B-2 (fig. 73a) is the only example that appears to retain the same diameter throughout the body, even though only half the body remains. In fact, there is very little narrowing at the shoulders where the head begins, as if the body continues right to the head, the neck nearly as thick as the body. This may indicate a different species representation than the rest of the quadruped effigies.

Effigy 12-Kiva G (fig. 73b) also differs somewhat in form from the basic cylindrical body. The body is very

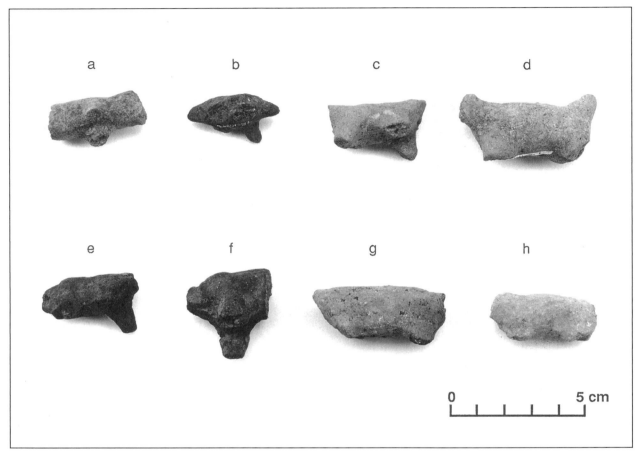

Figure 73. Round Body Quadrupeds: a, *12-G-38B-2;* b, *12-Kiva G;* c, *12-C-3-9;* d, *12-H-3-7;* e, *12-5-9-14-1;* f, *12-5-9-14-2;* g, *12-4-2-III-1;* h, *12-K-14-II & III.*

wide in the middle and almost round when viewed from above. It measures 3.54 cm in length and sits only 1.63 cm high, probably shorter than any other Round Body Quadruped. In addition, this is the smallest of the quadruped effigies, and although the head and tail are both intact, they cannot be distinguished from each other. The one intact leg also differs from those on most quadrupeds in that it protrudes down and slightly out from the body, whereas other legs, for the most part, extend straight down. The peculiarities of this effigy indicate that this is probably the image of a turtle.

Effigy 12-C-3-9 (fig. 73c) retains the same form as the other quadrupeds but has a very thin hole extending through the body from just below the neck and exiting just below the tail area. This could have been formed by drilling with a thin tool after firing but more likely by inserting a very thin, straight twig and either removing it before firing or letting it burn in the firing—a process similar to creating the vent for a ceramic pipe. This shaft

may have been intended to represent an anal orifice (Scott 1960:16). Fulton and Tuthill (1940:50) speculate that these holes, appearing on both human and animal figures at the Gleeson site in Arizona, are evidence of a support, such as a twig, running through the body, which was used as a handle to facilitate the modeling of the effigy before it was fired. This effigy is 2 cm tall from foot to back.

The head and tail are still distinguishable on effigy 12-H-3-7 (fig. 73d), the tail consisting of a simple 1-cm conical protrusion at a 45-degree angle to the rear of the body. The head is very small in proportion to the body, and although most of the front portion is missing, it appears to have only one ear represented, on the left side. Effigy 12-5-9-14-1 (fig. 73e) is similar in features to effigy 12-Kiva G, but it has a less circular shape and sits higher, 2.3 cm from foot to back. Unfortunately, both head and tail are missing from the effigy. The one remaining leg also extends at a significant angle from the

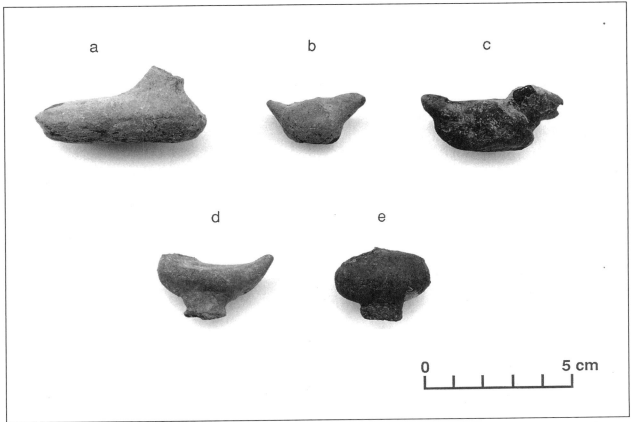

Figure 74. Folded-Wing Bird effigies: a, 12-K-15-I; b, 12-K-3; c, 12-H-2-4; d, 12-C-2-2; e 12-G-25C-2.

body; however, this is not as clear a turtle representation as effigy 12-Kiva G. Effigy 12-5-9-14-2 (fig. 73f) is either the front or back half of a large, crude effigy with short, thick appendages, with an unusually clean break just behind two legs. One leg remains, indicating the figure's height of 3.33 cm. Effigies 12-4-2-III-1 and 12-K-14-II&III (fig. 73g and h) are featureless bodies, the former being larger with more attention to surface treatment.

FOLDED-WING BIRD

The bird forms have very round bodies, representing sitting birds with the wings closely folded against the backs (fig. 74). No birds with spread wings were found at Arroyo Hondo. In fact, wings are absent or consist of only slight swellings on the sides of the body. Only two effigies have heads remaining; one "head" is a 1 cm protrusion with no detailed features, and the other extends 1.7 cm from the body, has two fragmented areas on the top, and has a notch that may represent an open beak. There is either no tail on these effigies or a small V-shaped projection extending approximately 0.8 cm from the back

of the body. Also, no feet or legs are represented on these bird effigies.

Effigy 12-K-15-I (fig. 74a) is a very large bird with a flat, oval body measuring 5.4 cm in length and tapering toward the tail, suggestive of a bird floating on water, such as a duck. Although large in surface area, the body measures only 1.52 cm from the bottom to the top of the back. The head is missing, but a portion of the neck remains, measuring 0.8 cm from the top of the back. There is no distinct tail on this effigy; however, it is interesting to note that a 1.3 cm by 1 cm section of the tail area has flaked off. This effigy is very different in form from the rest of the birds at Arroyo Hondo, possibly indicating a different species.

Effigy 12-K-3 (fig. 74b) is the most intact effigy from Arroyo Hondo, although a section on the bottom of the bird is very cracked and is missing some clay. This is also the smallest bird of the collection, measuring only 3.23 cm in length and 1.8 cm in height. The head and neck section is just a 1 cm protrusion tapering from the front of the body and tilting down slightly at the end, suggesting a beak. The tail extends 0.6 cm from the rear of the body, forming a V-shaped dovetail. From the general form of the body, head, and tail, this could be a dove or similar bird. Although the features of this effigy are simple, it is probably the most finely crafted of all the animals in the collection.

The open beak of effigy 12-H-2-4 (fig. 74c) is the most detailed feature on the typed effigies at Arroyo Hondo. The overall effigy is crudely shaped, with two fragmented areas on the top of the head, but the front of the head tapers to form a beak cut with a 0.2-cm notch. The beak was probably formed by simply squeezing the head between two fingers. The tail is the same V-shaped protrusion found on most of the birds, extending 0.86 cm from the rear, but it does not taper quite as sharply and is larger and more rectangular. This effigy measures 4.5 cm in total length and sits 2.33 cm high. The two fragmented areas on the head may have been projected portions of the effigy, since no other areas have been damaged, including the tail and beak. Another possibility is that these areas were destroyed intentionally, for reasons now unknown.

FOLDED-WING BIRD WITH BASE

These two effigies are similar in form and other characteristics to the previous type, but each has a round base about 0.8 cm in height and 1.3 cm in diameter directly below the body (fig. 74d and e). It is uncertain whether these bases were used to attach the effigies to another object, such as a ceramic vessel, or whether they were a crude means of depicting legs and giving the effigies a support on which to stand. Cushing (1883:29) notes that in ceremonials at Zuni this base, or pedestal, was necessary when bird effigies were set on the floor rather than suspended.

Effigy 12-C-2-2 (fig. 74d) measures 3.70 cm from the tail to the front of the breast and 1.10 cm from the top of the back to the beginning of the base. The very sharp tail extends from the body, and the head is missing. The folded wings on this bird are slightly more prominent than those in the rest of the collection, but the bulges are still barely distinguishable from the main body. Other than the head, the effigy is intact except for a small area on the underside near the rear that has chipped off.

Effigy 12-G-25C-2 (fig. 74e) has an extremely rounded, oval body, almost egglike in form. The body measures 3.04 cm in length and sits 1.5 cm above its base. This effigy is missing both the head and the tail, although there is a slightly flaked area where the tail might have been. A very thin hole penetrates the center of the body to a depth of about 0.08 cm. There is also a shallow, thin hole extending diagonally back about 0.03 cm from

the fragmented area where the head and neck once were. These two holes do not appear to have ever been connected, but they may have served some purpose in attaching separate head and tail pieces. The hole in the tail area may also represent an anal orifice, similar to that of effigy 12-C-3-9.

UNKNOWN ANIMALS

There are three small ceramic forms that were likely components of some animal effigies at one time. Effigy 12-H-3-7 is a head, probably of some quadruped, and 12-5-9-14-1 could also be a head, although the form is not as readily familiar. The third fragment, effigy 12-11-2-2, could be the leg, ear, or tail of almost any animal.

Effigy 12-H-3-7 is lizardlike, with bulging eyes on the sides of the head and a small, slightly open mouth at the end of a narrow snout. The figure is slightly arched, and the thick neck tapers gradually to form the head. This fragment measures 3.3 cm in length. Effigy 12-5-9-14-1 appears to be the head segment of an animal, but the form is very different from others in the collection. There is a protruding "snout," and another 1.1-cm protrusion at a right angle to this snout. This feature may represent an ear; however, there is only a very small bulge at right angles to both snout and protrusion to suggest another ear. A tiny puncture about 1 cm penetrates the snout; its purpose is unknown. The length of this head section is 3 cm. Effigy 12-11-2-2 measures 1.6 cm in length and resembles the legs on some of the Round Body Quadrupeds, tapering gradually from the hip area to a rounded foot.

Provenience

Eleven of the 16 effigies were located in either plazas or kivas, though there was no apparent concentration of effigy types in specific areas of the site. One bird was excavated in kiva C-2, and kiva G held one Round Body Quadruped. Effigy 12-11-2-2 was found in a room designated solely as a storage facility. Effigy 12-C-3-9 was found in the gate of plaza C in Component I trash. The rest of the effigies, which were all either Round Body Quadrupeds or unknown animals, were found in combination living and storage rooms (Creamer 1993).

Only effigy 12-4-2-III-1 was found in situ, in contact with the floor of room 4-2, a living room converted to storage. This is a Round Body Quadruped with no appendages or features intact. All three effigies from room 5-9 came from level 14, a trash level just below the floor. As with the pipes at Arroyo Hondo and the effigies from Pecos, most of the effigies were excavated from general trash.

Chronology

Although Kidder (1932:133) states that all the effigies at Pecos occur relatively late, from A.D. 1550 to 1650, it would seem that ceramic animal effigies enjoyed popularity somewhat earlier in the northern Rio Grande and other areas of the Southwest. The two occupations at Arroyo Hondo fall into the late Pueblo III to early Pueblo IV (late Coalition–early Classic) period, and during the same period, similar ceramic animal effigies appear at several sites in the region, such as Pindi, Paa-ko, Las Madres, and Unshagi (Stubbs and Stallings 1953:92; Lambert 1954:116; Dutton 1966:5; Reiter 1938:156). The same types of effigies have also been recovered from sites in northern Arizona during the Pueblo III period (Scott 1960:11). Animal effigies are a diagnostic feature of the Upper Gila culture, as well, and similar quadrupeds were reported from the excavation of a site near Point of Pines in east-central Arizona dated to either A.D. 1350–1400 or 1400–1450 (Wendorf 1950:85–89, 92).

At Arroyo Hondo, almost all the effigies were recovered from Component I proveniences, dated to about A.D. 1285–1345 (Creamer 1993). Of the two effigies from Component II, however, only effigy 12-C-2-2, a Folded-Wing Bird with Base, could be typed. This effigy was dated by three tree-ring samples to A.D. 1386; these were the only tree-ring dates recovered from Arroyo Hondo that were associated with an effigy. Effigy 12-11-2-2 is a fragment from an unknown animal, probably a leg from a quadruped. The limited representation of Component II effigies at Arroyo Hondo suggests that these effigies were used primarily during the earlier occupation.

Function

Ethnographic comparison can be very useful for putting effigy figures in a context of use. Accounts from the modern Pueblos can give at least a general idea of what the function of an object may have been six hundred years ago. Although most effigies in use historically have been made of stone rather than clay, it can be assumed that the images still provide some useful parallels.

The central purpose, and probably the reason the animal effigy was originally created in the Southwest, has been to ensure continued success in hunting local game animals. Judd (1954:296) does note, however, that the Hopi, Zuni, and Navajo have used effigies of domestic animals for their herds and flocks to promote healthy and increased stock. Very few domesticated animals were present at Arroyo Hondo. Of those that were found, the most prominent was the turkey (Lang and Harris 1984:

87). Although several turkey pens were identified in plaza areas at Arroyo Hondo, none of the bird effigies were recovered in proximity to these assemblages. Effigy 12-K-14-II&III, a Round Body Quadruped, was associated with a jacal, or wattle-and-daub, enclosure in plaza K, but the function of this feature is unknown.

Eventually, prey animal effigies became general tokens of good fortune and protection in all endeavors, similar to the amulets and talismans employed by other tribes in North America (Gunnerson n.d.:3; Cushing 1883:39). At Zuni, the hunter chose an effigy representing the natural hunter of the intended quarry, such as a mountain lion effigy if the individual wished to hunt elk (Cushing 1883:31). In some accounts, the effigy has the power to change into the actual predator and chase down the game for the hunter (Gunnerson n.d.:3). The six main effigies used for the hunt at Zuni represent the six prey animals that guard each of the six directions: north, south, east, west, upper, and lower. The mountain lion is the guardian of the north, the most sacred region, and is generally regarded as the most powerful prey animal; it is therefore very popular as an effigy. The coyote, with a sacred status even higher than the mountain lion's, is another valued image (Cushing 1883:31). The bear has also been a popular image for effigies historically (Jeançon 1923:66). It is likely that many quadruped effigies of unknown species may have been intended to represent mountain lions, bears, or coyotes.

Although some effigies may be kept by individuals, most are in the care of ceremonial leaders when not in use, primarily to receive the proper care. Because the figures are generally regarded as mediators between the medicine societies and the actual animals, they are cared for very carefully with prayers and ceremony (Cushing 1883:19). At Zuni, one large ritual was performed annually for the prey gods or fetishes, and abbreviated versions were held before any major tribal hunt (Cushing 1883:32–33). The effigies are fed as though they were real animals. Usually, they are fed cornmeal or pollen, but the main "meal" occurs, for the mountain lion, at least, just after a deer has been killed. The effigy is then either smeared with the blood of the slain animal or placed within its chest. Accounts of this practice exist from the pueblos of Taos, Zuni, Acoma, Zia, Santa Ana, Cochiti, and Laguna (Gunnerson n.d.:20–22).

In addition to the hunting significance of effigies, certain images were helpful to the warriors in the tribe. The Priesthood of the Bow at Zuni used only the mountain lion and bear of the prey animal fetishes, and its members carried a favorite fetish for protection from enemies when traveling through foreign regions. Unlike the hunting effigies, these fetishes were kept and cared

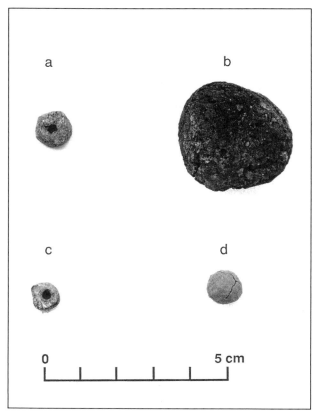

Figure 75. Clay beads and balls: a, *bead 12-G-104B-2;* b, *ball 12-H-3-7;* c, *bead 12-12-4-6;* d, *ball 12-16-30-2.*

for personally by the individual (Cushing 1883:41); like the hunting effigies, however, these also were "fed on the life-blood of the slain" (Cushing 1883:43).

As well as assisting with the ability to take life, the images of powerful animals have been helpful at many pueblos in curing illness. Again, the bear and mountain lion have been most popular for this purpose, especially at the pueblos of Cochiti, Isleta, Santo Domingo, San Felipe, and San Juan (Gunnerson n.d.:11–12). At Cochiti, the *chaiani*, or medicine man, may leave a mountain lion or bear effigy with the patient in the case of illness caused by witchcraft, because the animal *chaiani* has the power to ward off any repeated witch attack (Dumarest 1919:161).

Ceramic Beads

Two circular ceramic beads were recovered from Arroyo Hondo (fig. 75a and c), one from plaza G fill and one, associated with a straight conical pipe, from a midden below the second floor of Component I room 12-4. Bead

12-G-104B-2 (fig. 75a) measures 0.87 cm in diameter and 0.44 cm in thickness; its drilled hole is approximately 0.15 cm in diameter. Bead 12-12-4-6 (fig. 75c) measures 0.64 cm in diameter and 0.41 cm in thickness; its drilled hole is 0.18 cm in diameter. Unlike the shell beads from Arroyo Hondo, which they resemble in form and size (Venn 1984:233), on these beads the surface and edges are not smoothed.

Ceramic Balls

Twelve ceramic balls of varying size and shape were recovered from Arroyo Hondo. The average diameter is 1.8 cm, ranging from 0.8 cm to 3 cm. The color of these spheres also varies, ranging from red-buff to light grayish white, with grayish brown predominant. None of the balls were pierced, although one has a conical hole penetrating 0.35 cm toward the center; none exhibits any decoration or surface attention beyond cursory smoothing. This suggests that these balls were not used as beads. Most balls have a rough or pitted surface texture, often with cracks or fragments of clay missing. Very few are near-perfect spheres: most are slightly oval, and ball 12-H-3-7 (fig. 75b) is almost cubelike. Similar balls have been found at other sites in the region, including Pecos (Kidder 1932:141) and Paa-ko (Lambert 1954:123). Their function remains unclear, but Kidder (1932:141) suggests that the smaller balls may be clappers, since several were found in ceramic bells at Pecos. Although one very small ball (fig. 75d) was recovered from Arroyo Hondo, no ceramic bells or bell fragments were found.

Miniature Vessels

The most readily identifiable forms included in the miniature vessels category are bowls, jars, and dippers or ladles. Some other, more aberrant forms are included because they resemble some kind of vessel, but many are too fragmented to allow recognition of the complete form. Fifteen miniature vessels were recovered from Arroyo Hondo: four bowls, four jars, five ladles, and two unknown forms. In general, these objects are crudely formed, unslipped, unpolished, with no paint or other evidence of decoration. The paste ranges from light brown or buff to dark gray in color, and generally has a coarse temper. Twelve vessels were excavated from Component I and three from Component II. Six vessels came from trash fill of rooms, one unknown form from the floor of a Component I room, and five vessels from plaza fill. Four vessels—a bowl, a jar, a ladle, and an unknown

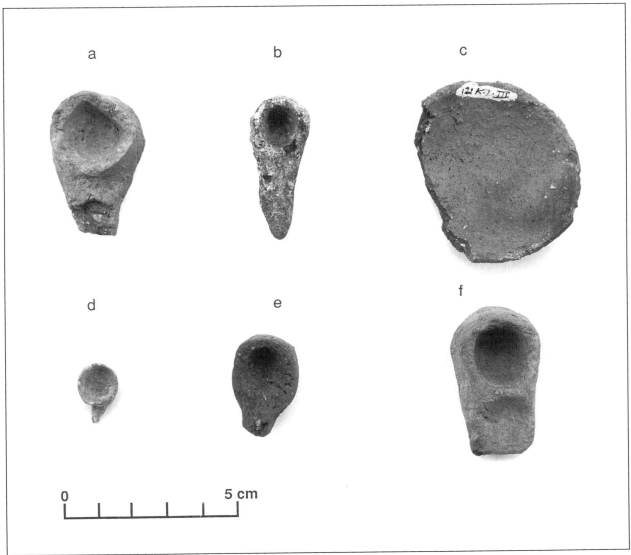

Figure 76. Miniature vessels: a, *ladle 12-G-5-V;* b, *ladle 12-C-3C-4-1;* c, *bowl 12-K-1-III;* d, *ladle 12-5-14-IVE;* e, *ladle 12-12-4-7;* f, *ladle 12-G-C35-3.*

form—were excavated from kivas. In addition, vessel 12-K-1-III (fig. 76c), the most intact and best-formed miniature bowl, was associated in plaza K fill with a Straight Conical Undecorated pipe.

The bowls ranged from 1.2 cm to 2 cm in height and 1.61 cm to 2 cm in rim diameter. The jars ranged from 2.1 cm to 4 cm in height and 0.85 cm to 1.7 cm in rim diameter. Many of the bowl and jar forms can only be inferred from fragments of the original vessels. Vessels 12-K-1-III and 12–15a-7-1, however, remain virtually intact and exhibit the most regular form, although the

latter has an uneven surface. The paste is dark with a coarse temper and resembles many of the culinary wares from Arroyo Hondo. None of the jars are intact, but the remaining fragments generally reveal flat, broad bases with restricted orifices.

Two basic forms are represented in the collection of miniature ladles from Arroyo Hondo. Four of the ladles are very thick walled with stout handles; only one of these remains fully intact (fig. 76a, b, e, f). For the most part, these specimens are crudely manufactured with coarse temper; two cases exhibit some cracking. Vessel

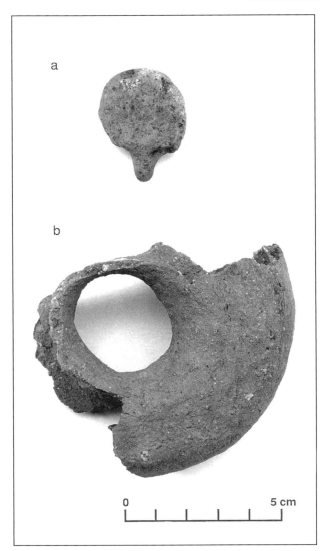

bowl, 1.17 cm in width at the bowl, and 1 cm in rim diameter.

Although miniature vessels of these types are common at sites in the northern Rio Grande and other parts of the Southwest, their function has not been very well defined. Kidder (1932:137) suggests that they served a function similar to the effigies' as toys or cult objects. Reiter (1938:155) concurs with this opinion and adds the possibility that they were used to test potential clay sources. Considering the fact that one-third of the miniature vessels recovered at Arroyo Hondo were in kivas and that one bowl was associated with a ceramic pipe, a possible ceremonial function is indicated. But because there is limited additional contextual evidence at Arroyo Hondo, and because parallels with the modern pueblos offer little insight, the true function of these vessels at Arroyo Hondo remains ambiguous.

Prayer Plume Base

Object 12-kiva G (fig. 77a) is very similar to a prayer plume base, or *tiponi*, reported by Jeançon (1923:64–65, pl. 51) from the site of Poshu in the Chama Valley of northern New Mexico. The prong of the tiponi's base would be pushed into the sand of an altar or shrine, and prayer feathers can be inserted into a tiny hole on the top along the edge. The base of the Arroyo Hondo specimen measures approximately 3 cm in diameter and 1.23 cm in thickness; the prong is 1 cm long. This artifact was recovered from kiva G, supporting the belief that it was used in a ceremonial context at Arroyo Hondo, as Jeançon asserts that the base from Poshu was used.

Ring Vessel

One fragmented ring vessel (12-K-13-III-2) (fig. 77b) was recovered from plaza K at Arroyo Hondo. It is possible that it could be a stirrup spout handle, although this form usually involves two separate tubes attached to the top of a globular vessel, with the orifice at the top over the center of the vessel (Dixon 1964:456). The Arroyo Hondo form suggests a complete ring, although the location of the orifice is unknown. The inner diameter of the ring measures 3.4 cm, but the outer diameter is unknown. The diameter of the tube itself is 2.2 cm by 2.95 cm on the inside and 3.95 cm on the outside. The thickness of the tube walls is 0.57 cm. The color of the vessel is buff-brown, although one side shows evidence of burning or smudging during firing. The paste is similar to some of the culinary wares at Arroyo Hondo, but

Figure 77. Prayer plume base and ring vessel: a, prayer plume base 12-Kiva G; b, ring vessel 12-K-13-III-2.

12-G-C35–3 (fig. 76f) is an exception to these general characterizations: it has a slightly squared bowl, a smoothed surface, and a thumb-size depression just behind the bowl. The fifth ladle (fig. 76d) is much smaller than the others and has very thin walls and a thin handle, most of which is missing. Its overall delicate characteristics, compared to the other ladles, imply a different function, possibly ceremonial. The ladles ranged from 1.24 cm to 1.86 cm in height at the bowl; from 1.7 cm to 2.72 cm in width at the bowl; and from 1.2 cm to 1.8 cm in rim diameter. These ranges do not include the fifth ladle, which measures 0.7 cm in height at the

the rock temper is unusually coarse in some places and is present in large amounts. In general, the features of this vessel are unusual, as ring vessels are normally painted, well made, and unburned (Dixon 1964:455).

Ring vessels first appeared in the Southwest in the San Juan region about A.D. 500 and in the Kayenta region and the northern Rio Grande around A.D. 1300 (Dixon 1964:458). This form does not seem to have any practical advantage over other vessels, rendering its function and acceptance by the Anasazi uncertain. One ethnographic account from Santa Clara indicates a ring vessel's use during a ceremony to end a drought (Jeançon 1923:72). A ring vessel was also recovered from a ceremonial context at Te'ewi (Wendorf 1953:55). Unfortunately, the vessel at Arroyo Hondo came from plaza fill, and because its characteristics certainly do not suggest ceremonialism, its particular function must remain conjecture.

Part II

The Stone Artifacts from Arroyo Hondo Pueblo

Carl J. Phagan

The Stone Artifacts from
Arroyo Hondo Pueblo

Carl J. Phagan

The analysis of stone artifact assemblages from archaeological contexts has moved into the modern era of archaeological research relatively more slowly than have some other kinds of analysis. This may be particularly true in the American Southwest, in part because of the nonlithic character of much of its most obvious archaeological material. Two major characteristics of the analytical efforts of the past twenty years are (1) the changing function of quantification from primarily descriptive purposes to those of explicit comparison and interpretation, and (2) a realization that the most convincing behavioral comparisons are those based on carefully defined content from carefully controlled contexts.

The reconstruction and interpretation of lithic data from Arroyo Hondo Pueblo contained in this report focus specifically on these concerns. Archaeological content is as clearly and consistently defined as possible. The relationships between lithic variability and behavior are explicitly stated. Archaeological contexts with independently determined temporal or spatial association, or both, are identified, and quantification of their lithic content is expressly for comparison and behavioral interpretation, as well as for assemblage description.

The Arroyo Hondo lithic materials were originally analyzed over a five-year period from 1970 to 1974, in two distinctly different systems. These analytic systems are briefly described below, and a third system is introduced that combines the first two into a single, more generalized lithic content structure for the entire site. Both whole-site and sub-site contexts are then identified, into which various segments of the Arroyo Hondo lithic content are grouped for temporal, spatial, and organizational comparison and interpretation.

Analytic Procedures
Background

RACHEL BONNEY, 1971–72

The analytic typological structure adopted by Rachel Bonney, the first analyst, for the 1971 and 1972 lithic materials from Arroyo Hondo was basically that formulated by Kidder (1932) at Pecos Pueblo, expanded somewhat to include categories and terminology from Binford (1963), Honea (1965), and Woodbury (1954) (Bonney 1971:1–6). This basic typological approach had dominated Southwestern lithic analysis for several decades. It was appropriate for the stated goals of the Arroyo Hondo project (Schwartz 1971:15) and was, in fact, virtually required for a comparison of Arroyo Hondo materials with those from other large late Coalition–early Classic sites in the northern Rio Grande region. The initial 1971 analysis included 25 ground-stone categories and 26 flaked- or chipped-stone categories (Bonney 1971). These artifact types were a mixture of morphological (i.e., shape, form, or "formal"), technological, and functional categories, without explicit definition; today they would be called descriptive or "convenient" types.

The 1972 analysis was expanded to include 41 ground-stone and 30 flaked-stone types (Bonney 1972:232–35). This expansion was due, at least in part, to an extensive search of the ethnographic literature for descriptions of stone tool use (Bonney 1972:158–225). The added types were primarily rather specialized functional categories, and they were represented in the Arroyo Hondo collection by very few items. By the end of the 1972 analysis, 1,842 (84%) ground-stone artifacts and 341 (16%) flaked-stone artifacts had been analyzed, and 9,995 "unworked stones" had been counted. These unworked stones included "cores, flakes, slabs, ground-stone chips, fire-box stones, and minerals" (Bonney 1972:vi–viii).

On the basis of the 1971 and 1972 analyses, Bonney made several observations and preliminary data interpretations. She noted, for example, relatively small proportions of both ground-stone tools and "ceremonial objects" in the Classic period Component II assemblage (Bonney 1972:145). After briefly considering and rejecting environmental or subsistence-related behavioral change, she concluded that the explanation for such data variability is probably a limited, inaccurate, or biased sample (Bonney 1972:146–48). Bonney also noted, but did not interpret, several rooms or roomblocks with noticeably high proportions of one or another tool type (Bonney 1972:148–50). After considering the sources of lithic raw materials observed in the Arroyo Hondo assemblage, she concluded that a very large majority were locally available and that a much smaller proportion of regionally available and exotic materials were probably acquired through some kind of trade (Bonney 1972: 151–57). Bonney examined three background topics in some detail: ethnographic analogy (Bonney 1972:158–93), functional use-wear interpretation (Bonney 1972: 194–207), and functional "tool complexes" (Bonney 1972:207–25). These discussions present the basis for her addition in 1972 of a number of functional types to supplement the more traditional descriptive types of Kidder and Woodbury that were used in the 1971 analysis.

LAURANCE LINFORD, 1973–74

Major changes in personnel, analytic approach, and procedure were made after the 1972 season. Analysis by Laurance D. Linford resulted in a further expansion of the recognized artifact categories to 62 ground-stone and 38 flaked-stone types (Linford 1974:iii–iv). In addition, cores, hammerstones, and several previously unanalyzed smaller categories became types within the ground-stone analysis system, and both used and unused flakes became types within the flaked-stone analysis system. This resulted in both a much larger tool assemblage in 1973 than in the previous two years, and a major shift in the proportions of ground- and flaked-stone artifacts in the assemblage: 2,212 (25%) ground-stone and 6,703 (75%) flaked-stone items, or an approximate reversal in proportions from those of 1971–72 (Linford 1974:183–85).

Two factors in this 1973 restructuring of the lithic analysis are of major significance in attempting to sum-

marize and interpret the total Arroyo Hondo lithic assemblage. First, correspondence between the individual artifact categories of the two analysis systems (1971–72 and 1973–74) is uncertain. Some categories were renamed, but the included materials apparently remained largely unchanged; thus, there may be greater similarity between the two analysis systems than is apparent from their data summaries. Some categories, however, were clearly different in both name and content. In still others the type name apparently remained unchanged, but the implicit category definition was either expanded or contracted to include more or less variability in the type; thus, there also may be greater difference between the two analysis systems than is apparent from the data summaries. In a draft copy of a chart showing the correspondence of type names (only) between the 1971–72 and the 1973 ground-stone analytic variables, only 11 of 45 artifact type names remained essentially the same in both systems (Linford n.d.a). Assuming that these type-name changes mean variation in category constituency, which appears quite likely, either direct comparison of the two systems or any reduction of the two into a single system of ground-stone tool types must be approached with considerable caution. If a similar listing of between-systems changes for flaked-stone tool types exists, it was not located in the site records.

A second analytic restructuring factor of major importance for this report concerns the retroactive application of the revised 1973–74 analytic system to 1971–72 materials. The final project summary manuscript (Linford n.d.b:1.12) does indicate that "a very small proportion" of the *unanalyzed* 1971–72 material had been included. It is unclear, however, just how much of the *analyzed* 1971–72 materials were included in the final total of 23,640 items (Linford n.d.b:1.20) and whether any such included materials were individually reanalyzed into the 1973–74 categories or whether they were simply transferred as categories from one system to the other.

These changing sets of types describe the analytic content variability in the Arroyo Hondo lithic assemblage, but in terms that are sufficiently inconsistent to make summary comparisons and interpretations difficult or uncertain at best. In addition, the assignment of these content data to temporal and spatial grouping variables is inconsistently reported in the analysis records, so that most behaviorally interpretable context data groupings are difficult to evaluate with confidence. Roomblock, room, and such major spatial contexts as kivas, middens, gates, or plazas are integral parts of the field specimen (FS) numbering system, and such context groupings can be confirmed or reproduced only to the extent that individual FS numbers have been preserved in the analysis records; this is itself quite inconsistent. In most cases the assignment of materials to one of two temporal components at the Arroyo Hondo site is made on a summary basis and cannot be confirmed from the analysis records. Temporal groupings smaller than components, such as those used by Lang and Harris (1984:14–18) for the Arroyo Hondo faunal materials, and spatial groupings smaller than those inherent in the FS numbering system are dependent on excavation provenience information that is not included in the lithic analysis records or summaries.

The yearly lithic analysis summaries (Bonney 1971, 1972; Linford 1974) are arranged primarily as cumulative totals for artifact types, without indication of the types' occurrence in either temporal or spatial contexts. The 1971 and 1972 analysis summaries do contain artifact lists in FS format, giving catalog numbers, artifact types, and numbers of items. These artifact lists are absent in the 1973 analysis summary (Linford 1974), which does, however, include a by-components division of each artifact type, plus by-components totals for raw material categories and a functional analysis of flakes. No 1974 analysis summary is available.

The final manuscript summarizing the 1973–74 analysis (Linford n.d.b) includes a number of data summaries and interpretations. Linford (n.d.b:7.1) calls the total Arroyo Hondo assemblage "fairly typical" with reference to other large contemporaneous sites in the northern Rio Grande region, particularly Paa-ko (Lambert 1954), Pindi (Stubbs and Stallings 1953), and the later materials from Pecos (Kidder 1932). The comparisons on which this interpretation is based are made largely on the presence or absence of trait-list characteristics. They are necessarily rather subjective, since quantitative descriptions or summaries are rarely available in the literature and were not calculated for Arroyo Hondo. In such comparisons, Linford also indicates that the Arroyo Hondo materials are generally "unaesthetic" and that "almost without exception, the artifacts from Arroyo Hondo are utilitarian in nature. No examples of high quality craftsmanship were recovered" (Linford n.d.b:7.1). He attributes this to abandonment or post-abandonment factors, rather than prehistoric systemic factors (Linford n.d.b:7.2), and to the fact that the Arroyo Hondo analysis included all excavated materials, rather than being limited to the "visually pleasing" (Linford n.d.b:1.6).

Linford provides extensive description of ground-stone (Linford n.d.b:chap. 2) and flaked-stone (Linford n.d.b:

chap. 3) tool types, with much attention to individual items. Each tool type has a summary data table in which the artifacts are grouped by component, either late Coalition (Component I) or early Classic (Component II). In a discussion of lithic raw materials (Linford n.d.b: chap. 4), he describes 59 material types, further categorized as local, regional ("within foraging distance"), or "so distant that they were most likely traded into the pueblo" (Linford n.d.b:4.1). By equating frequency of occurrence with raw material preference, Linford concludes that Arroyo Hondoans strongly preferred local cherts, followed by regional cherts and obsidians, and last by distant materials (Linford n.d.b:4.15). He notes a tendency for items with greater production input to be made from "better quality" raw material (Linford n.d.b: 4.15). A tabular arrangement of raw materials by component (Linford n.d.b:5.25–5.26, tables 1.4, 1.5) is not interpreted, perhaps because there are very few obvious between-components differences.

CARL J. PHAGAN, 1989–90

Four principles guided my reconstruction of summary data that can be used for reliable, broad-level comparison and interpretation of the Arroyo Hondo lithic assemblage. First, I have relied primarily on the original analysis notes, which consistently contain more explicit description and definition than do the various data summaries. These notes often include the FS number, which permits the reconstruction of at least gross-level spatial or contextual groupings. A major problem in applying this principle is that some original notes may be missing from the site records, particularly for the 1973–74 materials. This skews the reconstructed data samples in favor of materials excavated and analyzed earlier in the Arroyo Hondo project, a result judged both acceptable and consistent with other data manipulations described below. The fact that 1971 and 1972 fieldwork combined intensive excavation of two roomblocks (9 and 16) with representative excavations across all major site contexts (Schwartz 1972:5–6; Schwartz and Lang 1973:10) also makes a sample emphasis on these earlier materials appropriate.

Second, I have combined many smaller categories of noncomparable or uncertain content into a few much larger categories. These larger categories, while quite general in character, are much more likely than smaller categories to be equivalent, and therefore are more reliably comparable and interpretable. This approach limits the questions to which the data can respond to those of a rather general character, but this is seen as an appropriate concession for purposes of this report.

Third, I have generated several data sets rather than a single omnibus data set. Each set focuses on a particular temporal or spatial context grouping or on a particular analytic problem. This has allowed as much data as possible to be used for each set, rather than requiring all data to be usable for all such analytic applications. Since some data can be rather securely grouped by component but cannot be grouped by spatial context, and vice versa, this approach has permitted maximum data use for each problem. No overall data set description or presentation is possible, however.

Finally, I have eliminated questionable data, as well as data from uncertain, unspecified, or inadequately defined content or context groupings. The remaining data sets, considerably reduced in size, represent the entire Arroyo Hondo lithic assemblage in statistically unspecifiable ways, but they appear subjectively to be quite adequate in size and reliable in character to support general-level comparisons and interpretations.

Tables 16 and 17 provide the correspondences of ground-stone and flaked-stone artifact types employed in the 1971–72 and 1973–74 analyses with the more generalized types of this 1989–90 data reconstruction. Type descriptions provided by Bonney (1971, 1972) and Linford (1974, n.d.b) vary considerably in extent and character, and precise definitions for the more generalized data groupings or types formed by combining their types are clearly not possible. These larger groupings are simply broad categories that are generally descriptive in character, though they may also have functional or technological implications. They have been selected as appropriate compromise categories into which similar items and types from the 1971–72 and 1973–74 analysis systems may be grouped for useful description, comparison, and interpretation of as much of the Arroyo Hondo lithic assemblage as possible.

The more inclusive artifact types, presented below with only generalized definitions, have several advantages for this report: (1) they allow the 1971–72 and 1973–74 data to be expressed in the same terms and to be combined for maximum data utility; (2) they avoid large numbers of data units with very few or no items when the data are grouped by temporal and/or spatial context; and (3) they provide more appropriate support for the broader contextual data groupings (described below) than do extremely narrow content units. This explicitly coarse-grained approach to data structure and interpretation seems useful, convincing, and consistent with this summary presentation.

Reconstructing Summary Data Sets: Content

Systems for analyzing stone tools in Southwestern assemblages have traditionally been largely descriptive rather than classificatory, with categories used primarily for simplifying the description of large collections. This is not bad, but neither is it adequate for responding to the kinds of problems archaeologists address today. More recent analytic systems have begun to reflect such concerns. The worth of any analysis system or any included artifact category is directly related to its interpretability or its potential to organize information in response to relevant problems. Both analytic categories and individual observations should be restricted to such interpretable variability: in other words, measure only what can be interpreted. In a data reconstruction such as this, taxonomic groupings must necessarily be few and large— in part because of some uncertainty in combining results from two analytic systems, and in part because of the generalizing level of the interpretation.

GROUND-STONE ARTIFACT TYPES

The basic food-processing tool systems of the agricultural northern Southwest, with its active manos and passive metates, clearly and expectedly dominates the ground-stone tool assemblage at Arroyo Hondo. Though both the 1971–72 and 1973–74 lithic analysis systems divided shape variability into numerous categories, particularly for manos (see table 16), this variability was not used as the basis for behavioral interpretation. Little is therefore lost for this data reconstruction by collapsing this variability into a few very basic categories that do indicate general behavior, in this case those that differentiate between two distinct food-processing systems. One is the more specialized and temporally later two-hand mano/slab or trough metate system, with design features that make it especially effective for grinding corn. The other is the one-hand mano/basin metate or grinding slab system, with a much longer tradition of use in the Southwest, commonly interpreted as indicating the more generalized processing of a wide range of plants and minerals (Phagan and Hruby 1984:85–87). The two systems can usually be identified by their manos or metates, since both items from both systems often exhibit clear distinctions in size, production input, and use modification; however, considerable confusion surrounds the terms used in the literature to describe these distinctions. "Slab metate," "basin metate," "flat metate," and "grinding slab" are notably inconsistent. Only the distinctions between "one-hand" and "two-hand" manos,

TABLE 16
Artifact type correspondence: ground stone.

Phagan 1989	Bonney 1971–72	Linford 1973–74
One-hand manos	One-hand manos	One-hand manos; one-hand mano/ hammerstones
Two-hand manos	Manos with one grinding surface; manos with two opposing grinding surfaces; manos with four grinding surfaces; manos with two adjacent grinding surfaces; manos with three grinding surfaces; mano blanks; unused/ roughened manos; unidentified manos	Unifacial/rectangular manos; bifacial/rectangular manos; bifacial/trapezoidal manos; bifacial/acute triangular manos; bifacial/ biconvex manos; bifacial/plano-convex manos; bifacial/concavo-convex manos; bifacial/obtuse triangular manos; trifacial/obtuse triangular manos; quadrifacial/diamond manos
Mano fragments	Mano fragments	Mano fragments
Metates	Flat metate; slab metate; slab metate with red ochre	Flat metates; basin metates; metate preforms
Grinding stones	Grinding and polishing stones; floor polishers, abraders, or one-hand manos	Grinding stones; grinding/hammerstones; grinding/scrapers; grinding/choppers; pestles; abraders
Grinding slabs	Grinding slab; sandstone grinding slab; round grinding slab; palettes; griddle/grinding slab; griddle; miscellaneous slab fragments	Unifacial palettes; bifacial palettes; palette/ manos; palette/hammerstones; palette/grinding stones; ground slabs; griddles
Polishing stones	Pot polishing stones	Polishing stones
Hafted items	Axes; mauls; hoes; *tchamahia*	Axes; mauls; digging implements
Hammerstones	Polishing/hammerstones; hammerstones	Polishing/hammerstones; hammerstones
Ornaments	Pipe; beads; disc beads; tubular beads; pendants	Beads; pendants
Minerals	Hematite balls; hematite objects; minerals and unworked stones; mica flakes; turquoise; red ochre; yellow ochre; pyrite; azurite; mica ornaments	Turquoise; muscovite artifacts; muscovite flakes; pigment materials
Shaped slabs	Pot covers; sipapu covers	Pot lids
Miscellaneous	Arrowshaft smoothers; awl smoothers; lightning stones; concretion fetishes; earth mother fetishes; mountain lion fetishes; miscellaneous ceremonial stones; vein quartz pebbles or spheres; quartz crystals; quartz cylinders; phyllite object; selenite block; polished ceremonial stones; kiva ringing stones; firebox stones; miscellaneous slabs; selenite/ gypsum flakes; petrified wood; crinoid stems; micaceous stones	Anvil stones; awl sharpeners; arrowshaft smoothers; ceremonial stones; problematical stones; coping slabs; fireplace slabs; kiva floor stones; perforated stones; pit covers; slab entry covers; stone firedogs; tempering materials; turkey gizzard stones
Ground-stone fragments	Ground-stone chips; miscellaneous fragments	Miscellaneous ground-stone fragments

and between well-used "trough metates" and all other metate forms, are consistently applied.

The one-hand and two-hand manos can be consistently distinguished on the basis of a distinct bimodal size distribution, as well as frequent obvious differences in production input, use modification, and general suitability for use with either one or two hands grasping the tool. Two-hand manos are of two major kinds: those used with trough metates and those used with slab metates. This distinction is far more difficult to make because it is based on much less obvious variability. The two-hand mano/trough metate grinding system predominates in the northern Southwest during the Pueblo I and II periods. Metates are quite large and heavy, often simply rather flat-topped boulders or large, thick slabs, since it is their own mass that is primarily responsible for maintaining their stability during use. Their trough gradually develops during their use-life as a result of the reciprocal motion of the mano; the deeper the trough, the more easily this metate is recognized. Little-used trough metates on large rock slabs, however, are difficult to distinguish from, and are often confused with, slab and/or basin metates. Consistent with the site's relatively late date, trough metates are apparently either very rare or completely absent from the Arroyo Hondo assemblage.

During the later Pueblo II and III periods in the northern Southwest, the two-hand mano/slab metate system replaces the two-hand mano/trough metate system, sometimes completely. These slab metates are much less massive than trough metates. They are held stable during use by being mortared into place, sometimes in bins of upright slabs, and they often demonstrate considerable production input or shape modification. Corresponding manos are quite long and narrow, sometimes nearly cylindrical, and their reciprocal use motion extends across the entire upper side of the metate, which is quite flat perpendicular to the motion direction and gently concave parallel to the motion direction.

The terminology used during both the 1971–72 and 1973–74 Arroyo Hondo lithic analysis, and descriptions of the various mano and metate categories (see table 16), makes it clear that trough metates, and presumably their corresponding two-hand manos as well, were not present. Most of the eight 1971–72 and ten 1973–74 two-hand mano categories appear to distinguish—in quite different terms—shape variability that is, in all probability, the result of idiosyncratic use-wear patterns within the basic two-hand mano/slab metate system. Multiple and/or faceted use-wear surfaces, as opposed to single and/or flat (or rounded) surfaces, are not particularly interpretable as the result of distinct cultural patterns; at least, they have not yet been so interpreted. Consequently, the only mano distinction recognized in this data reconstruction is that between one-hand manos and two-hand manos. Mano fragments, most of which are probably from two-hand manos, are maintained as a distinct category because their isolation maintains the integrity and interpretability of the other two mano categories.

The analytic uncertainty caused by the definition and description problems surrounding various metate categories, discussed above, and the need for maximum data use from both 1971–72 and 1973–74 analyses argue for collapsing all metate forms into a single metate class. This permits maximum data use while maintaining general context comparability, but it sacrifices recognition within this tool class of the relative presence of the specialized or generalized mano/metate systems. Such a distinction is still recognizable, however, in the one-hand and two-hand mano categories, and a ratio of all manos to all metates should still provide a useful index suggesting the relative intensity of associated processing behavior for major contexts.

Grinding stones and grinding slabs are generalized artifact categories that include a range of 1971–72 and 1973–74 types. These combination categories appear to maintain, though in a less formalized way, the active and passive functional characters, respectively, of manos and metates. They may or may not have been involved in a generalized food-processing system, and their range of possible uses is clearly much greater and less specialized than that of the mano/metate systems. They have been included with manos and metates in most reconstructed data tables as a total subset of grinding tools, with broad behavioral interpretability.

Polishing stones are small, smooth river pebbles, sometimes with worn and even faceted areas, that are interpreted as ceramic production tools for polishing vessel surfaces prior to firing. Whether or not all items in this category are such specialized ceramic production tools is uncertain. Bonney (1972:109–10), however, specifically calls them "pot polishing stones," and the emphasis of this reconstructed data set on her 1971–72 material increases the confidence with which this artifact class is so interpreted.

Hafted items include all ground-stone tools with an obvious hafting element, usually a partially or completely encircling groove or opposing notches. The attachment of a haft or handle increases the amount and accuracy of the chopping, pounding, or digging forces that can be applied with such tools. Hammerstones are unspecialized and unhafted force-delivering implements, normally recognized by a distinctive use-wear pattern created by the impact of stone on stone, as in the production and maintenance of both ground- and flaked-stone tools. A much wider range of actual uses for hammerstones is certain, but these are unrecognizable in most analytic procedures.

All ornaments, mostly beads and pendants, have been subsumed in a single category. Mineral items have been grouped into three readily distinguishable material categories: turquoise, mica (mostly muscovite), and various pigments such as hematite and azurite. Since such min-

TABLE 17
Artifact type correspondence: flaked stone.

Phagan 1989	Bonney 1971–72	Linford 1973–74
Notched projectile points	(Nine unnamed categories of "stemmed and side-notched points and knives"); aberrant forms	(Nine unnamed categories of "stemmed and side-notched points and knives"); aberrant forms
Unnotched projectile points and knives	(Three unnamed categories of "stemless lanceolate blades"); (three unnamed categories of "stemless triangular projectile points and knives")	Preforms; (six unnamed categories of "stemless points"); knives; knife/scrapers
Projectile point fragments	Type I.A. fragments; knife and projectile point fragments	Point/knife fragments
Drills, gravers	(Seven unnamed categories of drills with "modified shafts," plain shafts," and "reworked knives and flakes")	Gravers; (six unnamed categories of drills)
Scrapers	End scrapers; double-side scrapers; (convergent-side scrapers; side-and-end scrapers; single-side scrapers; transverse scrapers; knife-scrapers	End scrapers; side-end scrapers; single-side scrapers; double-side scrapers; convergent-side scrapers; transverse scrapers; unclassifiable scraper fragments; spokeshaves; gouges
Used flakes	Utilized flakes	Utilized flakes
Flakes	Flakes	Unutilized flakes
Cores	Cores	Cores; core/nuclei; core/hammerstones
(Not included)	"Ceremonial obsidian crescent" (one item); miscellaneous unworked lithics	Ceremonial stones; problematical stones

erals sometimes occur as ornaments (i.e., these two categories are not mutually exclusive), an analytic convention was used in which an item's "mineralness" superceded its "ornamentness." This was done to preserve the integrity and interpretability of the mineral categories, which are important trade indicators. It does so, of course, at the expense of ornaments, which may be status indicators.

Shaped slabs are usually rather small, thin sandstone items, with minimal production input to regularize their plan shape. They are generally thought to have functioned as pot lids or covers for small floor pits; a "portable countertop" function seems reasonable, as well. The miscellaneous category is, in this case, exactly that. It includes a large number of small categories, some of which—from both the 1971–72 and 1973–74 analysis systems—contain a single or very few items. The primary purpose of this category is to maintain the content integrity of the major tool types and to focus interpretation on the apparent central tendencies of the data sets, or on the peaks of the data distribution. This purpose is achieved at the expense of the distributional tails, and much interesting descriptive detail is lost. Still, this

analytic focus is viewed as appropriate for this summary interpretation of the reconstructed Arroyo Hondo lithic data. Ground-stone fragments are those many fragmentary items too small for identification, except as possible remains of early-stage ground-stone tool production or as severely broken tools themselves. They are not included as ground-stone tools, but *are* considered artifacts.

FLAKED-STONE ARTIFACT TYPES

Table 17 contains a summary of the 1971–72 and 1973–74 flaked-stone artifact types that comprise the reconstructed data categories used in this analysis. Projectile points have long been among the types most often identified and interpreted in Southwestern archaeological literature, and in some cases they have been the only flaked-stone tools described, particularly from ceramic period sites. On the one hand, this focus on projectile points is well deserved: they have clearly received much production input, they have strong functional and technological implications, and they have a wide range of morphological (shape) variability that can be correlated with time, space, other archaeological content, or the expression of personal or group ideology. On the other hand, however, no aspect of lithic analysis has been as problematic or confusing as constructing categories for and interpreting projectile point types. The selection and assignment of importance to projectile point variables, the manner of their combination into analytic categories, and the attachment of meaning to those categories are continuing problems of special concern (Phagan 1988).

Both the 1971–72 and 1973–74 analyses consistently recognized a basic distinction between projectile points with notches or stems and those that lacked such specialized hafting characteristics (Bonney 1972:16–49; Linford n.d.b:3.13–3.39). In addition, both analyses recognized nine similarly described subtypes of "stemmed and side notched points and knives." The definitions provided for these subtypes are brief, qualitative, and descriptive in character: for example, "stemmed and side-notched points with tapering stems," "large triangular stemmed and side-notched points and/or knives," "stemless, triangular, straight sides, flat or concave base," and so on (Bonney 1972:16–49; Linford n.d.b:3.13–3.39). Photographic illustrations of selected items from the 1971–72 subtypes (Bonney 1972:16–49) demonstrate that quite similarly shaped items are in different subtypes, and quite differently shaped items are in the same subtype. This appears to violate the basic taxonomic principle that categories should demonstrate both internal cohesion and external distinction. The problem appears to be not so much that the definitive type attributes have been applied inconsistently, but that the selected attributes (or combinations thereof) simply fail to distinguish patterned shape regularities in the Arroyo Hondo projectile point assemblage. Linford (n.d.b:3.15) provides only schematic outline drawings of the 1973–74 subtypes, so it is not possible to evaluate their characteristics or their similarity to the 1971–72 materials. Both the 1971–72 and 1973–74 analyses simply report the numbers of items in the projectile point subtypes; in other words, the groups are used only for assemblage description and are not interpreted in terms of behavioral variability.

An additional matter of some concern for this data reconstruction is the inclusion of "knives" among the projectile point types and subtypes (Bonney 1972:16–49; Linford n.d.b:3.13–3.39). In both analysis systems, the term "knife" has apparently been used to designate both notched/stemmed and unnotched items that appear on the basis of unspecified evidence to have served cutting rather than, or in addition to, penetrating functions. Linford states that "the majority of the knives and scrapers

are merely conchoidal flakes . . . that were used without modification" (Linford n.d.b:3.1). The possibility exists, therefore, that some low-input and/or asymmetrical items are included in the 1971–72 and 1972–73 projectile point groupings.

Given these major problems of definition and correspondence, in this data reconstruction only the presence or absence of notches and/or stems have been retained as criteria to divide projectile points into two large classes. This basic distinction does not necessarily imply that unnotched items were unhafted; but any hafting certainly involved a technologically different procedure than was used for notched/stemmed items, and it is quite likely that the functions of the two basic forms were different as well.

The large category of notched projectile points, then, contains all of the high-input, symmetrical, pointed bifaces with distinct hafting elements; in addition, it may or may not contain a few lower-input or asymmetrical items with hafting elements that were judged to have functioned as knives (see table 17). The unnotched projectile points and knives category definitely contains both high-input, symmetrical, pointed bifaces without distinct hafting elements and lower-input, asymmetrical bifaces judged to have served as knives. It may also contain some very low input 1973–74 items that are unshaped or only marginally shaped. Interpretations based on the proportions of these categories in given context assemblages will therefore necessarily be tentative and suggestive. Projectile point fragments may represent either notched or unnotched items, and they are included in a collected subtotal of all projectile points and knives.

The 1971–72 and 1973–74 analyses included, respectively, seven and six unnamed categories of drills, and the 1973–74 system added a "gravers" category (Bonney 1972:50–59; Linford n.d.b:3.53–3.59). Like projectile points and knives, these categories have observed morphological and presumed functional homogeneity that serve descriptive rather than interpretive ends. Also as with projectile points and knives, photographs of selected 1971–72 items and schematic drawings of 1973–74 categories indicate some lack of clear internal cohesion among and external distinction between subtypes. For this data reconstruction, then, all drill subtypes, along with the 1973–74 gravers, have been collected into a single large category of drills and gravers. This category has little significance with reference to the production technology(ies) involved, but it should contain most of the tools associated with etching, incising, drilling, piercing, or boring of holes into harder or softer materials.

Seven 1971–72 and nine 1973–74 scraper subtypes are

similarly employed as descriptive rather than interpretive categories (Bonney 1972:61–72; Linford n.d.b:3.39–3.52). These subtypes were based on a typology "suggested by Honea (1965)" (Bonney 1972:2; Linford n.d.b:1.14), and they include such categories as "end," "side-and-end," "transverse," and "convergent side" scrapers—categories that rely on the orientation of the scraping edge(s) to the long axis of the flake on which they are made. Such categories may be very appropriate for assemblages dominated by very regular flakes and/or blades, such as many Arctic or Old World Paleolithic assemblages, but they do not distinguish among the kinds and ranges of extremely diverse variability in most Southwestern Puebloan assemblages. Indeed, few of Bonney's selected photographic illustrations (Bonney 1972:61–74) bear even slight resemblance to Linford's schematic drawings for the same subtypes (Linford n.d.b:3.40). The very large majority of scraper assemblages in the Puebloan Southwest, including that from Arroyo Hondo, simply do not contain the kinds of specialized production input that are effectively managed by such a typological structure. This data reconstruction therefore combines all Arroyo Hondo scrapers into a single generalized category, with only very broad functional or technological implications.

Used flakes are explicitly recognized in both the 1971–72 and 1973–74 analyses, though the criteria used to identify them were quite different (Bonney 1972:75; Linford n.d.b:3.64–3.65). Used flakes comprise less than 1 percent of the 1971–72 flaked-stone artifacts, but 47 percent of the 1973–74 materials. Because of this major analytic difference, used flakes are omitted from the flaked-stone tool category here. In order to preserve comparability of categories, while allowing as much of the two original data sets as possible to be used, used flakes are included along with flakes and cores as flaked-stone artifacts. Flakes are either the identifiable by-products of flaked-stone tool production and maintenance or the intended end result of that production on which no traces of use can be detected. Cores are the parent blocks of lithic raw material from which flakes are removed. Cores may be large or small and vary considerably in shape, but they always bear the distinctive negative, or concave, scars of flake removals.

ARTIFACT TYPE RATIOS

In addition to both the absolute and relative frequencies of individual data categories for given contexts, this reconstruction of the Arroyo Hondo lithic data also employs a number of artifact ratios. Such ratios can simplify context comparison and interpretation by converting "size" variability into "shape" variability. For example, grinding tools comprise 73 percent and 71 percent, respectively, of the ground-stone tool assemblages from first-floor and second-floor rooms. These figures suggest that associated grinding behavior in the two contexts was quite similar (at least in extent), even though the numbers of both artifacts and observations (rooms) are in this case quite dissimilar. However, when these data are arranged as a ratio of "grinding tools per room," a concept not unlike that of relating length and width to define shape, first-floor rooms average 10 such tools per room, while second-floor rooms average 26. This indication of strong behavioral dissimilarity is the more appropriate, and it is much easier to conceptualize when relevant data categories are arranged into the mathematical interrelationships provided by ratios.

Seven ground-stone tool ratios are presented: ground-stone tools per room, grinding tools per room, ground-stone fragments per room, and total ground stone per room are convenient ways to compare and interpret the differential expression of major tool groupings in room contexts. In addition, manos per metate, two-hand manos per one-hand mano, and ground-stone fragments per ground-stone tool ratios present data with technological and behavioral interpretability that will be detailed later. A similar set of five ratios is provided for flaked-stone artifacts: flaked-stone tools per room, all flakes per room, total flaked stone per room, all flakes per core, and all flakes per flaked-stone tool. Two ratios are then presented in the flaked-stone tool tables that relate ground-stone to flaked-stone artifacts: ground-stone tools per flaked-stone tool, and total ground stone per total flaked stone.

One must be cautious in interpreting these ratio data. In the first place, it is important to demonstrate the relevance and comparability of all individual data groupings that comprise the ratio. For example, not all excavation contexts at Arroyo Hondo that are designated as "rooms" are architectural and/or social equivalents; some, such as "midden" and "plaza" contexts, are more administrative units than architectural units. Such nonarchitectural units are readily identified by their names, and their individual or collective interpretation is avoided. Second, one cannot assume that the artifact assemblages from all similarly described units, such as architectural rooms, have been similarly collected and are, in fact, directly comparable. A detailed study of the Arroyo Hondo excavation notes was not made to confirm this comparability; it seems reasonable to assume, however, that architectural rooms within roomblocks were excavated with the same procedures, and so the comparison and interpretation of "per room" ratios will be restricted to these contexts.

Reconstructing Summary Data Sets: Context

The same principles that have guided the reconstruction of data content for this summary interpretation of the Arroyo Hondo lithic assemblage have also been used to produce a restructured set of data contexts—the temporal and spatial groupings into which the data are arranged for interpreting content variability. These principles are: (1) primary reliance on artifact analysis notes rather than on preliminary data summaries; (2) production of fewer and larger data categories; (3) elimination of questionable data; and (4) production of multiple data structures to maximize data use. The effect of these data-structuring principles is to improve both content and context reliability, but at some expense in the amount of data available for use. Restructuring only the confirmed data into fewer, larger, and more inclusive content and context categories improves the confidence with which data comparisons can be made and interpreted, and also reduces the level of interpretive detail to a rather coarse-grained analysis. Such an analytic approach seems appropriate for this Arroyo Hondo interpretive summary.

Original records for the 1971, 1972, and 1973 lithic analyses were examined (no 1974 analysis records were available), and lists of artifacts were constructed. Both specific FS (field specimen) identification and artifact-type designation were required for inclusion on these lists, either as individual items or as small groupings of contextually and/or typologically related items. These artifact lists, the roomblock and individual room contexts identifiable from the FS designations, and the correspondence of 1971–72 and 1973–74 artifact types with the newly produced and more general types (see tables 16 and 17) formed the basis for the reconstructed data sets, as briefly described below. These basic data were supplemented by more specific context information provided by School of American Research staff (Winifred Creamer, Jonathan Haas, Judith Habicht-Mauche, personal communication, 1989). These data were entered into a computerized set of interactive SYSTAT (version 3.0) data files on an IBM-compatible personal computer. Summary data tables were produced and converted to a standardized and simplified tabular format (tables 18–34).

The data tables are discussed and interpreted in the following section; they are briefly introduced here to provide a comprehensive preview of the data structure. Data appear as sets of two tables for each context and/or data set: one each for ground-stone and flaked-stone artifacts. Two sets of tables (tables 18 and 19, 20 and 21) summarize the maximum possible Arroyo Hondo lithic data.

Tables 18 and 19 present a comparison of the 1971–72 and 1973–74 Arroyo Hondo analysis results, clearly illustrating the need for multiple data structures and for collapsing content categories into fewer and larger artifact types. Tables 20 and 21 present the maximum possible Arroyo Hondo data assemblage, expressed in these more generalized artifact types. These two tables are simply content rearrangements (see tables 16 and 17) of Linford's (n.d.b) summary data tables. Because this maximum data set cannot be contextually identified in the original analysis notes—and therefore cannot be contextually subdivided—its use is limited to a very generalized view of the entire Arroyo Hondo lithic assemblage.

The only temporal context into which the Arroyo Hondo lithic data can be grouped is that of component: the Coalition period occupation (Component I) from approximately A.D. 1300 to 1350 and the Classic period reoccupation (Component II) from approximately A.D. 1375 to 1425 (Habicht-Mauche and Creamer 1989: 2–3; Schwartz 1981b:ix). Linford's maximum Arroyo Hondo summary data presentation (tables 19 and 20) is arranged by component. The component assignment of these summary data, however, cannot be confirmed in the project analysis records. A smaller data set of FS-confirmed component assignments is presented for comparison and interpretation as tables 22 and 23; the component assignments in these tables were made from a listing of room-component correspondences provided by School of American Research staff (Creamer, personal communication, 1989).

The fundamental spatial contexts identifiable for the Arroyo Hondo materials, structured into the FS numbering system, are room and roomblock, plaza, midden, gate, and kiva. In addition, a listing provided by School of American Research staff (Creamer, personal communication, 1989) identifies many rooms as either first-floor or second-floor contexts. By far the majority of the FS-confirmable Arroyo Hondo data are from structural rooms in roomblocks, and these data are presented as tables 24, 25, 26, and 27. Several roomblocks are of particular interest because of such factors as construction materials or plans, site formation sequence, reoccupation, or excavation intensity (Schwartz 1972; Schwartz and Lang 1973:11, fig. 2). Tables 24 and 25 summarize ground-stone and flaked-stone artifact data from roomblocks with at least 40 tools per roomblock. These data are presented and interpreted as relative frequencies. Tables 26 and 27 summarize as raw data frequencies the lithic data from roomblocks with fewer than 40 tools per roomblock. Interpretation of roomblock data will focus on the larger assemblages. Tables 28 and 29 present the

TABLE 18
Ground-stone artifacts from Arroyo Hondo Pueblo, by analysis years.

	Bonney 1971–72[a]		Linford 1973–74[b]	
	No.	%	No.	%
Ground-stone tools				
One-hand manos		3		5
Two-hand manos		25		6
Mano fragments		13		2
(Subtotal: manos)		(40)		(13)
Metates		10		9
Grinding stones		6		18
Grinding slabs		13		7
(Subtotal: grinding tools)		(69)		(47)
Polishing stones		4		3
Hafted items		2		7
Hammerstones		5		11
Ornaments		2		2
Mineral, turquoise		1		7
Mineral, mica		5		6
Mineral, pigment		3		3
Shaped slabs		<1		3
Miscellaneous		9		11
Total ground-stone tools	1,779	100/38	613	100/82
Ground-stone fragments	2,906	62	134	18
Total ground stone	4,685	100	747	100
Ratios				
Ground-stone tools/room		24		47
Grinding tools/room		17		22
Ground-stone fragments/room		40		10
Total ground stone/room		64		57
Manos/metate		4.0		1.4
Two-hand/one-hand mano		9.8		1.3
Ground-stone fragments/ground-stone tool		1.6		0.2

[a] Number of rooms = 73.
[b] Number of rooms = 13.

lithic data that are identifiable with reference to major site contexts other than roomblock: first-floor rooms, second-floor rooms, other (mixed) rooms, plazas, and middens.

Because of its extensive level of excavation—35 rooms—and its occupation in Components I and II, roomblock 16 was selected for a detailed study of room use at Arroyo Hondo (Habicht-Mauche and Creamer 1989:3). Lithic data from roomblock 16 are presented in tables 30, 31, 32, and 33, arranged as several "residence unit" types (Habicht-Mauche and Creamer 1989:10–11) in each component (tables 30 and 31) and as first- and second-floor rooms (tables 32 and 33). Each of these data structures is examined and interpreted below.

Interpretation
Intrasite Comparisons

CONTENT

Tables 18 and 19 present a comparison of the 1971–72 and 1973–74 analysis results for ground-stone and flaked-stone artifacts, respectively. The relatively small number of specifically identifiable room contexts in the 1973–74 analysis reflects both the absence of any 1974 analysis records and a tendency for the 1973 materials to be summarized into multiple FS data groupings other than individual room contexts. Tables 18 and 19 reveal strong assemblage dissimilarities that are almost certainly the

TABLE 19
Flaked-stone artifacts from Arroyo Hondo Pueblo, by analysis years.

	Bonney 1971–72[a]		Linford 1973–74[b]	
	No.	%	No.	%
Flaked-stone tools				
Notched projectile points		28		10
Unnotched projectile points, knives		21		9
Projectile point fragments		10		4
(Subtotal: projectile points and knives)		(58)		(23)
Drills, gravers		6		5
Scrapers		36		71
Flaked-stone tools	315	100/4	294	100/5
Used flakes	35	<1	2,510	47
Flakes	6,400	91	2,470	46
Cores	318	4	95	2
Total flaked stone	7,068	100	5,369	100
Ratios				
Flaked-stone tools/room		4		23
Flakes/room		88		383
Total flaked stone/room		97		413
Flakes/core		20		52
Flakes/flaked-stone tool		20		17
Ground-stone tools/flaked-stone tool		5.6		2.1
All ground stone/all flaked stone		0.7		0.1

[a] Number of rooms = 73.
[b] Number of rooms = 13.

result of different analytic emphases rather than of interpretable content differences. Such strong variability would be very difficult to interpret as prehistoric behavioral differential. A careful examination of the Arroyo Hondo field reports (Schwartz 1971, 1972; Schwartz and Lang 1973) reveals no obvious differences in fieldwork objectives or procedures that would explain differences of such magnitude, and it is difficult to imagine that chance selection of excavation contexts would result in such extreme content variability. Certainly the 73 rooms from the 1971–72 analysis and the 13 rooms from the 1973–74 analysis were drawn, in whatever fashion, from the total population of Arroyo Hondo rooms, and there are no indications from other analytic results (Dickson 1979; Kelley 1980; Lang and Harris 1984; Palkovich 1980; Rose, Dean, and Robinson 1981; Wetterstrom 1986) to suspect such extreme content variability on any basis, particularly such an apparently arbitrary one as the year of excavation and analysis.

Closer examination of tables 18 and 19 indicates a number of probable analytic differences, some of which were mentioned earlier. For ground stone (table 18) these include a very strong differential in the recognition of two-hand manos, mano fragments, grinding stones, grinding slabs, hafted items, and hammerstones. It is also clear that ground-stone fragments are quite different entities in the two analyses, comprising 62 percent of the total 1971–72 ground-stone assemblage, and only 18 percent of the 1973–74 materials. Five of the seven ground-stone artifact ratios demonstrate differences of at least two orders of magnitude; only grinding tools per room and total ground stone per room demonstrate general similarity. The differences between the 1971–72 and 1973–74 flaked-stone assemblages (table 19) are at least as great as those in the ground-stone artifacts. Only the proportions of drills and gravers and of flaked-stone tools as a proportion of total flaked stone are generally similar. Four of the five internal flaked-stone artifact ratios and both flaked-to-ground-stone ratios demonstrate very strong differences.

Tables 18 and 19 clearly demonstrate how difficult it is to construct a single Arroyo Hondo data set from which convincing behavioral interpretations can be made. Combining the contextually identifiable 1971–72 and 1973–

TABLE 20
Ground-stone artifacts from Arroyo Hondo Pueblo.

	Component I		Component II		Total	
	No.	%	No.	%	No.	%
Ground-stone tools						
One-hand manos		3.2		1.8		2.9
Two-hand manos		20.0		20.9		20.2
Mano fragments		2.7		4.1		3.0
(Subtotal: manos)		(25.8)		(26.9)		(26.1)
Metates		3.3		5.0		3.7
Grinding stones		15.4		14.2		15.1
Grinding slabs		18.0		21.8		18.9
(Subtotal: grinding tools)		(62.4)		(67.9)		(63.8)
Polishing stones		3.3		1.7		2.9
Hafted items		2.1		2.7		2.2
Hammerstones		10.0		6.3		9.1
Ornaments		0.9		1.1		1.0
Mineral, turquoise		1.8		0.6		1.5
Mineral, mica		6.3		6.4		6.3
Mineral, pigment		1.6		1.6		1.6
Shaped slabs		0.3		1.0		0.5
Miscellaneous		11.4		10.8		11.2
Ground-stone tools	2,830	100/42.7	941	100/44.0	3,771	100/43.0
Ground-stone fragments	3,800	52.3	1,200	56.0	5,000	57.0
Total ground stone	6,630	100	2,141	100	8,771	100
Ratios						
Manos/metate		7.9		5.4		7.1
Two-hand/one-hand mano		6.2		11.6		7.1
Ground-stone fragments/ ground-stone tool		1.3		1.3		1.3

SOURCE: Linford n.d.b:table 2.1.

74 materials is only a partial solution, since simply averaging this extreme variability clearly does not guarantee correct or appropriate comparability. Furthermore, it is unclear just how the "sample" of 13 identifiable 1973–74 room contexts might represent the entire 1973–74 assemblage, or how its combination with the entire 73-room 1971–72 assemblage might constitute some sample of the total Arroyo Hondo lithic assemblage.

Tables 20 and 21 are presented as a basis for assessing these concerns in a general fashion and as the maximum possible Arroyo Hondo lithic data presentation. These tables are simply a rearrangement of Linford's final summary data tables (Linford n.d.b, tables 2.1, 3.1) into the more general content categories of this report. Comparison of tables 18 and 19 demonstrates that the relative proportions of ground-stone artifact categories and ratios for the 13 identifiable 1973–74 room contexts are quite different from the total Arroyo Hondo assemblage: that is, Linford's ground-stone artifact "profile" for the total Arroyo Hondo assemblage (table 20) differs greatly from that of the "sample" of his 13 identifiable room contexts (table 18). A comparison of flaked-stone artifacts from the same contexts (tables 19 and 21) similarly reveals important differences in about half the data groupings. Some of this difference may be due to the various sampling and/or analytic factors already mentioned (or others) and some may be due to prehistoric behavioral variability in these Arroyo Hondo contexts, but it is not possible to determine to what extent these factor(s) are involved. Because of these data uncertainties, interpretation of the more comprehensive Arroyo Hondo data sets will be generally avoided. Instead, several smaller data groupings will be used for the majority of data interpretation; these are analytically much more consistent,

TABLE 21
Flaked-stone artifacts from Arroyo Hondo Pueblo.

	Component I		Component II		Total	
	No.	%	No.	%	No.	%
Flaked-stone tools						
Notched projectile points		15.3		20.2		17.2
Unnotched projectile points, knives		33.3		28.5		31.4
Projectile point fragments		7.5		8.3		7.8
(Subtotal: projectile points and knives)		(56.1)		(57.0)		(56.4)
Drills, gravers		8.0		7.7		7.9
Scrapers		35.9		35.3		35.7
Flaked-stone tools	535	100/5.6	337	100/6.3	872	100/5.8
Used flakes	2,990	31.3	2,070	38.4	5,060	33.9
Flakes	5,651	59.2	2,895	53.8	8,546	57.3
Cores	366	3.8	84	1.6	450	3.0
Total flaked stone	9,542	100	5,386	100	14,928	100
Ratios						
All flakes/flaked tool		16.2		14.7		15.6
All flakes/core		23.6		59.1		30.2
Ground-stone tools/flaked-stone tool		5.3		2.8		4.3
All ground-stone/all flaked stone		0.7		0.4		0.6

SOURCE: Linford n.d.b:table 3.1.

and they have been contextually confirmed through the project FS numbering system. These sets of data are presented in standardized table format (tables 22–33) and are breifly interpreted below as temporally and spatially structured data groupings.

TIME

The occupation of Arroyo Hondo has been securely dated by several independent means to the 125-year period between A.D. 1300 and 1425. It was characterized by two major population peaks, or components, separated by a short period of virtual or complete abandonment. Component I represents a large Coalition-period occupation between approximately A.D. 1300 and 1350, and Component II represents a much smaller Classic-period occupation between approximately A.D. 1375 and 1425 (Habicht-Mauche and Creamer 1989:2–4; Schwartz 1981b:ix; Schwartz and Lang 1973:17–34).

The lithic data from Arroyo Hondo are arranged by component in tables 20 and 21, which present Linford's final unconfirmed data summaries (Linford n.d.b), and in tables 22 and 23, which present a smaller set of FS-verified data comprising mostly 1971–72 materials (Bonney 1971, 1972). Smaller temporal divisions, such as those used by Lang and Harris (1984:14–18, table 1) for

the Arroyo Hondo faunal data, are not possible. My interpretation will focus on the smaller data set presented in tables 22 and 23 for three reasons: (1) the content of the smaller data set is confirmable in the project analysis records; (2) the analysis is known to be generally consistent; and (3) the data are known to come from most of the roomblocks at the site.

The proportional occurrences of tool types in the ground stone assemblages of the two components (table 22) demonstrate quite similar profiles (Phagan 1984:144–50). To the extent that such ground-stone tool profiles can be used to distinguish among major subsistence patterns, the two Arroyo Hondo components suggest strong similarity with reference to plant processing and consumption. It is likely that none of the between-components differences in tool type proportions is statistically significant, though sampling uncertainties make such tests questionable for use with these data.

The internal proportions of the ground-stone assemblages in table 22 and the per-room expressions of those assemblages, however, suggest rather marked between-components distinctions. Component II has far fewer ground-stone tools, grinding tools, and total ground stone per room; it shows slightly fewer ground-stone fragments per room. These data suggest a considerably reduced

TABLE 22
Ground-stone artifacts from Arroyo Hondo Pueblo, by component.

	Component I[a]		Component II[b]	
	No.	%	No.	%
Ground-stone tools				
One-hand manos		2		2
Two-hand manos		25		26
Mano fragments		12		16
(Subtotal: manos)		(39)		(44)
Metates		11		11
Grinding stones		7		5
Grinding slabs		14		11
(Subtotal: grinding tools)		(71)		(71)
Polishing stones		4		3
Hafted items		2		1
Hammerstones		5		3
Ornaments		1		1
Mineral, turquoise		1		2
Mineral, mica		3		5
Mineral, pigment		3		3
Shaped slabs		<1		1
Miscellaneous		9		11
Ground-stone tools	1,064	100/45	301	100/26
Ground-stone fragments	1,281	55	862	74
Total ground stone	2,345	100	1,163	100
Ratios				
Ground-stone tools/room		33		12
Grinding tools/room		24		8
Ground-stone fragments/room		40		33
Total ground stone/room		73		45
Manos/metate		3.7		4.0
Two-hand/one-hand mano		11.6		12.8
Ground-stone fragments/ground-stone tool		1.2		2.9

[a] Number of rooms = 32.
[b] Number of rooms = 26.

level of plant-food processing and consumption during Component II, perhaps simply because there were fewer occupants per room. Both components, then, demonstrate the same basic kinds and relative proportions of ground-stone tool–associated behavior, but at very different levels of intensity. Such differences would appear to be related more to differential population sizes rather than to occupation nature or duration, with simply a much smaller Component II population (Habicht-Mauche and Creamer 1989:2–3). This conclusion is confirmed in a general way by the Arroyo Hondo skeletal and mortuary remains: 102 burials were associated with Component I and only 12 with Component II (Palkovich 1980:1).

A ratio of about 12 two-hand manos per each one-hand mano for both components indicates a similar strong subsistence focus on specialized corn processing, with relatively minor attention given to the more generalized processing of native plants (Phagan and Hruby 1984:85–86). This ratio confirms the general similarity in subsistence patterns of the two Arroyo Hondo components: their differences, in other words, appear more quantitative than qualitative, at least for the ground-stone data.

Component II demonstrates nearly three times as many ground-stone fragments per each ground-stone tool as does Component I, suggesting either a technological

TABLE 23

Flaked-stone artifacts from Arroyo Hondo Pueblo, by component.

	Component I[a]		Component II[b]	
	No.	%	No.	%
Flaked-stone tools				
Notched projectile points		22		27
Unnotched projectile points, knives		21		23
Projectile point fragments		11		11
(Subtotal: projectile points and knives)		(54)		(61)
Drills, gravers		5		7
Scrapers		41		32
Flaked-stone tools	143	100/5	106	100/6
Used flakes	16	<1	5	<1
Flakes	2,821	90	2,112	91
Cores	161	5	93	4
Total flaked stone	3,141	100	2,316	100
Ratios				
Flaked-stone tools/room	4		4	
Flakes/room	83		73	
Total flaked stone/room	92		80	
Flakes/core	18		23	
Flakes/flaked-stone tool	20		20	
Ground-stone tools/flaked-stone tool	7.4		2.8	
All ground stone/all flaked stone	0.7		0.5	

[a]Number of rooms or units = 34.
[b]Number of rooms or units = 29.

difference in production methods or location, a site-formation difference in the accumulation of ground-stone debris, or both. The process of reoccupying a site and rebuilding and retooling at least in part from its ruins would seem to be sufficient explanation for such a difference.

Table 23 presents Arroyo Hondo flaked-stone tool data by component. As with the ground-stone tools, the two components demonstrate very similar profiles of proportional tool representation, suggesting a general between-components similarity of technologically and functionally associated behavior. This conclusion is in general agreement with Lang and Harris's (1984:47–54) interpretation of the Arroyo Hondo faunal remains, in which they find broad between-components similarity with minor changing emphases in deer, elk, bison, and antelope remains. A slightly increased proportion of notched projectile points, along with a somewhat decreased proportion of scrapers in Component II, might reflect any of several circumstances involving differential reliance on these animal resources and/or differential lo-

cations and procedures for their acquisition, processing, storage, and consumption.

Both the internal flaked-stone artifact ratios and the per-room artifact distributions shown in table 23 indicate general qualitative and quantitative between-components similarity. Very little change appears through time in the technology of flaked-stone tool production, the behavior associated with the use of these tools, or the manner of their discard. Such similarity is anticipated given the brief interval between Arroyo Hondo components, the broad cultural similarity of the two occupations, and the relative stability (or conservatism) of lithic technological systems (Phagan 1986:103–4).

The major between-components variation suggested by the data presented in tables 22 and 23, then, is the marked decrease in intensity of ground-stone tool–associated behavior in Component II, which produces the strong relative differences in the ground-stone tool per flaked-stone tool ratio given in table 23. This variation might best be explained by hypothesizing a much smaller Component II population that was relatively less involved with corn production and processing than was its earlier counterpart, but which did not differ significantly in the *kinds* of plant- or animal-processing tools or associated behavior.

SPACE

ROOMBLOCKS. The Arroyo Hondo spatial context most readily identifiable in both the 1971–72 and 1973–74 lithic analyses is that of the roomblock. Nineteen such major contiguous room groupings were identified (Schwartz and Lang 1973:10–11, fig. 2) and structured into the FS numbering system. The maximum possible Arroyo Hondo lithic data set that can be confirmed contextually from the analysis records has been formed by combining roomblock data from both the 1971–72 and 1973–74 analyses (tables 24, 25, 26, and 27). The content correspondences of the 1971–72 and 1973–74 analysis system types with the more general artifact categories used throughout this report have been discussed; they are summarized in tables 16 and 17. Materials included from the 1971–72 analysis records are the accumulated individual artifact totals. Materials from the 1973–74 analysis had been grouped by roomblock in the analysis records, and these totals have simply been restructured into the more general artifact categories for presentation here. The 1973–74 analysis records included only flaked-stone data for several of the roomblocks reported; ground-stone data were missing from roomblocks 7, 8, 9, 10, and 15A (Linford 1974). Because 1971–72 materials were also reported for these roomblocks (Bonney 1971, 1972), they have been included in tables 24, 25, 26, and 27. Their interpretation, however, must be tempered by the fact that they contain only flaked-stone data (i.e., no ground-stone data) from 1973–74.

Tables 24 and 25 contain ground-stone and flaked-stone artifact data, respectively, from roomblock contexts with at least 40 tools each. These data are presented and will be interpreted as proportional data. Tables 26 and 27 contain ground-stone and flaked-stone artifact data, respectively, from roomblock contexts with fewer than 40 tools each. These data are presented as numbers of items, and they are interpreted only minimally because of their generally small numbers. With two exceptions, all roomblock groupings contain data from only one to three rooms each; they are therefore considered minimal samples in representing the entire roomblocks. Interpretations based on these small and uncertain samples must be considered suggestive rather than conclusive. The two exceptions are roomblocks 11 and 16, from which excavated room samples are quite good (9 rooms

and 35 rooms, respectively). Only two other roomblocks, roomblocks 9 and 10, have at least 40 tools in both ground- and flaked-stone assemblages. These four roomblocks—9, 10, 11, and 16—surround a single plaza, plaza C (Schwartz and Lang 1973:11, fig. 2). Considerable interpretive attention will be directed to these four roomblocks because of their larger sample size, particularly roomblocks 11 and 16. It should be recalled that this arrangement of data by roomblock (tables 24, 25, 26, and 27) includes some distinctly different data groupings that make comparison and interpretation difficult. Several of the roomblocks contain only 1971–72 materials (roomblocks 4, 11, 12, 13, 15, 15A, 19, 20, 21, 23, 24), while others contain both 1971–72 and 1973–74 materials (roomblocks 3, 6, 7, 8, 9, 10, 14). Furthermore, the 1973–74 ground-stone artifact data from roomblocks 7, 8, 9, 10, and 15A are missing, so that these five roomblocks contain ground-stone artifact data from only 1971–72, but flaked-stone data from 1971–72 and 1973–74. Data columns in tables 24, 25, 26, 27, 28, and 29 have been marked to indicate this variability.

Table 24 suggests a relatively low and evenly distributed level of the generalized grinding activities represented by one-hand manos across all Arroyo Hondo roomblocks. In contrast, the data indicate an extremely varied intensity and spatial distribution of the more specialized grinding behavior represented by two-hand manos and mano fragments. Variability in the manos subtotal, which is considerable, is therefore judged to be at least in part the result of differentially patterned specialized corn-grinding behavior.

Metates appear to be more evenly and systematically distributed than manos, in part because of their smaller numbers, and perhaps in part because their greater mass makes them less likely to be moved about and therefore more likely to remain in or near their use context. This factor is closely related to their frequent designation as "site furniture" (Binford 1977). If the distribution of manos and metates, which are functional partners in a single task, differs markedly, it is probably safest to interpret behavioral intensity from manos, and behavioral type and location from metates. At Arroyo Hondo, therefore, the distribution of metates suggests a relatively even distribution of specialized corn-grinding behavior (i.e., type of behavior) among roomblocks, while the distribution of manos suggests that some roomblocks were processing considerably more corn than others (i.e., amount of behavior). This interpretation is supported by the grinding tools subtotal, which varies from 50 percent to 88 percent of the roomblock ground-stone tool assemblages.

Several of the minor ground-stone tool types in table 24

TABLE 24

Ground-stone artifacts from Arroyo Hondo roomblocks with at least 40 ground-stone tools.

Roomblock Number

	6[b] (N[c] = 2)		7[a] (N = 3)		8[a] (N = 3)		9[a] (N = 3)		10[a] (N = 2)		11[a] (N = 9)		14[b] (N = 2)		15[b] (N = 2)		15A[a] (N = 2)		16[a] (N = 35)	
	No.	%	No.	%	No.	%	No.	%	No.	%	No.	%	No.	%	No.	%	No.	%	No.	%
Ground-stone tools																				
One-hand manos		2		4		2		4		4		4		2		3		2		2
Two-hand manos		28		33		27		17		8		32		19		18		4		29
Mano fragments		7		18		2		11		25		12		3		24		13		9
(Subtotal: manos)		(38)		(56)		(31)		(32)		(37)		(48)		(23)		(45)		(19)		(40)
Metates		14		7		11		7		10		5		7		7		11		12
Grinding stones		4		6		5		5		6		4		8		6		6		6
Grinding slabs		10		19		18		13		21		8		13		13		15		15
(Subtotal: grinding tools)		(66)		(88)		(65)		(57)		(73)		(65)		(51)		(70)		(50)		(73)
Polishing stones		6		1		5		2		4		8		5		–		2		4
Hafted items		–		1		–		2		2		4		2		–		–		1
Hammerstones		6		4		5		12		8		2		14		10		11		4
Ornaments		3		–		9		1		2		5		–		–		–		1
Mineral, turquoise		–		–		–		2		–		2		1		–		–		1
Mineral, mica		10		–		5		11		2		5		3		–		24		4
Mineral, pigment		1		1		2		2		–		1		5		–		2		5
Shaped slabs		–		–		–		–		–		–		4		–		–		1
Miscellaneous		8		4		7		9		10		8		17		20		11		7
Ground-stone tools	125	100/48	72	100/35	55	100/50	82	100/40	52	100/17	201	100/37	111	100/67	71	100/70	54	100/33	698	100/46
Ground-stone fragments	138	52	132	65	56	50	121	60	254	83	346	63	55	33	31	30	111	67	808	54
Total ground stone	263	100	204	100	111	100	203	100	306	100	547	100	166	100	102	100	165	100	1,506	100
Ratios																				
Ground-stone tools/room	63		24		18		27		26		22		56		36		27		19	
Grinding tools/room	41		21		12		16		19		14		29		25		14		15	
Ground-stone fragments/room	69		44		19		40		127		38		28		16		56		23	
Total ground stone/room	132		68		37		68		153		61		83		51		83		43	
Manos/metate	2.8		8.0		2.8		4.3		3.8		9.6		3.3		6.4		1.7		3.3	
Two-hand/one-hand mano	11.7		8.0		15.0		4.7		2.0		8.0		10.5		6.5		2.0		18.3	
Ground-stone fragments/ground-stone tool	1.1		1.8		1.0		1.5		4.9		1.7		0.5		0.4		2.1		1.2	

[a] 1971–72 data only.   [b] 1971–72 plus 1973–74 data.   [c] N = number of rooms.

suggest the possibility of differentially distributed associated behavior(s), such as high proportions of ceramic-polishing stones and hafted items in roomblock 11, a high proportion of ornaments in roomblock 8, a high proportion of mica (muscovite) items in roomblock 15A, and high proportions of pigment materials in room-blocks 14 and 16. Because the numbers of items represented by these proportions are sometimes rather small, however, and because other kinds of data cannot be similarly structured for verification, any behavioral inferences based on this variability should be very tentative.

A strong differential in recognizing ground-stone fragments characterizes the 1971–72 and 1973–74 analytic systems, resulting in an unknown, but probably considerable, amount of the table 24 variability in total ground stone. The small number of rooms in most roomblocks makes the per-room ratio values of questionable utility except for roomblocks 11 and 16, which have generally similar per-room profiles for all categories other than ground-stone fragments and the totals and ratios involving fragments. Both roomblocks 11 and 16 include only 1971–72 materials, so any difference is not likely to be analytic (see discussion on table 25, below). These two roomblocks also demonstrate considerable difference in the ratios of manos to metates and of one-hand to two-hand manos. Roomblock 16 has only one-third as many manos per metate as roomblock 11, and more than twice as many two-hand manos per one-hand mano. These ratios imply the occurrence of less intense but more specialized grinding activity in roomblock 16, and conversely, more intense and less specialized grinding activity in roomblock 11. Any explanations of this grinding behavior differential are speculative without specifically organized data of other kinds, but it may be related in some way(s) to the differential construction materials and/or historical development of the two roomblocks. Roomblock 16 is constructed of adobe, and roomblock 11, the earliest Arroyo Hondo roomblock, is constructed of masonry (Schwartz 1981a:81). Since roomblock 11 has relatively fewer Component II rooms than roomblock 16 (see below), however, these data may also support the earlier suggestion of more specialized resource procurement behavior during the Component II occupation.

Table 25 presents flaked-stone artifact data from the four Arroyo Hondo roomblocks having at least 40 flaked-stone tools. These data are problematic, in that most of the typological categories with relatively large numbers (and proportions) of items clearly occur as a strongly patterned dichotomous distribution among the four roomblocks. Roomblocks 9 and 10 are generally similar, as are roomblocks 11 and 16, but the two groupings are quite different from each other. This pattern holds for the projectile points and knives subtotal, and for scrapers, flaked tools, used flakes, flakes, all three per-room ratios, and both ground stone-to-flaked stone ratios. There are no obvious culturally associated reasons that would account for this patterning: the four roomblocks surround a single plaza, all contain first-floor and second-floor rooms, and all contain rooms from components I and II, though in differing proportions. There are, however, two analytic and data-structuring factors that probably account for most of the variability.

First, roomblocks 9 and 10 contain materials analyzed in both 1971–72 and 1973–74, while roomblocks 11 and 16 contain only 1971–72 materials. Several differences between the 1971–72 and 1973–74 analysis systems have been discussed, and particularly important here is the differential recognition of used flakes. In arranging the data for this report, an attempt was made to minimize the effect of this analytic difference by removing used flakes from the flaked-stone tools category and considering them, along with flakes and cores, as "nontool" elements of the total flaked-stone assemblage. Combining flakes and used flakes into an "all flakes" category should then subsume the analytic differences into a single, more generalized and comparable data category. This has been successful at least in part, in that the "all flakes" proportion of the total flaked-stone roomblock assemblages demonstrates very little of the dichotomous pattern mentioned above. In addition, no such dichotomous pattern appears in the "all flakes per core" and "all flakes per flaked-stone tool" ratios. However, the projectile points and knives subtotal, scrapers, both ground stone per flaked stone ratios, and the three "per-room" ratios, which should all be independent of any flakes versus used flakes analytic difference, still clearly demonstrate the dichotomous pattern. Some, but not all, of this apparent dichotomy may be due to a second data-structuring factor: the number of rooms from which the materials came.

The number of rooms in roomblocks 11 and 16 from which table 25 data are derived is certain and can be traced in the project analysis records. The number of rooms represented in the roomblock 9 (3 rooms) and 10 (2 rooms) data, however, is far less secure. These are in fact a minimum number of rooms: that is, it is certain that data are from at least this minimum number of rooms, but they may be from more—even considerably more. The minimum number of rooms is used here—even though problems are associated with its use—in order to provide some very rough indication of the volume of fill from which the materials were derived, or some

TABLE 25

Flaked-stone artifacts from Arroyo Hondo roomblocks with at least 40 flaked-stone tools.

	Roomblock Number							
	9[b] (N[c] = 3)		10[b] (N = 2)		11[a] (N = 9)		16[a] (N = 35)	
	No.	%	No.	%	No.	%	No.	%
Flaked-stone tools								
Notched projectile points		13		16		28		22
Unnotched projectile points, knives		13		16		19		20
Projectile point fragments		2		5		5		11
(Subtotal: projectile points and knives)		(29)		(37)		(52)		(53)
Drills, gravers		10		3		–		7
Scrapers		61		60		48		39
Flaked-stone tools	83	100/4	62	100/4	42	100/6	147	100/6
Used flakes	770	40	516	33	4	1	1	<1
Flakes	1,049	55	921	60	622	91	2,429	91
Cores	22	1	45	3	14	2	90	3
Total flaked stone	1,924	100	1,544	100	682	100	2,667	100
Ratios								
Flaked-stone tools/room	28		31		5		4	
All flakes/room	606		719		70		69	
Total flaked stone/room	641		772		76		76	
All flakes/core	22		23		15		27	
All flakes/flaked-stone tool	83		32		45		17	
Ground-stone tools/flaked-stone tool[d]	1.0		0.8		4.8		4.7	
All ground stone/all flaked stone[d]	0.1		0.2		0.5		0.6	

[a] 1971–72 data only.
[b] 1971–72 plus 1973–74 data.
[c] N = number of rooms.
[d] Ground stone data from table 24, this volume.

measure of artifact density. It will be especially helpful in comparing and interpreting data contexts that can be clearly demonstrated as comparable, and will hereafter be restricted to such situations.

When the effects of both the known 1971–72 versus 1973–74 analytic differences and the number of rooms from which the data are derived are discounted, however, there still remains some indication of a dichotomous variability pattern in flaked-stone artifacts between roomblocks 9 and 10 and roomblocks 11 and 16. This pattern is seen in the assemblage proportions of projectile points and knives, scrapers, flaked-stone tools, and the two ground stone per flaked stone ratios. No such dichotomous pattern for these roomblocks is evident from the ground-stone data in table 24, even considering the comparison problem caused by the missing 1973–74 ground-stone data from roomblocks 9 and 10, though conceivably such a pattern might appear with the addi-

tion of the missing data. No satisfying reasons can be offered for this dichotomous flaked-stone artifact pattern, but I am inclined to suspect some unrecognized analytic factor(s).

Certainly the most reliable flaked-stone artifact comparison among these data is that between roomblock 11 and roomblock 16; it is hampered only slightly by the relatively small size of the roomblock 11 tool assemblage (N = 42). Some small but potentially interesting differences between the two roomblocks might be anticipated on the basis of either component (I or II) or floor (first or second story). Roomblock 11 includes five Component I rooms, three Component II rooms, and one room of unassigned component status, all nine of which are first-floor rooms. Roomblock 16 includes 13 Component I rooms, 11 of which are second-floor rooms; 20 Component II rooms, all of which are first-floor rooms, and 2 rooms of unassigned component status (Creamer, personal communication, 1989). Roomblock 11, therefore, contains all first-floor rooms and a majority of Component I rooms; roomblock 16 contains both first- and second-floor rooms, and a majority of Component II rooms (see tables 22 and 23 for component data).

Roomblocks 11 and 16 demonstrate broadly similar flaked-stone artifact profiles (table 25). Over half of the flaked tools are projectile points, knives, and their identifiable fragments; this seems to be a rather large proportion of these mostly bifacial, high-production-input items. There are, however, few directly comparable data from which to confirm this impression (see Intersite Comparisons, below). In addition, it should be recalled that minimally modified or simply used items are not included here as tools. Nevertheless, to have more projectile points and knives than other clearly modified flaked-stone items in these roomblocks suggests either some behavioral focus on animal procurement and/or generally light-duty processing of softer materials for which such items are best suited, or tool maintenance and short-term storage.

Among flaked-stone tools other than projectile points and knives, the absence of drills and gravers in roomblock 11 may be a small-sample problem; this is reflected also in the higher proportion of scrapers, the only other tool category. The two ratios "all flakes per core" and "all flakes per flaked-stone tool" are technological indicators of lithic reduction patterning, and both, especially the latter, demonstrate some differential between roomblocks 11 and 16. Several inductive interpretations of these ratios are possible, and those suggested here are simply likely examples. More flakes per core in roomblock 16 may suggest greater intensity in reduction activity. Other factors being equal, more flakes per tool may also suggest the possibility of either greater reduction intensity, such as the later stages of biface reduction, or the spatial separation of tool production from tool use and/or discard, or both. In this case the latter interpretation is preferred for roomblock 11, since the former would contradict the flakes-per-core evidence. Such interpretive hypotheses must remain tentative and deductively untested, however, as these data cannot be contextually rearranged to examine their further implications.

Both roomblocks 11 and 16 have almost five ground-stone tools for each flaked-stone tool, which seems to be an unusually heavy emphasis on ground-stone technology and its associated behavior. It must be recalled, however, that minimally or unmodified flakes—usually the most common stone tool in Southwestern Puebloan assemblages (Phagan 1986:105)—are not included here as tools. A comparison of total flaked-stone with total ground-stone assemblages for both roomblocks 11 and 16 demonstrates about two flaked-stone items for each ground-stone item, a more "normal" Puebloan expression (Phagan 1986:105).

Tables 26 and 27 present ground-stone and flaked-stone artifact data, respectively, for Arroyo Hondo roomblocks with fewer than 40 tools. The rather large ranges of variability demonstrated for many of the artifact categories is expected as the result of the small and irregular sample sizes. In addition, the differences between the 1971–72 and 1973–74 analytic systems are particularly apparent in the ground-stone fragments (table 26) and used flakes (table 27) categories.

MAJOR CONTEXT TYPES. To the extent possible, the Arroyo Hondo lithic data have also been arranged for this summary reconstruction into major context types: first-floor rooms, second-floor rooms, plazas, middens, and so on. Tables 28 and 29 present ground-stone and flaked-stone artifact data, respectively, for these major site contexts. Plaza, midden, and individual room contexts are identifiable in the project FS structure, and a listing of first- and second-floor rooms was provided by School of American Research staff (Creamer, personal communication, 1989). However, neither the 1971–72 (Bonney 1971, 1972) nor the 1973–74 (Linford 1974, n.d.b) analyses consistently grouped the data into such categories, and it was necessary to examine the analysis records themselves to make these context assignments. As a result, far more 1971–72 materials could be included than 1973–74 materials, particularly for individual first-floor and second-floor rooms, which consist entirely of 1971–72 materials. Mixed room, plaza, and midden contexts contain both 1971–72 and 1973–74 materials.

Habicht-Mauche and Creamer, in their detailed study of Arroyo Hondo roomblock 16, have indicated that "in two story units the upper story was favored for habitation while the lower story was used primarily for storage" (Habicht-Mauche and Creamer 1989:5). The distribution of ground-stone artifacts in these major site contexts (table 28), however, demonstrates very little proportional difference in the ground-stone tool assemblages of first-floor and second-floor rooms. With reference to ground-stone tool–related behavior, this suggests that there is little difference between the two, except for a noticeably greater proportion of ground-stone fragments in first-floor rooms. Although there appears to be little difference in the *kinds* of ground-stone tool–related behavior in first-floor and second-floor contexts, there is strong and consistent evidence for differing *amounts* of such behavior. All four per-room ratios indicate considerably

TABLE 26
Ground-stone artifacts from Arroyo Hondo roomblocks
with fewer than 40 ground-stone tools.

	Roomblock Number								
	3^b (N^c = 1) No.	4^a (N = 1) No.	12^a (N = 1) No.	13^a (N = 1) No.	19^a (N = 1) No.	20^a (N = 2) No.	21^a (N = 1) No.	23^a (N = 1) No.	24^a (N = 1) No.
Ground-stone tools									
One-hand manos	–	–	1	–	1	–	–	2	–
Two-hand manos	2	2	2	5	4	5	8	1	3
Mano fragments	–	4	9	–	1	6	–	2	1
(Subtotal: manos)	(2)	(6)	(12)	(5)	(6)	(11)	(8)	(5)	(4)
Metates	1	1	1	3	–	1	1	–	–
Grinding stones	–	2	4	–	2	1	3	–	–
Grinding slabs	–	–	3	–	1	7	2	–	1
(Subtotal: grinding tools)	(3)	(9)	(20)	(8)	(9)	(20)	(14)	(5)	(5)
Polishing stones	–	–	2	2	–	–	–	–	1
Hafted items	–	–	1	2	–	–	1	–	1
Hammerstones	1	–	4	1	–	1	1	1	–
Ornaments	–	–	–	–	4	–	1	–	–
Mineral, turquoise	–	–	–	–	–	–	–	1	–
Mineral, mica	–	–	1	–	–	–	–	3	–
Mineral, pigment	–	–	–	–	–	1	–	–	–
Shaped slabs	2	–	–	–	–	–	–	–	–
Miscellaneous	2	1	5	1	10	16	1	–	2
Ground-stone tools	8	10	33	14	23	38	18	10	9
Ground-stone fragments	–	39	37	5	4	19	39	6	2
Total ground stone	8	49	70	19	27	57	57	16	11
Ratios									
Ground-stone tools/room	8	10	33	14	23	19	18	10	9
Grinding tools/room	3	9	20	8	9	10	14	5	5
Ground-stone fragments/room	–	39	37	5	4	10	39	6	2
Total ground stone/room	8	49	70	19	27	29	57	16	11
Manos/metate	2.0	6.0	12.0	1.7	–	11.0	8.0	–	–
Two-hand/one-hand mano	–	–	2.0	–	4.0	–	–	2.0	–
Ground-stone fragments/ ground-stone tool	–	3.9	1.1	0.4	0.2	0.5	2.2	0.6	0.2

[a] 1971–72 data only.   [b] 1971–72 plus 1973–74 data.   [c] N = number of rooms.

more tools, fragments, and total ground stone in second-floor than in first-floor contexts. Such an increased level of (presumedly) plant-processing behavior in second-floor rooms seems consistent with Habicht-Mauche and Creamer's conclusion that these were more frequently used as living rooms than as storage rooms.

Ground-stone artifacts from plaza contexts provide a rather mixed picture of associated behavior. With reference to generalized grinding or plant processing, there are increased proportions of both one-hand manos and

grinding stones but relatively fewer of the grinding slabs with which they presumedly would have been used. In addition, while there are far fewer specialized two-hand manos, there are also slightly more associated metates. These metates, plus the very low ratios of both manos per metate and two-hand manos per one-hand mano, suggest a more generalized set of ground-stone tool–related behavior in plazas than in other major contexts. Consistently fewer fragments and broken items, as well as fewer fragments per tool, imply a behavior pattern in plazas

TABLE 27

Flaked-stone artifacts from Arroyo Hondo roomblocks with fewer than 40 flaked-stone tools.

	Roomblock Number														
	3[b] (N[c]=1) No.	4[a] (N=1) No.	6[b] (N=2) No.	7[b] (N=3) No.	8[b] (N=3) No.	12[a] (N=1) No.	13[a] (N=1) No.	14[b] (N=2) No.	15[a] (N=2) No.	15A[a] (N=2) No.	19[a] (N=1) No.	20[a] (N=2) No.	21[a] (N=1) No.	23[a] (N=1) No.	24[a] (N=1) No.
Flaked-stone tools															
Notched projectile points	–	1	2	2	4	–	–	–	3	1	5	–	–	1	–
Unnotched projectile points	–	–	2	5	2	–	–	–	2	4	–	1	2	2	–
Projectile point fragments	–	–	2	–	1	1	–	–	1	2	–	–	–	–	–
(Subtotal: projectile points and knives)	(–)	(1)	(6)	(7)	(7)	(1)	(–)	(6)	(7)	(5)	(1)	(3)	(2)	(3)	(–)
Drills, gravers	–	–	2	–	1	–	–	–	–	–	–	1	1	–	–
Scrapers	–	1	6	4	2	3	3	8	3	3	2	1	–	3	–
Flaked-stone tools	0	2	14	11	10	4	3	8	9	10	7	3	3	3	0
Used flakes	8	16	59	37	39	2	–	54	–	2	1	–	2	–	3
Flakes	–	–	143	114	102	77	17	94	88	190	24	46	98	29	22
Cores	–	8	6	11	7	4	2	23	13	6	2	3	6	–	1
Total flaked stone	8	26	222	173	158	87	22	179	110	208	34	52	109	32	26
Ratios															
Flaked-stone tools/room	–	2	7	4	3	4	3	4	5	5	7	2	3	3	–
All flakes/room	8	16	101	50	47	79	17	74	44	96	25	23	100	29	25
Total flaked stone/room	8	26	111	58	53	87	22	90	55	104	34	26	109	32	26
All flakes/core	–	2	34	14	20	20	9	6	7	32	13	15	17	–	25
All flakes/flaked-stone tool	–	8	14	14	14	20	6	19	10	19	4	15	33	10	25
Ground-stone tools/flaked-stone tools[d]	–	5.0	8.9	6.5	5.5	8.3	4.7	13.9	7.9	5.4	3.3	12.7	6.0	3.3	–
All ground stone/all flaked stone[d]	1.0	1.9	1.2	1.2	0.7	0.8	0.9	0.9	0.9	0.8	0.8	1.1	0.5	0.5	0.4

[a] 1971–72 data only.
[b] 1971–72 plus 1973–74 data.
[c] N = number of rooms.
[d] Ground stone data from tables 24 and 26, this volume.

227

TABLE 28

Ground-stone artifacts from major Arroyo Hondo site contexts.

	First-Floor Rooms[a] (N[c] = 31)		Second-Floor Rooms[a] (N = 21)		Mixed Rooms[b] (N = 19)		Plaza[b]		Midden[b]	
	No.	%	No.	%	No.	%	No.	%	No.	%
Ground-stone tools										
One-hand manos		2		2		3		6		3
Two-hand manos		26		27		23		6		6
Mano fragments		14		11		7		2		33
(Subtotal: manos)		(43)		(40)		(33)		(14)		(42)
Metates		11		11		5		13		–
Grinding stones		5		6		6		20		5
Grinding slabs		14		14		11		6		–
(Subtotal: grinding tools)		(73)		(71)		(55)		(53)		(47)
Polishing stones		5		4		4		2		2
Hafted items		2		2		2		8		–
Hammerstones		3		6		9		8		16
Ornaments		1		1		4		1		–
Mineral, turquoise		2		<1		1		8		–
Mineral, mica		3		4		7		5		11
Mineral, pigment		5		2		2		2		16
Shaped slabs		–		1		1		2		–
Miscellaneous		7		10		13		10		8
Ground-stone tools	447	100/36	784	100/48	430	100/46	536	100/79	63	100/18
Ground-stone fragments	788	64	833	52	508	54	144	21	295	82
Total ground stone	1,235	100	1,617	100	938	100	680	100	358	100
Ratios										
Ground-stone tools/room		14		37		23		N/A		N/A
Grinding tools/room		10		26		13		N/A		N/A
Ground-stone fragments/room		25		40		20		N/A		N/A
Total ground stone/room		40		77		34		N/A		N/A
Manos/metate		4.0		3.7		6.5		1.1		N/A
Two-hand/one-hand mano		10.5		13.2		7.5		1.0		2.0
Ground-stone fragments/ ground-stone tool		1.8		1.1		0.9		0.3		4.7

[a] 1971–72 data only.
[b] 1971–72 plus 1973–74 data.
[c] N = number of rooms.

focused on generalized tool use (rather than production?), perhaps with regular clean-up of broken items and of production and maintenance debris.

The sample of confirmable ground-stone artifacts from Arroyo Hondo midden contexts is considerably smaller than that from other major contexts, but a very different assemblage pattern is nevertheless quite clear. High proportions of small and fragmentary items, an absence of larger metates and grinding slabs, and a greatly increased number of fragments per tool are consistent with the accumulation of midden deposits.

Flaked-stone artifact assemblages from the same major site contexts are presented in table 29. There are approximately two-thirds as many flaked-stone items per room, both tools and flakes, for first-floor rooms as for second-floor rooms. This finding lends support to Habicht-Mauche and Creamer's (1989:5) contention that first-floor rooms were favored for storage and second-floor rooms for habitation. Not all first-floor rooms had second-floor rooms above them, however, and though most second-floor rooms may have been living rooms, certainly many first-floor rooms served the same func-

TABLE 29
Flaked-stone artifacts from major Arroyo Hondo site contexts.

	First-Floor Rooms[a] (N^c = 31)		Second-Floor Rooms[a] (N = 21)		Mixed Rooms[b] (N = 19)		Plaza[b]		Midden[b]	
	No.	%	No.	%	No.	%	No.	%	No.	%
Flaked-stone tools										
Notched projectile points		30		17		17		13	7	
Unnotched projectile points, knives		23		22		15		5	2	
Projectile point fragments		11		9		4		6	1	
(Subtotal: projectile points and knives)		(64)		(48)		(36)		(24)	(10)	
Drills, gravers		7		5		7		5	–	
Scrapers		29		47		57		71	1	
Flaked-stone tools	107	100/5	95	100/5	210	100/5	163	100/6	11	2
Used flakes	7	<1	3	<1	1,487	38	1,036	39	6	1
Flakes	1,817	89	1,878	91	2,203	56	1,372	52	691	95
Cores	103	5	97	5	61	2	75	3	18	2
Total flaked stone	2,034	100	2,073	100	3,961	100	2,646	100	726	100
Ratios										
Flaked-stone tools/room	3		5		11		N/A		N/A	
All flakes/room	59		90		194		N/A		N/A	
All flaked stone/room	66		99		208		N/A		N/A	
All flakes/core	18		19		60		32		39	
All flakes/flaked-stone tool	17		20		18		15		63	
Ground-stone tools/flaked-stone tool[d]	4.2		8.3		2.0		3.3		5.7	
All ground stone/all flaked stone[d]	0.6		0.8		0.2		0.3		0.5	

[a] 1971–72 data only.
[b] 1971–72 plus 1973–74 data.
[c] N = number of rooms.
[d] Ground stone data from table 28, this volume.

tion, particularly during the Component II occupation (Creamer, personal communication, 1989). The table 29 data, then, tend to support a functional distinction between first- and second-floor rooms.

The differential distribution of two flaked-stone tool types—notched projectile points and scrapers—in first- and second-floor rooms suggests some sort of patterned behavioral difference, but the nature of that difference is not at all clear from such coarsely structured data groupings. If the living-versus-storage functional dichotomy of second- and first-floor rooms is expected to dominate the flaked-tool variability in these contexts, we should expect to see evidence for differing amounts of behavior, as well as for appropriately differing kinds. It is difficult to envision storage rooms regularly being the scene of flaked-stone tool production, maintenance, or use, and it is also difficult to envision stone tools requiring much in the way of storage. Assuming a general similarity in site formation and of data recovery processes, the greater number of notched projectile points in first-floor Arroyo

Hondo rooms would seem to indicate a relatively greater amount of production or use of these items for light-duty cutting of softer materials in storage contexts. This interpretation seems enigmatic, at least. The increased number of ground-stone tools per flaked tool in second-floor contexts may suggest a relatively greater focus on plant- than on animal-processing behavior in living rooms.

The data for mixed rooms and plaza contexts in table 28 contain both 1971–72 and 1973–74 materials; this is especially evident in the strongly differing proportions of used flakes and flakes compared with the first- and second-floor rooms. The indication of relatively fewer projectile points and knives in these contexts, along with correspondingly more scrapers, may be due in part to the 1973–74 analytic tendency to classify more items as scrapers, as previously discussed. The suggestion remains, however, that more scraper-associated behavior was occurring, especially in plazas. The ratio of flakes per core provides a rough measure of lithic reduction intensity, with more flakes per core indicating increased reduction. While there is some reason to agree with the increased reduction behavior in Arroyo Hondo plazas suggested by table 29, the extremely high values of this ratio in mixed rooms is problematic, particularly when compared with first- and second-floor rooms.

The very small numbers of flaked tools identifiable from Arroyo Hondo midden contexts in table 29 precludes detailed interpretation, but the implication is that relatively few tools and many flakes occur in middens. Such a pattern would be quite consistent with anticipated behavioral variability in site formation.

The general picture provided by this rather coarse-grained data summary and interpretation of major Arroyo Hondo site contexts (tables 28 and 29) is, despite some uncertainty in data comparability, one of distinct behavioral variation among the contexts. Furthermore, this behavioral variation seems to be in general agreement with inductive behavioral expectations for contexts such as plazas and middens, with proposed functional hypotheses of room use (Habicht-Mauche and Creamer 1989:5), or both. Several obvious deviations from these expected data distributions may be due to analytic variability, to sample size problems, or to a limited set of inductive behavioral hypotheses.

ROOMBLOCK 16. The recent work of Judith Habicht-Mauche and Winifred Creamer (1989; personal communication, 1989; this volume) has been of considerable importance in shaping this summary reconstruction of Arroyo Hondo lithic data and in using those data to examine hypotheses with clearly stated social and behavioral implications. Only very preliminary results of their analyses have been available, but these have been incorporated to the extent possible in tables 30, 31, 32, and 33. Habicht-Mauche and Creamer's approach has been to focus analytic attention on a single Arroyo Hondo roomblock, roomblock 16, because

> it was at the core of the earliest occupation during Component I and was rebuilt and reoccupied during Component II times. It, therefore, provided an excellent opportunity to study changes in roomblock and residence unit structure throughout the history of the site. Another important factor in this choice was that Roomblock 16 was the focus of extensive excavations by the School of American Research during the early 1970's. It thus provided the most complete set of data regarding horizontal room relationships at the site. (Habicht-Mauche and Creamer 1989:3)

Because all roomblock 16 lithic materials were analyzed in 1971–72 (Bonney 1971, 1972), selecting this roomblock for detailed analytic attention (a) avoids any major analytic inconsistency, and (b) permits most materials to be traced through the analysis records to their FS-designated contexts.

Habicht-Mauche and Creamer have independently provided three kinds of contextual arrangements for roomblock 16 rooms: first-floor versus second-floor location, "residence unit" type (see below), and component (Creamer, personal communication, 1989). Arrangement of the roomblock 16 lithic data into these contexts permits comparison with similar contexts (floors and components) for the entire site data, as well as an internal comparison and interpretation of the new context, the residence unit.

Table 30 presents roomblock 16 ground-stone artifacts, arranged by floor context. It is clear that the ground-stone assemblages from the two contexts are virtually identical, with no major differences in either the kinds of associated behavior or the relative proportions of such behavior. It is equally clear, however, that there are differing amounts of that behavior, with considerably more activity occurring in second-floor rooms, as evidenced by all four of the per-room artifact ratios. This result agrees well with the entire site profile presented in table 28, but the agreement occurs in large part because a major portion of the floor-identifiable rooms from the site are from roomblock 16 (29 out of 31 first-floor rooms, and 5 out of 21 second-floor rooms). The ground-stone tool profile of both first- and second-floor rooms suggests behavior heavily focused on grinding activity and/or the storage of associated tools, particularly the specialized corn processing presumably associated with two-hand manos.

The flaked-stone artifact data from roomblock 16 first- and second-floor rooms are presented in table 31. These flaked-stone profiles demonstrate considerably more tool type variability between first- and second-floor rooms than did the ground-stone assemblages in table 30, but the magnitude of the differences is not great. Although the number of flaked-stone tools per room is only very slightly greater in second-floor than in first-floor rooms (and the sample is quite small in absolute numbers), the numbers of both flakes per room and flakes per tool are much greater in second-floor rooms. A considerably greater intensity of flake-producing and/or discard behavior (production? maintenance?) in these second-floor rooms is thus suggested, but not a particularly greater amount of tool-using behavior. Second-floor rooms have nearly four times as many ground-stone tools per

TABLE 30

Ground-stone artifacts from Arroyo Hondo roomblock 16, by floor context.

	First-Floor Rooms (N^a = 29)		Second-Floor Rooms (N = 5)	
	No.	%	No.	%
Ground-stone tools				
One-hand manos		2		1
Two-hand manos		28		30
Mano fragments		12		7
(Subtotal: manos)		(42)		(38)
Metates		13		11
Grinding stones		5		7
Grinding slabs		14		17
(Subtotal: grinding tools)		(74)		(73)
Polishing stones		3		5
Hafted items		1		2
Hammerstones		3		4
Ornaments		<1		1
Mineral, turquoise		2		<1
Mineral, mica		3		4
Mineral, pigment		8		2
Shaped slabs		–		1
Miscellaneous		7		7
Ground-stone tools	287	100/48	380	100/48
Ground-stone fragments	315	52	405	52
Total ground stone	602	100	785	100
Ratios				
Ground-stone tools/room		13		35
Grinding tools/room		10		25
Ground-stone fragments/room		14		37
Total ground stone/room		27		71
Manos/metate		3.2		3.5
Two-hand/one-hand mano		14.0		30.0
Ground-stone fragments/ground-stone tool		1.1		1.1

$^a N$ = number of rooms.

flaked-stone tool as do first-floor rooms, suggesting a much greater level of associated plant-processing than of animal-processing behavior in these second-floor, predominantly habitation-room contexts. These interpretations of roomblock 16 data also tend to confirm those suggested for the entire site in the table 29 data, again in large part because a major proportion of the floor-identifiable Arroyo Hondo rooms are from roomblock 16. Division of these roomblock 16 data into first-floor living rooms, first-floor storage rooms, second-floor living rooms, and second-floor storage rooms results in content assemblages too small for confident interpretation.

Much of the interpretive uncertainty in all these data groupings results from the rather coarse level of analysis in both context and content units. Data categories as inclusive as component, roomblock, or even first-floor rooms clearly involve much site formation variability, which tends to obscure any associations between specific contexts and their interpretable content. Habicht-Mauche and Creamer have produced a more finely textured analytic approach for roomblock 16 at Arroyo Hondo by assigning each room a functional type on the basis of "size and location, presence and location of entryways, internal room features, and the distribution of floor contact artifacts" (Habicht-Mauche and Creamer

231

TABLE 31

Flaked-stone artifacts from Arroyo Hondo roomblock 16, by floor context.

	First-Floor Rooms (N^a = 29)		Second-Floor Rooms (N = 5)	
	No.	%	No.	%
Flaked-stone tools				
Notched projectile points		25		16
Unnotched projectile points, knives		20		24
Projectile point fragments		11		8
(Subtotal: projectile points and knives)		(56)		(48)
Drills, gravers		8		8
Scrapers, used flakes		36		44
Flaked-stone tools	114	100/6	25	100/4
Flakes	1,646	90	610	93
Cores	66	4	22	3
Total flaked stone	1,826	100	657	100
Ratios				
Flaked-stone tools/room		4		5
Flakes/room		57		122
Total flaked stone/room		63		131
Flakes/core		24.9		27.7
Flakes/flaked-stone tool		14.4		24.4
Ground-stone tools/flaked-stone tool[b]		2.5		15.2
All ground stone/all flaked stone[b]		0.3		1.2

[a] N = number of rooms.
[b] Ground stone data from table 30, this volume.

1989:4). Hearths were especially important in distinguishing living from storage rooms. "Residence units" were then identified for each component as "at least one habitation room . . . and any connecting rooms. Residence units ranged in size from a single habitation room to a unit containing 6 first floor storage rooms and 3 second floor living rooms" (Habicht-Mauche and Creamer 1989:10).

Data from these residence units are interpreted by Habicht-Mauche and Creamer as representing the behavior of Arroyo Hondo social-economic groups. This analytic framework indicates that such residence units were often physically rearranged and that they tended to become smaller through time, a tendency that is interpreted as a "trend toward social and economic units that may indicate a shift from extended to nuclear family residence units" (Habicht-Mauche and Creamer 1989:11).

Tables 32 and 33 arrange the ground-stone and flaked-stone artifacts from roomblock 16 into the residence unit groupings of Habicht-Mauche and Creamer (1989:

figs. 1 and 3; personal communication, 1989). The data are grouped within each component as individual storage rooms, single living rooms, smaller residence units, and larger residence units. Because of the restricted nature of the Component II data contexts in roomblock 16, only the single living room and the larger residence unit categories have sufficient artifact numbers to be interpreted proportionally. The most direct functional comparison of rooms per se is that between the single storage room and the single living room categories. Here too, however, samples are quite small, especially for Component II, and interpretations are very tentative.

Ground-stone artifacts from roomblock 16, presented in table 32, suggest that single storage rooms consistently have fewer tools than do living rooms or residence units containing living rooms, certainly an expected and confirming characteristic of such storage contexts. Artifact types occurring in these storage contexts include relatively fewer fragments of any kind, fewer metates (though nearly average proportions of two-hand manos) with cor-

TABLE 32
Ground-stone artifacts from Arroyo Hondo roomblock 16,
by residence unit type and component.

	Component I								
	Single Storage Rooms (N^a = 2)		Single Living Rooms (N = 2)		Two–Three Room Units (N = 4)		Four or More Room Units (N = 5)		Total (N = 13)	
	No.	%	No.	%	No.	%	No.	%	No.	%
Ground-stone tools										
One-hand manos		2		–		2		2		2
Two-hand manos		22		22		30		31		28
Mano fragments		2		9		9		6		7
(Subtotal: manos)		(26)		(31)		(41)		(39)		(37)
Metates		5		12		10		16		12
Grinding stones		10		14		10		3		8
Grinding slabs		19		27		18		10		17
(Subtotal: grinding tools)		(60)		(84)		(79)		(68)		(74)
Polishing stones		14		–		2		7		5
Hafted items		–		1		1		3		2
Hammerstones		5		3		4		5		4
Ornaments		2		–		–		2		1
Mineral, turquoise		–		–		1		1		1
Mineral, mica		5		4		3		1		3
Mineral, pigment		14		4		5		2		5
Shaped slabs		–		1		–		–		<1
Miscellaneous		–		3		5		10		6
Ground-stone tools	42	100/68	74	100/63	220	100/62	161	100/46	497	100/56
Ground-stone fragments	20	32	43	37	134	38	189	54	386	44
Total ground stone	62	100	117	100	354	100	350	100	883	100
Ratios										
Ground-stone tools/room	21		37		55		32		38	
Grinding tools/room	13		31		43		22		28	
Ground-stone fragments/ room	10		22		34		38		30	
Total ground stone/room	31		59		89		70		68	
Manos/metate	5.5		2.6		4.1		2.4		3.1	
Two-hand/one-hand mano	9.0		–		15.0		15.5		14.0	
Ground-stone fragments/ ground-stone tool	0.5		0.6		0.6		1.2		0.8	

^{a}N = number of rooms.

(Continued on next page)

respondingly fewer total grinding tools, and increased proportions of polishing stones and mineral pigment items. It seems reasonable that fragments would rarely find their way into storage contexts and that relatively few metates would be effectively removed from the functioning systemic context into storage contexts. Two-hand manos, on the other hand, might well be stored in anticipation of future use with the same metates. The high proportions of polishing stones, which in this case are primarily ceramic polishers (table 32), and mineral pigments may represent the short-term storage of ceramic-manufacturing equipment, as well as seldom-used items.

TABLE 32   (continued)

	Single Storage Rooms (N[a] = 3) No.	%	Single Living Rooms (N = 3) No.	%	Two-Room Units (N = 4) No.	%	Three-Room Units (N = 6) No.	%	Total (N = 16) No.	%
Ground-stone tools										
One-hand manos	—			—	1			1		1
Two-hand manos	—			34	2			27		25
Mano fragments	1			3	2			18		14
(Subtotal: manos)	(1)			(37)	(5)			(46)		(40)
Metates	—			13	5			12		14
Grinding stones	—			—	—			—		—
Grinding slabs	—			28	1			8		12
(Subtotal: grinding tools)	—			(78)	(11)			(66)		(66)
Polishing stones	—			6	—			2		3
Hafted items	—			—	—			1		1
Hammerstones	—			—	2			2		3
Ornaments	—			—	—			—		—
Mineral, turquoise	—			—	3			—		2
Mineral, mica	—			3	—			12		8
Mineral, pigment	1			3	1			2		4
Shaped slabs	—			9	—			—		2
Miscellaneous	2			—	3			13		12
Ground-stone tools	4	100/17	32	100/32	20	100/45	83	100/36	139	100/35
Ground-stone fragments	19	83	69	68	24	55	148	64	260	65
Total ground stone	23	100	101	100	44	100	231	100	399	100
Ratios										
Ground-stone tools/room	1		11		5		14		9	
Grinding tools/room	<1		8		3		9		6	
Ground-stone fragments/room	6		23		6		25		16	
Total ground stone/room	7		34		11		39		25	
Manos/metate	—		3.0		1.0		3.8		2.9	
Two-hand/one-hand mano	—		—		2.0		27.0		25.0	
Ground-stone fragments/ground-stone tool	4.8		2.2		1.2		1.8		1.9	

Other ground-stone types occur in roughly the same proportions as in the residence unit contexts.

Among the three residence unit categories, which increase in size and complexity, are several notable differences in the occurrence of ground-stone artifacts. Single living room residence units, with less storage area than other units, contain slightly fewer two-hand manos, correspondingly fewer total manos, and more generalized grinding slabs. In addition, all categories of grinding tools are sufficiently high (or other categories sufficiently low) in these rooms to produce the highest proportion of grinding tools among the residence unit types. This may be because all grinding equipment for that residence unit was kept and used in a single room, though the relatively low numbers of items per room would seem to contradict this interpretation.

Two- and three-room residence units, having at least one living and one storage room, demonstrate the greatest numbers of ground-stone artifacts per room, perhaps indicating that the greatest intensity of associated behavior occurred in these "average-sized" residence units. If there is a typical residence unit at Arroyo Hondo, it is probably these two- and three-room units. The larger four-plus-room residence unit type has generally higher proportions of specialized two-hand manos and their metates, with lower proportions of the more generalized grinding stones and slabs. In addition, there are considerably more ground-stone fragments in two- and three-room units. These data proportions suggest that such large residence units could represent communal suites of rooms for specialized grinding and other tasks, a possibility explored below.

Among the Component II residence units, the virtual absence of one-hand manos and grinding stones and the relatively high proportions of two-hand manos and their metates suggest that plant processing in this later Arroyo Hondo occupation may have focused on corn rather than on more generalized processing. But this sample from one roomblock is too small to be extended to the entire Arroyo Hondo site, and contradictory evidence is present in the noticeably high proportion of generalized grinding slabs in Component II single living room residence units.

In general, Component I demonstrates relatively more grinding tools, many of which are the less specialized forms, than does Component II, along with significantly more items per room and far fewer fragmentary items. Even though this sample of ground-stone artifacts from roomblock 16 components is not large, particularly in the numbers of rooms and items in Component II contexts, the results are very similar to those reported in table 22 for all Arroyo Hondo ground-stone data assignable to components. Only the proportions of fragments and tools are noticeably different, which may be due in part to the small roomblock 16 sample.

Table 33 presents flaked-stone artifact data from roomblock 16 at Arroyo Hondo, arranged by component into the same residence unit types as table 32. Because of the small numbers of tools in the residence unit type groupings, raw data are presented rather than percentages, and proportional interpretations of tool assemblages are generally avoided except for component totals. The very small numbers of flaked-stone items in Component I single storage rooms precludes confident interpretation, but the high proportion of cores, the low number of flakes per room, and the large number of ground-stone tools per flaked-stone tool should perhaps be noted as appropriate characteristics of storage contexts.

Among the three residence unit types, the flaked-stone assemblages are dominated by flakes, with relatively few tools and cores. The number of flakes per room generally increases with residence unit size, suggesting more flake-related behavior (production, use, maintenance, or discard) in the larger units. The largest four-plus-room residence unit type in Component I has especially large numbers of flakes, along with correspondingly lower proportions of both tools and cores, suggesting some distinctive behavior in such units. Habicht-Mauche and Creamer (1989:8–9) have also noted this unusually high proportion of flakes, and they suggest that it may represent the manufacture of hunting equipment in specialized contexts, as noted in other Southwestern pueblos (Hill 1970:53). The technological characteristics that could confirm whether or not these flakes in fact represent such manufacturing activity have not been recorded. They could be large flakes suitable for generalized scraping and cutting, small biface reduction flakes, or some combination of these and other characteristics. The flake data, coupled with the high proportions of specialized grinding tools in these residence units, do appear to indicate some distinctive behavior pattern. Whether this is ritual-ceremonial, as suggested by Habicht-Mauche and Creamer (1989:8–9), or shared and perhaps specialized domestic-economic activity in a suite of communally used rooms, seems open to further analysis and the application of additional data.

Roomblock 16 residence unit contexts from Component II have even smaller samples of flaked-stone artifacts than do those from Component I, but they seem generally similar in character—with the exception of very low numbers (and proportions) of cores and correspondingly high numbers of flakes per core. There is also little interpretable flaked-stone variability among the Component II residence unit types, except for the same kind (and degree) of assemblage domination by flakes in the larger residence unit type.

A comparison of the flaked-stone assemblages from each component in roomblock 16 residence units demonstrates more projectile points and knives, more drills and gravers, and correspondingly fewer scrapers in Component II than in Component I. This suggests the possibility that Component II subsistence may have been somewhat more focused on hunting than was that of Component I, a perspective generally supported by a per-capita conversion of Lang and Harris's (1984:47–51) faunal data, though the very small sample size could be partly responsible, as well. Component II also demonstrates considerably fewer flakes per room than Component I, with far fewer cores—data that indicate less intense flake production activity in Component II residence units. The much lower number of ground-stone tools per flaked-stone tool in Component II—that is, a

TABLE 33
Flaked-stone artifacts from Arroyo Hondo roomblock 16,
by residence unit type and component.

	Component I									
	Single Storage Rooms (N[a] = 2)		Single Living Rooms (N = 2)		Two–Three Room Units (N = 4)		Four or More Room Units (N = 5)		Total (N = 13)	
	No.	%	No.	%	No.	%	No.	%	No.	%
Flaked-stone tools										
Notched projectile points	1		1		7		4		19	
Unnotched projectile points, knives	1		1		3		6		16	
Projectile point fragments	1		1		4		2		12	
(Subtotal: projectile points and knives)	(3)		(3)		(14)		(12)		(47)	
Drills, gravers	–		1		1		2		6	
Scrapers, used flakes	–		1		19		11		46	
Flaked-stone tools	3	100/10	5	100/5	34	100/8	25	100/4	67	100/6
Flakes	22	71	89	95	370	86	610	93	1,091	90
Cores	6	19	–	–	27	6	22	3	55	4
Total flaked stone	31	100	94	100	431	100	657	100	1,213	100
Ratios										
Flaked-stone tools/room	2		3		9		5		5	
Flakes/room	11		45		93		122		84	
Total flaked stone/room	16		47		108		131		93	
Flakes/core	3.7		–		13.7		27.7		19.8	
Flakes/flaked-stone tool	7.3		17.8		10.9		24.4		16.3	
Ground-stone tools/ flaked-stone tool[b]	14.0		14.8		6.5		6.4		7.4	
All ground stone/all flaked stone[b]	2.0		1.2		0.8		0.5		0.7	

[a] N = number of rooms.
[b] Ground stone data from table 32, this volume.

(Continued on next page)

much-diminished emphasis on ground-stone tools—is the result of the presence of unusually few ground-stone tools (see table 31) rather than of many flaked-stone tools.

These profiles of components I and II flaked-stone assemblages from roomblock 16 residence units, despite their small sample size, are very similar to those given in table 23, which are based on much larger samples from all assignable Arroyo Hondo flaked-stone materials. This similarity is particularly strong for Component I. It differs for Component II only in that the roomblock 16 profile (table 33) has fewer flakes (and, correspondingly, total flaked stone) per room, and fewer cores (and, corre-

spondingly, more flakes per core). These well-controlled roomblock 16 data therefore tend to confirm the reconstruction procedures used for the larger Arroyo Hondo data sets and, as a result, the reliability of the interpretations based on them.

Intersite Comparisons

The archaeological literature reporting lithic assemblages from relatively large, late sites in the northern Rio Grande region has been heavily influenced by A. V. Kidder. His seminal work at Pecos Pueblo (Kidder 1932; Kidder and Shepard 1936) set the basic descriptive tone,

TABLE 33 (continued)

	Single Storage Rooms (N^a = 3)		Single Living Rooms (N = 3)		Two-Room Units (N = 4)		Three-Room Units (N = 6)		Total (N = 16)	
	No.	%	No.	%	No.	%	No.	%	No.	%
Flaked-stone tools										
Notched projectile points	3		4		6		4			32
Unnotched projectile points, knives	2		3		1		6			23
Projectile point fragments	–		–		1		2			6
(Subtotal: projectile points and knives)	(5)		(7)		(8)		(12)			(61)
Drills, gravers	1		3		1		1			11
Scrapers, used flakes	1		6		2		6			28
Flaked-stone tools	7	100/8	16	100/8	11	100/8	19	100/4	53	100/6
Flakes	71	88	188	90	124	91	468	94	851	92
Cores	3	4	4	2	1	1	13	2	21	2
Total flaked stone	81	100	208	100	136	100	500	100	925	100
Ratios										
Flaked-stone tools/room	2		5		3		3		3	
Flakes/room	24		63		31		78		53	
Total flaked stone/room	27		69		34		83		58	
Flakes/core	23.7		47.0		124.0		36.0		40.5	
Flakes/flaked-stone tool	10.1		11.8		11.3		24.6		16.1	
Ground-stone tools/flaked-stone tool[b]	0.6		2.0		1.8		4.4		2.6	
All ground stone/all flaked stone[b]	0.3		0.5		0.3		0.5		0.4	

[a] N = number of rooms.
[b] Ground stone data from table 32, this volume.

typological approach, and reporting structure for at least the next four decades in dealing with such sites throughout much of the Southwest (Brew 1946; Judge 1974; Lambert 1954; Stubbs and Stallings 1953; Wendorf 1953; Woodbury 1954).

Kidder's basic approach to lithic analysis and reporting, employed even earlier in the region by such researchers as Jeançon (1923), is characterized by (1) considerably more attention being paid to ground-stone than to flaked-stone assemblages; (2) generally implicit typological structures with broadly described, rather than defined, categories or types; (3) types that are used primarily for assemblage description (i.e., "convenient" or "descriptive" types) rather than for behavioral comparison and interpretation; (4) detailed description of many individual items considered important or unusual; (5) very little actual measurement; (6) description of entire site assemblages with little intrasite contextual or temporal differentiation; (7) qualitative intersite comparison and interpretation focused on the descriptive similarity of individual items or types and on the presence or absence of descriptive types or items (i.e., trait-list comparisons); and (8) interpretation that is normally focused on artifact types rather than site contexts. Such an approach was, of course, simply the way archaeology was done. Besides description, major attention was given to ceramic chronology, tree-ring dating, population growth, architectural variability, and site and regional occupation sequences. All these concerns were critical for building culture history, and all could be addressed

TABLE 34
Comparison of lithic data from Arroyo Hondo and Tijeras pueblos.

	Arroyo Hondo Pueblo[a]		Tijeras Pueblo[b]	
	No.	%	No.	%
Flaked stone				
Projectile points and knives		56		76
Scrapers		36		24
Other		8		–
Flaked-stone tools	872	100/6	794	100/4
Used flakes		34		16
Flakes		57		79
Cores		3		1
Total flaked stone	14,928	100	20,693	100
Ground stone				
Manos		26		68
Metates		4		20
Other		70		12
Ground-stone tools	3,771	100	512	100
Ratios				
All flakes/flaked tool		16		25
All flakes/core		30		101
Manos/metate		7.1		3.5
Ground-stone tools/flaked-stone tool		4.3		0.6

[a] From tables 20 and 21, this volume.
[b] From Judge 1974:47.

very adequately with only incidental reference to lithic variability. The recent development of more processual concerns with subsistence-related behavior and organizational variability have brought about very different analytical and reporting procedures, in which lithic data have become much more central.

The Arroyo Hondo lithic analysis structure was explicitly patterned after Kidder's Pecos model (Bonney 1971, 1972; Linford 1974, n.d.b), at least partly to promote comparison with other large late sites in the northern Rio Grande region. Linford was instructed by the project director to compare

> the excavated pueblos of Pecos, Paa-ko, and Pindi, chosen because of their proximity to Arroyo Hondo, their similarity in time (all have at least one component of comparable time-frame), and the fact that they each have the data collected from them widely disseminated and easily accessible. (Linford n.d.b:1.1)

The lithic data presented in these reports (Kidder 1932;

Lambert 1954; Stubbs and Stallings 1953), while generally similar typologically and structurally, are nevertheless quite different descriptively and proportionally. Quantitative comparisons among them are not possible without major, and probably unjustified, assumptions of typological correspondence.

Linford nevertheless indicates that "for the most part, the lithic assemblages from the four sites strongly resemble one another" (Linford n.d.b:1.1). His assessment is necessarily qualitative and descriptive in character, and it cannot be quantitatively confirmed. A subjective examination of published artifact illustrations does, in fact, suggest a general morphological similarity in gross artifact form, at least among those items selected for illustration. However, the difficulty of extending this apparent morphological artifact similarity to broader assemblage similarity may be illustrated by even a superficial comparison of the lithic assemblage reported from Pindi Pueblo (Stubbs and Stallings 1953) with that from Arroyo Hondo.

Pindi Pueblo is a large Coalition–early Classic period

site on the Santa Fe River about seven miles southwest of Santa Fe (Ahlstrom 1989; Stubbs and Stallings 1953). The Pindi site is the type site for the early, or Pindi, phase of the Coalition period (Dickson 1979:10–13; Wendorf and Reed 1955:144–45; Wetherington 1968: 90–91). It was excavated in the early 1930s and reported in 1953 (Stubbs and Stallings 1953), using Kidder's general descriptive typological approach. The flaked-stone assemblage is reported briefly in about two pages of text, with three pages of illustration (Stubbs and Stallings 1953:97–102). Fifteen types are used to describe a total of only 57 flaked-stone items. Arroyo Hondo, on the other hand, contained at least 872 flaked-stone tools, plus over 14,000 flakes and cores, and was described by Bonney (1972:232–35) with 30 types, by Linford (1974: iii–iv) with 38 types, and in this reconstruction with 8 types. Stubbs and Stallings (1953:102–26) also describe, in much more detail, just over 1,000 ground-stone items with 51 types, many of which have a single included item. Arroyo Hondo contained at least 3,771 ground-stone tools, plus over 5,000 fragments, described by Bonney (1972:232–35) with 41 types, by Linford (1974:iii–iv) with 62 types, and in this reconstruction with 16 types.

A solidly quantitative comparison—and a resulting interpretation of close cultural similarity—of these Pindi Pueblo and Arroyo Hondo lithic assemblages is clearly not appropriate. There are, for example, over four times as many flaked-stone tools per ground-stone tool at Pindi. In any case, such whole-site comparisons would not address the kinds of between-components temporal differences and within-site organizational differences that are of major concern to this Arroyo Hondo data reconstruction and summary. They do, perhaps, confirm the general trait-list similarities anticipated among large,

roughly contemporaneous sites in the northern Rio Grande region.

Tijeras Pueblo is another large late Coalition–early Classic period site. Located approximately 20 miles east of Albuquerque, New Mexico, it was excavated during the 1970s by the University of New Mexico archaeological field school. Judge provides some preliminary whole-site lithic data from the 1971–73 field seasons that can be arranged into a form relatively comparable to some of the data used in this Arroyo Hondo presentation, largely because Judge's data, too, are presented in Kidder's basic typological structure (Judge 1974:47). Apparent analytic similarities in recognizing some data classes, such as ground-stone fragments and used flakes, suggest that the most appropriate comparison of the Tijeras Pueblo data is with Linford's rearranged Arroyo Hondo data summary (tables 20 and 21). This data comparison is presented in table 34.

Despite the strong likelihood that there are analytic and data recognition differences between the Arroyo Hondo Pueblo and Tijeras Pueblo lithic artifact profiles, particularly in the ground-stone assemblages, it is abundantly clear from the comparison given in table 34 that all large late Coalition–early Classic sites in the northern Rio Grande area are not alike with reference to their lithic assemblages and the behavior they represent. Some of this lithic variability may, of course, be due to differential subsistence patterns or organizational variability associated with environmental-ecological differences between the two sites, which are about 100 miles apart. Identifying, quantifying, and comparing such lithic variability in the archaeological record is in fact at the center of modern archaeological interpretation, and the evidence presented here both demonstrates that such comparisons are possible and begins that analytic process.

References

Adams, E. Charles
  1990 "Origins of the Pueblo Katsina Cult: Iconographic
        Evidence." Paper presented at the 55th annual meet-
        ing of the Society for American Archaeology, Las
        Vegas.
  1991 *The Origins and Development of the Pueblo Katsina
        Cult.* Tucson: University of Arizona Press.
Ahlstrom, Richard V. N.
  1989 "Tree Ring Dating of Pindi Pueblo, New Mexico.
        The Kiva 54:361–84.
Allen, J. W.
  1971 "The Pueblo Alamo Project: Archaeological Salvage
        at the Junction of U.S. 85 and U.S. 285 South of
        Santa Fe, New Mexico." Museum of New Mexico,
        Laboratory of Anthropology Note no. 86. Ms., Lab-
        oratory of Anthropology, Santa Fe.
Anderson, Dana, and Yvonne Oakes
  1980 "A World View of Agriculture." In *Tijeras Canyon:
        Analysis of the Past,* ed. Linda S. Cordell, pp. 12–40.
        Albuquerque: University of New Mexico Press.
Anschuetz, Kurt F.
  1987 "Pueblo III Subsistence, Settlement, and Territori-
        ality in the Northern Rio Grande: The Albuquerque
        Frontier." In *Secrets of the City: Papers on Albuquer-
        que Area Archaeology,* eds. Anne V. Poore and John
        Montgomery, pp. 148–64. Papers of the Archaeo-
        logical Society of New Mexico, no. 13. Santa Fe:
        Ancient City Press.
Ariss, Robert
  1939 "Distribution of Smoking Pipes in the Pueblo Area."
        New Mexico Anthropologist 3(3–4):53–57.
Arnold, Dean E.
  1985 *Ceramic Theory and Cultural Process.* Cambridge:
        Cambridge University Press.
Atkinson, William W., Jr.
  1961 *Geology of the San Pedro Mountains, Santa Fe
        County, New Mexico.* State Bureau of Mines and
        Mineral Resources Bulletin 77. Socorro: New Mex-
        ico Institute of Mining and Technology.
Bandelier, Adolph F.
  1881 *Historical Introduction to Studies Among the Seden-
        tary Indians of New Mexico, Report on the Ruins of
        the Pueblo of Pecos.* Papers of the Archaeological In-
        stitute of America, American Series, no. 1. Boston.

  1890 *Final Report of Investigations Among the Indians of
        the Southwestern United States, Part I.* Papers of the
        Archaeological Institute of America, American Se-
        ries, no. 3. Cambridge.
  1892 *Final Report of Investigations Among the Indians of
        the Southwestern United States, Part II.* Papers of the
        Archaeological Institute of America, American Se-
        ries, no. 4. Cambridge.
Barth, Fredrik
  1969 "Introduction." In *Ethnic Groups and Boundaries:
        The Social Organization of Cultural Difference,* ed.
        Fredrik Barth, pp. 9–38. Boston: Little, Brown.
Baugh, Timothy G.
  1984 "Southern Plains Societies and Eastern Frontier
        Pueblo Exchange During the Protohistoric Period."
        In *Collected Papers in Honor of Harry L. Haddock,*
        ed. Nancy L. Fox, pp. 157–67. Papers of the Ar-
        chaeological Society of New Mexico, no. 9.
Beach, Marshall A., and Christopher S. Causey
  1984 "Bone Artifacts from Arroyo Hondo Pueblo." In *The
        Faunal Remains from Arroyo Hondo Pueblo, New
        Mexico: A Study in Short-Term Subsistence Change,*
        by Richard W. Lang and Arthur H. Harris, pp. 187–
        225. Arroyo Hondo Archaeological Series, vol. 5.
        Santa Fe: School of American Research Press.
Beckett, Patrick H.
  1985 "Distribution of Chupadero Black-on-White, or The
        Black and White of Jug Use." In *Southwestern Cul-
        ture History: Collected Papers in Honor of Albert H.
        Schroeder,* ed. Charles H. Lange, pp. 27–30. Papers
        of the Archaeological Society of New Mexico, no.
        10. Santa Fe: Ancient City Press.
Bice, Richard A., and William M. Sundt
  1972 *Prieta Vista: A Small Pueblo III Ruin in North-
        Central New Mexico.* Albuquerque: Albuquerque
        Archaeological Society.
Binford, Lewis R.
  1963 "A Proposed Attribute List for the Description and
        Classification of Projectile Points." In *Miscellaneous
        Studies in Typology and Classification,* Anthropo-
        logical Papers 19:193–221. Ann Arbor: Museum of
        Anthropology, University of Michigan.
  1977 "Forty-seven Trips: A Case Study on the Character
        of Archaeological Formation Processes." In *Stone*

Tools as Cultural Markers: Change, Evolution, and Complexity, ed. R. V. S. Wright, pp. 24–36. Prehistory and Material Culture Series, no. 12. Atlantic Highlands, NJ: Humanities Press.

Bohrer, Vorsila L.
1986 "The Ethnobotanical Pollen Record at Arroyo Hondo Pueblo." In *Food, Diet, and Population at Prehistoric Arroyo Hondo Pueblo, New Mexico*, by Wilma Wetterstrom, pp. 187–250. Arroyo Hondo Archaeological Series, vol. 6. Santa Fe: School of American Research Press.

Bonney, Rachel A.
1971 "A Preliminary Analysis of the Lithic Artifacts from Arroyo Hondo." Ms., School of American Research, Santa Fe.
1972 "Arroyo Hondo 1972 Lithic Analysis: Typology, Distribution, and Functions." Ms., School of American Research, Santa Fe.

Bower, Nathan W., and David H. Snow
1984 "A Comparative Study of Early Historic 'Tewa' Pottery." In *Rio Grande Rift: Northern New Mexico*, ed. W. S. Baldridge, P. W. Dickerson, R. E. Riecker, and J. Zidek, pp. 291–95. New Mexico Geological Society Guidebook, 35th Field Conference.

Braun, David P., and Stephen Plog
1982 "Evolution of 'Tribal' Social Networks: Theory and Prehistoric North American Evidence." *American Antiquity* 47(3):504–25.

Breternitz, David A.
1966 *An Appraisal of Tree-Ring Dated Pottery in the Southwest*. Anthropological Papers of the University of Arizona, no. 10. Tucson: University of Arizona Press.

Brew, J. O.
1946 "The Use and Abuse of Taxonomy." In *Archaeology of Alkali Ridge, Southwestern Utah*, pp. 44–66. Papers of the Peabody Museum of American Archaeology and Ethnology, vol. 21. Cambridge: Harvard University.

Bronitsky, Gordon
1983 "Economic Change in the Rio Grande Valley." In *Ecological Models in Economic Prehistory*, ed. Gordon Bronitsky. Anthropological Research Papers 29: 168–88. Tempe: Arizona State University.

Carlson, Roy L.
1970 *White Mountain Redware: A Pottery Tradition of East-Central Arizona and Western New Mexico*. Anthropological Papers of the University of Arizona, no. 19. Tucson: University of Arizona Press.

Castetter, Edward F.
1943 "Early Tobacco Utilization and Cultivation in the American Southwest." *American Anthropologist* 45: 320–25.

Collins, Susan M.
1975 "Prehistoric Rio Grande Settlement Patterns and the Inference of Demographic Change." Ph.D. dissertation, University of Colorado.

Colton, Harold S.
1953 *Potsherds: An Introduction to the Study of Prehistoric Southwestern Ceramics and Their Use in Historic Reconstruction*. Museum of Northern Arizona Bulletin, no. 25. Flagstaff.

Conkey, Margaret W.
1978 "Style and Information in Cultural Evolution: Toward a Predictive Model for the Paleolithic." In *Social Archeology: Beyond Subsistence and Dating*, ed. C. L. Redman, M. J. Berman, E. V. Curtin, W. T. Langhorne, Jr., N. M. Versaggi, and J. C. Wanser, pp. 61–85. New York: Academic Press.

Cordell, Linda S.
1979a *Cultural Resources Overview of the Middle Rio Grande Valley, New Mexico*. Washington, D.C.: U.S. Government Printing Office.
1979b "Prehistory: Eastern Anasazi." In *Handbook of North American Indians*, vol. 9, *Southwest*, ed. Alfonso Ortiz, pp. 131–51. Washington, D.C.: Smithsonian Institution Press.
1980 *Tijeras Canyon: Analyses of the Past*. Albuquerque: University of New Mexico Press.
1984 *Prehistory of the Southwest*. Orlando: Academic Press.
1989 "Northern and Central Rio Grande." In *Dynamics of Southwest Prehistory*, ed. Linda S. Cordell and George J. Gummerman, pp. 293–335. Washington, D.C.: Smithsonian Institution Press.

Cordell, Linda S., Amy C. Earls, and Martha R. Binford
1984 "Subsistence Systems in the Mountainous Settings of the Rio Grande Valley." In *Prehistoric Agricultural Strategies in the Southwest*, eds. Suzanne K. Fish and Paul R. Fish, pp. 233–41. Anthropological Research Papers, no. 13. Tempe: Arizona State University.

Cordell, Linda S., and Fred Plog
1979 "Escaping the Confines of Normative Thought: A Reevaluation of Puebloan Prehistory." *American Antiquity* 44(3):405–29.

Creamer, Winifred
1993 *The Architecture of Arroyo Hondo Pueblo, New Mexico*. Arroyo Hondo Archaeological Series, vol. 7. Santa Fe: School of American Research Press.

Creamer, Winifred, and Jonathan Haas
1989 "Demographic Change and European Contact in the Northern Rio Grande Valley." Ms., Field Museum of Natural History, Chicago.

Crotty, Helen
1990 "Protohistoric Anasazi Kiva Murals: Variation as a Reflection of Differing Social Contexts." Paper presented at the 55th annual meeting of the Society for American Archaeology, Las Vegas.

Crown, Patricia L.
1990 "Converging Traditions: Salado Polychrome Ceramics in Southwestern Prehistory." Paper presented at the 55th annual meeting of the Society for American Archaeology, Las Vegas.

241

Cushing, Frank Hamilton
1883 "Zuni Fetishes." In *2nd Annual Report of the Bureau of American Ethnology, 1880–81*, pp. 3–45. Washington, D.C.: Smithsonian Institution. Reprinted in 1988 by KC Publications, Las Vegas.

Dick, Herbert W.
1965 *Picuris Pueblo Excavations.* Santa Fe: National Park Service, Southwest Region.

Dickson, D. Bruce, Jr.
1979 *Prehistoric Pueblo Settlement Patterns: The Arroyo Hondo, New Mexico, Site Survey.* Arroyo Hondo Archaeological Series, vol. 2. Santa Fe: School of American Research Press.

Disbrow, Alan E., and Walter C. Stoll
1957 *Geology of the Cerrillos Area, Santa Fe County, New Mexico.* State Bureau of Mines and Mineral Resources Bulletin, no. 48. Socorro: New Mexico Institute of Mining and Technology.

Dixon, Keith A.
1964 "The Acceptance and Persistance of Ring Vessels and Stirrup Spout-Handles in the Southwest." *American Antiquity* 29(4):455–60.

Dixon, Roland B., and John B. Stetson, Jr.
1922 "Analysis of Pre-Columbian Pipe Dottles." *American Anthropologist* 24:245–46.

Douglass, Amy A.
1985 "The Pottery of Rowe Ruin: A Stylistic Analysis of the Black-on-White Ceramics." Paper presented at the 50th annual meeting of the Society for American Archaeology, Denver.

Dumarest, Noel
1919 *Notes on Cochiti, New Mexico.* Memoirs of the American Anthropological Association, vol. 6, no. 3.

Dutton, Bertha P.
1966 *Prehistoric Migrations into the Galisteo Basin, New Mexico.* 36 Congreso Internacional de Americanistas, separata del vol. 1. Sevilla, Spain.

Ellis, Florence Hawley, and J. J. Brody
1964 "Ceramic Stratigraphy and Tribal History at Taos Pueblo." *American Antiquity* 29(3):316–27.

Ferg, Alan
1982 "Fourteenth Century Kachina Depiction on Ceramics." In *Collected Papers in Honor of John W. Runyon*, ed. Gerald X. Fitzgerald, pp. 13–29. Papers of the Archaeological Society of New Mexico, no. 7. Albuquerque.

Ferring, C. Reid, and Timothy K. Perttula
1987 "Defining the Provenance of Red-Slipped Pottery from Texas and Oklahoma by Petrographic Methods." *Journal of Archaeological Science* 14(4):437–56.

Ford, Richard I.
1972a "Barter, Gift, or Violence: An Analysis of Tewa Intertribal Exchange." In *Social Exchange and Interaction*, ed. Edwin N. Wilmsen, pp. 21–45. Anthropological Papers, no. 46. Ann Arbor: Museum of Anthropology, University of Michigan.
1972b "An Ecological Perspective on the Eastern Pueblos." In *New Perspectives on the Pueblos*, ed. Alfonso Ortiz, pp. 1–18. Albuquerque: School of American Research and University of New Mexico Press.

Ford, Richard I., Albert H. Schroeder, and Stewart L. Peckham
1972 "Three Perspectives on Puebloan Prehistory." In *New Perspectives on the Pueblos*, ed. Alfonso Ortiz, pp. 22–40. Albuquerque: School of American Research and University of New Mexico Press.

Fulton, William Shirley, and Carr Tuthill
1940 *An Archaeological Site near Gleeson, Arizona.* The Amerind Foundation, Inc., no. 1.

Galusha, Ted, and John C. Blick
1971 *Stratigraphy of the Santa Fe Group, New Mexico.* Bulletin of the American Museum of Natural History, vol. 144, no. 1.

Graves, Michael W.
1985 "Ceramic Design Variation within a Kalinga Village: Temporal and Spatial Processes." In *Decoding Prehistoric Ceramics*, ed. Ben A. Nelson, pp. 9–34. Carbondale: Southern Illinois University Press.

Gunnerson, James H.
n.d. "Mountain Lions and Pueblo Shrines in the American Southwest." Ms., University of Nebraska State Museum, Lincoln.

Guthe, Carl E.
1925 *Pueblo Pottery Making: A Study at the Village of San Ildefonso.* Department of Archaeology, Phillips Academy, Andover. New Haven: Yale University Press.

Habicht-Mauche, Judith A.
1988a "An Analysis of Southwestern-Style Utility Ware Ceramics from the Southern Plains in the Context of Protohistoric Plains-Pueblo Interaction." Ph.D. dissertation, Harvard University. Ann Arbor: University Microfilms.
1988b "Town and Province: Regional Integration and Economic Interaction among the Classic Period Rio Grande Pueblos." Paper presented at the 53rd annual meeting of the Society for American Archaeology, Phoenix.

Habicht-Mauche, Judith A., and Winifred Creamer
1989 "Analysis of Room Use and Residence Units at Arroyo Hondo." Paper presented at the 54th annual meeting of the Society for American Archaeology, Atlanta.

Habicht-Mauche, Judith A., John Hoopes, and Michael Geselowitz
1987 "Where's the Chief?: The Archaeology of Complex Tribes." Paper presented at the 52nd annual meeting of the Society for American Archaeology, Toronto.

Hagstrum, Melissa
1985 "Measuring Prehistoric Ceramic Craft Specialization: A Test Case in the American Southwest." *Journal of Field Archaeology* 12(1):65–75.

Hargrave, L. L.
1932 *Guide to Forty Pottery Types from Hopi Country and the San Francisco Mountains, Arizona.* Museum of Northern Arizona Bulletin, no. 1. Flagstaff.

Haury, F. W., and L. L. Hargrave
1931 *Recently Dated Pueblo Ruins in Arizona.* Smithsonian Miscellaneous Collections, vol. 82, no. 11. Washington, D.C.

Hawley, Florence
1950 *Field Manual of Southwestern Pottery Types* (rev. ed.). University of New Mexico Bulletin, Anthropological Series, vol. 1, no. 4.

Hayes, Alden C.
1981 *Excavations at Mound 7, Gran Quivira National Monument, New Mexico.* Publications in Archeology, no. 16. Washington, D.C.: National Park Service.

Hegmon, Michelle
1990 "Organizational Scale and Social Relations in the Ninth Century Kayenta and Mesa Verde Regions." Paper presented at the Southwest Symposium: Prehistoric Community Dynamics in the North American Southwest, Albuquerque.

Hewett, Edgar Lee
1930 *Ancient Life in the American Southwest.* Indianapolis: The Bobbs-Merrill Co.

Hibben, Frank C.
1937 *Excavation of the Riana Ruin and Chama Valley Survey.* The University of New Mexico Bulletin, no. 300, Anthropological Series, vol. 2, no. 1. Albuquerque: University of New Mexico Press.
1975 *Kiva Art of the Anasazi at Pottery Mound.* Las Vegas: KC Publications.

Hill, James N.
1970 *Broken K Pueblo: Prehistoric Social Organization in the American Southwest.* Anthropological Papers, no. 18. Tucson: University of Arizona.

Hodder, Ian
1979 "Economic and Social Stress and Material Culture Patterning." *American Antiquity* 44(3):446–54.
1986 *Reading the Past.* Cambridge: Cambridge University Press.

Hodge, Frederick W. (ed.)
1907 "The Narrative of the Expedition of Coronado by Castañeda." In *Spanish Explorers in the Southern United States, 1528–1543,* ed. Frederick W. Hodge, pp. 281–387. New York: Charles Scribner's Sons.

Honea, Kenneth H.
1965 "A Morphology of Scrapers and Their Methods of Production." *Southwestern Lore* 31:25–40.
1968 "Material Culture: Ceramics." In *The Cochiti Dam: Archaeological Salvage Project, Part 1: Report on the 1963 Season,* ed. Charles H. Lange, pp. 111–69. Museum of New Mexico Research Records, no. 6. Santa Fe: Museum of New Mexico Press.

1973 "The Technology of Eastern Puebloan Pottery on the Llano Estacado." *Plains Anthropologist* 18(59): 73–88.

Hunter-Anderson, Rosalind
1979 "Explaining Residential Aggregation in the Northern Rio Grande: A Competition Reduction Model." In *Archeological Investigations in Cochiti Reservoir,* vol. 4, *Adaptive Change in the Northern Rio Grande,* eds. Jan V. Biella and Richard C. Chapman, pp. 169–75. Albuquerque: Office of Contract Archeology, University of New Mexico.

Jeançon, J. A.
1923 *Excavations in the Chama Valley, New Mexico.* Bureau of American Ethnology Bulletin, no. 81. Washington, D.C.: U.S. Government Printing Office.

Jones, Volney H.
1944 "Was Tobacco Smoked in the Pueblo Region in Pre-Spanish Times?" *American Antiquity* 9:451–56.

Jorde, L. B.
1977 "Precipitation Cycles and Cultural Buffering in the Prehistoric Southwest." In *For Theory Building in Archaeology: Essays on Faunal Remains, Aquatic Resources, Spatial Analysis and System Modeling,* ed. Lewis R. Binford, pp. 385–96. New York: Academic Press.

Judd, Neil M.
1922 *Archaeological Investigations at Pueblo Bonito, New Mexico.* Smithsonian Miscellaneous Collections, vol. 72, no. 15. Washington, D.C.: Smithsonian Institution.
1954 *The Material Culture of Pueblo Bonito.* Smithsonian Miscellaneous Collections, vol. 124. Washington, D.C.: Smithsonian Institution. Reprinted in 1981, *Reprints in Anthropology,* vol. 23. Lincoln, NB: J & L Reprint Company.

Judge, W. James
1974 *The Excavation of Tijeras Pueblo 1971–1973: Preliminary Report.* Albuquerque: USDA, Forest Service, Southwest Region.

Kelley, N. Edmund
1980 *The Contemporary Ecology of Arroyo Hondo, New Mexico.* Arroyo Hondo Archaeological Series, vol. 1. Santa Fe: School of American Research Press.

Kidder, Alfred V.
1915 *Pottery of the Pajarito Plateau and Some Adjacent Regions in New Mexico.* Memoirs of the American Anthropological Association, vol. 2, part 6.
1927 "Southwest Archaeological Conference." *Science* 68: 489–91.
1932 *The Artifacts of Pecos.* Papers of the Phillips Academy South West Expedition, no. 6. New Haven: Yale University Press.
1958 *Pecos, New Mexico: Archaeological Notes.* Papers of the Robert S. Peabody Foundation for Archaeology, vol. 5. Andover: Phillips Academy.

Kidder, Alfred V., and C. A. Amsden
1931   *The Pottery of Pecos, Vol. 1: The Dull-Paint Wares.* Papers of the Phillips Academy, South West Expedition, no. 5. New Haven: Yale University Press.

Kidder, Alfred V., and Anna O. Shepard
1936   *The Pottery of Pecos, Vol. 2: The Glaze Paint, Culinary, and Other Wares.* Papers of the Phillips Academy, South West Expedition, no. 7. New Haven: Yale University Press.

Kidder, M. A., and A. V. Kidder
1917   "Notes on the Pottery of Pecos." *American Anthropologist* 19(3): 325–60.

Kintigh, Keith W.
1985   "Social Structure, the Structure of Style, and Stylistic Patterns in Cibola Pottery." In *Decoding Prehistoric Ceramics*, ed. Ben A. Nelson, pp. 35–74. Carbondale: Southern Illinois University Press.

Kohler, Timothy A.
1989   *Bandelier Archaeological Excavation Project: Research Design and Summer 1988 Sampling.* WSU Department of Anthropology Reports of Investigations, no. 61.

Lambert, Marjorie F.
1954   *Paa-ko: Archaeological Chronicle of an Indian Village in North Central New Mexico, Parts I–V.* Monographs of the School of American Research, no. 19. Albuquerque: University of New Mexico Press.

Lang, Richard W.
1975a   "The Ceramics from Arroyo Hondo Pueblo." Ms., School of American Research, Santa Fe.

1975b   "The Dating of Pindi Pueblo and Its Components." Ms., School of American Research, Santa Fe.

1977   *Archaeological Survey of the Upper San Cristobal Drainage, Galisteo Basin, Santa Fe County, New Mexico.* Contract Archaeology Program Report, no. 37. Santa Fe: School of American Research.

1982   "Transformation in White Ware Pottery of the Northern Rio Grande." In *Southwestern Ceramics: A Comparative Review*, ed. Albert H. Schroeder, pp. 153–200. *The Arizona Archaeologist* 15.

1984   "Artifacts of Hide, Fur, and Feathers from Arroyo Hondo Pueblo." In *The Faunal Remains from Arroyo Hondo Pueblo, New Mexico: A Study in Short-term Subsistence Change*, by Richard W. Lang and Arthur H. Harris, pp. 255–85. Arroyo Hondo Archaeological Series, vol. 5. Santa Fe: School of American Research Press.

1986   "Artifacts of Woody Materials from Arroyo Hondo Pueblo." In *Food, Diet, and Population at Prehistoric Arroyo Hondo Pueblo, New Mexico*, by Wilma Wetterstrom, pp. 251–76. Arroyo Hondo Archaeological Series, vol. 6. Santa Fe: School of American Research Press.

1989   "Pottery from LA 2, the Agua Fria Schoolhouse Site: Chronology, Change, and Exchange: Circa A.D. 1300–1957." In *Limited Excavations at LA 2, The Agua Fria Schoolhouse Site, Agua Fria Village, Santa Fe County, New Mexico*, eds. Richard W. Lang and Cherie L. Scheick, pp. 57–98. Southwest Report no. 216. Santa Fe: Southwest Archaeological Consultants Research Series.

Lang, Richard W., and Arthur H. Harris
1984   *The Faunal Remains from Arroyo Hondo Pueblo, New Mexico: A Study in Short-Term Subsistence Change.* Arroyo Hondo Archaeological Series, vol. 5. Santa Fe: School of American Research Press.

Lang, Richard W., and Cherie L. Scheick (eds.)
1989   *Limited Excavations at LA 2, The Agua Fria Schoolhouse Site, Agua Fria Village, Santa Fe County, New Mexico.* Santa Fe: Southwest Archaeological Consultants Research Series.

Lechtman, Heather, and Arthur Steinberg
1979   "The History of Technology: An Anthropological Point of View." In *The History and Philosophy of Technology*, eds. G. Bugliarello and D. B. Doner, pp. 135–60. Chicago: University of Illinois Press.

Lekson, Stephen
1990   "Sedentism and Aggregation in Anasazi Archaeology." In *Perspectives on Southwest Prehistory*, eds. Paul Minnis and Charles L. Redman. Boulder: Westview Press.

Leonard, Robert D.
1989   "Resource Specialization, Population Growth, and Agricultural Production in the American Southwest." *American Antiquity* 54(3): 491–503.

Lightfoot, Kent G.
1984   *Prehistoric Political Dynamics: A Case Study from the American Southwest.* De Kalb: Northern Illinois University Press.

Linford, Laurance
1974   "Arroyo Hondo 1973 Lithics Analysis: Typology and Component Comparisons." Ms., School of American Research, Santa Fe.

n.d.a   Unbound analysis notes, School of American Research, Santa Fe.

n.d.b   "The Lithic Artifacts from Arroyo Hondo, New Mexico." Ms., School of American Research, Santa Fe.

Mackey, James
1980   "Arroyo Hondo Population Affinities." In *Pueblo Population and Society: The Arroyo Hondo Skeletal and Mortuary Remains*, by Ann M. Palkovich, pp. 171–81. Arroyo Hondo Archaeological Series, vol. 5. Santa Fe: School of American Research Press.

1982   "Vallecitos Pueblo (A Fourteenth Century A.D. Ancestral Jemez Site) and LA 12761 (A Late Prehistoric–Early Historic Jemez Phase Farm House Site) in New Mexico." *Journal of Intermountain Archaeology* 1: 80–99.

Mauss, Marcel
1967   *The Gift: Forms and Functions of Exchange in Archaic Societies.* New York: W. W. Norton and Company.

Mera, H. P.
1931   *Chupadero Black-on-White*. Laboratory of Anthropology Technical Series Bulletin, no. 1. Santa Fe.
1933   *A Proposed Revision of the Rio Grande Glaze Paint Sequence*. Laboratory of Anthropology Technical Series Bulletin, no. 5. Santa Fe.
1934   *A Survey of the Biscuit Ware Area in Northern New Mexico*. Laboratory of Anthropology Technical Series Bulletin, no. 6. Santa Fe.
1935   *Ceramic Clues to the Prehistory of North Central New Mexico*. Laboratory of Anthropology Technical Series Bulletin, no. 8. Santa Fe.
1940   *Population Changes in the Rio Grande Glaze-Paint Area*. Laboratory of Anthropology Technical Series Bulletin, no. 11. Santa Fe.

Morrison, Kathleeen D.
1985   "1984 Rowe Pueblo Ceramic Analysis: Preliminary Report." In *Final Report to NSF*, ed. Linda S. Cordell, pp. 1–29. Ms., Department of Anthropology, University of New Mexico, Albuquerque.

Munsell Color
1975   *Munsell Soil Color Charts*. Baltimore: MacBeth Division, Kollmorgen Corporation.

Nelson, Nels C.
1913   "Ruins of Prehistoric New Mexico." *American Museum Journal* 13(2):63–81.
1914   *Pueblo Ruins of the Galisteo Basin, New Mexico*. Anthropological Papers of the American Museum of Natural History, no. 15, pt. 1. New York.
1916   "Chronology of the Tano Ruins, New Mexico." *American Anthropologist* 18(2):159–80.
1917   *The Archaeology of the Tano District, New Mexico*. Proceedings of the 19th International Congress of Americanists. Washington, D.C.

Olinger, Bart
1987a "Pottery Studies Using X-Ray Fluorescence, Part 1: An Introduction, Nambe Pueblo as an Example." *Pottery Southwest* 14(1):1–5.
1987b "Pottery Studies Using X-Ray Fluorescence, Part 2: Evidence for Prehistoric Reoccupation of the Pajarito Plateau." *Pottery Southwest* 14(2):2–5.

Palkovich, Ann M.
1980   *Pueblo Population and Society: The Arroyo Hondo Skeletal and Mortuary Remains*. Arroyo Hondo Archaeological Series, vol. 3. Santa Fe: School of American Research Press.

Paper, Jordan
1988   *Offering Smoke: The Sacred Pipe and Native American Religion*. Moscow: University of Idaho Press.

Parsons, Elsie Clews
1925   *The Pueblo of Jemez*. Papers of the South West Expedition, no. 3. Andover: Department of Archaeology, Phillips Academy.

Peacock, D. P. S.
1970   "The Scientific Analysis of Ancient Ceramics: A Review." *World Archaeology* 1(3):375–89.

Peckham, Stewart
1984   "The Anasazi Culture of the Northern Rio Grande Rift." In *Rio Grande Rift: Northern New Mexico*, eds. W. S. Baldridge, P. W. Dickerson, R. E. Riecker, and J. Zidek, pp. 275–81. New Mexico Geological Society Guidebook, 35th Field Conference.

Phagan, Carl J.
1984   "Lithic Profiles." In *Dolores Archaeological Program: Synthetic Report 1978–1981*, chap 5, sec. 6. Denver: U.S. Department of the Interior, Bureau of Reclamation, Engineering and Research Center.
1986   "Reductive Technologies." In *Dolores Archaeological Program Final Synthetic Report*, comp. David A. Breternitz, Christine K. Robinson, and G. Timothy Gross, chap 3. Denver: U.S. Department of the Interior, Bureau of Reclamation, Engineering and Research Center.
1988   "Projectile Point Analysis, Part I: Production of Statistical Types and Subtypes." In *Dolores Archaeological Program Supporting Studies: Additive and Reductive Technologies*, comp. Eric Blinman, Carl J. Phagan, and Richard H. Wilshusen, chap. 4. Denver: U.S. Department of the Interior, Bureau of Reclamation, Engineering and Research Center.

Phagan, Carl J., and Thomas H. Hruby
1984   *Dolores Archaeological Program Reductive Technologies Manual: Preliminary Analysis Systems and Procedures*. Dolores Archaeological Program Technical Reports, DAP-150, submitted to the U.S. Bureau of Reclamation, Upper Colorado Region, Salt Lake City.

Phillips, Phillip
1958   "Application of the Wheat-Gifford-Wasley Taxonomy to Eastern Ceramics." *American Antiquity* 24(2):117–25.

Plog, Stephen
1980   *Stylistic Variation in Prehistoric Ceramics*. New York: Cambridge University Press.
1983   "Analysis of Style in Artifacts." *Annual Review of Anthropology* 12:125–42.

Reed, Erik K.
1949   "Sources of Upper Rio Grande Culture and Population." *El Palacio* 56(6):163–84.

Reiter, Paul
1938   *The Jemez Pueblo of Unshagi, New Mexico, with Notes on the Earlier Excavations at Amoxiumqua and Giusewa*. Monographs of the School of American Research, nos. 5 and 6. Albuquerque: University of New Mexico Press.

Rice, Prudence M.
1984   "The Archaeological Study of Specialized Pottery Production: Some Aspects of Method and Theory." In *Pots and Potters: Current Approaches in Ceramic Archaeology*, ed. Prudence M. Rice, pp. 45–54. UCLA Institute of Archaeology Monograph no. 24. Los Angeles: University of California Press.

1987 *Pottery Analysis: A Sourcebook.* Chicago: University of Chicago Press.

Robbins, Wilfred William, John Peabody Harrington, and Barbara Freire-Marreco
1916 *Ethnobotany of the Tewa Indians.* Bureau of American Ethnology Bulletin, no. 55. Washington, D.C.: Smithsonian Institution.

Robinson, William J., John H. Hannah, and Bruce G. Harrill
1972 *Tree-Ring Dates from New Mexico I, O, U: Central Rio Grande Area.* Tucson: Laboratory of Tree-Ring Research, University of Arizona.

Rose, Martin R., Jeffrey S. Dean, and William J. Robinson
1981 *The Past Climate of Arroyo Hondo, New Mexico, Reconstructed from Tree Rings.* Arroyo Hondo Archaeological Series, vol. 4. Santa Fe: School of American Research Press.

Rye, Owen S.
1981 *Pottery Technology: Principles and Reconstruction.* Washington, D.C.: Taraxacum.

Sackett, James R.
1977 "The Meaning of Style in Archaeology: A General Model." *American Antiquity* 42(3):369–80.
1982 "Approaches to Style in Lithic Archaeology." *Journal of Anthropological Archaeology* 1(1):59–112.

Sahlins, Marshall D.
1968 *Tribesmen.* Englewood Cliffs: Prentice-Hall.
1972 *Stone Age Economics.* Chicago: Aldine.

Schaafsma, Curtis
1967 "Field Notes: LA 8843, LA 8844, LA 8845." Ms., Laboratory of Anthropology, Museum of New Mexico, Santa Fe.
1969 "The Pottery of Las Madres." Ms., Laboratory of Anthropology, Museum of New Mexico, Santa Fe.
1979 "Fourteenth Century Galisteo Basin Trade Networks as Viewed from Las Madres Pueblo." In *Collected Papers in Honor of Bertha Dutton,* ed. Albert H. Schroeder, pp. 33–39. Papers of the Archaeological Society of New Mexico, no. 4.

Schaafsma, Polly
1990 "War Imagery and Magic: Petroglyphs at Comanche Gap, Galisteo Basin, New Mexico." Paper presented at the 55th annual meeting of the Society for American Archaeology, Las Vegas.

Schaafsma, Polly, and Curtis F. Schaafsma
1974 "Evidence for the Origins of Pueblo Katchina Cult as Suggested by Southwestern Rock Art." *American Antiquity* 39(4):535–45.

Schwartz, Douglas W.
1971 *Background Report on the Archaeology of the Site at Arroyo Hondo: First Arroyo Hondo Field Report—1971.* Santa Fe: School of American Research.
1972 *Archaeological Investigations at the Arroyo Hondo Site: Second Field Report—1971.* Santa Fe: School of American Research.
1981a "Population, Culture, and Resources: A Rio Grande Pueblo Perspective." *Geoscience and Man* 22:77–84.
1981b "Foreword." In *The Past Climate of Arroyo Hondo, New Mexico, Reconstructed from Tree Rings,* by Martin R. Rose, Jeffrey S. Dean, and William J. Robinson, pp. ix–xv. Arroyo Hondo Archaeological Series, vol. 4. Santa Fe: School of American Research Press.
1986 "Foreword." In *Food, Diet, and Population at Prehisoric Arroyo Hondo Pueblo, New Mexico,* by Wilma Wetterstrom, pp. xiii–xxi. Arroyo Hondo Archaeological Series, vol. 6. Santa Fe: School of American Research Press.

Schwartz, Douglas W., and R. W. Lang
1973 *Archaeological Investigations at the Arroyo Hondo Site: Third Field Report—1972.* Santa Fe: School of American Research.

Scott, Stuart D.
1960 "Pottery Figurines from Central Arizona." *The Kiva* 26(2):11–26.

Scully, Virginia
1970 *A Treasury of American Indian Herbs: Their Lore and Their Use for Food, Drugs, and Medicine.* New York: Crown Publishers.

Service, Elman R.
1971 *Primitive Social Organization* (2nd ed.). New York: Random House.

Shepard, Anna O.
1942 *Rio Grande Glaze Paint Ware: A Study Illustrating the Place of Ceramic Technological Analysis in Archaeological Research.* Contributions to American Anthropology and History, no. 39, publ. 528. Washington, D.C.: Carnegie Institution of Washington.
1965 "Rio Grande Glaze-Paint Pottery: A Test of Petrographic Analysis." In *Ceramics and Man,* ed. Frederick R. Matson, pp. 62–87. Viking Fund Publications in Anthropology, no. 41. New York: Wenner-Gren Foundation for Anthropological Research.
1980 *Ceramics for the Archaeologist* (10th printing). Publication 609. Washington, D.C.: Carnegie Institution of Washington.

Smiley, Terah L., Stanley A. Stubbs, and Bryant Bannister
1953 *A Foundation for the Dating of Some Late Archaeological Sites in the Rio Grande Area, New Mexico: Based on Studies in Tree-Ring Methods and Pottery Analysis.* Laboratory of Tree-Ring Research Bulletin, no. 6. University of Arizona Bulletin, vol. 24, no. 3.

Smith, R. E., G. R. Willey, and J. C. Gifford
1960 "The Type-Variety Concept as a Basis for the Analysis of Maya Pottery." *American Antiquity* 25(3):330–40.

Smith, Watson
1971 *Painted Ceramics of the Western Mound at Awatovi.* Papers of the Peabody Museum of Archaeology and Ethnology, vol. 38. Cambridge: Harvard University.

Snow, David H.
1974 *The Excavation of Saltbush Pueblo, Bandelier National Monument, New Mexico, 1971.* Laboratory of Anthropology Notes, no. 97. Santa Fe.

1976 "Summary." In "Section B: The Ceramics and Mineral Resources of LA 70 and the Cochiti Area," by A. H. Warren, in *Archaeological Excavations at Pueblo del Encierro, LA 70, Cochiti Dam Salvage Project, Cochiti, New Mexico, Final Report: 1964–1965 Field Seasons*, ed. David H. Snow, pp. B170-B184. Laboratory of Anthropology Notes, no. 78. Santa Fe: Museum of New Mexico.

1981 "Protohistoric Rio Grande Economics: A Review of Trends." In *The Protohistoric Period in the North American Southwest*, A.D. 1450–1700, eds. David R. Wilcox and W. Bruce Masse, pp. 354–77. Arizona State University Research Papers, no. 24.

1982 "The Rio Grande Glaze, Matte-Paint, and Plainware Tradition." In *Southwestern Ceramics: A Comparative Review*, ed. Albert H. Schroeder, pp. 235–78. *The Arizona Archaeologist* 15.

Spaulding, Albert C.
1953 "Statistical Techniques for the Discovery of Artifact Types." *American Antiquity* 18(4):305–13.

Spiegel, Zane, and Brewster Baldwin
1963 *Geology and Water Resources of the Santa Fe Area, New Mexico*. Geological Survey Water-Supply Paper, no. 1525, U.S. Geological Survey. Washington, D.C.: United States Printing Office.

Spielmann, Katherine A.
1982 "Inter-societal Food Acquisition among Egalitarian Societies: An Ecological Study of Plains/Pueblo Interaction in the American Southwest." Ph.D. dissertation, University of Michigan. Ann Arbor: University Microfilms.

Spinden, Herbert J.
1950 *Tobacco is American: The Story of Tobacco Before the Coming of the White Man*. New York: New York Public Library.

Stearns, Charles E.
1953 "Early Tertiary Vulcanism in the Galisteo-Tonque Area, North-Central New Mexico." *American Journal of Science* 251:415–52.

Stephen, Alexander M.
1936 *Hopi Journal of Alexander Stephen*, ed. Elsie C. Parsons. Columbia Contributions to Anthropology, no. 23. New York: Columbia University.

Stevenson, Matilda Coxe
1904 "The Zuni Indians: Their Mythology, Esoteric Societies, and Ceremonies." *Bureau of American Ethnology, Annual Report*, 23:3–608. Washington, D.C.: Smithsonian Institution.

Stone, Glenn Davis, Robert McC. Netting, and M. Priscilla Stone
1990 "Seasonality, Labor Scheduling, and Agricultural Intensification in the Nigerian Savanna." *American Anthropologist* 92(1):7–23.

Stuart, David E., and Rory P. Gauthier
1981 *Prehistoric New Mexico: Background for Survey*. Santa Fe: Historic Preservation Bureau.

Stubbs, Stanley A., and W. S. Stallings, Jr.
1953 *The Excavation of Pindi Pueblo, New Mexico*. Monographs of the School of American Research, no. 18. Santa Fe: Museum of New Mexico Press.

Sundt, William M.
1972 "Ceramics." In *Prieta Vista: A Small Pueblo III Ruin in North-Central New Mexico*, eds. Richard A. Bice and William M. Sundt, pp. 98–176. Albuquerque Archaeological Society.

1984 *Typological Analysis of Potsherds in Collections from LA 85 (Old Santo Domingo Pueblo) and Other Sites near Tent Rocks, New Mexico*. Report no. TA85–1. Albuquerque: William M. Sundt, Consultant.

1987 "Pottery of Central New Mexico and its Role as Key to Both Time and Space." In *Secrets of the City: Papers on Albuquerque Area Archaeology*, eds. Anne V. Poore and John Montgomery, pp. 116–47. Papers of the Archaeological Society of New Mexico, no.13. Santa Fe: Ancient City Press.

Switzer, Ronald R.
1969 *Tobacco, Pipes, and Cigarettes of the Prehistoric Southwest*. El Paso Archaeological Society Special Report, no. 8.

Talmage, Sterling B., and Thomas P. Wootton
1937 *The Non-Metallic Resources of New Mexico and their Economic Features*. New Mexico School of Mines Bulletin, no. 12. Socorro: Bureau of Mines and Mineral Resources.

Traylor, Diane, Nancy Wood, Lyndi Hubbell, Robert Scaife, and Sue Waber
1977 "Bandelier: Excavations in the Flood Pool of Cochiti Lake, New Mexico." Ms., Southwest Cultural Resource Center, National Park Service, Santa Fe.

Traylor, Diane E., and Robert P. Scaife
1982 "Ceramics." In *Bandelier: Excavations in the Flood Pool of Cochiti Lake, New Mexico*, eds. Lyndi Hubbell and Diane Traylor, pp. 239–94. Submitted by National Park Service, Southwest Cultural Resource Center, to Interagency Archeological Services Division. Denver: National Park Service.

Tschopik, Harry, Jr.
1941 *Navaho Pottery Making: An Inquiry into the Affinities of Navaho Painted Pottery*. Papers of the Peabody Museum of American Archaeology and Ethnology, vol. 17, no. 1. Cambridge: Harvard University.

Upham, Steadman
1982 *Polities and Power: An Economic and Political History of the Western Pueblo*. New York: Academic Press.

1984 "Adaptive Diversity and Southwestern Abandonment." *Journal of Anthropological Research* 40(2):235–56.

Venn, Tamsin
1984 "Shell Artifacts from Arroyo Hondo Pueblo." In *The Faunal Remains from Arroyo Hondo Pueblo, New Mexico: A Study in Short-Term Subsistence Change,*

by Richard W. Lang and Arthur H. Harris. Arroyo Hondo Archaeological Series, vol. 5. Santa Fe: School of American Research Press.

Warren, A. Helene
1968 "Petrographic Notes on Glaze-Paint Pottery." In *The Cochiti Dam Archaeological Salvage Project, Part 1: Report on the 1963 Season*, ed. Charles H. Lange, pp. 184–97. Museum of New Mexico Research Records, no. 6. Santa Fe: Museum of New Mexico Press.

1969 "Tonque: One Pueblo's Glaze Pottery Industry Dominated Middle Rio Grande Commerce." *El Palacio* 76(2):36–42.

1970 "Notes on the Manufacture and Trade of Rio Grande Glazes." *The Artifact* 8(4):1–7.

1976 "Section B: The Ceramics and Mineral Resources of LA 70 and the Cochiti Area." In *Archaeological Excavations at Pueblo del Encierro, LA 70, Cochiti Dam Salvage Project, Cochiti, New Mexico, Final Report: 1964–1965 Field Seasons*, ed. David H. Snow, pp. B1–169. Laboratory of Anthropology Notes, no. 78. Santa Fe: Museum of New Mexico.

1979 "The Glaze Paint Wares of the Upper Middle Rio Grande." In *Archaeological Investigations in Cochiti Reservoir, New Mexico, vol. 4: Adaptive Change in the Northern Rio Grande Valley*, eds. Jan V. Biella and Richard C. Chapman, pp. 187–216. Albuquerque: Office of Contract Archeology, University of New Mexico.

1980 "Prehistoric Pottery of Tijeras Canyon." In *Tijeras Canyon: Analyses of the Past*, ed. Linda S. Cordell, pp. 149–68. Maxwell Museum of Anthropology Publication Series. Albuquerque: University of New Mexico Press.

1981 "A Petrographic Study of the Pottery." In *Contributions to Gran Quivira Archaeology*, ed. Alden C. Hayes, pp. 67–73. Publications in Archaeology, no. 17. Washington, D.C.: National Park Service, U.S. Department of the Interior.

Wendorf, Fred
1950 *A Report on the Excavation of a Small Ruin near Point of Pines, East Central Arizona*. University of Arizona Social Science Bulletin, no. 19. Tucson.

1953 *Salvage Archaeology in the Chama Valley, New Mexico*. Monographs of the School of American Research, no. 17. Santa Fe: School of American Research Press.

1954 "A Reconstruction of Northern Rio Grande Prehistory." *American Anthropologist* 56(2):200–227.

Wendorf, Fred, and Erik K. Reed
1955 "An Alternative Reconstruction of Northern Rio Grande Prehistory." *El Palacio* 62(5–6):131–73.

West, George A.
1934 *Tobacco, Pipes, and Smoking Customs of the American Indians*. Bulletin of the Public Museum of the City of Milwaukee, vol. 17. Reprinted in 1970 by Greenwood Press, Westport, CT.

Wetherington, Ronald K.
1968 *Excavations at Pot Creek Pueblo*. Fort Burgwin Research Center Publication, no. 6. Taos.

Wetterstrom, Wilma
1986 *Food, Diet, and Population at Prehistoric Arroyo Hondo Pueblo, New Mexico*. Arroyo Hondo Archaeological Series, vol. 6. Santa Fe: School of American Research Press.

Wheat, J. B., J. C. Gifford, and W. W. Wasley
1958 "Ceramic Variety, Type, Cluster, and Ceramic System in Southwestern Pottery Analysis." *American Antiquity* 24(1):34–47.

White, Leslie A.
1942 "Further Data on the Cultivation of Tobacco among the Pueblo Indians." *Science* 96:59–60.

1943 "Punche: Tobacco in New Mexico History." *New Mexico Historical Review* 18:386–93.

Wilbert, Johannes
1987 *Tobacco and Shamanism in South America*. New Haven: Yale University Press.

Wilcox, David R.
1981 "Changing Perspectives on the Protohistoric Pueblos, A.D. 1450–1700." In *The Protohistoric Period in the North American Southwest, A.D. 1450–1700*, eds. David R. Wilcox and W. Bruce Masse, pp. 378–409. Arizona State University Anthropological Research Papers, no. 24.

1984 "Multi-Ethnic Division of Labor in the Protohistoric Southwest." In *Collected Papers in Honor of Harry L. Haddock*, ed. Nancy L. Fox, pp. 141–54. Papers of the Archaeological Society of New Mexico, no. 9.

Willey, Gordon R., T. P. Culbert, and R. E. W. Adams
1967 "Maya Lowland Ceramics: A Report from the 1965 Guatemala City Conference." *American Antiquity* 32(3):289–315.

Wiseman, Regge N.
1980 *The Carnue Project: Excavation at a Late Coalition Period Pueblo in Tijeras Canyon, New Mexico*. Laboratory of Anthropology Note, no. 166. Santa Fe: Museum of New Mexico.

Wobst, H. Martin
1977 "Stylistic Behavior and Information Exchange." In *For the Director: Research Essays in Honor of James B. Griffin*, ed. Charles E. Cleland, pp. 317–42. Anthropological Papers, no. 61. Ann Arbor: University of Michigan, Museum of Anthropology.

Woodbury, Richard B.
  1954 *Prehistoric Stone Implements of Northeastern Arizona*. Papers of the Peabody Museum of American Archaeology and Ethnology, vol. 34. Cambridge: Harvard University.

Woodbury, Richard B., and Nathalie F. S. Woodbury
  1966 "Decorated Pottery of the Zuni Area." In *The Excavation of Hawikuh by Fredrick Webb Hodge: Report of the Hendricks-Hodge Expedition, 1917–1923*, eds. Watson Smith, Richard B. Woodbury, and Nathalie F. S. Woodbury, pp. 302–36. New York: Museum of the American Indian Heye Foundation.

Woosley, Anne I.
  1984 "Puebloan Prehistory of the Northern Rio Grande: Settlement, Population, and Subsistence." *The Kiva* 51(3):143–64.

Index